HOUGHTON MIFFLIN HARCOURT

JOURNEYS

Program Authors

James F. Baumann · David J. Chard · Jamal Cooks
J. David Cooper · Russell Gersten · Marjorie Lipson
Lesley Mandel Morrow · John J. Pikulski · Héctor H. Rivera
Mabel Rivera · Shane Templeton · Sheila W. Valencia
Catherine Valentino · MaryEllen Vogt

Consulting Author

Irene Fountas

HOUGHTON MIFFLIN HARCOURT
School Publishers

HOUGHTON MIFFLIN HARCOURT

JOURNEYS

HOUGHTON MIFFLIN HARCOURT
School Publishers

Finding Your Voice

Big Idea We all need to communicate.

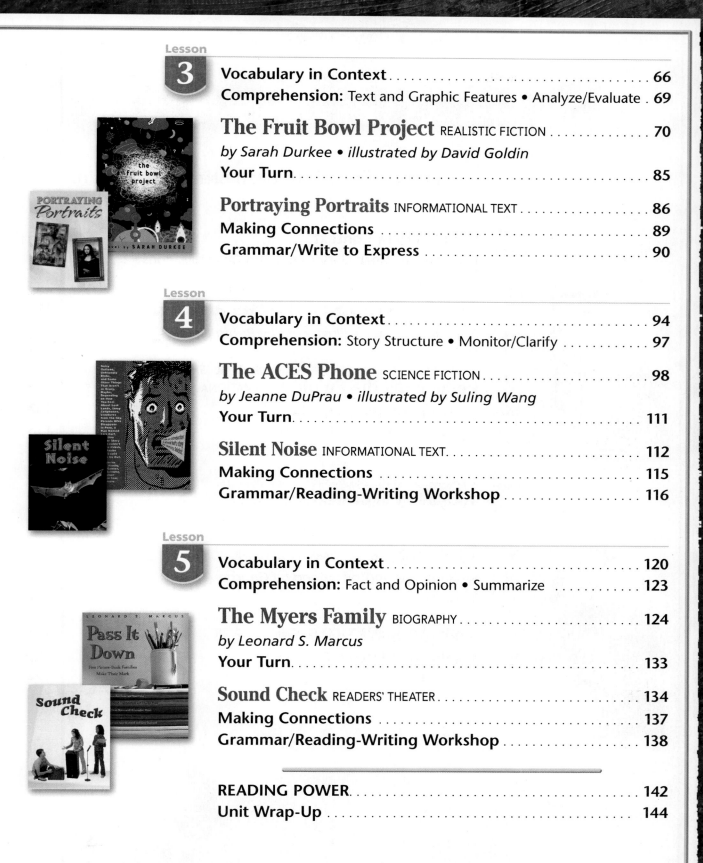

Common Ground

Big Idea When we connect with each other, we all gain.

Unit 3

Going the Distance

💡 **Big Idea** Sometimes you need to give it all you've got.

Treasures of the Ancient World

Big 💡 Idea The past is full of amazing stories.

Unit 5

Taking Charge of Change

Big Idea Changing things for the better is worth the challenge.

Welcome, Reader!

You're about to set out on a reading journey that will take you from ancient Egypt to the modern world of robots. On the way, you'll learn amazing things as you become a better reader.

Your reading journey begins with a story about a young girl writing a book of her own.

Plenty of other reading adventures lie ahead. Just turn the page!

Sincerely,

The Authors

The Authors

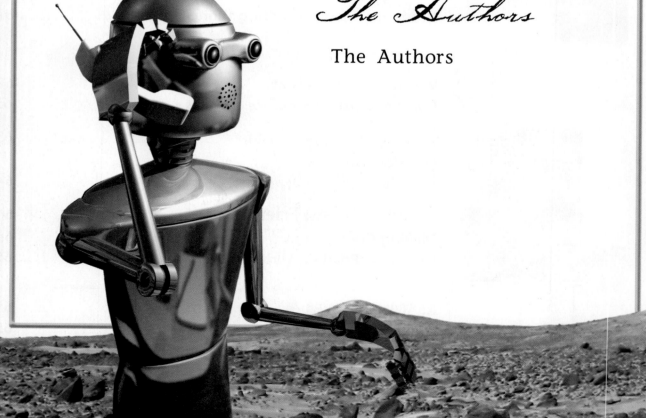

Finding Your Voice

Well?

Unit 1

Paired Selections

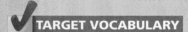

publishing

manuscript

editorial

pressuring

disclose

maze

literary

revisions

wry

muted

Vocabulary
Reader

Context
Cards

Vocabulary in Context

1 publishing

A publishing company prints millions of copies of books for people to buy and read.

2 manuscript

An author first writes a manuscript of a story. Later, those pages may become a book.

3 editorial

The editorial director is in charge of the department that corrects early versions of a book.

4 pressuring

Readers sometimes send letters pressuring, or urging, an author to bring back a favorite character.

- **Study each Context Card.**
- **Use two Vocabulary words to tell about an experience you had.**

5 disclose

The middle of a book might disclose, or reveal, a surprising event in the plot of the story.

6 maze

A writer's office may be a maze, a confusing path among books, papers, and computer equipment.

7 literary

A writer might need to hire a literary agent, someone whose business has to do with books.

8 revisions

An editor often asks the author to make revisions, or changes, to his or her writing.

9 wry

The author Studs Terkel wrote with a wry sense of humor, finding reasons to smile at the difficulties of life.

10 muted

A critic may include muted, or quiet, criticism in an otherwise favorable book review.

Background

How Is a Book Made? Suppose that you have written a manuscript. It includes wry humor and is sure to be a bestseller. Now you want to get it published. Working through the maze of people and places in the publishing business can be frightening. It helps to have an idea of what to expect.

Most authors need a literary agent who understands the professional, business-related details of what publishers want. An agent knows the right editorial people to contact. If a company decides to publish your book, an editor will suggest revisions. Perfecting a book can take months or even years.

At last your book will be printed. Muted publicity won't win you many readers, so go on a book tour. Reviewers will soon be pressuring the public to read your book. With luck, they won't disclose the ending!

Overview of the Publishing Process

Manuscript

Publisher/Editor

Book Store

Literary Agent

Printer

Comprehension

✔ **TARGET SKILL** **Understanding Characters**

The characters in "The School Story" reveal a great deal about their personalities through such clues as their words, thoughts, and actions. Use a chart like the one below to list details that help you understand each character in the selection.

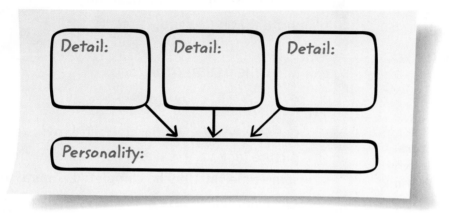

✔ **TARGET STRATEGY** **Question**

You can use your chart to help you generate questions about the characters and events in the selection. Asking questions and finding answers help you understand more about what you read.

Andrew Clements

✔ **TARGET VOCABULARY**

publishing	maze
manuscript	literary
editorial	revisions
pressuring	wry
disclose	muted

✔ **TARGET SKILL**

Understanding Characters
Use text details to explain why characters act, speak, and think as they do.

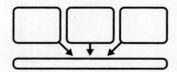

✔ **TARGET STRATEGY**

Question Ask questions before you read, as you read, and after you read.

GENRE

Realistic fiction has characters and events that are like people and events in real life.

Set a Purpose Before reading, set a purpose for reading based on what you know about the genre and your own experiences.

MEET THE AUTHOR

Andrew Clements

How has Andrew Clements written over fifty books, including such popular school stories as *Frindle*, *The Landry News*, and *Lunch Money*? He explains, "You don't have to do everything at once. You don't have to know how every story is going to end. You just have to take that next step, look for that next idea, write that next word."

MEET THE ILLUSTRATOR

C. F. Payne

C. F. Payne is known for his ability to make a picture look very real and very funny at the same time. In 1999 he completed a mural for Cincinnati Playhouse in the Park in his hometown of Cincinnati, Ohio. The mural depicts actors and playwrights whose work has been performed in that theater.

Natalie Nelson's widowed mother, Hannah, is a children's book editor at Shipley Junior Books. Hannah's boss, Letha, is pressuring *her to find a "school story" that will become the company's next best-selling book. Natalie thinks "The Cheater," a novel she just wrote, could be that book— but she doesn't want to* disclose *her true identity. Natalie's friend, Zoe Reisman, comes up with a daring plan: turn Natalie into author Cassandra Day and Zoe into her agent, Zee Zee from the Sherry Clutch Agency! All Natalie has to do is make sure her story ends up with Hannah rather than with Hannah's coworker, Ella, keeper of unread manuscripts.*

Natalie got off the elevator at Shipley Junior Books at 4:25. She walked to the desk and handed a thick brown envelope to the receptionist. Natalie smiled and said, "A messenger brought this— it's for my mom. Do you need to check it in, or can I take it right back to her?"

He looked at the address label and said, "All it needs is a date stamp and my initials." The stamp made a mechanical *ca-chonk* sound as he pressed it onto the front of the envelope, and then he scribbled his initials below the date. Now the package looked official. "Here you go." He handed the envelope back to Natalie, then pushed the security button to open the door for her.

Natalie wound her way through the maze to her mom's office. Her mouth was dry. Even though she'd been here a hundred times, she felt like a spy sneaking into a strange building.

"Hi, Mom."

As her mom swung her chair around and smiled, Natalie glanced at the phone console on the desk beside the computer screen. The Message Waiting light was dark. That meant her mom had already listened to Zee Zee's message.

"Here," Natalie said, and she handed the envelope to her mom. "This is for you."

STOP AND THINK

Author's Craft The author uses an example of **onomatopoeia**, a word that imitates the sound of the thing it describes, in paragraph two. What word does he use, and why do you think he chooses it?

Hannah Nelson looked at the envelope. The large address label was printed in bright green ink. She read the return address aloud. "'The Sherry Clutch Literary Agency'? I just had a message from this agent, but I don't think I know her. . . . Oh, well." And she dropped the envelope onto the papers beside her computer. "Could you get me a juice or something, Natalie? I didn't even stop for lunch today."

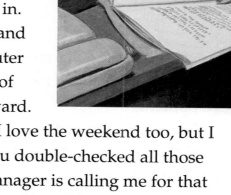

Natalie returned with two bottles of apple juice and some shortbread cookies. Her mom held up her bottle for a toast, and when Natalie clinked it, her mom said, "Here's to our weekend!"

And at that moment Letha walked in. She stepped across the space carefully and leaned over to look at Hannah's computer screen. Natalie caught the sharp scent of Letha's perfume and took a step backward.

With a strained smile Letha said, "I love the weekend too, but I don't think it's quite here yet. Have you double-checked all those revisions, Hannah? The production manager is calling me for that text every half hour, and we can't get out of here until it's released."

Glancing around Hannah's workspace, she snatched up the new envelope and said, "What's this?"

Hannah said, "That? It's just a manuscript. Must be a new agency—Sherry something."

Letha read the label. "Sherry Clutch . . . oh, yes, I believe I've heard of her. She's supposed to be very bright. Listen—buzz me the second you're sure all those revisions check out, okay? And I want you to give this a look over the weekend." Letha dropped the envelope on Hannah's lap and swept out of the office.

Hannah shook her head and gave Natalie a wry smile. "So much for the weekend, eh? Listen, I've got to get back to work. Tim is probably gone by now, so you can hang out over there, okay?"

Natalie said, "Sure, Mom."

As she walked over to Tim's cubicle, Natalie tried not to smile. The editorial director of Shipley Junior Books had just pretended that she knew all about the Sherry Clutch Literary Agency. And then she had ordered her best editor to read a novel written by a twelve-year-old.

Alone in Tim's office, Natalie grinned. For the first time ever she was glad that her mom's boss was a fire-breathing, stuck-up know-it-all.

After Letha told her mom to read the manuscript, Cassandra Day couldn't wait to tell her agent about this unexpected development.

Natalie actually picked up the phone in Tim's office and dialed half of Zoe's number. Then she stopped and asked herself, *Do I really want Zoe calling me every five minutes all weekend long asking me, "Has she read it? Has she read it yet?"* Natalie hung up the phone.

Then she picked it up and dialed the number again. Zoe deserved some kind of progress report. *But she doesn't need to know everything—bad enough that one of us has to worry the whole weekend.*

"Zoe Reisman's room at the Reisman residence, Zoe Reisman speaking."

Natalie kept her voice low because her mom's office was only ten feet away. "Zoe? It's me. The manuscript is here. It's in my mom's office."

STOP AND THINK

Understanding Characters What do Natalie's thoughts in paragraph six tell you about the kind of person Zoe is?

Zoe was excited. "Great! Is she going to read it? Did she listen to my message? Do you think she suspects anything?"

"I know she got your message, and she doesn't suspect a thing. And I'm pretty sure she's going to read it. So we'll just have to see what happens next."

"You know," said Zoe slowly, "you could maybe help things along. You know, like pick up the envelope and say, 'I wonder if this one's any good'—something like that."

Natalie smiled, but she talked in a serious voice. She wanted Zoe to calm down. "No, I think we better just let things move ahead on their own. If there's no action in a week or so, then maybe you can call her again."

Zoe did not like that idea. "A week? Are you crazy? A week is forever! If I don't hear from her in three days, then I'm going to turn the heat up—way up!"

"Look, Zee Zee, relax. I've got to get off the phone now, but I'll let you know if anything else happens, okay?"

Zoe said, "Hey! Maybe you could offer to read it for her—you know, help out around the office?"

"Zoe?" said Natalie. "No. No, no, no. Just be patient."

"Yeah," said Zoe, "easy for you to say."

"No, it isn't easy for me to say, Zoe. I want to know what she thinks about it as much as you do. But we're just going to have to let it move along one step at a time, okay?"

There was a pause, and then Zoe said, "Okay. You're right . . . I guess."

"I'll call you if there's any news, I promise."

"Okay," said Zoe. "Bye."

When they finally left the office at seven-fifteen on Friday night, Natalie could see the envelope from the Sherry Clutch Literary Agency sticking up from the outside pocket of her mom's briefcase.

Natalie tried to think. She tried to decide what she was feeling. She couldn't figure out if she was happy or scared or numb or what. Because what Zoe had said at the very beginning was true now. All of a sudden her mom wasn't just her mom. She was her editor. Hannah Nelson would be the first person to read "The Cheater" in a professional way. Her own mom would be comparing Natalie's story to all the other manuscripts she had read during the past five years at Shipley Junior Books—manuscripts written by successful, established, professional authors. Part of Natalie wanted to snatch that envelope out of her mom's briefcase and toss it into a trash barrel. But it was too late for that. The day of judgment had arrived.

But that day wasn't Friday. Friday night when they got home, Natalie and her mom went right out again and ate at a Chinese restaurant and then caught a late movie at the local theater—one of those British movies where half the actors wear fancy clothes and the other half look like beggars. It was a lively story with plenty of action and a little bit of romance, but Natalie couldn't stay focused on it. Her mind kept wandering back to that envelope, still in the briefcase, sitting on a chair in the entryway of their loft.

And Saturday wasn't judgment day either. In the morning they went grocery shopping, and then there was the laundry, and then they both spent two hours cleaning the loft from one end to the other. And then it was dinner time.

Natalie went to her room to read after dinner, hoping that if she left her mom alone, she'd remember the manuscript. At about nine o'clock Natalie opened her bedroom door and walked softly toward the living-room area. Peeking from behind the big, leafy plants that framed the living room, she saw her mom. She was asleep on the couch, feet propped up on the coffee table, open magazine on her lap, bathed in flickering light from the muted TV.

Lying in bed later, Natalie tossed and turned. She thought about the heap of envelopes stacked up in Ella's darkened office. For every envelope there was a person somewhere, and Natalie knew how each of them felt. Those people were out there tonight, sleeping in hundreds of different beds in hundreds of different towns in dozens of different states. Every day each person woke up and thought, "Maybe the editor will read my story today," or "Maybe the editor will call me today." Every day each writer wondered if the mail would bring a letter, maybe good news from New York City.

And Natalie felt guilty. *Her* envelope wasn't in a heap somewhere in a dark office. Her story was in the editor's briefcase. The editor's boss had assigned *her* story as homework.

Natalie sat up in bed and looked at the clock. It was almost midnight. She groped for the phone on her bed stand and punched the glowing buttons.

Zoe answered on the third ring, groggy and grumpy. "Hello?"

"It's me, Zoe. I've got to tell you what happened."

It took Natalie about two minutes to tell Zoe how her story found its way home with the editor for the weekend.

Zoe was wide awake now. "So she read it? Did she like it? What did she say when she finished it? C'mon, tell me, tell me!"

"Well . . . she hasn't read it . . . not yet."

"She hasn't read it? So why did you call me in the middle of the night?"

Natalie hesitated. "Because . . . because I feel bad. I feel like the girl in my book. I feel like I'm a cheater too. All those other stories at my mom's office, stories that she'll never even look at? And here's my story, and it's all the way up at the head of the line. It just doesn't feel fair. That's all."

"Not fair? Who said things are fair? It's never fair, Natalie. You're a great writer, and someone like me isn't—is that fair? Is it?"

"Well . . . no. I guess not," said Natalie. "But you're great at things I stink at."

"Exactly," said Zoe. "It all evens out. It seems unfair, but it's not. Your mom is a good editor at a good publishing company, and someone else's mom isn't. Is that fair?"

"No . . . not really."

"Of course it's not fair. It's just the way it is. Didn't you have to work hard to write your book—just as hard as those other writers did?"

Natalie nodded as she answered. "Yeah, I did. I worked hard."

"So do you know why your book is going to get looked at and some of those other ones aren't? It's because you are who you are, and your mom is who she is, and you worked hard to write a great book."

Zoe paused to let that sink in. Then she said, "And there's another reason your book will get published and most of those others won't."

Natalie asked, "Why's that?"

In her best agent voice Zoe said, "Because you have a great agent, and those other schnooks don't! Now listen, Cassandra. I'm giving you good advice, you hear me? You hang up now and get a good night's sleep. And just stop thinking so much. You artists are all alike—thinking, thinking, thinking! Not to worry, darling. Zee Zee is going to take good care of you."

After hanging up, Natalie felt better, but it still took her another hour to get to sleep.

And even after her lecture to Cassandra, Zee Zee lay awake doing some thinking of her own.

STOP AND THINK

Question What question or questions might you ask yourself after reading Zoe's advice?

Then on Sunday it happened. It was late in the afternoon, and after finishing her math and English, Natalie settled into her beanbag chair to read about ancient Egypt in her social studies book. The chair was so comfortable, and she had stayed up too late the night before. The next thing Natalie knew, her mom was shaking her awake.

"Natalie, you won't believe this! You know this manuscript Letha made me bring home? Well, I opened it up, you know, just so I could tell her I looked at it? And I started reading it, and it's just . . . well, I couldn't stop reading! It's one of the best things I've read in a long time—and besides that, it's even a school story! Isn't that great?"

Natalie wanted to throw her arms around her mom's neck and burst into tears. She wanted to say, "It's mine, Mom! I wrote that! I wrote it for you, and I wrote it for Dad, and I'm so happy that you like it!"

But she couldn't, so she didn't. Instead Natalie gulped, and she smiled and said, "That's great, Mom. So, it's really good?"

Her mom nodded excitedly. "It's got such a wonderful feeling all through it . . . I mean, it needs some work here and there, but this Cassandra Day—that's the author—it's her first novel, and for a first novel it's terrific. I can't wait for you to read it."

And Natalie nodded and said, "I'd love to."

Your Turn

Undercover Author

Share Your Opinion Natalie uses a pen name (Cassandra Day), invents an agent (Zee Zee), and gives her manuscript directly to an editor (her mother). In your opinion, was Natalie "cheating" or just carrying out a daring plan? Write a paragraph that answers this question and explains why you think as you do. PERSONAL RESPONSE

Buy My Book!

Role-Play Literary agents try to persuade publishers to publish books. Work in a small group. One of you takes the role of a publisher, while the rest role-play literary agents. Each agent thinks of a story and tries to "sell" it to the publisher by describing it. The publisher accepts or rejects it, explaining why. SMALL GROUP

Building Character

Turn and Talk Authors create characters who may be a little like themselves or people they know. Think about what you learned about the characters Natalie and Zoe. With a partner, discuss what these characters might reveal about the author of "The School Story." UNDERSTANDING CHARACTERS

History of the Book

Throughout history, people have found ways to disclose their ideas. Writers have been recording their thoughts for thousands of years. These expressions from the past are not muted, but vibrant and meaningful.

Books have an important place in the timeline of recorded thought. This timeline spans from the ancient Chinese symbols that were scratched into tortoise shells to the electronic books of our own time.

2300 B.C.E.
Babylonian clay tablets

3000 B.C.E.   **2000 B.C.E.**   **1000 B.C.E.**

3200 B.C.E.
Egyptian papyrus scrolls

From Papyrus to Print

People are always looking for better ways to record information and ideas. The ancient Egyptians used a form of paper called papyrus. Papyrus was made from a plant that grew along the Nile River.

The ancient Babylonians used clay tablets to record everything from goat sales to literary works. They even used clay tablets to record the first known map of the world. With this system, though, it was not easy to make revisions to manuscript.

Parchment was a material made from the skin of sheep or goats. It was developed during the Roman Empire. Parchment lasted longer than papyrus.

Until the late 700s C.E., text had to be written and copied by hand. Book printing began in China around 868, but the type could be used only once. Around 1050, a Chinese printer named Bi Sheng invented movable type. Movable type could be used over and over.

Perhaps the biggest printing breakthrough came in the 1440s in Germany when Johannes Gutenberg developed a printing press. Movable type was set in a wooden form. The letters were coated with ink. Then a sheet of paper was laid on the letters and pressed with a wooden plate. Gutenberg began building his first large printing press in 1450.

1440–1450 C.E.
The Gutenberg press

868 C.E.
Early printed book

100 B.C.E.　　　　**500 C.E.**　　　　**1500 C.E.**

190 B.C.E.
Parchment codex

1050 C.E.
Movable type

From Linotype to Online Type

In the 1880s, the publishing industry was drastically changed. A man named Ottmar Mergenthaler invented the Linotype machine. It allowed its operator to use a keyboard to type the text. Then the Linotype machine gathered molds of whole lines of type. This gave the machine its name. Text became cheaper to produce. The public began pressuring the industry to print more of it. People wanted both the wry humor of Mark Twain and the serious news of the day.

The first audio books were developed in 1931 by the American Foundation for the Blind. These books were known as "talking books." In the 1960s, talking books became popular with the public. Many books are now available on CD and MP3.

Today, the fastest way to publish a book is electronically. An author can publish his or her own work on the Internet, as an e-book. The editorial process saves paper. However, an e-book may still go through a maze of procedures before publication.

Many e-books are available free in electronic form on several web sites, including one named Project Gutenberg in honor of one of the giants in the history of the book.

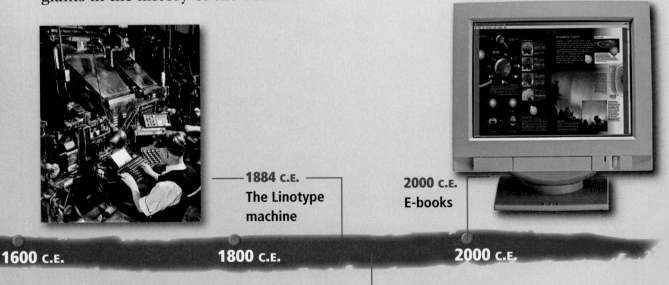

1884 C.E.
The Linotype machine

2000 C.E.
E-books

1600 C.E.　　　**1800 C.E.**　　　**2000 C.E.**

1931 C.E.
Audio books

Making Connections

 Text to Self

Write a Character Sketch In "The School Story," Natalie writes a novel called "The Cheater." If you were to write a fiction story, who would your main character be? Write a description of the character. Include details about his or her personality, appearance, and background.

 Text to Text

Discuss Bookmaking With a partner, use the information in "History of the Book" to discuss how Natalie's novel in "The School Story" might have been written and "published" before 700 C.E., in 1500 C.E., and today. Which publishing method would have reached the widest audience? Why? If you were an author, which method would you have preferred? Why?

 Text to World

Connect to Social Studies A study of the history of books takes a person all over the world. On a map, locate the important places mentioned in "History of the Book." You may need to do research to find out where some of the ancient places were located. Share what you learned by giving an oral report to a small group.

Grammar

Academic Language

sentence

complete subject

complete predicate

fragment

run-on sentence

What Is a Sentence? A **sentence** is a group of words that expresses a complete thought. A sentence must include a **complete subject**, all the words that tell whom or what the sentence is about, and a **complete predicate**, all the words that tell what the subject does, is, has, or feels. A **fragment** is missing one or both of these sentence parts.

	complete subject complete predicate
Complete Sentence	My friend writes books about her school.
Fragment (missing a subject)	Writes a chapter every week.
Fragment (missing a predicate)	A skillful and determined writer.

A **run-on sentence** is two or more sentences that are run together with commas or without any punctuation. It is hard to tell where one thought ends and the next one begins.

Run-on Sentence	I like mysteries, I also like adventure stories.
Corrected Sentence	I like mysteries. I also like adventure stories.

 **The items below are sentence fragments and run-on sentences. On another sheet of paper, correct and rewrite them as complete sentences.**

1 A career in writing.

2 The book has colorful characters, its plot is fascinating.

3 Are often excellent writers.

4 Editors study a manuscript carefully, they look at every detail.

Sentence Fluency You can sometimes fix sentence errors in your writing by combining fragments with sentences or other fragments to make complete sentences.

Sentence and Fragment	Combined into One Sentence
Natalie trusted her mother's judgment. And hoped for a good reaction to the manuscript.	Natalie trusted her mother's judgment and hoped for a good reaction to the manuscript.

Connect Grammar to Writing

As you edit your dialogue, make sure you correct any run-on sentences. Rewrite fragments, or combine them with other sentences or fragments to make complete sentences.

Write to Express

✔ **Voice** A good writer develops characters through their conversations as well as their actions. For example, when Natalie and Zoe first talk in "The School Story," their **dialogue** reveals that Zoe is impatient and that Natalie is cautious. Dialogue can take the place of description.

Isaiah drafted a dialogue between two friends who are discussing what to give another friend for his birthday. Later, Isaiah revised the dialogue to reveal more about the characters who are talking.

Writing Traits Checklist

✔ **Ideas**
Does each character have unique traits?

✔ **Organization**
Does the dialogue flow in a natural way?

✔ **Sentence Fluency**
Did I combine sentence parts to avoid run-ons?

✔ **Word Choice**
Does the dialogue use formal or informal language appropriately?

✔ **Voice**
Does my dialogue reveal the characters' personalities?

✔ **Conventions**
Did I use correct spelling, grammar, and punctuation?

Revised Draft

I think
"Maybe we should get Max a photo
! He's always taking pictures.
album."

Derek waved off Flor's idea and sighed.
Nah,
" He'd rather keep his photos on the

computer."
gazed into the distance
Flor was still enthusiastic. "Okay then,
since
he could use a new backpack his has holes

in it."

Final Copy

The Gift Question

by Isaiah Jackson

"I think we should get Max a photo album! He's always taking pictures."

Derek waved off Flor's idea and sighed. "Nah, he'd rather keep his photos on the computer."

Flor gazed into the distance. "Okay then, he could use a new backpack since his has holes in it."

Derek shook his head. "A backpack is kind of a personal decision. That won't work."

"Wait, I've got it! How about a year's membership to the science museum?"

"Nope," mumbled Derek. "His grandpa always gives him that."

Flor stared at him. "All right, you grump. What do YOU think we should give him?"

Derek shrugged. "Why don't we just get him another computer game?"

In my final paper, I added words and punctuation to show the characters' personalities more clearly. I also fixed a run-on sentence by making it a complex sentence.

Reading as a Writer

How does Isaiah's dialogue show the differences between Flor's and Derek's personalities? How can you use dialogue to make your characters' differences clearer?

mentor

employed

scholastic

grimly

contested

tumult

pursuit

culprit

deprived

miraculous

Vocabulary
Reader

Context
Cards

Vocabulary in Context

1   mentor

The job of a mentor, or experienced teacher, is to guide and encourage a person who is learning.

2   employed

Men and women who have done well in sales jobs probably used, or employed, a friendly style.

3   scholastic

Employers look at the scholastic record of a person they might hire. Achievement in school is important.

4   grimly

People who work long hours for low pay often do their work grimly, with no satisfaction.

- **Study each Context Card.**
- **Make up a new context sentence that uses two Vocabulary words.**

5 contested

A referee makes many decisions in a game. Some are contested, or challenged, by players.

6 tumult

People preparing meals in the kitchen of a restaurant often work in a scene of tumult, or noisy confusion.

7 pursuit

A police officer might use flashing lights in pursuit of someone trying to get away after breaking a law.

8 culprit

A librarian may not always charge a fine when a culprit, or guilty person, brings back an overdue library book.

9 deprived

Workers who are deprived of sleep don't have the energy to do their jobs well.

10 miraculous

Scientists have discovered miraculous cures for diseases that were thought to be incurable.

Background

✔ TARGET VOCABULARY **What Goes into an Autobiography?** An autobiography includes the events of a person's life, written by that person. The author might tell about the pursuit of success, a nasty culprit who got away with something, or a wise mentor who taught an important skill. You might read about the author's scholastic experiences, a miraculous recovery from an accident, or how he or she found fame despite being deprived of opportunities. Autobiographies have employed different styles and techniques. Some events are told grimly, propelled, or pushed forward, by history. Results may seem inevitable, as if they had to happen. The facts may even be contested. It's all based on memory, after all, and it's about the confusing tumult of life! Look for some of these characteristics in the next selection about and by author Jerry Spinelli.

A Jerry Spinelli Timeline

1940   **1955**   **1970**   **1985**   **2000**

1941 Born in Norristown, PA

1954 Goes to Stewart Junior High School

1956 Goes to Norristown High School

1982 Publishes *Space Station Seventh Grade*

1991 Wins Newbery Medal for *Maniac Magee*

1947 Goes to Hartranft Elementary School

In "Knots in My Yo-yo String," author Jerry Spinelli writes about his experiences while living in Norristown, Pennsylvania, in 1957.

Comprehension

✔ **TARGET SKILL** **Author's Purpose**

Authors write their books for specific reasons, such as entertaining readers or informing readers about a particular topic. As you read "Knots in My Yo-yo String," think about why the author wrote the selection. Make a chart like the one below to help you keep track of details that reveal the author's purpose in writing "Knots in My Yo-yo String."

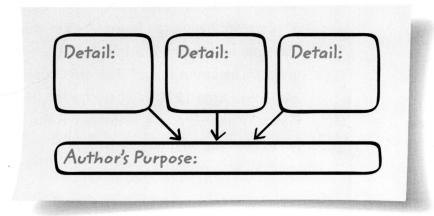

Detail: Detail: Detail:

Author's Purpose:

✔ **TARGET STRATEGY** **Infer/Predict**

As you read the selection, use the details in your chart to make inferences and predictions about Jerry Spinelli's purpose. Learning to make inferences and predictions helps you understand what the author is telling the reader.

JOURNEYS DIGITAL | Powered by DESTINATIONReading
Comprehension Activities: Lesson 2

✔ TARGET VOCABULARY

mentor	tumult
employed	pursuit
scholastic	culprit
grimly	deprived
contested	miraculous

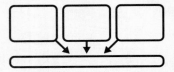

✔ TARGET SKILL

Author's Purpose Use text details to figure out the author's viewpoint and reasons for writing.

✔ TARGET STRATEGY

Infer/Predict Use text clues to figure out what the author means or what might happen in the future.

GENRE

Autobiography tells about events in a person's own life, written by that person.

Set a Purpose Before reading, set a purpose for reading based on what you know about the genre and your own experiences.

MEET THE AUTHOR
Jerry Spinelli

Jerry Spinelli once wanted to be a cowboy and a baseball player. Then, in the eleventh grade, a football game—which you'll read about in *Knots in My Yo-yo String*—turned him into a writer. Spinelli says, "Writing is a way of completing my experience. It's like things that I see and feel have not totally happened to me until I write about them." Spinelli's book *Maniac Magee* won the 1991 Newbery Award. His wife, Eileen Spinelli, is also a writer and is the first person to read anything he writes.

Knots in My Yo-yo String

by Jerry Spinelli

Writing about his childhood in Pennsylvania, author Jerry Spinelli remembers Haws Avenue, his dentist, and all the neighbors, bullies, girlfriends, zep sandwiches, and pesky yo-yo-string knots that filled his days between Hartranft Elementary and Norristown High, and that later filled his books.

On Friday evening, October 11, 1957, at Roosevelt Field, site of my fifty-yard-dash triumph five years before, Norristown High School played Lower Merion in a football game under the lights. Lower Merion was a powerhouse. Over the preceding three years they had won thirty-two games in a row. But Norristown was good, too. It figured to be a close, fiercely contested game, and it was. I was a junior now, sixteen years old, and my autumn sport had become soccer, but I still loved football. I was one of thousands in the grandstand.

As the teams changed field direction for the start of the fourth quarter, Norristown was leading, 7–6. Each team had scored a touchdown, but the Aces of Lower Merion had missed the extra point. But now a Lower Merion halfback was breaking free and racing downfield, blue-and-white-shirted Norristown Eagles in pursuit. The Eagles stopped him on the one-yard line, and the stage was set for one of the great moments in Norristown's scholastic sports history.

First down and goal to go on the one. One little yard. Thirty-six little inches. Lower Merion. Thirty-two straight victories. Who could stop them? In the bleachers across the field the Lower Merion fans celebrated. Norristown fans grimly awaited the inevitable.

The first Ace ball carrier plunged ahead helmet-first, the Lower Merion side erupted in a touchdown roar—but, strangely, no touchdown sign came from the referee. The ball carrier was crumpled in the rude arms of Eagle defender Mike Branca. The ball had advanced nary an inch.

Twice more the Aces ran the ball, attacking different points in the Eagle defense. The results were the same. The sound from the Lower Merion side was rising and falling as if directed by a choirmaster. But now, as the Ace quarterback bent over the center for the fourth time and barked out the count, Roosevelt Field fell silent. For the fourth time the Ace quarterback handed the ball to a running back—they refused to believe anyone could stop them from ramrodding the ball thirty-six little inches—and for the fourth time the ball failed to penetrate the end zone.

The impossible had been done.

Now it was the Norristown side that erupted, with a roar and a celebration that continued through the end of the game and burst from the stadium and spread out across the town and late into the night. I rode the tide. Lower Merion! We had beaten *Lower Merion!* I couldn't believe it. At home in my room I could hear the blaring horns, the shrieks of victory.

Again and again, following my old habit, I replayed the miraculous Eagle goal-line defense in my head. I went to sleep re-experiencing the event, re-feeling the thrill. In the morning I woke up and daydreamed on—and began to realize that I had a problem. For no matter how many times I replayed the goal-line stand in my head, I kept falling short of satisfaction. The scoreboard had said the game was over, but for me it wasn't, for me it was somehow frustratingly incomplete. I discovered that Roosevelt Field was not the only field that the game had been played on; the other was inside myself. The game kept happening and happening within me. I could not come to the end of it.

✔ STOP AND THINK

Author's Purpose What clues on pages 48 and 49 hint at the author's purpose for writing this selection?

And then for no reason that I can recall, I sat down at my study desk and reached for a pencil and paper and wrote down a title. Then I began to write rhyming verse. And the verses became a poem:

Goal to Go

The score stood 7—6
With but five minutes to go.
The Ace attack employed all tricks
To settle down its stubborn foe.

It looked as though the game was done
When an Ace stepped wide 'round right.
An Eagle stopped him on the one
And tumult filled the night.

Thirty-two had come their way
And thirty-two had died.
Would number thirty-three this day
For one yard be denied?

Roy Kent, the Eagle mentor, said,
"I've waited for this game,
And now, defense, go, stop 'em dead,
And crash the Hall of Fame!"

The first Ace bolted for the goal
And nothing did he see
But Branca, swearing on his soul,
"You shall not pass by me."

The next two plays convinced all
The ref would make the touchdown sign,
But when the light shone on the ball
It still lay inches from the line.

Said Captain Eastwood to his gents,
"It's up to us to stop this drive."
Said Duckworth, Avery, Knerr, and Spence,
"Will do, as long as we're alive."

The halfback drove with all his might,
His legs were jet-propelled,
But when the dust had cleared the fight,
The Eagle line had held.

At last, for me, the game was over.

STOP AND THINK

Infer/Predict Why do you think the author says on page 51 that after finishing the poem "Goal to Go," the game was over for him at last?

On a September day in 1992, thirty-five years after Norristown High's historic goal-line stand, I stood before an audience of children and adults in Fargo, North Dakota. I was there in connection with my novel *Maniac Magee*, which had recently won the Newbery Medal for children's literature. The important award on this day, however, was the Flicker Tale, which had been voted to *Maniac Magee* as a favorite of North Dakota's young readers. A hundred elementary-school kids sat cross-legged on the floor as I accepted the plaque.

After giving a little talk, I invited the audience to ask questions. There were many. One of them stays with me still. It came from a boy, who said, "Do you think being a kid helped you to become a writer?"

Good question.

After writing "Goal to Go," I gave it to my father and forgot about it. Several days later I opened the *Times Herald* to the sports section, and there was my poem, printed in a box with the headline "Student Waxes Poetic." At school the next day everyone—kids, teachers, football coaches—told me how much they liked it.

That, I believe, was the beginning. By the time I went off to Gettysburg College two years later, I knew I wanted to be a writer.

I graduated from Gettysburg, attended the Writing Seminars at the Johns Hopkins University, spent six months on active duty with the Naval Air Reserve, got a job as a menswear editor for a department store magazine, and in my spare time began to write my first novel.

Three years later I finished it, but no one wanted to publish it. So I wrote another.

And another.

And another.

Wrote them on my lunch hours, after work, weekends. Four novels over thirteen years.

Nobody wanted them.

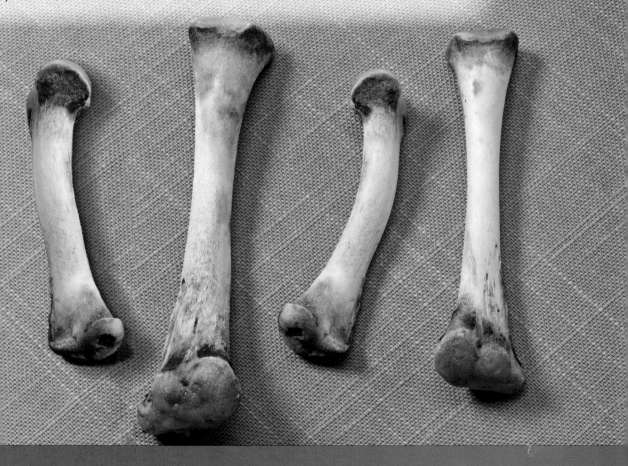

In the meantime I gained a wife, Eileen, also a writer, and six kids. One day for dinner we had fried chicken. There were leftovers. I packed the unclaimed pieces into a paper bag and put it in the refrigerator, intending to take it to work for lunch the following day. But when I opened the bag early the next morning, I found only chicken bones. The meat had been eaten away.

No doubt this was the work of one of the six little angels sleeping upstairs. Knowing no one would confess (I'm still waiting), I went to work that day lunchless and began to imagine how it might have gone had I known who the culprit was and confronted him or her in the kitchen. By noon I had decided to write down my imaginings. I was about to do so, intending to describe the scene from the point of view of the chicken-deprived father, when it suddenly occurred to me that there was a more interesting point of view here—namely, the kid's.

And so with ballpoint pen and yellow copy paper in a tiny windowless office on the fifth floor of the Chilton Company in Radnor, Pennsylvania, I wrote these words:

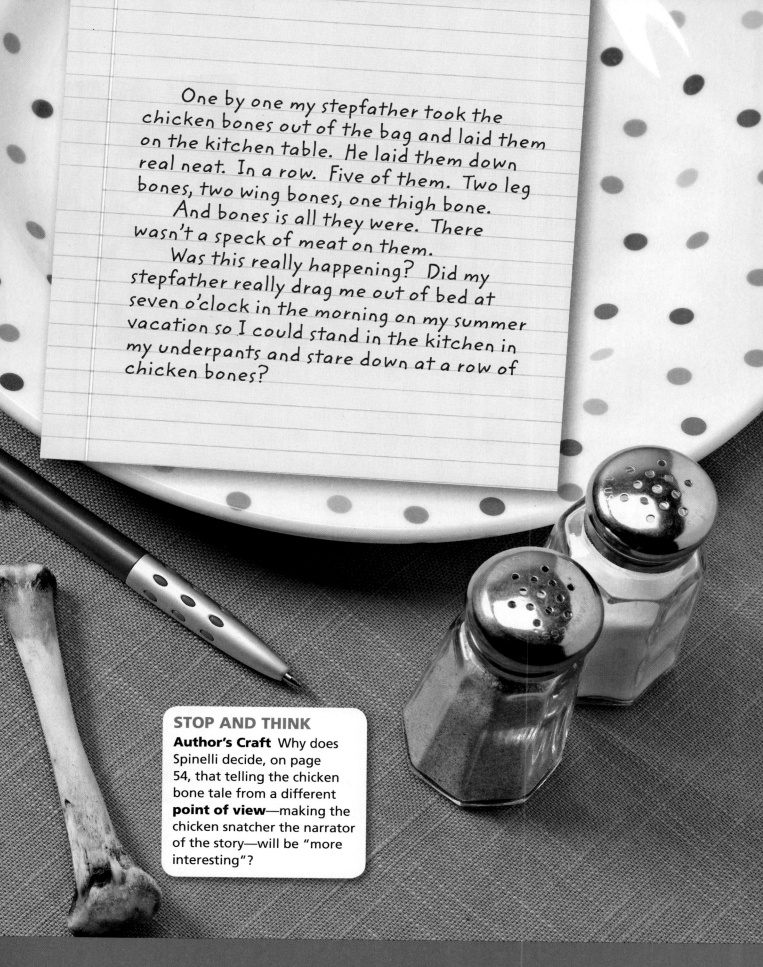

One by one my stepfather took the chicken bones out of the bag and laid them on the kitchen table. He laid them down real neat. In a row. Five of them. Two leg bones, two wing bones, one thigh bone.

And bones is all they were. There wasn't a speck of meat on them.

Was this really happening? Did my stepfather really drag me out of bed at seven o'clock in the morning on my summer vacation so I could stand in the kitchen in my underpants and stare down at a row of chicken bones?

STOP AND THINK

Author's Craft Why does Spinelli decide, on page 54, that telling the chicken bone tale from a different **point of view**—making the chicken snatcher the narrator of the story—will be "more interesting"?

That night at home I kept writing. I gave the chicken snatcher a name, Jason, and an age, twelve. And I started remembering. Remembering when I was twelve, when I lived in the West End, when I went to Stewart Junior High School, when I wanted to be a shortstop, when I rode a bike, when I marveled at the nighttime sky. In my head I replayed moments from my kidhood. I mixed my memories with imagination to make stories, to make fiction, and when I finished writing, I had a book, my fifth novel, my first about kids. I called it *Space Station Seventh Grade*.

It became my first published book.

In the years that followed, I continued to write stories about kids and to rummage through the attic of my memories. Norristown became Two Mills in my fiction, George Street became Oriole. There is a prom in one book and a girlfriend named Judy in another. There is a beautiful blonde who lives on an avenue called Haws and a mysterious man on whose front steps no kid dares sit. There is a zep and a mulberry tree, a Little League field, a park, a zoo, a band shell, a red hill, and a mother who whistles her kids home to dinner. There is a river called Schuylkill and a creek called Stony and a grocery store on a corner next to a house whose address is 802. And a brown finger in a white mouth. And a boy who is a wizard at untying knots in yo-yo strings.

Do you think being a kid helped you to become a writer?

I could have taken days to answer the boy's question, but neither he nor Fargo had that much time. So I simply nodded and smiled and said, "Yes, I believe it did."

**A budding ballplayer
(age 4, 1945)**

**Shortstop, Green Sox
(age 12, 1953)**

Your Turn

Take My Advice!

Share Your Thoughts There is a saying in publishing: "Write about what you know." Write a paragraph explaining how the events in Jerry Spinelli's life, as described in "Knots in My Yo-yo String," support this saying. End your paragraph by explaining what you would write about if you were going to follow this advice.

PERSONAL RESPONSE

Game Time!

Write Songs A football game inspired the poem "Goal to Go." In a group, play a game such as tic-tac-toe, rock-paper-scissors, or a board game you have in the classroom. Then create an entertaining song about the experience.

PARTNERS OR SMALL GROUPS

Life Becomes Literature

Turn and Talk With a partner, discuss how Jerry Spinelli used events from his life in "Knots in My Yo-yo String." Answer these questions: Why does the author tell about the football game in detail? Why does he tell about the chicken bones? What does he want the reader to understand about his childhood?

AUTHOR'S PURPOSE

Poetry

✓ TARGET VOCABULARY

mentor	tumult
employed	pursuit
scholastic	culprit
grimly	deprived
contested	miraculous

GENRE

Poetry uses the sound and rhythm of words in a variety of forms to suggest images and to express feelings.

TEXT FOCUS

Line breaks vary the rhythm of a poem. A **limerick** has regular breaks after each rhyme. Other poems may break lines in unusual ways.

Sporty Poetry

A poem about sports, like Jerry Spinelli's "Goal to Go," can capture the tumult of an exciting game or a pursuit downfield. It can capture a miraculous victory or a contested call by an umpire who said a base-stealer was "safe" when the culprit seemed to be "out"! A sports poem can scold a mentor, as "Quitter" does. It can recall the good and bad times in many seasons, as "We Have Our Moments" does. Sports poems can also be funny, like the two limericks on page 60.

Quitter

Coach calls me a quitter
He mutters it under his breath
Loud enough for me to hear,
But quiet enough
So no one knows
When I prove him wrong.

Janet Wong

We Have Our Moments

Sometimes we leap and land.
Sometimes we trip and fall.
Sometimes we catch the other team before they score.
Sometimes we jump too soon and get faked out of our
socks.

We can be sharp on the pick-up play at third.
Or
we can have rocks in our heads and miss that
softly batted ball,
and miss that
one
sweet chance to
save
the
day.

I lose. I win. We lose. We win.
The team finishes in last place.
The team is
in the play-offs at last
and past defeats f a d e
fast.
We have our moments.

Arnold Adoff

When I step on the basketball court,
They all jeer, "In your dreams! You're too short!"
Do I get in a funk?
Nope. I calmly slam dunk.
I would say I'm a pretty good sport.

Rob Hale

A bicycle racer named Raleigh
Told the cheering crowd, "Thanks! But, by golly,
I couldn't have done it—
I'd never have won it—
Without my dear passenger, Wally!"

Rob Hale

Write a Sports Poem

Write a poem about a sport you enjoy. Try a poem about a team deprived of a win, going grimly home. Write about a scholastic athlete who has employed a tricky move to score. Any idea will do!

Making Connections

Text to Self

Write About Inspirations A football game and leftover chicken bones inspired Jerry Spinelli to write. Make a list of five things or events in *your* life that could inspire a poem or story. Explain why each subject is inspirational.

Text to Text

Compare Poetry Choose a poem from "Sporty Poetry" and compare it to Jerry Spinelli's poem "Goal to Go" in "Knots in My Yo-yo String." Compare and contrast the poems' purposes and details. Share your ideas in a small group.

Text to World

Connect to Social Studies Well-known authors, like Jerry Spinelli, are not the only people who write autobiographies. Use online or print resources to find an autobiography of a famous person. List the three most interesting facts you learned about the person. Share these facts with a partner, and have him or her guess the identity of your subject.

Grammar

What Are the Four Kinds of Sentences? A **declarative sentence** makes a statement. It ends with a period. An **interrogative sentence** asks a question. It ends with a question mark. An **imperative sentence** gives a command. It ends with a period. An **exclamatory sentence** expresses strong feeling. It ends with an exclamation point.

Academic Language

declarative sentence
interrogative sentence
imperative sentence
exclamatory sentence

Sentence	Kind of Sentence
Jerry Spinelli watched an exciting football game.	declarative
Did he write a poem about it?	interrogative
Turn to the sports section.	imperative
The paper has printed Jerry's poem!	exclamatory

Work with a partner. Read each sentence below. Tell what kind of sentence it is.

1. What is your favorite sport?
2. Think of a memorable game or match.
3. You can write a poem about it.
4. Create pictures with your words.
5. What an exciting match it must have been!

Sentence Fluency You can make your writing more interesting by varying the types of sentences you use and the ways the sentences begin. Writing that includes questions, exclamations, and commands, as well as declarative sentences, can help hold readers' attention.

Same Sentence Type

Some people thought Norristown could beat Lower Merion. Norristown won, and blaring horns and shrieks of victory announced the result.

Varied Sentence Types

Could Norristown actually beat Lower Merion? Blaring horns and shrieks of victory announced that Norristown had won!

Connect Grammar to Writing

As you revise your story scene, make sure you vary the types of sentences you use. Look for places where changing a sentence to a different type could add interest and variety to your writing.

Write to Express

☑ **Voice** A **story**, or fictional narrative, is more interesting and more like real life when the writer shows the characters' reactions and feelings to events that take place. As you revise your fictional narrative, add your characters' thoughts and feelings.

Willow drafted a **scene** for a story about Margie, a girl who is a gifted public speaker. Later, she added Margie's inner thoughts.

Writing Traits Checklist

☑ **Ideas**
Did I make the action and dialogue interesting?

☑ **Organization**
Did I use the elements of story structure?

☑ **Sentence Fluency**
Did I vary sentence types?

☑ **Word Choice**
Are the pronouns correct for my first- or third-person point of view?

☑ **Voice**
Did I reveal my characters' thoughts and feelings?

☑ **Conventions**
Did I use correct spelling, grammar, and punctuation?

Revised Draft

On Monday morning, Tiffany opened her locker next to Margie's and then turned to look at her. "Hey, I heard your speech Saturday at the Prospectors Day festival." held her breath. She had no idea what to say. Margie ∧ waited. Tiffany and her crowd rarely gave Margie the time of day. Now they knew something that made her even Would they spread gossip and make fun of her? more different from them. ∧

64

The Speaker
by Willow Tucker

On Monday morning, Tiffany opened her locker next to Margie's and then turned to look at her. "Hey, I heard your speech Saturday at the Prospectors Day festival."

Margie held her breath. She had no idea what to say. Tiffany and her crowd rarely gave Margie the time of day. Now they knew something that made her even more different from them. Would they spread gossip and make fun of her?

But Tiffany smiled warmly. "What a cool thing it is that you can tell about the town's history in front of so many people! I could never do that!"

In my final paper, I made sure the description and dialogue reveal the characters' feelings. I also varied the sentence types.

Reading as a Writer

Which of Willow's changes do you think is most effective? Where can you reveal more about your characters' thoughts and feelings?

✔ **TARGET VOCABULARY**

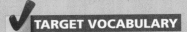

manipulated

menace

resolve

precisely

conclusion

emphatically

agony

demeanor

vigorously

revolting

Vocabulary
Reader

Context
Cards

Vocabulary in Context

1 manipulated

Clay is one material that is manipulated, or controlled, by sculptors when they create.

2 menace

Rust can be a menace to art objects made of iron. It can damage them if they are not protected.

3 resolve

A screenplay writer may try to have problems resolve by the end of a movie to create a happy ending.

4 precisely

A careful painter knows precisely, or exactly, how much paint to use with every brushstroke.

- **Study each Context Card.**

- **Discuss one picture. Use a different Vocabulary word from the one in the card.**

5 **conclusion**

A theater critic may reach the conclusion, or final opinion, that a play has been poorly written.

6 **emphatically**

When an audience claps emphatically, with force, performers often return to the stage.

7 **agony**

Without words, a good actor can communicate agony as well as joy.

8 **demeanor**

A cartoonist's drawing might show a character's demeanor, or behavior, in a few pen-and-ink lines.

9 **vigorously**

Street dancers perform their moves vigorously, with strong movements.

10 **revolting**

People react to art in different ways. Some may love it, while others may find it revolting.

Background

✔ **TARGET VOCABULARY** **What Do Writers Do?** Writers write in many different genres, but whether they create fiction or nonfiction, most writers would agree they have manipulated words to express ideas.

A screenwriter might write a script for a horror movie describing the agony of a revolting creature with a frightening demeanor. A songwriter might dash off lyrics with gusto, or energy. A cookbook writer might explain precisely how to bake a pie. A graphic novelist might tell about the shenanigans, or mischief, of a character who is a menace until a hero comes along to resolve the problem emphatically and vigorously.

What conclusion can you make about writers? As long as people have ideas, they will write to entertain, inform, and persuade.

A writer's ideas can fit many different genres.

Comprehension

✔ TARGET SKILL **Text and Graphic Features**

In "The Fruit Bowl Project," visual clues add another layer of meaning to the text. Look for text and graphic features such as headings, illustrations, unusual punctuation, and styles of lettering. Make a chart like the one below to record examples of text and graphic features and their purpose in "The Fruit Bowl Project." Add more rows for more examples.

Text or Graphic Feature	Page Number	Purpose
Example:		

✔ TARGET STRATEGY **Analyze/Evaluate**

You can use your graphic organizer to help you analyze the content and design of each part of this selection. Then you can evaluate the author's and illustrator's decisions. As you read "The Fruit Bowl Project," think about which text format and graphic features are most effective.

and stormy night...

TARGET VOCABULARY

manipulated	emphatically
menace	agony
resolve	demeanor
precisely	vigorously
conclusion	revolting

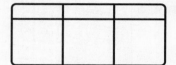

TARGET SKILL

Text and Graphic Features
Examine how the arrangement of text and visuals makes ideas clearer.

TARGET STRATEGY

Analyze/Evaluate Think carefully about the text and form an opinion about it.

GENRE

Realistic fiction has characters and events that are like people and events in real life.

MEET THE AUTHOR

Sarah Durkee

Sarah Durkee has written Emmy-winning scripts and songs for *Sesame Street*, *Between the Lions*, *Arthur*, and *Dora the Explorer*. She has written stand-up comedy, musicals, rock lyrics, plays, and poetry for children and adults. She has also sold skis. She lives in New York City.

MEET THE ILLUSTRATOR

David Goldin

David Goldin's childhood in New York City was spent exploring the city and reading comic books. In addition to drawing and painting, he does animation and makes collages and unusual toys. He also travels the world collecting objects that he can use in his work.

THE FRUIT BOWL PROJECT

by Sarah Durkee

selection illustrated by David Goldin

Essential Question

How can text and graphics retell a story?

Ms. Vallis has invited her brother-in-law, rock songwriter Nick Thompson, to visit her eighth-grade class at West Side Middle School. Nick tells the students that a writer's words are like an artist's paints. Words can be manipulated *in a million different ways to "paint" the same bowl of fruit. To demonstrate, Nick gives the class a writing assignment that is to be their "fruit bowl." Each student has to craft a piece of writing, in any genre or format, containing the following seven elements:* **school, sixth grade, a reading test, a boy who drops a pencil, a girl who gets angry, lunch, and milk coming out of a boy's nose.** *Here is a selection from the class's "fruit bowl."*

JUST THE FACTS
By Greta Stern

One morning in a sixth-grade classroom in New York City, a boy dropped a pencil during a test. Stooping to pick it up, he bumped the arm of a girl sitting next to him. She got mad at him, the bump having caused her to make a mark on her test, and accused him of trying to cheat. Later, in the cafeteria, the same boy told a joke to another boy, who then laughed, making his drink come out of his nose. They had to throw their lunches away.

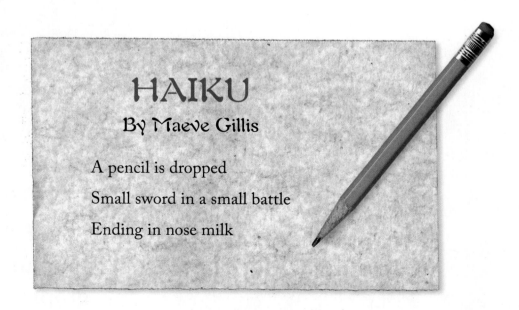

HAIKU

By Maeve Gillis

A pencil is dropped

Small sword in a small battle

Ending in nose milk

NEWSPAPER

By Deena Prajapati

NEW YORK—When is an accident not an accident?

When it's "totally on purpose," said Zoe Blass, eleven, of Manhattan. The sixth-grader at I.S. 280 said it began innocently enough. The kids were taking a citywide reading test the morning of April 20 and Blass was, she insists, doing very well.

"I always do well on those tests," she said. "I always think I might flunk, but then I always do well. It's weird."

Weirder still was what happened next, reported Blass. A classmate, Kevin Marchetti, dropped his pencil on the floor and bent to pick it up.

"He, like, slammed into me," said Blass emphatically. "I mean, not just a little bump. He hit my elbow really, really hard." Blass also claims Marchetti was attempting to cheat, though she's unable to prove it. The incident left her close to tears and with an ugly pencil mark on her test.

Blass claimed Marchetti gave no apology.

Other students backed up Blass's account. "He, like, slammed her," agreed Franny Stabenau. "He totally did," chimed in Lindsey Edwards.

But there is, the girls reported, some justice. Later on in the cafeteria, another student, Jason Allen, laughed so hard at a joke Marchetti told, chocolate milk sprayed out of his nose and all over his and Marchetti's lunch.

"It was gross," Blass said. "But he deserved it."

"Totally," agreed Stabenau.

STOP AND THINK
Analyze/Evaluate On pages 72 and 73, "HAIKU" and "NEWSPAPER" present the same story in very different ways. What are some differences between the two pieces?

EXAGGERATION
By Talisa Guzman

It was *easily* 100 degrees in there, the room felt like a *pottery kiln* for goodness sake. The poor sixth graders were practically *fainting*. As usual, the teacher was hovering like some predatory *hawk* while the kids were taking yet another test in an *endless* series of *completely* pointless tests. One huge boy threw his pencil on the floor in absolute *disgust*. He hit the sweet little girl next to him when he picked it up and she cried out in *agony*, the kids all stopped dead they were so worried about her! It was totally obvious to everyone that he was probably *cheating*, and the teacher did exactly *nothing* about it. The incredible thing is he practically *laughed*, the stupid thug! He's lucky he didn't get *expelled*. She was a *crumpled heap* of sobs. It was *so* awful.

Later in the cafeteria something *hysterical* happened! The same exact horrible boy told the funniest joke you've ever heard in your entire *life*! The boy he told it to laughed so hard chocolate milk gushed out of his nose like an open *fire hydrant*, I mean *torrents* of chocolate milk, all over *everybody's* lunch trays! It was the most disgusting mess you've ever *seen*! People were lining up at the trash cans having a total *fit*, screaming and laughing and dumping *tons* of revolting food into the trash! It was complete, total *pandemonium*!!!

✔️ **STOP AND THINK**

Text and Graphic Features In the story "EXAGGERATION," words are often shown in italics (a special sloping typeface used to emphasize text). What do the italics tell you about this story?

TWENTY WORDS OR LESS
By Brendan Torres

School. Hot. Test. Boy. Restless. Pencil. Drop. Retrieve.
Bump. Girl. Angry. Lunch. Boys. Joke. Laughter. Milk.
Nose. Food. Gross. Trash.

Instant Message

By Justin Sirk

 Fizzykat:
hi

 bwaygrrl1010:
hi

 Fizzykat:
where r u?????

 bwaygrrl1010:
home

 Fizzykat:
do you have school were
on spring break still

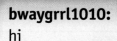 **bwaygrrl1010:**
aaaaaaaaaaaaaaagggghhhhh!!!
:(((((((((((((((((((((
I'm sooooo jelouse!!!!!!!!

 Fizzykat:
☺ lol what's up

 bwaygrrl1010:
nm

 Fizzykat:
r u still frds w / Zoe?

bwaygrrl1010:
yeah sort of
she was so insane today we had
a test and this kid hit her arm and she made a
pencil mark and sh went INSANE!!!!!!! ☺

Fizzykat:
who hit her

bwaygrrl1010:
she said he was cheating a
kid named Kevin you don't
know him I don't think

Fizzykat:
i dont know him.
is he wierd?

bwaygrrl1010:
YES!!!!!!!!!!!!!!!!!!!!!!!!!!!

Fizzykat:
☐..☐..☐......
(I just felt like doing that)

bwaygrrl1010:
u r insane

Fizzykat:
☺☺☺☺☺☺☺☺☺☺☺☺☺☺☺

bwaygrrl1010:
have u ever had a drink come
out ur nose at lunch?

Fizzykat:
NOOOOOOOO did u??????

bwaygrrl1010:
No but a kid did today

Fizzykat:
!!!!!!!!!!!??????????

bwaygrrl1010:
brb

Fizzykat:
k

Fizzykat:
zzzzzzzzzzzzzzzzz

Fizzykat:
dum dee dum de dummm

Fizzykat:
WHERE R UUUUUU??????

bwaygrrl1010:
gtg bye!

Fizzykat:
k bye c u

CROSS-EXAMINATION
By Danielle Nesby

Q: *Exactly where did this happen?*

A: A sixth-grade classroom.

Q: *And how do you know it was the sixth grade, and not the seventh or even the fifth?*

A: It's my classroom and I'm in the sixth.

Q: *How many children were involved?*

A: Twenty-something. Plus a teacher.

Q: *Twenty-two? Twenty-eight?*

A: Probably more like twenty-eight.

Q: *Did you notice anything strange in particular? Anything at all?*

A: Strange?

Q: *Strange behavior, perhaps?*

A: Well, Kevin seemed very restless.

Q: *Let the record show that the witness is indicating Mr. Marchetti. So, Mr. Marchetti seemed very restless, you say. And how did you draw this conclusion?*

A: He kept jiggling his leg and tapping his pencil like he was, y'know, restless.

Q: *I see. And this was what you would call "strange behavior" . . . ?*

A: Well, you said did I notice anything at all—

Q: *—stranger than the behavior that followed? The girl's behavior?*

A: That was kinda strange, too.

79

Q: *Would you tell us precisely what happened, please, in your own words.*

A: Sure. Um . . . Kevin was acting restless, and then he dropped his pencil on purpose.

Q: *And what made you think that he dropped his pencil on purpose?*

A: I dunno. He just seemed like he wanted to get everybody's attention.

Q: *"Seemed." I see. So in your opinion, Mr. Marchetti simply enjoys attention?*

A: Yeah. Yes, I would say that. And he enjoyed making the girl mad.

Q: *Did Mr. Marchetti say anything that would make you think he enjoyed getting the girl mad?*

A: Noooo, but . . . he was kinda smiling . . .

Q: *Could he, in fact, have felt very badly about the dropped pencil, very badly indeed? And might he have been smiling about something else entirely at that moment?*

A: Well, yeah, I guess that's possible.

Q: *And who was this girl?*

A: Zoe, the girl sitting next to him. She got furious because he bumped her arm when he picked up his pencil.

Q: *Did he injure the girl?*

A: No, not really . . . but he made her make a mark on the test we were taking, and she said he was trying to cheat.

Q: *This was merely her opinion, correct?*

A: Yeah. Correct.

Q: *Would you say the girl's reaction was extreme?*

A: Um . . . maybe a little . . .

Q: *Overly emotional?*

A: Maybe. Yeah, definitely . . .

Q: *Inappropriately intense? Violent?*
(Lawyer: Objection! Leading the witness . . .)
(Judge: Sustained. Please continue.)
Q: *How did the incident resolve?*
A: The teacher calmed her down.

Q: *Which was no doubt quite difficult to do, as hysterical as the girl was . . . ?*
(Lawyer: Objection!)
(Judge: Sustained.)
Q: *Did you then witness Mr. Marchetti's demeanor in the lunchroom?*
A: Demeanor?

Q: *His behavior, his mood?*
A: Yeah, I witnessed him having a very funny demeanor.

Q: *Funny amusing, or funny peculiar?*
A: Funny amusing. He told a redheaded kid a joke that made him laugh milk out of his nose.

Q: *Were there other witnesses to this?*
A: Tons. They had to throw chicken nuggets away that had nose milk on them.

Q: *And how do you know they threw their lunches away because they had nose milk on them?*
A: I just figured that was why . . .

Q: *Isn't it possible that they threw those chicken nuggets away NOT because of nose milk, indeed NOT because of anything Mr. Marchetti said or did, but because the chicken nuggets simply TASTED BAD, as they do EVERY time they are served?*
A: I . . . I guess that's possible.

Q: *Thank you. That will be all.*

INSTRUCTIONS

By Sandra Bruce

Congratulations on the purchase of your SIXTH-GRADE SHENANIGANS™ MILK OUT THE NOSE! kit! Ready to start? Have fun!

You will need:

1 classroom
1 cafeteria
28 children (11 and 12 years, assorted sizes)
1 teacher

Enclosed items:

Pencils (28)
Test booklets (28)
Chicken nuggets (16)
Chocolate milk container (1)

Step 1:

Preheat classroom to 93 degrees. Fill with children. Insert teacher.

Step 2:

Place enclosed pencils and test booklets on desks. Watch children work! (Note: Children will be drowsy. This is normal.)

Step 3:

Let children sit undisturbed 30–35 minutes or until knee of largest boy begins jiggling vigorously. Pencil of largest boy will then drop to floor.

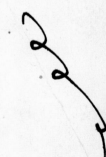

Step 4:

Allow largest boy to pick up pencil. When he sits up, he will strike arm of small girl seated next to him and her pencil will scratch across her test. WATCH WHAT HAPPENS!

Step 5:

Move children to cafeteria. (Caution: CHILDREN WILL BE LOUD. Adjust volume as necessary.)

Step 6:

Divide enclosed chicken nuggets onto 2 plastic plates (plates, cutlery, and additional food not included). Seat largest boy across from red-haired boy.

Step 7:

Place enclosed chocolate milk container in hand of red-haired boy. Largest boy will begin telling a joke!

Step 8:

Sit back and watch the wacky result!!!

STOP AND THINK

Author's Craft On page 83 the author uses the word *wacky* to describe the result the kit is supposed to produce. What other **word choices** on pages 82 through 84 help create a funny, persuasive tone?

(Note: It is very important that the red-haired boy takes a gulp of milk at the precise moment the largest boy tells "punch line." If largest boy finishes joke and red-haired boy laughs without performing expected squirting action from nose, repeat steps 5–7.)

Enjoy these crazy SHENANIGANS™ again and again!

More kits available from
SIXTH-GRADE SHENANIGANS™:

SLEEPLESS SLEEPOVER!
PUBLIC SCREAMING!
UNBELIEVABLY EMBARRASSING MOM!
ZIT SNIT!
SKATEBOARD MENACE!

Your Turn

Show Your Style!

Rewrite a Story Think of a short fairy tale or fable you know. Rewrite it in one of the styles used by the students in "The Fruit Bowl Project." Include the appropriate graphic features, and share the purpose of each feature with a partner. TEXT AND GRAPHIC FEATURES

Say It with Art

Sketch an Event Think of a funny event that happened to you recently. Draw three sketches that show the beginning, middle, and end of the event. Trade sketches with a partner. Try to guess your partner's event. PARTNERS

Telling Tales

Turn and Talk Flip through "The Fruit Bowl Project" with a partner, and discuss the different ways the story is told. Then think of three more ways to tell the story. Talk about which text and graphic features you would use in each version. With your partner, determine which of the three versions is most effective and why.

TEXT AND GRAPHIC FEATURES

PORTRAYING Portraits

by Mary Sloan

Artists have many ways of painting portraits. A portrait is a picture of a person. It might show agony or joy, kindness or menace. An artist might use paint lightly or vigorously. A portrait may reveal a little or a lot about a person.

Many early portraits are of rulers. This portrait is of the early Chinese Emperor Taizong. He has a strong, serious look. It shows that his demeanor, or behavior, was probably forceful.

Leonardo da Vinci painted *Mona Lisa* in 1503. It may be the most well-known portrait in the world. Da Vinci had come to a key conclusion. He thought a portrait should give a glimpse of its subject's inner life. That glimpse can be seen in *Mona Lisa*. People are captivated by her mysterious smile.

Mary Cassatt painted *At the Opera* in 1879. Cassatt liked to paint people in real settings. She was an American who spent many years in Paris. While there, she was influenced by the Impressionists. These artists wanted to show light and color at a moment in time. They did not paint details precisely.

Pablo Picasso was a Spanish painter. He believed emphatically in trying new techniques. He painted *Le Guitariste* in 1910. As an example of Cubism, it shows a subject from many angles at once. Many viewers found Cubism exciting; others considered it revolting. This debate would resolve as people grew used to Cubism.

Margo Humphrey created *The History of Her Life Written Across Her Face* in 1991. She manipulated words and images to represent herself. The painting shows her experiences as an African American female artist. Some of her ideas came from traditional body art.

Making Connections

 Text to Self

Write About Expression In "The Fruit Bowl Project," students work by themselves on their writing. In some other forms of expression, such as bands or choirs, artists express themselves by working together. Write about how you like to express yourself. Is it working alone or with a group? Explore the benefits and challenges of working with others and working alone.

 Text to Text

A Different Approach Painters in "Portraying Portraits" take different approaches to one form of art. Students in "The Fruit Bowl Project" take different approaches to one writing assignment. In a small group, choose one portrait from "Portraying Portraits." Each member should then describe it using the "Twenty Words or Less" form.

 Text to World

Connect to Art Cut out of old magazines two different portraits, either illustrations or photographs. Discuss how the portraits are similar and different in style or expression.

Grammar

What Are Compound Subjects and Predicates? The main word (or set of words) in a complete subject is the **simple subject**. The **simple predicate** is the main word (or words) in a complete predicate. A **compound subject** contains two or more simple subjects joined by the **conjunction** *and* or *or*. A **compound predicate** contains two or more simple predicates joined by *and* or *or*.

Academic Language

simple subject
simple predicate
compound subject
conjunction
compound predicate

Sentence with a Simple Subject and Predicate	simple simple subject predicate A pencil fell to the floor.
Sentence with a Compound Subject	compound subject simple simple simple subject subject predicate A pencil and a pen fell to the floor.
Sentence with a Compound Predicate	compound predicate simple simple simple subject predicate predicate A pencil fell to the floor and rolled beneath a desk.

Try This! **Write the sentences below on a sheet of paper. Draw a box around the simple subjects, underline the simple predicates, and circle the compound subjects and compound predicates.**

1 The teacher and her brother talked to the class.

2 He writes and sings rock songs.

3 I download his songs and listen to them often.

4 The words and phrases suggest a story to me.

Sentence Fluency When you write, you can make your sentences less repetitive by eliminating extra words. Try using a conjunction, such as *and,* to combine sentences that have the same subject but different predicates or the same predicate but different subjects.

Same Subject, Different Predicates

The pencil fell.

The pencil rolled toward the girl's feet.

Compound Predicate

The pencil fell and rolled toward the girl's feet.

Connect Grammar to Writing

As you revise your descriptive paragraph, look for sentences that have the same subjects or predicates. Try combining these sentences to form sentences with compound subjects or predicates.

Write to Express

✓ Word Choice Description is vital to realistic fiction because readers want to imagine each scene. Descriptive writing is most effective when it uses sensory words that bring the action to life. As you revise your description, add sensory words.

Mustafa drafted a **descriptive paragraph** about a cafeteria disrupted when a frog gets loose. Later, he imagined what the characters would see and hear, and then he added sensory words.

Writing Traits Checklist

✓ Ideas
Did I include details that put the reader at the scene?

✓ Organization
Did I use a logical order to present the details?

✓ Sentence Fluency
Did I combine sentences by using compound subjects or predicates?

✓ Word Choice
Did I use words that appeal to multiple senses?

✓ Voice
Did I try adding personification?

✓ Conventions
Did I use correct spelling, grammar, and punctuation?

Revised Draft

The next fifteen minutes were ~~confusing.~~ sheer mayhem. Screams and yells

~~Noises~~ from all over the room revealed

which way the frog ~~went.~~ hopped Some kids ran

toward the frog while others ran away.

Teachers ^and janitors darted here and there. ~~The~~

~~janitors ran around, too.~~ Only when a boy

caught the frog in his lunchbox did all the

~~noise go away.~~ racket fade

One Wild Lunch

by Mustafa Barifi

Ali breathed deeply, inhaling the warm smell of pepperoni pizza as he carried his tray toward friends waving at him from a far cafeteria table. The hard, narrow benches guaranteed he wouldn't take long to eat. Before he finished his first bite, though, a girl at the table behind him shrieked. "Oh no! Tuba got away! Hey, everybody, help me catch my frog!" The next fifteen minutes were sheer mayhem. Screams and yells from all over the room revealed which way the frog hopped. Some kids ran toward the frog while others ran away. Teachers and janitors darted here and there. Only when a boy caught the frog in his lunchbox did all the racket fade.

In my final paper, I added sensory words to enliven the action. I also combined sentences using a compound subject.

Reading as a Writer

How do Mustafa's changes add life to his description? Where can you add sensory words in your own descriptive paragraph?

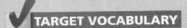

torrent
accustomed
void
swiveled
clustered
transmissions
doleful
clamor
urgent
coaxed

Vocabulary
Reader

Context
Cards

Vocabulary in Context

1 torrent
Like a torrent, or a rushing stream, people pour out of the subway on their way to work.

2 accustomed
City pigeons are accustomed to sharing their home with humans. They are used to people.

3 void
A vacant lot is a void among city buildings. Most big cities have these empty spaces.

4 swiveled
This revolving door has swiveled, or turned, to let people in and out of the building.

- **Study each Context Card.**

- **Ask a question that uses one of the Vocabulary words.**

5 clustered

At lunchtime, hungry customers can be found clustered around street vendors selling food.

6 transmissions

Police officers in the city communicate by sending and receiving radio transmissions.

7 doleful

An abandoned building can be a doleful sight. It may give a sad look to a neighborhood.

8 clamor

A crowd in a city stadium might make a deafening clamor after an exciting victory.

9 urgent

This ambulance answers an urgent call. Cars move aside so it can rush to an emergency.

10 coaxed

Many store owners have easily coaxed, or persuaded, customers to come in for big sale events.

Background

What Is Science Fiction? Astronauts journey into the void of space after receiving urgent transmissions from aliens. Robots rampage, or storm, around a city while scientists clustered in a lab search for solutions. Friends investigating a loud clamor in a cave find a prehistoric creature in distress. These are examples of science fiction—fantasy stories based on science and technology.

A torrent of scientific discoveries has provided an immense range of science fiction ideas. Some writers have coaxed a story from science by going slightly beyond what's possible. Others have swiveled their thinking to imagine a weird, doleful future. But many stories, like the one that follows, take place in a setting that most of us are accustomed to seeing.

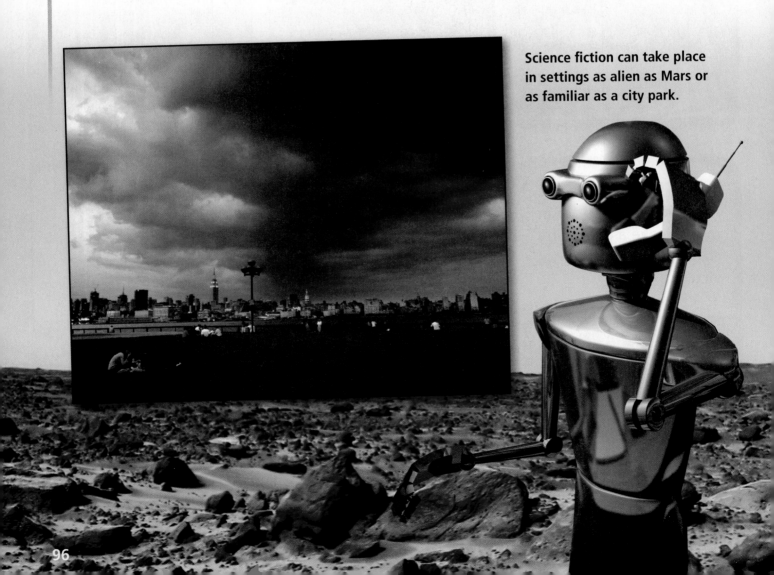

Science fiction can take place in settings as alien as Mars or as familiar as a city park.

Comprehension

TARGET SKILL Story Structure

As you read "The ACES Phone," identify story elements such as characters, setting, and plot, which includes the story's events, conflict, and resolution. These elements work together, so that if any were to change, the story might develop differently. Make a story map like the one below to keep track of story elements as you read.

Characters:	Setting:
Plot:	

TARGET STRATEGY Monitor/Clarify

Organizing the story elements in a story map will help you to monitor, or pay attention to, what you are reading and to clarify parts of the story that you may not understand.

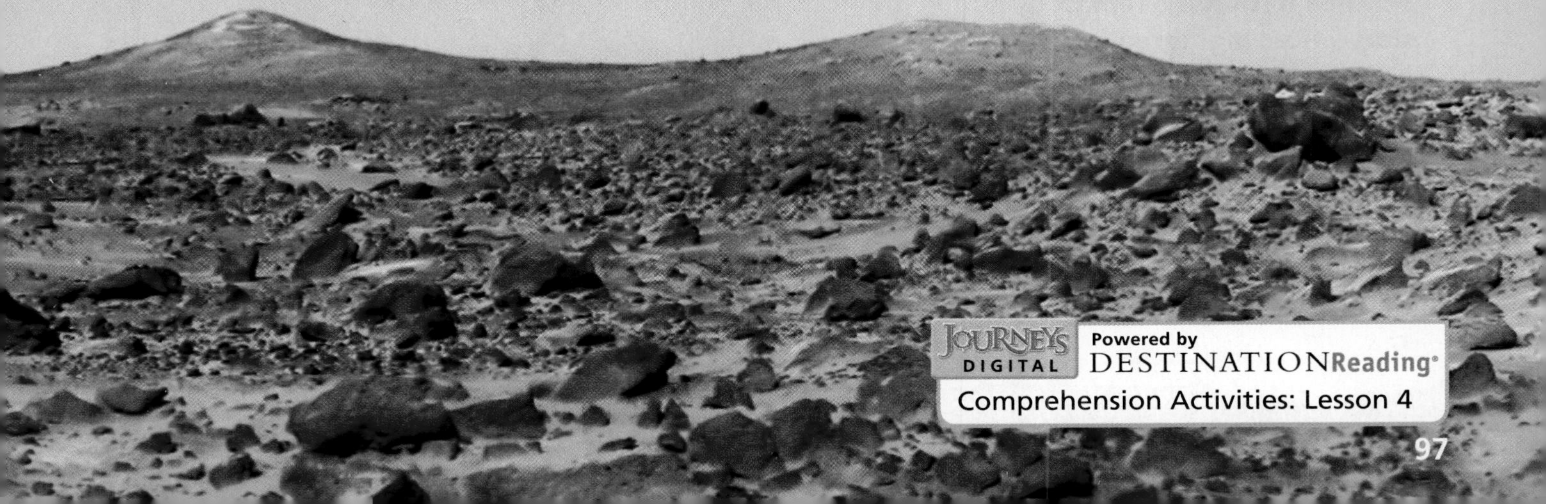

Main Selection

✔ TARGET VOCABULARY

torrent	transmissions
accustomed	doleful
void	clamor
swiveled	urgent
clustered	coaxed

✔ TARGET SKILL

Story Structure Examine details about characters, setting, and plot.

✔ TARGET STRATEGY

Monitor/Clarify As you read, notice what isn't making sense. Find ways to figure out the parts that are confusing.

GENRE

Science fiction is a fantasy story whose plot often depends on scientific ideas.

Set a Purpose Before reading, set a purpose for reading based on what you know about the genre and your own experiences.

MEET THE AUTHOR

Jeanne DuPrau

When she was five, Jeanne DuPrau wrote a book in crayon about a snowman. Since then she has written five novels, including *The City of Ember* series. She urges young writers to read a lot, write a lot, and be curious about the world. Besides writing, DuPrau enjoys puttering in her garden with her dog, Ethan.

MEET THE ILLUSTRATOR

Suling Wang

Among the books Suling Wang has illustrated are two by Lawrence Yep: *The Magic Paintbrush* and *When the Circus Came to Town*. Wang also creates computer animation.

THE ACES PHONE

from **NOISY OUTLAWS, UNFRIENDLY BLOBS, AND SOME OTHER THINGS...**

by Jeanne DuPrau

selection illustrated by Suling Wang

Essential Question

How might a character solve a problem by listening?

Martin loves his big family, but there's barely enough room for him in his crowded urban apartment. He spends a lot of time skating outdoors, feeling that there is a void in his life he ought to fill. When he finds a cell phone in the park one day, Martin presses the speed-dial numbers to see if he can identify its owner. He gets nowhere until he presses the number 5....

The phone rang only once. Then there was a click and a brief silence. And then came a sound unlike anything he'd heard before. It seemed to come from both far away and near, a clamor made up of a thousand thread-like voices—and along with the noise came a blast of feeling so strong it nearly knocked him off the bench. He pitched forward, as if he'd gotten a sudden terrible cramp. The feeling poured into his ear and flooded down through his chest and into his blood and raced like fire all through his body. It wasn't rage or fear or joy or love but a mixture of all of them, so strong that he cried out and dropped the phone on the ground.

The pigeons, thinking it might be something to eat, flocked around it. He bent down to pick it up, shaking. Cautiously, he put the phone near his ear—not right against it this time—and listened. The strange, immense chorus of sound still poured out, and the feeling jolted him again. It was so strong that he couldn't stay sitting on the bench. He had to get up and move.

He paced furiously around the playground, under the swings, over to the slide, around the jungle gym. It was a good thing no one was there—he knew he looked very odd, as if the wind was blowing him this way and that. After a long time, he began to notice something.

The feeling that shot through him changed slightly as he changed his direction. When he walked toward the baseball diamond, his heart beat harder, as if he were afraid. When he walked toward Avenue B, he grew calmer. When he went out of the park and down 14th Street, he felt weighed down by sadness.

It was like that game where you're looking for something and the other person says, "You're hot! No, you're getting colder! No, *really* cold! Now you're hot again!" But what was he looking for? He had no idea.

The next day he had a terrible time concentrating at school. He was wildly impatient to try out the phone again. It wasn't quite as cold, so a few people were in the park when he got there—a mother pushing her toddler on a swing, a couple of kids going backward down the slide, and an old woman in a knit hat and a lumpy purplish coat trudging along the path by the baseball diamond.

> **STOP AND THINK**
>
> **Author's Craft** On page 100 the author uses **alliteration**, repeating the beginning consonant sounds of words to emphasize important ideas or to create a mood, in "a thousand thread-like voices." Why do you think she repeats the *th* sound? Find another example of alliteration in the first paragraph on page 102.

Martin stood within a clump of trees at the corner of the park, turned on the phone, and pressed 5. Once again, the torrent of sound-feeling rushed through him and forced him to start walking. He went toward Avenue B, since that had made the feeling calmer yesterday. But it didn't work today. Everything was different. He felt a pang of fear as he went toward the jungle gym, and a jolt of joy as he neared the picnic tables. Finally, when he got back to the park bench, he just stopped. He turned off the phone and sat down, completely confused.

That was when he felt a poke in his back, and a voice said, "That phone you got. That's mine."

He whirled around. Behind him stood the old woman he'd seen before. She was glaring at him from under the rim of her knit hat, which looked like a purple pancake drooping just above her eyes. She pointed to the phone in his hand and said again, "That's mine. I musta dropped it yesterday."

Martin held onto it tighter. "Prove it," he said.

The old woman laughed. "Easy. I bet you called my number 5. Right?"

He just stared at her. All of a sudden he recognized her—Mrs. DeSalvio was her name, though she was usually called just Mrs. D. He'd seen her for years around the neighborhood, always tramping along with a phone held to her ear. People joked about her. They said she must have the most long-winded family in the world, because she always seemed to be listening, hardly ever talking.

"Ever heard anything like that before?" she said.

He shook his head. "What is it?"

She came around to his side of the bench and sat down beside him with a thump, wafting out a smell that reminded Martin of a pastrami sandwich. "Why should I tell *you*?" she said.

"Because you want your phone back," said Martin, edging away and putting the phone in his pocket.

She pinned him with her eyes. They were clear eyes, Martin saw. "First," she said, "you tell me about you. Who are you? Talk to me."

He could have just stood up and walked away. Or run. She could never have caught him. But he thought the phone probably *was* hers, which meant she knew what was going on with it. And he wanted to know, too. So he talked.

She listened. She said, "Good, good," when he told her about skating. She frowned and bunched her lips up when he told her about where he lived, the too-small, too-crowded, too-noisy apartment that he didn't want to go home to after school. "You should have a job after school," she said.

"Yeah," said Martin. "But I don't know how to do anything."

She leaned close to him and spoke in a low voice. "Do you like animals?"

"Animals? Sure."

"What kind?"

"All kinds, I guess."

"You like dogs?"

"Yeah. Wish I had one."

"Why don't you, then?"

"No dogs allowed in the building."

"Awright," said the old woman. She took some crumbs out of her pocket and tossed them to the pigeons who clustered around her feet. "Now. Can you handle the strange?"

"What?"

"The strange," she said irritably. "You know, the strange, the unusual, the slightly weird. Can you handle that?"

"Sure," said Martin. He *liked* the strange and unusual.

"I wouldn't tell you this if I thought you were going to laugh," she said. "Or spread it around to your friends."

"I wouldn't," said Martin, which was the truth.

"I have this hunch you might be the one, that's why I'm telling you," she said.

"The one?" said Martin. "What one?"

But she didn't answer. She just studied his face, as if his brown eyes, his wavy black hair, and his chipped front tooth were giving her some kind of clue about him. "Awright, then," she said finally. "That number you called—" she paused. She squinched up her eyes. She lowered her voice to a hoarse whisper. "That number taps you into the dogs."

Martin stared at her. He didn't get it. "What?" he said.

A gust of wind blew some crumpled food wrappers across the playground. The pigeons rose into the air and settled again.

"Let's walk around," the old woman said. "I'm freezing to death, sitting here like this."

So they walked around the path that circled the playground, around and around, and she explained. "You know, dogs," she said, "they don't talk. They don't have the words, just the feelings. They got feelings so strong they fill up the air, like . . . like . . ." She waved her hands around. "Like a big network of radio waves. This phone taps into the network. If you're not used to it, you call that number and the feelings come roaring through and knock you down."

"That's what happened to me," Martin said. "But what's the point of a phone like that? And where did you get it?"

"An old guy in my building gave it to me," she said, "a long time ago. And the point of it is: ACES."

"What's that?"

"Assistance for Canines in Emergency Situations. ACES."

"I don't understand," said Martin.

"Let's sit down," she said. "My feet hurt, walking around like this."

So they sat down again. "You figured out that the feeling changes when you change direction," she said. "I saw you doing it."

"Yeah," Martin said. "But I don't know why."

"Let me have the phone," she said, holding out her hand. Martin gave it to her. She punched in the number. She frowned, clenched her jaw, and put the phone to her ear. For a few seconds she listened; then she nodded and handed the phone to Martin. "Hold yourself strong," she said, "and you can take it."

He tightened all his muscles and listened. Again the feelings rampaged through him, but they didn't strike him down.

"Okay," said Mrs. D. "That's good." She took the phone back and turned it off. "Now, here's what you're hearing. This network here covers about twenty blocks. There's others, all over the city—you don't have to worry about them. For this one, the park is the center. We're getting the vibes of all the dogs in that twenty-block area, pets and strays both. What you're hearing is like hundreds of little streams all running together in one huge river. You listen real hard and careful, and you can hear the different—well, not *voices*, exactly, more like transmissions."

"I figured that out," said Martin. "If you keep trying, you can find the way that feels better."

"That," said the old woman, "is exactly what you *don't* want to do. You gotta go the way that feels *worst*, that's the whole point." She fastened the top button of her coat and turned the collar up. "Come on," she said. "I'll show you."

She made the call again. She stood up, listening. She took a few steps, changed direction, took a few more steps, and kept doing this for a minute or so. Then she handed the phone to him. "Okay," she said. "Listen hard, and you'll hear a sort of wail, and you'll feel something kind of heavy and sad. Walk this way"—she pointed toward Avenue B—"and the sadness will get worse. What you want is to find where it's coming from. So you keep going toward it. It's hard, but the more you do it, the stronger you get."

So Martin walked. He set out up Avenue B, gritting his teeth because the sad feeling was indeed getting worse. The wail was thin and far away, like a needle of sound, and the sadness was like a stone in his chest. Every time the stone grew lighter, he knew he was going the wrong way. He had to pick out the faint wail from the chorus and turn toward it, again and again.

The whole time, Mrs. DeSalvio kept talking. "Last week, out near Anderson Avenue, I found a little mutt that got the worst of a dogfight. One side of him all bloody." She stamped along beside him, shaking her head. "We got an arrangement with the animal shelter, by the way," she said. "They fix up ACES dogs for free."

STOP AND THINK

Monitor/Clarify In the second paragraph above, what does Mrs. DeSalvio mean by saying "You gotta go the way that feels *worst*, that's the whole point"? For a clue, go back to page 105, where she explains what ACES stands for.

They were in Martin's neighborhood now. "That's where I live," he said, pointing at his building. "On the third floor. There's seven of us." He would have told her more—about how his father wanted to look for a better place but never had time, about how he had to share his room with a four-year-old and a five-year-old—but the stone in his chest was dragging on his words, making them heavy and hard to say. He fought against the desire to sit down on the sidewalk and curl up into a ball.

"Then there's the worst ones," said Mrs. D after a quick glance at his building. They turned the corner onto 18th Street. "That's when you find people being cruel to their dogs. Now this I can't stand."

Martin put his free hand over his other ear. He didn't want to hear about it. The sadness coming at him over the phone was almost more than he could stand. The stone in his chest felt like a load of bricks now, attached by a chain to his heart.

They turned up Carter Street, and went by the Chinese grocery and the noodle shop and the dry cleaners. Every now and then, Mrs. D took the phone from him and listened herself to make sure he was doing it right. "This is a real heavy one for your first time," she said. "Sorry about that."

Past the used bookstore they went, past the ice cream place. Martin's knees wanted to crumple. His feet weighed ten pounds apiece.

"But it isn't all bad, I want you to know," Mrs. D went on. "I can't tell you how many lost dogs I've returned to their families."

Martin wasn't listening. He was afraid he couldn't stand it any more. He thought he might collapse onto the curb and start sobbing. "I can't do this." He gasped out the words, and at first she didn't hear him. "I can't—" he said again, but he kept going anyhow, and in a minute he realized something odd. He'd come to a spot where, no matter what direction he took, the feeling grew just a tiny bit weaker. If he stood still, it was horribly strong. He told her so.

"Then we're here," she said. "This is it."

They'd come to a big apartment building—350 Lincoln Avenue—with wide steps leading up to a double door. The door was open, because two men carrying a table between them were coming out.

"Grab the door," Mrs. D whispered to Martin. He did, and they slipped inside.

"Awright. Now listen again. You should hear that one voice all by itself now."

He listened. The doleful feeling led him up the first flight of stairs and down a hall. At the end was an open door. It was clear that whoever lived here had moved out. Big taped-up cardboard boxes stood in the hall.

"You want me to take over now?" said Mrs. D.

Martin shook his head. He wasn't going to go through all this just to quit at the end.

"Then go in there and find out what's going on," she said. "I'll wait for you out here."

Martin turned off the phone and handed it to Mrs. D. He stepped into the apartment. It was nearly empty, except for a rolled-up carpet. He smelled paint. The only noise was a faint scraping sound coming from another room. He followed the sound.

In the living room, which overlooked the street, stood a man facing the windows, with his back to Martin. He was taping a piece of paper to the glass.

"Excuse me," Martin said.

The man turned around. "Who are you, kid?"

Martin said his name. "Is there a dog here?" he asked.

"Sure is," said the man. "In there, in the kitchen." He pointed across the hall. "People left him behind, can you believe it? Just left him, without a

word." He turned back to his taping. "So I gotta take him to the pound, unless you want him."

Martin went into the kitchen. There, under the kitchen table, tied to a table leg with a piece of rope, was a curled-up heap of sorrow—a small dog, white with brown patches and triangle ears. Without raising his head, he swiveled his eyes to look up at Martin. His tail was tucked down around his rump. He was trembling.

Martin squatted down and put his hand on the dog's back. "Hey, dog," he said quietly. "Hey, good dog, I'm here now." He untied the rope from the table leg and coaxed the dog to his feet. Slowly, he led him out of the kitchen.

The man was sweeping the floor of the living room now. Martin looked at the piece of paper taped to the window. It said: FOR RENT.

"How much?" he asked.

The man told him. Martin's heart sped up. "How many bedrooms?"

"Four," the man said.

Martin's heart beat so hard it made his voice shake. "I know a family that might like it," he said. "Nice people. *My* family. Will you hold it till I can get my father to come look?"

"Okay," said the man. "But you better get him right now. This place is going to go fast."

✔ **STOP AND THINK**

Story Structure What events have to take place in order for Martin to find out about the apartment for rent?

109

When Martin came out, Mrs. D (who'd been listening by the door) cast a glance at the little dog and told Martin her hunch had been right: she was turning over the ACES job to him. "Meant to be," she said. "Meant to be, no doubt about it. Just in time, too, my feet are too old for this." She frowned at him, and her purple hat fell down over her eyebrows. "Now, you won't get sick of this and quit, will you?"

"No," said Martin.

"And if you do ever want to quit, you'll find someone to take over, won't you?"

"Yes," said Martin.

She nodded once and handed him the phone. Then she reached out and snatched it back again. She hit the 5 button and held the phone to her ear. "Just want to listen one more time," she said. She stood there for a minute or so. Then she turned and stumped away.

And in the months and years that followed, people in the neighborhoods around the 14th Street Park became accustomed to seeing a tall boy on his inline skates every afternoon, gliding along the streets with a cell phone pressed to his ear. They figured he was a delivery boy of some kind. He never told anyone what his job really was. To his family and friends, he said he was out practicing his skating. It was true that he got a lot of practice. Some days he skated for miles, answering dozens of urgent calls. Other days there might be only two calls, or only one. And now and then came a day when the feelings pouring through the phone contained not a single thread of distress, when all the dogs in all the twenty blocks were well-fed and contented, either safe at home or romping happily with their people. On those afternoons, Martin left his skates in the apartment (at 350 Lincoln Avenue), went to the 14th Street Park, and played ball with his own dog, who was no longer sad.

Your Turn

Wanted: Dog Lover

Write a Want Ad Mrs. DeSalvio wanted to make sure that Martin had the right personal qualities to rescue dogs. Make a list of the qualities Martin needed in order to be successful at his job. Then write a want ad to advertise the position of dog rescuer. Include the qualities you identified, and explain why these qualities are necessary to do the job well. MEDIA

Speed Dial

Invent More Uses Number five on the ACES phone taps the listener into the emotions of dogs. With a partner, discuss what some of the other numbers on the ACES phone might tap into. Use your imagination to come up with two or three other ways the phone could serve as a tool to help the right listener do good things. PARTNERS

Listen Up

Turn and Talk Think about the two main characters in the story. Discuss with a partner how Martin and Mrs. DeSalvio demonstrate that listening is a vital part of communication. Talk about how listening in "The ACES Phone" helped to solve at least three problems. STORY STRUCTURE

Silent Noise

by Jacqueline Adams

Dog owners are accustomed to seeing their pets prick their ears when everything seems silent. Like many animals, dogs hear sounds that are beyond human reach.

Biologist Katy Payne listened to elephants communicate at a zoo in Portland, Oregon. Even when the elephants seemed to be silent, she felt the air throb. It reminded her of the throbbing from a pipe organ's low, doleful tones.

Payne began to wonder if elephants made noises not heard by humans. She recorded the elephants with devices that pick up sounds below the range of human hearing. She discovered a torrent of rumbling. "There was a whole communication system down there that people hadn't known about," she said. This would help solve an elephant mystery that had puzzled biologists for years.

Elephants pick up frequencies too low for humans to hear.

How Low Can You Go?

Biologists have heard a wide range of elephant sounds, from mothers' gentle rumblings as they coaxed their calves along to urgent trumpeting that warned of danger. But how elephants kept track of each other in the wild remained a mystery. Elephants lived clustered in groups that stayed a couple miles apart but traveled in the same direction. When one group changed direction, other groups swiveled to follow. How did the elephants know what faraway groups were doing?

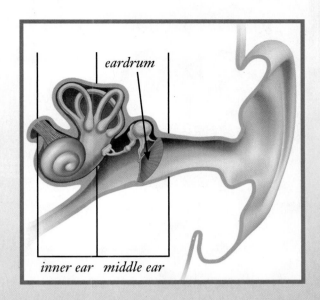

eardrum

inner ear middle ear

The mystery was solved when Payne discovered that elephants communicate with infrasonic sound. Because low-pitched transmissions travel farther, elephants can communicate over long distances.

Catch the Wave

Sound energy travels in waves. When sound waves reach the outer ear, they are funneled inside, starting a chain reaction. The eardrum vibrates, moving tiny bones in the middle ear and passing the waves to the inner ear.

The number of waves that travel each second is a sound's frequency, measured in hertz (Hz). The human ear is tuned to hear frequencies between 20 and 20,000 Hz.

Animals such as dogs, dolphins, and bats go to the opposite extreme. They pick up supersonic, or ultrasonic, sound frequencies. These sounds are above the range of human hearing.

Even though bats can see, sight isn't enough for finding insects at night. Bats send out a clamor of supersonic chirps into what looks like a dark void. These high-frequency waves bounce off insects and come back to tell the bat where the insects are. To humans, what seems like a quiet night is filled with "silent" noise!

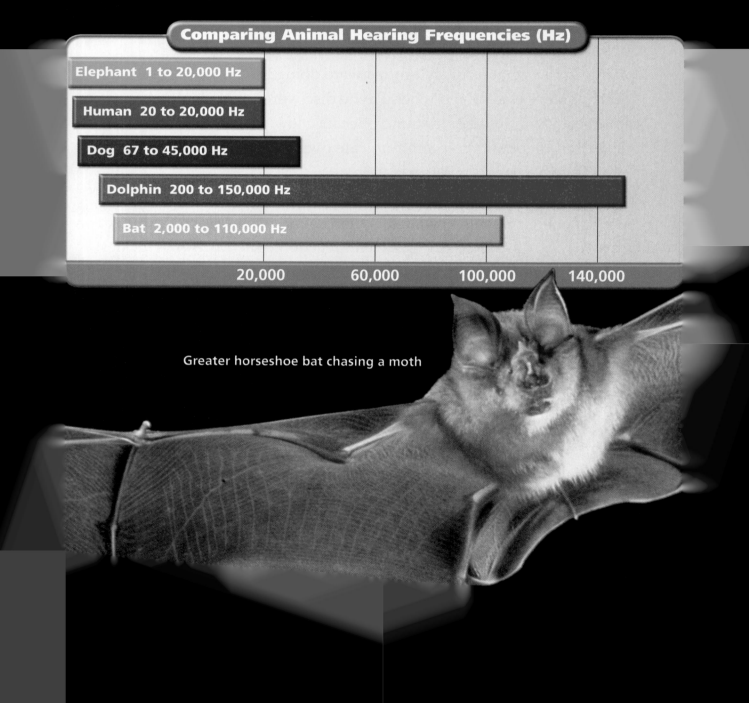

Comparing Animal Hearing Frequencies (Hz)

Elephant 1 to 20,000 Hz

Human 20 to 20,000 Hz

Dog 67 to 45,000 Hz

Dolphin 200 to 150,000 Hz

Bat 2,000 to 110,000 Hz

20,000   60,000   100,000   140,000

Greater horseshoe bat chasing a moth

Making Connections

Text to Self

Translate a Message In "The ACES Phone," Martin hears dogs in distress. Think about a time, either from experience or from a book, movie, or TV show, when you could tell what an animal was trying to communicate. Write a brief explanation of how the animal's noises, behaviors, or movements revealed a message. Include an illustration and a speech balloon to show what the animal's message was.

meow

Text to Text

Connect to Science The animals in "Silent Noise" use different frequencies to communicate. In "The ACES Phone," Martin tunes in to dogs' distress signals by using a special phone. Use details about animals from the selections to make a poster showing why animals need to use sound frequencies. Include pictures and descriptions on your poster.

Text to World

Animal Rescue "The ACES Phone" is a science fiction story that features a fanciful way of helping dogs in distress. Find out about real-life animal rescue organizations that exist to help animals in need. Use a local telephone book or online resources to help you locate information.

Grammar

What Is a Common Noun? What Is a Proper Noun? When you talk or write in a general way about a person, place, thing, or idea, you use a **common noun**. When you talk or write about a particular person, place, thing, or idea, you use a **proper noun**. Names of people, places, and organizations are proper nouns. In a proper noun with more than one word, capitalize the first word, the last word, and all other important words.

Common Nouns	Proper Nouns
woman	Mrs. DeSalvio
street	Avenue B
organization	Assistance for Canines in Emergency Situations

An **appositive** is a word or group of words that comes right after the noun it explains.

noun   appositive

The flier is from Friends of the Park, a community organization.

Turn and Talk **With a partner, read aloud each sentence below. Identify common and proper nouns. Then find the two appositives. Identify the noun that each appositive explains.**

1. Pilar Burgos, my best friend, loves animals.

2. She volunteers at the Oceanside Aquarium.

3. The aquarium is located at the intersection of Beach Road and Railroad Street.

4. Pilar is also a member of Cat Companions, a group of volunteers.

Word Choice You can make your writing clearer by adding appositives after proper nouns. Using precise common nouns instead of general ones will make your writing more interesting.

Proper Noun Without Appositive General Noun	Proper Noun with Appositive Precise Noun
Mrs. DeSalvio asked Martin to give her the device.	Mrs. DeSalvio, an older woman wearing a knit hat and purple coat, asked Martin to give her the cell phone.

Connect Grammar to Writing

As you write your fictional narrative, think about replacing general nouns with proper nouns or precise common nouns. Also, remember that some nouns can be explained by adding appositives.

Write to Express

✔ Organization Every **fictional narrative** needs an interesting conflict, or problem, involving its characters. As you explore the topic for your story, think about different kinds of conflicts you might choose. Develop a plot with a conflict your readers will like.

Antoine made a chart to generate story conflicts for his main character. Then he chose his favorite idea and created a story map to organize his narrative.

Writing Process Checklist

▶ **Prewrite**

☑ Will the setting, characters, and plot interest my readers?

☑ Will I enjoy writing about this story idea?

☑ Does my plot have a conflict and resolution?

☑ Have I planned a dramatic, exciting climax?

☑ Do I know how I will develop my characters?

Draft

Revise

Edit

Publish and Share

Exploring a Topic

Person Against Person	Person Against Supernatural Forces	Person Against Self
A boy can communicate with birds & tries to stop the town millionaire from cutting down the town forest.	A boy finds markers that make drawings come to life but his brother ∧accidentally creates monsters that chase them.	A boy superhero develops a fear of heights & has trouble rescuing people.

Story Map

Setting	Characters
Place: Jake's home, a two-story house in a quiet suburban neighborhood Time: the present	Jake: ordinary kid, likes to draw, brave Ralph: Jake's younger brother, causes trouble, easily frightened

Conflict: Jake has special markers but his brother finds them and creates monsters.

Event 1: Jake finds markers at a flea market that make drawings come to life.

Event 2: Jake sets up a booth where he draws anything people request.

Event 3: Ralph finds the markers and draws monsters.

Climax: The monsters come to life and chase Jake and Ralph.

Resolution: Jake erases the drawings, and the monsters disappear.

When I organized my fictional narrative, I included interesting events that show how the conflict unfolds.

Reading as a Writer

What elements of Antoine's plan will make the conflict interesting? What can you do to your story's conflict to make the plot more interesting?

✔ **TARGET VOCABULARY**

aspect

tendency

aptly

genuinely

tension

parallel

welfare

credit

predominantly

innovation

Vocabulary
Reader

Context
Cards

Vocabulary in Context

1 aspect

Being in a family has many sides to it. One aspect is doing things together.

2 tendency

Some family members have a tendency, or are likely, to enjoy the same kinds of food.

3 aptly

The composer J. S. Bach had twenty children. Aptly, or fittingly, seven of them also became famous musicians.

4 genuinely

Even though brothers and sisters may fight, they genuinely, or truly, care about each other.

- **Study each Context Card.**
- **Tell a story about two or more pictures, using Vocabulary words of your choice.**

5 tension

Disagreements about chores can cause tension, or stress, among family members.

6 parallel

This father and son have parallel interests. They both enjoy cooking the family meal.

7 welfare

Parents are often concerned for their children's welfare—their health and safety.

8 credit

An author's family members often receive credit, or recognition, on a page of a book.

This book is dedicated to my parents, with gratitude.

9 predominantly

Going to the movies is what this family predominantly, or mostly, does.

10 innovation

Children often teach their grandparents how to use a new gadget, or technological innovation.

Background

TARGET VOCABULARY **Authors and Illustrators** Writing and illustrating a book are two parallel tasks. Both jobs are creative, but sometimes there can be tension between the creators. The illustrator might have a tendency to be a bit farfetched, or wild. The author may feel that the book is predominantly about the words. It helps if both partners are genuinely interested in the welfare of the whole book, so that one aspect is just as important as another. Each person can bring an innovation, a new idea, to the project. In the end, the words should work aptly with the pictures. When they do, both the author and the illustrator deserve credit!

The author and illustrator create a dummy, or early version of the book, before it is published.

The competition at the talent show was fierce. Stefanie juggled while riding a unicycle.

Carlos played a brisk medley of jazz tunes on the saxophone.

Comprehension

✔ **TARGET SKILL** **Fact and Opinion**

As you read "The Myers Family," distinguish between facts, which give information that can be proved, and opinions, which give personal views and beliefs. Words that signal opinions include *thinks, wants, believes*, and *feels*. Make a chart like the one below to help you keep track of facts and opinions.

Fact	Opinion
Example:	Example:

✔ **TARGET STRATEGY** **Summarize**

An awareness of facts and opinions can help you summarize the main ideas and important details of "The Myers Family" as you read. Summarizing helps you stay focused on the most important ideas.

Main Selection

✓ TARGET VOCABULARY

aspect	parallel
tendency	welfare
aptly	predominantly
genuinely	credit
tension	innovation

✓ TARGET SKILL

Fact and Opinion Decide whether an idea can be proved or is a feeling or belief.

✓ TARGET STRATEGY

Summarize Briefly tell the important parts of the text in your own words.

GENRE

Biography tells about events in a person's life, written by another person.

Set a Purpose Before reading, set a purpose for reading based on what you know about the genre and your own experiences.

MEET THE AUTHOR

Leonard S. Marcus

Leonard S. Marcus knows the history and art of young people's literature as few others do. An author of children's fiction and nonfiction himself, Marcus has curated museum exhibits of book illustrations and written many books about illustrators and authors, including *Author Talk* and *The Wand in the Word: Conversations with Writers of Fantasy*. Marcus also reviews books for magazines, judges literary awards, and has participated in *The Night Kitchen Radio Theater* on satellite radio.

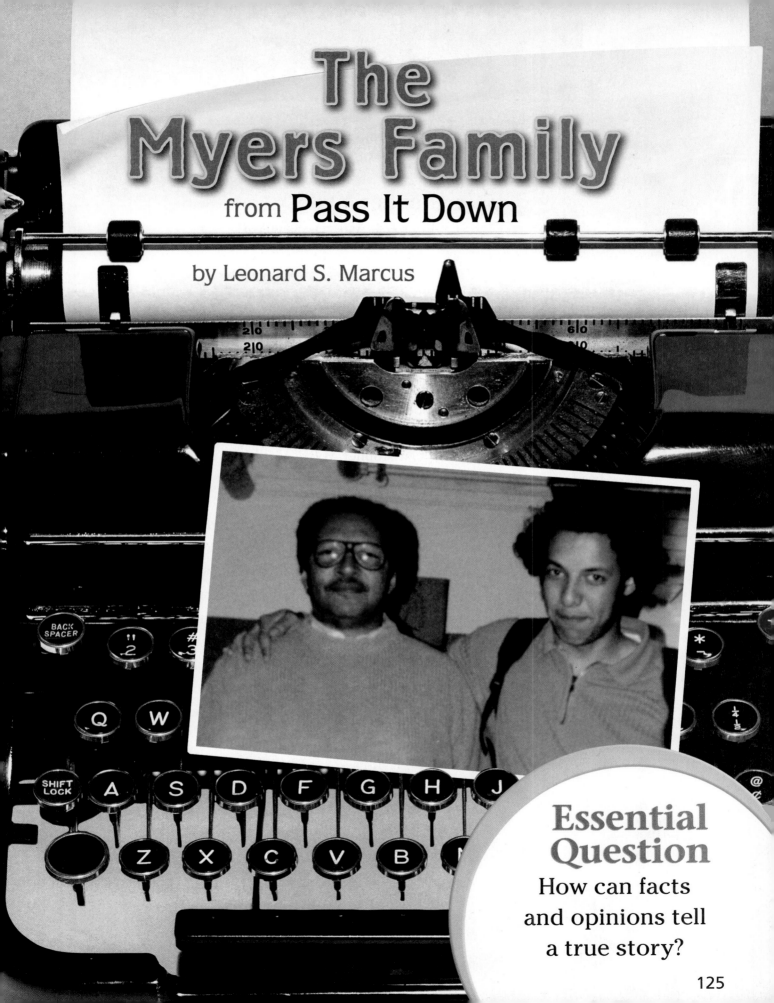

The Myers Family

from Pass It Down

by Leonard S. Marcus

Essential Question

How can facts and opinions tell a true story?

Walter Dean Myers
(born August 12, 1937, Martinsburg, West Virginia)

Christopher Myers
(born October 17, 1974, Astoria, New York)

"We lived on the cusp," Walter Dean Myers says of the Jersey City home where his son, Christopher, grew up during the 1970s. "On one side of our house, the neighborhood was all white. On the other side it was predominantly black. Christopher was a mixed-race kid. Because he could read at four, he started school early. His classmates were all two years older than him. He was not a good athlete. So he was pushed around a bit in school."

"Classmates looked at me," Christopher Myers recalls, "as if I had three heads."

Walter, the author of *Bad Boy* (Amistad/HarperCollins, 2001), grew up knowing a lot about not getting along well at school. Raised by foster parents in the economically depressed Harlem of the 1940s, he was a restless, inward-looking, overtall boy with a lisp and a serious tendency to take a fist to anyone who made fun of him. His foster parents worked long hours to make ends meet. Although genuinely concerned about his welfare, they were often unaware when their son skipped entire weeks of school.

Walter was lucky enough to have a few teachers who, despite his record as a troublemaker, wanted to help him. Some gave him books that made him hungry for more books. Reading—and by middle school, writing—became his life preservers.

Walter Dean Myers and Christopher Myers

As a teenager, as Walter became more aware that "blacks did not have the same chances as whites," his doubts about the future multiplied. It never occurred to him that he might one day write a book. Even as a first-time author, as a man in his thirties, Walter says, "I didn't think I was going to have a career. I thought that maybe I would get published occasionally." After years of earning his living as an editor, Walter became a full-time writer in 1977. He was forty. Christopher was three.

"I'm an early riser, and when Christopher was going to day care," Walter recalls of that time, "I'd finish work in the late morning and pick him up, and we would hang out together in the afternoon, which was very cool. We talked, very often solving the world's problems. I enjoyed his company.

"We read together: first comics, which had been forbidden to me as a child, and *Reader's Digest*, because we both loved jokes. Later, we read poetry." On weekends, father and son took the train into Manhattan and headed for their "Golden Triangle"—their three favorite bookstores, including one called Forbidden Planet—from which they always returned with armloads of books.

Walter, as his foster father had done with him, often told Christopher farfetched stories that he presented as true. Christopher remembers: "I wouldn't eat Brussels sprouts for years because of a story he told me. I had asked him, 'What *are* they? They're so odd-looking.' He responded with a long, involved story about a war we had fought in the sixties with a race of very small aliens. Brussels sprouts were the aliens' leftover heads. I was glad to find this out because now I knew why I was *never* going to eat Brussels sprouts again."

STOP AND THINK

Author's Craft In the first paragraph, the sentence "It never occurred to him that he might one day write a book" is an example of **foreshadowing**: hinting at a future event. What foreshadowing can you find in the last paragraph on page 129?

Christopher, age two

127

This was not the only way that Walter taught his son not to believe everything he heard or read. "Pop," Christopher says, "would go through my school history texts and write corrections in them. When a book referred to 'bringing the slaves from Africa,' he would cross that out, wanting to be sure I understood that African *people* had been *enslaved*. I was a good student, but I learned early on that education didn't necessarily happen in school. And I learned from Pop that books did not come down from on high: that people wrote them, and that there was work for me to do."

Christopher was drawing two hours a day by the time he was nine. Walter takes no credit for this. "His mom, who paints, must have noticed he had talent, because I didn't! Connie would put his drawings up on the refrigerator or the wall. At about ten, he won some contests, but I still wasn't paying much attention. Then he had a picture published in a children's magazine. I saw it—a drawing of an antelope or something—and said, 'That's really *good*.'"

Connie took Christopher to museums and comic book fairs and once, on his birthday, on a tour of Marvel Comics. Walter, meanwhile, involved his wife and their son in every aspect of his work.

Christopher remembers: "My father wrote ten pages a day. When he was done, he would come down and have me read it out loud so that my mother and he could talk about it."

As a teenager, Christopher accompanied his mother to the library to help research Walter's books. "Digging up information about African-American history strengthened my link to my cultural background," Christopher says. "I also realized that there were true stories worth finding, and that it was possible to unearth them."

Christopher and Walter at an event celebrating the publication of Harlem, *Stapleton Branch Library (Staten Island), New York Public Library, May 1998.*

Collage self-portrait made by Christopher, age fourteen.

When Walter discussed a new publishing contract with his wife, he encouraged Christopher to join in the discussion. "He wanted me even at nine and ten to see," Christopher says, "that a contract is part of the process by which books are made."

What Christopher most wanted, however, was to draw the pictures for his father's books. He recalls the first time he and his father talked about this: "I was ten and reading fantasy novels when Pop said one day, 'Let's do a fantasy together. What would you like to see in it?'

'How about a black unicorn?' I said.

'That's cool,' he said. 'What's his problem? We need to give him a problem.'" Years passed before Walter was able to answer his own question and finish *Shadow of the Red Moon* (Scholastic, 1995). Christopher, then a college student, illustrated the book, finally getting his wish.

> **STOP AND THINK**
> **Summarize** Summarize the ways in which Christopher's parents involve him in the world of publishing.

In all, Christopher illustrated two of his father's books while still at college: *Shadow of the Red Moon* and a picture book called *Harlem* (Scholastic, 1997). Both times, Walter suggested the idea and both times, Walter says, "the publisher was not happy about it. It gets too personal. They did not want to have to turn down my son. So Christopher did sample illustrations and had them accepted. When *Harlem* won a Caldecott Honor, everyone began saying, 'Father, son; father, son!' It's been much easier since then."

In 1999, Christopher launched his solo career with *Black Cat* (Scholastic, 1999), a haunting picture book that, aptly, traces the wanderings of a stray cat as he makes a place for himself in a big and not always welcoming city.

The next picture book Walter wrote for Christopher to illustrate was about the blues. As in the past, Christopher showed his father the artwork for *Blues Journey* (Holiday House, 2003) only after he had finished it.

Walter says, "I think he's still afraid of that father-and-son thing, the father as judge." Christopher agrees. "If we talked about it sooner, he might make some comment that would 'get into my head.'" But Christopher is not alone in his worries. Walter adds, "We're both nervous because we both want to hold up our end. We feed on the tension."

"Writing *Blues Journey*," Walter recalls, "was easy for me. I am comfortable with the blues lyric form." For Christopher, however, illustrating his father's poems was anything but easy. "I wanted the images to tell a parallel story, not just link one-to-one to the poems."

Walter admired his son's artwork but was puzzled by "a picture with a fisherman and his net. It didn't seem to go with any of the poems. So I wrote another poem to go with the image.

✔ STOP AND THINK

Fact and Opinion In the second paragraph, the information that Christopher illustrated *Black Cat* in 1999 is a fact. What opinion does the author give about the book in the same paragraph?

"Years earlier," Walter says, "I learned about the power of images from Christopher. My wife and I collect photographs. We have about ten thousand, most of black life between 1855 and 1940. I began collecting them when I was teaching a writing workshop for middle-school kids in Jersey City. Christopher, who was thirteen, was there too, drawing the illustrations for their yearbook. The kids were so into the images Christopher was making, I thought, let's bring in some photographs. That experience also led to *Brown Angels*" (HarperCollins, 1993).

Pencil study by Christopher for Blues Journey.

Finished art in mixed media on brown-bag paper for the fisherman poem in Blues Journey.

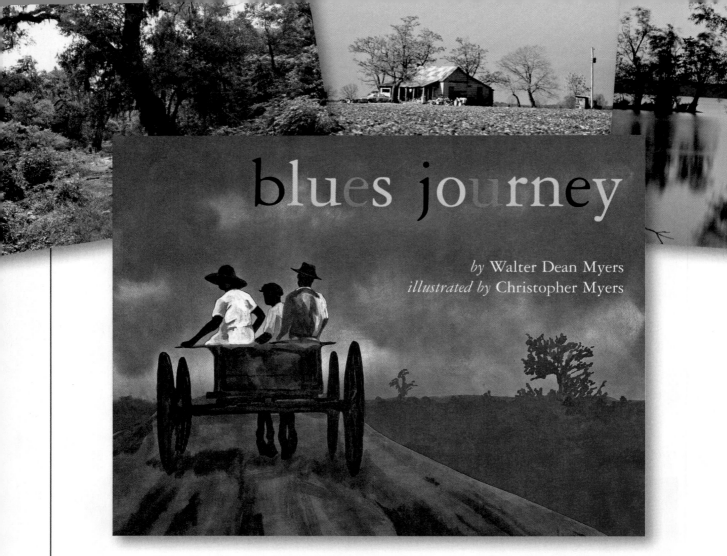

blues journey

by Walter Dean Myers
illustrated by Christopher Myers

Blues Journey *(mixed media on brown-bag paper, Holiday House, 2003).*

Looking back, Walter says, "I think that probably I have gained more from Christopher than he has from me. I've published more than eighty books. After a while you repeat yourself. But with Christopher's constant push toward innovation, I feel refreshed."

When Walter first saw the art for *Blues Journey*, he paid Christopher his version of a high compliment: "If I'd known you were going to do something that good," he told his son, "I would have written it better."

By now, Christopher usually knows when his father is teasing. "Oftentimes," he says, "he'll call me. I'll pick up the phone and he'll say, 'Why you talking on the phone?' And I'll say, 'Because you called me.' 'Well, I'm working,' he'll say. 'I can't talk to people like you!' Then he'll hang up the phone. In that joking way of his there's also a seriousness—the idea that he's always working, and that my life has to be about always working too."

Your Turn

Now Presenting . . .

Develop a Plan Write a paragraph explaining how Christopher Myers developed as an artist. Then write a second paragraph about a talent you would like to develop and how you might go about doing so. Include any problems you think you might encounter, and offer possible solutions. PERSONAL RESPONSE

Get Creative

Combine Talents Work in a small group. Make a list of all the group members' talents. One person may be a good writer, artist, or athlete. Others may be good at acting, singing, telling jokes, playing a musical instrument, or dancing. Think of a way in which all of your talents could be combined to create a product, a performance, or some other activity. Present your idea to the class. SMALL GROUP

Terrific Teamwork!

Turn and Talk With a partner, discuss what Walter Dean Myers says about his son on the last page of the selection. What facts does he present? What opinion does he give? What do his words tell you about the ways in which two creative talents can work together? FACT AND OPINION

Readers' Theater

Sound Check

by Joel Mallery

CAST OF CHARACTERS

Elisa Santos, age 12
Manny Santos, age 15
Anna Santos, age 10
Pedro Santos (Dad)
Elena Santos (Mom)

Setting: Elisa's middle school, Portland, Oregon.

Elisa: Hurry up, Manny! We still have tons to do.

Manny: Elisa, relax. You have this annoying tendency to get worked up before a show. I don't need the tension.

Elisa: Aren't you concerned about my welfare? We're singing in front of *my* school and *my* friends.

Manny: You should give your family a little more credit. We're professionals. Dad knows every aspect of the music business.

Elisa: I know, but what if I hit a wrong note?

Anna: La-la-la-la-la . . . What? I'm just doing my scales.

Manny: I think we should all focus predominantly on setting up the sound system. Read me the directions, Elisa.

Elisa: Okay. I'm sure I did the first one.

1. Plug in the amplifier.
2. Put the instruments and the microphones where they belong on the stage.

Anna: I'm on it!

Elisa: Shh! Where was I?

3. Connect the correct cords to the guitar, keyboard, and microphones.
4. Plug all cords into the amplifier.
5. Connect the speaker cords to the amplifier and then to the speakers.

Manny: Nothing is happening. Hmm, I think we may genuinely have a problem.

Mom: Is everything ready for the performance?

Elisa: Mom, Dad, thank goodness you're here. We don't have any sound!

Dad: Really? I can hear you just fine.

Elisa: Dad! This is my worst nightmare and you're making jokes!

Mom: Did you check that the correct cords are connected?

Manny: Yes. See where they're running parallel to the stage?

Mom: The speakers are plugged in to the amplifier.

Anna: Hey, did we try this plug?

Manny: Wow! Plugging in the amp! What an innovation!

Elisa: I guess I forgot to do Step 1.

Dad: That's okay. Luckily, Anna was here.

Anna: I guess I supply the power in this family.

Mom: Aptly put, Anna!

Dad: Great idea for a new song! Here's to Anna, the hero of the hour! Just plug her in and she'll supply the power!

Making Connections

Write a Story Walter Dean Myers told his son that Brussels sprouts were "aliens' leftover heads." Draw a picture of a food you don't like. Write an imaginative story that explains what it "really" is.

 Text to Text

Connect to Technology Think about the Myers family's experience with writing and illustrating books and the Santos family's experience with making music. With a partner, create a chart that lists details about the technology that is used in writing, in illustrating, and in making music.

Guitar   Writing   Drawing

 Text to World

Explore Careers Writing, making music, and illustrating are valuable skills. With a partner, brainstorm a list of careers that use these talents. Try to list at least five careers for each artistic talent. Then, choose one career and research the education and training that students need to reach this career goal. In a small group, give a brief how-to explanation that summarizes what you learned.

Grammar

How Are Plural and Possessive Nouns Formed?
A **singular noun** names one person, place, thing, or idea.
A **plural noun** names more than one. To form most
plural nouns, add **s** or **es** to the end of the noun. A
possessive noun names who or what owns or has
something. To form a singular possessive noun, add an
apostrophe (') and **s**. When plural nouns end with **s**, add
only an apostrophe to form the possessive. When they do
not end with **s**, add **'s**.

Academic Language

singular noun

plural noun

possessive noun

apostrophe

Nouns			
Singular	**Plural**	**Singular Possessive**	**Plural Possessive**
museum	museums	museum's	museums'
process	processes	process's	processes'
story	stories	story's	stories'
shelf	shelves	shelf's	shelves'
woman	women	woman's	women's

Try This! Copy the chart of nouns below onto another sheet of paper. Write the missing forms of each singular noun.

	Singular	Plural	Singular Possessive	Plural Possessive
1	contest	_____	contest's	_____
2	child	_____	child's	_____
3	class	classes	_____	_____
4	library	_____	_____	libraries'

138

Conventions When you write possessive nouns, make sure you use the correct noun form and put the apostrophe in the correct place.

Incorrect	Corrected
Blues Journey has Walter Dean Myers's poems and his sons illustrations. This book can be found on many library's shelves.	*Blues Journey* has Walter Dean Myers's poems and his son's illustrations. This book can be found on many libraries' shelves.

Connect Grammar to Writing

As you edit your fictional narrative, check each possessive noun to make sure it is written correctly.

Write to Express

☑ **Word Choice** In "The Myers Family," the author chooses words and phrases carefully, thinking about the feelings and images his language will communicate. As you revise your **fictional narrative**, think about what details will create a vivid picture for your readers. Add words and phrases to include those details.

Antoine drafted his story about a boy whose drawings come to life. Later, he added details to make his writing vivid and to make his readers curious about what will happen.

Writing Process Checklist

Prewrite

Draft

▶ Revise

☑ Does my beginning introduce the characters and setting?

☑ Does my plot contain an interesting conflict, climax, and resolution?

☑ Did I include suspenseful details and dialogue?

☑ Does my ending resolve the conflict and wrap up the story?

☑ Did I combine sentences correctly?

Edit

Publish and Share

Revised Draft

Everything he drew came to life! Next to
his drawing of a ⌃tropical bird, a real bird suddenly
appeared⌃, singing and chirping. Next to his drawing of a
motorcycle, a real motorcycle appeared!⌃, crushing his desk

Much more excitement was yet to come.
Jake⌃'s had a secret. When it got out, people
everywhere wanted him to draw something
for them. So he started ⌃his own booth at the flea market to draw for
customers.

Jake and the Remarkable Markers

by Antoine James

Jake Morris was an ordinary boy until he discovered some remarkable markers at a flea market. There were many bright colors in the set, plus one marker that didn't seem to have any color at all. When Jake took them up to his room and started drawing, he soon discovered that these were no ordinary art supplies. Everything he drew came to life! Next to his drawing of a tropical bird, a real bird suddenly appeared, singing and chirping. Next to his drawing of a motorcycle, a real motorcycle appeared, crushing his desk! Much more excitement was yet to come.

When Jake's secret got out, people everywhere wanted him to draw something for them. So he started his own booth at the flea market.

> In my final story, I added details to give readers a more vivid picture. I also used possessive nouns correctly.

Reading as a Writer

Where did Antoine use details to make his writing vivid? Where can you add vivid details to your own story?

141

Read the next selection. Think about how the main character changes by the end of the story.

Maddie's Changing Ways

The alarm clock buzzed for the second time. Eleven-year-old Maddie slowly dragged herself out of bed. She was tired from staying up late to watch a movie. This was not unusual. Maddie loved movies, and she often stayed up late to watch them on TV. She hurriedly got dressed, ate breakfast, brushed her teeth, and stuffed her notebook into her backpack on the way out the door. Walking to school, Maddie had a feeling she had forgotten something.

In class, Maddie had a hard time concentrating. Her mind wandered during a complicated math lesson. She was gazing out the window when her teacher, Ms. Lorenz, tapped her shoulder.

"Maddie, unless I'm mistaken, you've forgotten your homework again," Ms. Lorenz said. "I'm afraid you'll have to stay after school."

"I knew I had forgotten something," Maddie mumbled.

After school, Ms. Lorenz asked Maddie to choose a book and read quietly. Maddie picked up the nearest book on the shelf and yawned as she began to read. The book was about a girl who won a trumpet in a contest but didn't know how to play it. Then she met a famous musician who invited her to a movie set. Maddie came to an illustration of the movie set that sparked her interest. The picture made the character and plot come alive. She became so involved in reading that at first she didn't hear Ms. Lorenz tell her she could go home. Maddie asked Ms. Lorenz if she could borrow the book.

That night Maddie finished the book, but unfortunately, she forgot to do her homework. The next day she had to stay after school again. Ms. Lorenz told Maddie to write the story that she was supposed to have written the night before. Maddie thought about the assignment for a while. Then she decided to write about a girl who loves movies. To make the story more fun, she decided to have the girl be able to jump into the action of any movie she wanted. Maddie became very interested in writing her story. When she had finished it, she gave it to Ms. Lorenz.

When Ms. Lorenz returned the story, there was green ink everywhere. Ms. Lorenz used green ink to make corrections because she thought students associated red ink with negative feelings. Maddie appreciated the thought. Most of her papers came back covered in green because she made a lot of careless spelling and grammar errors. She tucked the story into her backpack to look at later.

That night, Maddie examined her story. Ms. Lorenz had written comments on the last page. They read, "Nice job, Maddie! I like the way you included details that make the character seem real. Your plot is exciting. I wish *I* could jump into movies! Write another draft to correct your errors, and turn it in next week." Maddie smiled. Ms. Lorenz was a hard grader, but her comments made Maddie want to do better. Right away, she wrote a new version. She took care to correct her previous errors. She forgot to do her other homework, though.

The next morning she put her story into the homework box. Ms. Lorenz looked at it. "I find it delightful that you are returning *anything* to the homework box, Maddie," she said. "But you still owe me your other homework. Please stay after school to do it."

That night, Maddie flipped through the television channels, looking for a movie to watch. Nothing was interesting enough. Then she started thinking. That book she had read in Ms. Lorenz's class would make a great movie! What if she wrote a movie treatment for the book? She sat right down and wrote one. She included the story plot and ideas for which scenes and characters to use. The next day she put her movie treatment into the homework box.

When Ms. Lorenz returned Maddie's movie treatment, there were many corrections in green ink. Maddie was pleased to see that there were also encouraging ideas. Ms. Lorenz had even included information about how to turn a movie treatment into a movie script.

Little by little, Maddie got better about completing homework and turning it in on time. She also worked and reworked new movie ideas and discussed them with Ms. Lorenz. Maddie noticed that her writing and her grades were steadily improving. She also realized that she liked writing scripts as much as she liked watching movies!

Unit 1 Wrap-Up

The Big Idea

Expression How do you communicate best? Do you express yourself best on the Internet, on the phone, or talking face to face? Is dancing, painting, or playing an instrument a way you communicate? Bring to class an object that represents your preferred form of communication. Explain its meaning to a small group.

Listening and Speaking

Play "Telephone" With five to ten students, play telephone. The first student writes down a message. That student then whispers the message to the next student, who whispers it to the next student, and so on. The last student says the message aloud. Compare the written message to the one the last student says aloud. Discuss how and why the message changed.

Common Ground

Unit 2

Big Idea

When we connect
with each other,
we all gain.

Paired Selections

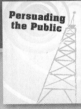

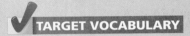
TARGET VOCABULARY

phenomenal
showdown
fundamental
flair
lingered
savor
gloat
berate
reserve
brainwashed

Vocabulary
Reader

Context
Cards

Vocabulary in Context

1 phenomenal
Winning a baseball game with a home run does not happen often. It is a phenomenal event.

2 showdown
Two rival football teams often meet each other in a showdown, or decisive contest.

3 fundamental
A glove is the fundamental, or basic, tool of an outfielder in a baseball game.

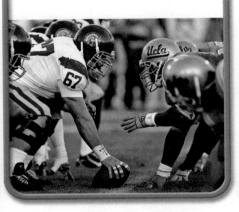

4 flair
A professional soccer player may display a lot of flair, or showy skill, during a game.

- Study each Context Card.
- Use two Vocabulary words to tell about an experience you had.

5 lingered

These fans have lingered on the field after the game. They are in no hurry to go home.

6 savor

This athlete takes a moment to savor, or enjoy, his feeling of accomplishment.

7 gloat

It is bad sportsmanship to gloat when you win, or to jeer about being better than another player.

8 berate

A coach might berate, or angrily scold, players for not trying hard enough during a game.

9 reserve

Reserve players don't start in a game, but they may be called upon to play at any moment.

10 brainwashed

This sign urges people to cheer. Are they being brainwashed, or can they decide for themselves?

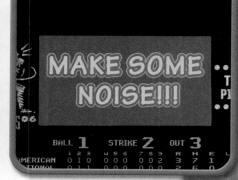

Background

The Power of the Media The next selection is about a small-town baseball game that is seen as a phenomenal event through the reporting of the media.

TV, radio, newspapers, magazines, and the Internet are all part of the media, a powerful force in our lives. They tell us stories that have lingered in our imaginations. One story might be about a reserve basketball player who comes off the bench to win a game, another about a showdown between two political rivals. The media keep us informed. An editorial might berate people for not voting. A reviewer might gloat about a bad movie with an "I told you so." If a story is written with flair, we savor it. However, we have a fundamental right to make up our own minds. By listening to many points of view, we won't become brainwashed.

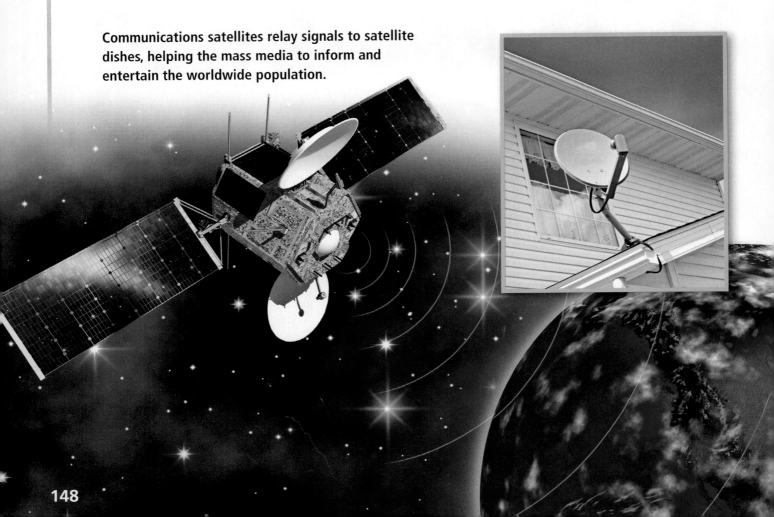

Communications satellites relay signals to satellite dishes, helping the mass media to inform and entertain the worldwide population.

Comprehension

Conclusions and Generalizations

As you read "The Boy Who Saved Baseball," look for details that support a conclusion or a generalization—a broad statement that is true about something or someone most of the time. Use a chart like the one below to gather text details and the conclusions or generalizations that those details support.

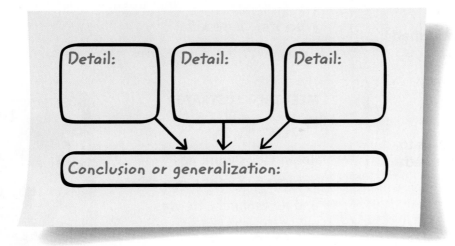

✔ **TARGET STRATEGY** **Analyze/Evaluate**

You can use the details and conclusions or generalizations in your chart to analyze events in the story and evaluate the author's decisions. Analyzing and evaluating help you form more accurate ideas about a story.

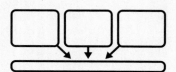

TARGET VOCABULARY

phenomenal	savor
showdown	gloat
fundamental	berate
flair	reserve
lingered	brainwashed

TARGET SKILL

Conclusions and Generalizations Use details to explain ideas that aren't stated or are generally true.

TARGET STRATEGY

Analyze/Evaluate Think carefully about the text and form an opinion about it.

GENRE

Realistic fiction has characters and events that are like people and events in real life.

MEET THE AUTHOR
John H. Ritter

"The driving force behind all my stories comes primarily from finding something that really bugs me," says John Ritter. With influences from Roberto Clemente to Bob Dylan, Ritter fondly remembers his titles in high school as both Senior Class President and Senior Class Clown. In 2009, he published a prequel to *The Boy Who Saved Baseball* titled *The Desperado Who Stole Baseball.*

MEET THE ILLUSTRATOR
Robin Eley

Robin Eley's work has appeared in books, magazines, and newspapers. He was born in London, grew up in Australia, and went to the Illustration Academy in Ringling, Florida. Eley lives in Adelaide, South Australia, where he teaches illustration and enjoys playing basketball.

The Boy Who Saved Baseball

by John H. Ritter   selection illustrated by Robin Eley

Local landowner Doc Altenheimer has promised his neighbors in Dillontown that he won't sell his land to a group of developers headed by Alabaster Jones, on one condition. Young Tom Gallagher's baseball team, the Dillontown Wildcats, will have to do what they've never done before—beat the all-star team from the camp down in Lake View Mesa. The task seems impossible until two things happen: a multitalented player, Cruz de la Cruz, joins the Wildcats' camp; and Cruz and Tom manage to persuade the gruff former star major-leaguer Dante Del Gato to be their coach. Over just a week, the team has grown in confidence and ability. Tom has even developed a computerized batting practice program called HitSim to help the team get ready for the big game. First the town, and now much of the country, is rooting for the Dillontown Wildcats.

By now, droves of reporters and photographers and television crews roamed the grounds. The dirt roadway cutting through Doc's land and heading to the ballpark was jammed, both sides, with satellite trucks, microwave trucks, radio vans, and SUVs.

All around the ball field, news crews set up lawn chairs, coolers, tripods, and umbrellas.

Some of the townspeople showed up with cookies and ice-cold lemonadeberry tea for the press, serving a few opinions to them as well. After he'd finished hitting, Tom heard one Los Angeles newscaster begin his interview with Mrs. Gleason by saying, "Folks, something phenomenal is happening in America today. There are more baseball games across the nation tonight than people have seen

in years. From little hamlets like this one to the last weed-filled vacant lots in cities everywhere, the Wild West showdown flavor of this Big Game has fired up interest and imaginations all over this land."

"Just focus on your hitting and fielding," Del Gato reminded everyone as the team finished its second round of batting practice. "Hitting, fielding."

Then came the sports network truck, and the players stopped what they were doing and stared as it all sank in. The Dillontown Wildcats were going *national.*

"Don't pay any attention," Del Gato called from the pitcher's mound. "Crying out loud, they got nothing better to do than hound a bunch of kids?"

Tom hustled out and sat atop the old stone wall in right field, pretending to be taking a break, while he spied on the guy from the sports network.

"How long's he going to pitch, fella?" he asked Tom.

"One more hitter, then we're done."

The reporter turned to a man with a camera on his shoulder, stepping out of the huge white truck. "Roy! Only one more batter. Get down there!" Then he slapped at his shirt pocket, retrieving a notebook and a pen. "What's your name, partner? How old are you? What's it like to have a legend like 'El Gato Loco' coaching your squad?"

Tom wanted to answer every question, but the last one reminded him that he needed to stay focused. "Sorry, I can't talk now." Then he couldn't help himself. He had to know. "Is that why you're here? All because of him?"

"Oh, no. Don't you see, kid? This Big Game, your whole situation here, has caught the attention of the entire nation. It's David versus Goliath! It's loyalty versus the big bucks. The small-market team fighting for its life against the big-money boys who want to come in and bulldoze right over them. It's a metaphor for the entire game of baseball."

"It is?"

"I'm telling you, buddy. It's *more* than a metaphor. This could be a meta*five*!"

With that, he stabbed the pen back into his pocket, folded the notebook, and ran toward the cameraman, followed by another guy wrapped in headgear and holding a furry microphone on a pole.

Luckily for the reporter, and for everyone in the stands, the last batter was Cruz. Because he put on a show.

"Ramón," he called out. "This one's for you." On the next pitch, he served up a low line into left field, two steps to the right of Ramón.

"María, get ready," he yelled, and the next one, a sharp ground ball, sizzled down the first-base line. María snagged it on the short hop.

The crowd *woo*ed at how easily she made the play.

By the time Cruz called Tom's name and sent him deep against the right-field wall, hoots and whistles ripped out of the stands for both hitter *and* fielder. More than that. Between pitches, Tom now heard a definite buzz of surprise, of discovery and awe.

"What're you feeding 'em for breakfast, Gallagher? A box of Wheaties and a pound of nails?"

Every hitter had done well that day, better than usual. The fielders had all displayed fundamental improvement, even over yesterday. But Cruz's show was full of flair and finesse. He could not miss. Like a pool player, he called his shots, hitting any pitch, high or low, toward any player. Hitting the ball as if it were standing still.

STOP AND THINK

Author's Craft In the first six lines, the reporter talks about the Dillontown baseball game as if it were a **symbol,** something that stands for something else. What kinds of things does the game represent?

Finally, the awesome display seemed to be sinking into the minds of the fans in the stands, particularly those, like Doc, who'd been there since Monday.

The ballpark became a canyon of quiet, save for Cruz's roll call and the slap of the ball on his maplewood bat. "Frankie, turn two!"

Frankie charged the hot grounder, stabbed it, tossed it to Tara at second, who relayed it to María at first. Smooth as *mole de chocolate* (MOH leh deh choh koh LAH teh). Again the crowd called out its admiration.

Tom felt a giddy light-headedness as he watched. For the first time, he felt happy to be here. Tara, running back to second, smiled and gave him thumbs-up.

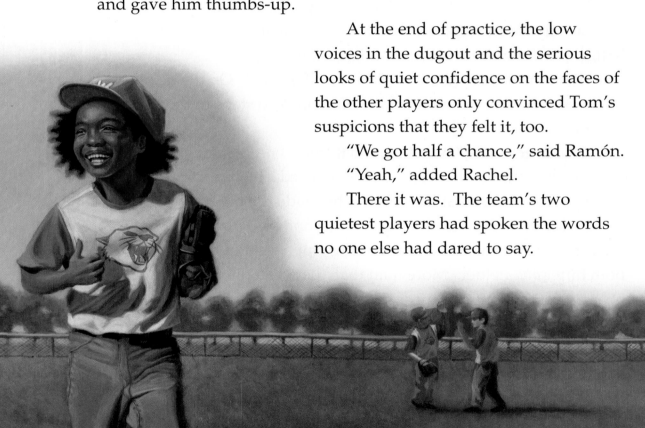

At the end of practice, the low voices in the dugout and the serious looks of quiet confidence on the faces of the other players only convinced Tom's suspicions that they felt it, too.

"We got half a chance," said Ramón.

"Yeah," added Rachel.

There it was. The team's two quietest players had spoken the words no one else had dared to say.

"Grab all your stuff," Del Gato growled, bringing a bucket of balls in from the mound. "We're going to jog out of here. And if those reporters come swarming around—well, you know the drill."

The players rose and filed out of the dugout. They started through the crowd and back to camp. Except for one. Tom lingered behind, sitting alone on the old pine bench. He wanted to savor the thrill of this moment. He wanted to allow everything that had happened to sink in. He let his thoughts fly loose, like leaves in the wind, like sagebrush whizzing past his face as he ran through the hillside chaparral. Then he reached for the sports bag next to his feet, pulled out his Dreamsketcher, and began to write.

Images of newscasters, landowners, outsiders, and locals who came to root or gloat, hate or berate, filled the movie screen of his mind. He painted the scenes in drawings and word pictures as fast as he could scratch. This awkward, ten-membered, twenty-legged caterpillar of a team, cocooned for days in the school library and on a sunken baseball field, was now breaking out into butterfly beauty, putting on a show, catching everyone's eye.

Tom pushed his pen along the paper, capturing the moment. He could still hear the roar, the drumbeats. He could hear footsteps. He looked up.

There stood Alabaster Jones.

157

"Well, Tom Gallagher," he said. "Just the man I'm looking for." He descended the dugout steps. "You boys must think you're pretty smart."

Tom only stared, afraid even to blink or breathe.

"Yes, sir," Mr. Jones continued, "I heard all about what you and that Mexican boy did. Think you're some clever *muchachos* (moo CHAH chohs), don't you?"

Tom managed a slight shrug.

Mr. Jones stepped closer, lowering his face into Tom's, and grabbed the neck of his T-shirt. "You ride off and bring back that no-good disgrace of a human being to coach this team of miserable misfits. Get him to show you a little something about hitting. Huh? Speak up!"

"Mr. Del Gato is not a disgrace. He has a lot of grace."

The man twisted his fists, tightening Tom's shirt around his neck.

"Shut up. Now, I'm only saying this once, so listen good. If by hocus or by pocus you happen to win tomorrow and this land deal falls through, you will sincerely regret it. I have associates in this town who promised me that they will personally shut down Scrub Oak Community School, fire the staff, and make all you kids hike down and back each day to that Lake View Mesa school if things don't go as planned. And why would we all do that? Simple lack of funds, my boy. It's big tax dollars you kids are playing with. Big money all around. Do you understand?"

He did. Instantly, Tom could see a whole chain of events, like dominoes falling whap-slap into each other. Either the Wildcats lose tomorrow, or Tom's parents lose their jobs. Then maybe even their home.

Compared to that, a few houses up on the hill didn't seem so bad.

Mr. Jones must've read the understanding on Tom's face. He let go of his shirt and smiled.

"Good," he said. "Because I can cause you more hurt than a heart attack." He grinned so wide, his sunburned lips turned white.

Tom stared back, blinking hard. But if Tom had learned anything during the past week, he'd learned when he had to speak up and when it was better to be silent.

And now was a time to speak.

"We're not trying to hurt you," said Tom. "We don't have anything against you at all. Why are you trying to hurt us?"

"Oh, you poor, poor boy. Listen, if you win that game, you'll be hurting me far more than what I could ever do to you. And I mean right here." He tapped his white sports jacket on the left side of his chest. "In my wallet."

Then Mr. Jones's face seemed to change, turning softer. Worry rose in his eyes. "You see, son, I was once a lot like you. I was young. I had stars in my eyes. But what you don't understand is that in the game of life, money wins. Brains can only take you so far. Talent barely gets you in the door these days. But this"—he held up his hand and rubbed his thumb against his first two fingers—"this opens more doors than dynamite. With this, you have instant respect, instant power."

Mr. Jones turned, but he did not leave. He looked off toward Rattlesnake Ridge as if imagining what all this land would be like after he was done with it.

"Remember," he said, "without money and the wish for even more money, Columbus never would've sailed to America. Then where would we all be today? Think about that."

 **STOP AND THINK**
Conclusions and Generalizations Do you agree or disagree with Alabaster Jones's generalization that "in the game of life, money wins"? Explain.

Under the stars that Friday night, all of the players joined in the wheel-spoke circle, and all eyes were wide open. Who could sleep with the weight of the fate of the town squeezing down on them?

Okay, Wil could. But he'd had three *burritos grandes*, four slices of watermelon, and a mango after catching batting practice all afternoon.

"No one expects us to win," said Clifford, lying with his knees up and hands behind his back. "I think somebody's going to be real surprised."

Ramón agreed. "My dad came by this morning saying, 'Don't worry. This game doesn't even matter. Sooner or later this whole place will be houses and eight-lane freeways.' I just smiled and said, 'Yeah, Dad, we know.'"

"That's what the mayor said, too," Frankie added. "But when he was watching batting practice today, he was white as a tortilla."

"Yeah," Cruz agreed. "But I think his true color was *alabaster*. Right, María? What are you going to say to him after we ruin his plans?"

Tom's gut clenched.

"Hey, look, you guys," María answered. "Don't get overconfident. Remember, batting practice is one thing. But in a game—especially this one—it's different. There's a lot of pressure."

"She's right," said Ramón. "But I think Cruz and Clifford are, too. The way I see it, as long as we think we have a chance, we have a chance."

Tom kept silent. His mind was still frozen under the snake eyes of a man named Jones who loomed above him like a viper over a rat. What did he expect Tom to do? Tell Cruz and everyone to throw the game? Tom was just the bench guy, the reserve player. Even if he got into the game, which would only happen if one team was way ahead of the other, he could strike out and make an error or two, but big deal. It would hardly affect the game.

Maybe, he thought, he could coach first and trip everyone as they ran the bases. Or maybe he could go out to the scoreboard with a mirror and shine sunlight into all the batters' eyes. But he hated these thoughts. In fact, he was tired of thinking.

"Tom," said Cruz. "What do you think?"

Boom went his heartbeat.

"About what?"

"About the neural receptors inside our brains."

"*What?*"

"Okay, then. Are we going to win tomorrow?"

"Oh, I don't know. It's up to you guys."

"*Aaapp!*" said Frankie. "Wrong answer."

"Well, he *doesn't* know." It was María coming to Tom's defense. "No one does. We spent three days swinging at the same stupid pitch a million times. But it was in the *library*. What about real life?"

"What about it?" asked Clifford. "You saw us today. We smashed the chips-and-dip out of the ball."

"So?" Rachel rustled inside her bag as she flipped over to her stomach. "I mean, I don't know what happened to us in the library. If we got hypnotized or reprogrammed or brainwashed or what. All I know is, we can't forget we're human beings. And human beings have control over their thoughts. And as long as we concentrate on doing our best, we shouldn't worry about winning or losing."

She paused, her voice lowered to a whisper. "I just believe that when people do things with good intentions, good things happen. Like when Tom and Cruz rode off to see Del Gato. But when we do stuff out of fear, bad things happen." She looked around. "A lot of people are afraid of what might happen tomorrow. But *we* can't be. Then, whatever happens will turn out okay."

"Even if we lose?" asked Frankie.

"Even if we lose. I mean, from where we are, losing may look like a total disaster. Like we just accidentally busted down someone's wall." Though he couldn't see her, Tom could hear the smile in her voice. "But you know, we only see it from here. How does it look from the hawk's nest? Or from the stars?"

No one said a word. Everyone, even Tom, searched the night sky, roamed the ether, bouncing around between the moon, the stars, and the eucalyptus trees.

From treetop, from the hawk's perch, Tom thought about the game, the town, the hillsides. In a million years—a short time, really, in space years—would it even matter whether they won or lost? In a thousand? What about a hundred?

Who could say? But he knew one thing. Rachel was right. He'd seen it too many times. When he froze up from fear, he did stupid things—like never talking to Doc about the ball field. And when he let his mind fly above the fear, he saw hitting a baseball as just another form of GPS tracking.

No matter if his parents got fired and his family had to move. No matter what trouble Alabaster Jones might cause. Tom determined that tomorrow he would play to win. And now he wondered how he could've considered doing anything else.

STOP AND THINK

Analyze/Evaluate In your opinion, do Tom's changes in making up his mind seem believable? Use story details and your own experience to back up your answer.

Land Grab

Write About Effects In "The Boy Who Saved Baseball," Alabaster Jones wants to develop Doc Altenheimer's land, but many townspeople do not want him to do so. What types of changes do you think might occur in the town if the land were developed? Would these changes be good or bad? Write a paragraph explaining your ideas.

SOCIAL STUDIES

Speak Out!

Role-Play Many reporters from around the country visit Dillontown before the big game. Work with a partner to role-play an interview that a reporter might have with either Mr. Jones or one of the townspeople. Use details from the story to help you think of questions and answers. Rehearse with your partner to make sure the questions and answers are clear, and then present your interview to a small group. PARTNERS

No Fear

Turn and Talk With a partner, consider how Tom's teammates help him overcome his fears of Alabaster Jones and what might happen to the community. Then discuss how Tom's courage might affect Dillontown and the strangers from around the nation who are following the story. CONCLUSIONS AND GENERALIZATIONS

Persuading the Public

by Cecelia Munzenmaier

Most Americans see or hear more than two hundred advertisements each day. They read them in magazines, newspapers, mail, and e-mail. They hear them on the radio. They see them on television, on billboards, and in skywriting.

The fundamental goal of commercial advertising is to persuade people to buy things. Other forms of persuasion try to influence how people think. Editorials or letters to the editor, for example, express an opinion. They might berate an official or give reasons why people should agree with a particular point of view.

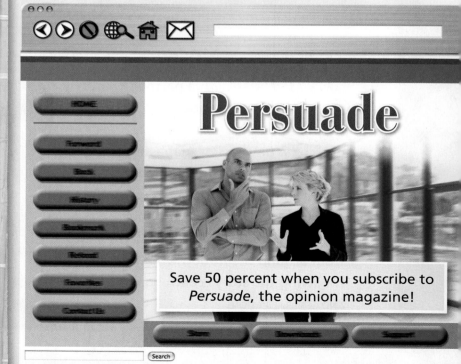

Persuade

Save 50 percent when you subscribe to *Persuade*, the opinion magazine!

Ads Attract Attention!

Advertisements use pictures, slogans, and celebrities to get people's attention. Ads often include a call to action. That message tells people how to improve their lives, usually by buying a certain product. Public service advertising campaigns also seek to persuade people. They do not promote a product. Instead, they give people information about how to make better choices. A public service announcement (PSA) might urge people to exercise, be tolerant of others, or recycle.

Chef Joe's Choice—

Soups to SAVOR

Chef Joe selects only the finest vegetables, bursting with garden-fresh flavor. For your health, choose Chef Joe's soups!

Chef Joe's Tomato & Red Pepper Soup

Keep It Clean!

This commercial ad (left) uses marketing flair—a slogan and a company celebrity—to promote a brand of soup. This public service ad (right) also uses a catchy slogan and effective pictures to persuade people not to litter.

Letters Express Opinions

Billions of dollars are spent on advertising each year. But mailing a letter to the editor of a local newspaper may be just as powerful. It can be an effective way to persuade people and change minds.

Letters to the editor are among the most popular features of newspapers and magazines. Radio and television stations also may share opinions and comments from listeners and viewers.

Whether in print or on the air, the most effective letters focus on one point and present facts and reasons to support it. Readers or listeners are not brainwashed. They are invited to consider, and perhaps share, a point of view. Here is an example.

Letters to the Editor

To the Editor of the *Sentinel*:

I believe our new gym should be named for Coach Len Burns.
Coach made all kids feel a part of the team, whether they were stars or reserve players. He taught us not to gloat when we won. He taught us not to give up when we lost. He gave us the confidence to face any showdown.

For thirty years, he has been a phenomenal coach. His lessons have lingered for many athletes. That's why the new gymnasium should be named for Len Burns. He is the man who taught us how to be good players and good sports.

Sincerely,
Alex Sims, basketball player
Hoyt Middle School

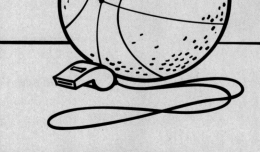

Making Connections

Text to Self

Write a Dialogue Alabaster Jones tries to persuade Tom to lose the big game. How would you react in a similar situation? Imagine that you are talking to a friend who is being pressured to do something. Write a short dialogue that shows what you and your friend might say to each other.

Text to Text

Make a Pitch Imagine that Tom wanted to persuade people in his town not to sell their land to Mr. Jones. Choose one of the persuasive forms you read about in "Persuading the Public." Think about how Tom might use it to make his message powerful. Share your ideas in a small group.

Text to World

Connect to Media Read an editorial or a letter to the editor in a newspaper or magazine. In an oral response, summarize the writer's main points. Explain why you agree or disagree with the writer. Include examples to support your opinion.

Grammar

What Is a Verb? A **verb** is a word that shows action or a state of being. When a verb tells what the subject does, it is an **action verb**. When a verb tells what the subject is or is like, it is a **being verb**. Some being verbs are called **linking verbs** because they link the subject to a word in the predicate. Most linking verbs are forms of the verb *be*.

Academic Language

action verb
being verb
linking verb
main verb
helping verb

Action Verb	Linking Verb
Tom opened his sports bag.	He was alone in the dugout.
He grabbed his Dreamsketcher.	The stands were empty.

A verb may be more than one word. The **main verb** expresses action or being. The **helping verb** works with the main verb but does not show action.

helping verb   main verb
Tom's teammates are talking.

helping verb   main verb
Rachel has shared her thoughts.

Turn and Talk   **With a partner, read aloud each sentence below. Find one sentence with a linking verb and three with action verbs. Which sentences have a main verb and a helping verb?**

1. Tom and the others searched the night sky.

2. The moon was large and bright.

3. Tom was thinking about the threats from Mr. Jones.

4. He would play without fear tomorrow.

168

Word Choice You can make your writing clearer and more vivid by choosing exact verbs.

Sentence with Vague Verb	Sentence with Exact Verb
 The player went to second base.	 The player sprinted to second base.
 Tom caught the long fly ball with his glove.	 Tom snagged the long fly ball with his glove.

Connect Grammar to Writing

As you revise your opinion paragraph, replace vague verbs with exact verbs.

Write to Respond

✓ **Voice** In a response to literature you state an opinion, using your own individual voice, about a story you have read. Your opinion can be a conclusion that you draw or a generalization that you make. Thinking about how your own life connects to the setting, characters, and plot events can help you support your opinion.

Jesse drafted an **opinion paragraph** about a character in "The Boy Who Saved Baseball." Then she added sentences to draw her readers into her writing, using a voice that shows her personality.

Writing Traits Checklist

✓ **Ideas**
Did I use logic to draw conclusions and make generalizations?

✓ **Organization**
Did I state my opinion and then support it with reasons and examples?

✓ **Sentence Fluency**
Did I use a variety of verb types?

✓ **Word Choice**
Did I use vivid and specific words?

✓ **Voice**
Does my writing show my personality and individuality?

✓ **Conventions**
Did I use correct spelling, grammar, and punctuation?

Revised Draft

As Rachel says in "The Boy Who Saved Baseball," losing feels worse up close. From a distance, it doesn't seem that bad. I learned that lesson last month. My soccer team lost a home game to our biggest rival, the Westside Wolverines. ^Imagine how awful we felt! After that, we watched a video of the game, identified our weak spots, and worked on our defense. ^All our hard work paid off. A week later, we ~~won against~~ blanked the Oaktown Titans, 2–0.

170

Lose Some, Win Some

by Jesse Ureste

As Rachel says in "The Boy Who Saved Baseball," losing feels worse up close. From a distance, it doesn't seem that bad. I learned that lesson last month. My soccer team lost a home game to our biggest rival, the Westside Wolverines. Imagine how awful we felt! After that, we watched a video of the game, identified our weak spots, and worked on our defense. All our hard work paid off. A week later, we blanked the Oaktown Titans, 2–0. Now our loss to the Wolverines is ancient history. We are too busy training for our next match to give it a second thought. Time gave us the distance we needed to see that losing is not so bad after all—as long as you win some, too.

> In my final paper, I added sentences to draw readers into my writing. I also used a variety of verbs.

Reading as a Writer

How does Jesse draw readers into her writing and let her voice show her personality? How can you make your own writing voice stronger?

reflect

multitude

agility

originated

jubilant

commemorates

initially

recollects

intense

customary

Vocabulary Reader

Context Cards

Vocabulary in Context

1 reflect
The images on this pot reflect the culture of Mexico. They recall a god found in Mexican myths.

2 multitude
Today, a multitude of people, over twenty million, live in and around Mexico City.

3 agility
Mexican dancers need great agility for the quick and graceful movements of regional folk dances.

4 originated
Many foods we enjoy today, such as corn, originated in Mexico. It was first grown there.

- **Study each Context Card.**

- **Tell a story about two or more pictures, using Vocabulary words of your choice.**

5 jubilant

Dancers may be jubilant as they joyfully perform to the lively music of a Mexican mariachi band.

6 commemorates

The Cinco de Mayo festival commemorates, or serves as a reminder of, Mexico's victory over the French in 1862.

7 initially

Stones like this are now valued as art, but initially the ancient Aztecs used them as calendars.

8 recollects

Seeing this carving from the ancient city of Palenque, one recollects, or remembers, an early Mayan ruler.

9 intense

Cactus plants can survive the Mexican desert's intense heat, so strong it has topped 120 degrees Fahrenheit.

10 customary

A quinceañera is a customary, or traditional, party for a Mexican girl celebrating her fifteenth birthday.

Background

What Are Folk Dances? Folk dances are traditional dances that each generation recollects and teaches to the next. The distinctive dance rhythms and costumes reflect a multitude of cultures. *La Bamba* is a customary dance at weddings in the Mexican state of Veracruz. The limbo originated in West Africa and took root in the Caribbean island of Trinidad. It tests the agility of dancers who try to pass under a low bar without touching it or falling.

Many dances are expressions of history, while others are still evolving. An African Tutsi dance commemorates the bravery of warriors who defended their kingdom against cattle thieves. English morris dancing was initially performed by men only, but today both men and women perform in jubilant morris teams at festivals.

In *La Bamba*, dancers tie a knot in a scarf with their feet.

The intense movements of the dragon dance are performed by teams in many Chinese New Year celebrations.

Comprehension

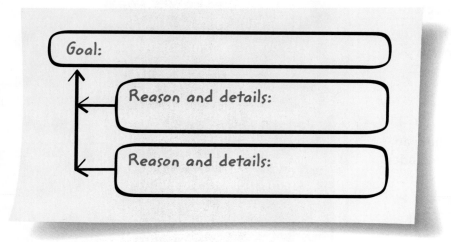

✔ **TARGET SKILL** **Persuasion**

As you read "Dancing Kane," think about how the author uses words and ideas to persuade the reader. Persuasive writing has a specific goal and includes reasons and details to support that idea. You can make a chart like the one below to help you keep track of persuasion in "Dancing Kane."

Goal:

Reason and details:

Reason and details:

✔ **TARGET STRATEGY** **Summarize**

You can use your graphic organizer to help you summarize the author's persuasive ideas about Kane's dancing, as well as other important information from the text.

Main Selection

✓ **TARGET VOCABULARY**

reflect	commemorates
multitude	initially
agility	recollects
originated	intense
jubilant	customary

✓ **TARGET SKILL**

Persuasion Examine how an author tries to convince readers to support an idea.

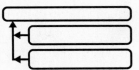

✓ **TARGET STRATEGY**

Summarize Briefly tell the important parts of the text in your own words.

GENRE

Narrative nonfiction gives factual information by telling a true story.

Set a Purpose Before reading, set a purpose for reading based on what you know about the genre and your own experience.

MEET THE AUTHOR AND PHOTOGRAPHER

George Ancona

George Ancona grew up in Coney Island, New York, where his father practiced photography as a hobby. Ancona says that "as a photographer, I can participate in other people's lives . . . producing something that can be shared and has a life of its own." He has created books about horses and helicopters, cowboys and carnivals, migrant workers and murals. Mexican culture is often the focus of Ancona's work. He has also explored other cultures in books such as *Powwow* and *Capoeira*, about a complex dance that is also a game from Brazil and Africa.

DANCING KANE

by George Ancona

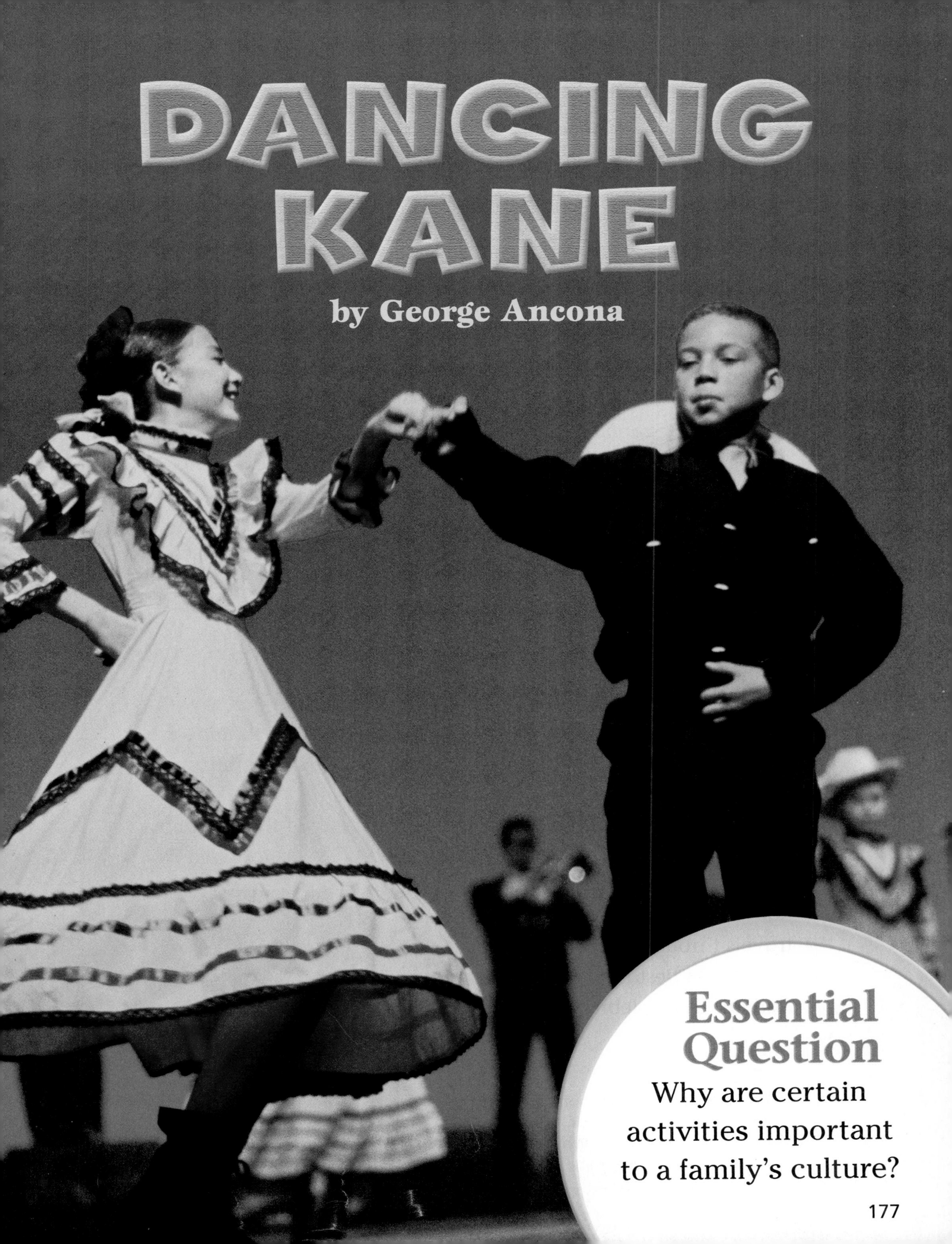

Essential Question

Why are certain activities important to a family's culture?

177

Kane Romp today

On stage, mariachi (mah ree AH chee) musicians dressed in elegant black and silver suits and silver braided sombreros burst out with jubilant Mexican music and song. From the wings of the stage, a line of girls swirling their colorful skirts and boys with their hands clasped behind their backs dance out into the spotlights. Their boots stomp out staccato rhythms.

Leading the line of boys is young Kane, spinning and stamping his boots on the stage. Kane loves to dance. The audience picks up his excitement and begins to clap to the music. This is Kane's first performance, and he is eager to show what he has been practicing for months.

"I was very excited to dance in my first performance," says Kane, remembering that time. "I wasn't nervous or scared, just excited. I wanted to show what I had learned. I was carefree and having fun."

Kane Romp began dancing when he was five years old. Today he is thirteen and is accomplished enough to dance with the adults of the dance company called *Los Niños de Santa Fe y Compañía* (lohs NEE nyohs deh sahn tah FEH ee kohm pah NYEE ah).

The city of Santa Fe, New Mexico, the home of the company, is the oldest capital city in the United States. It was founded by Spanish settlers over four hundred years ago. *Los Niños de Santa Fe y Compañía* travels throughout the Southwest to perform at fiestas, the traditional festivals that celebrate a town's history.

STOP AND THINK

Author's Craft The author opens the selection with a **flashback**, showing a scene from Kane's past. Why do you think the author introduces Kane this way?

178

Kane's mother, Antonina, dancing with the company

The Fiesta of Santa Fe takes place on the second weekend in September. It commemorates the peace between the Spaniards and the Pueblo Indians in 1692. There are parades with the horsemen dressed in the armor of the *conquistadores* (kohn kee stah DOH rehs). There are cowboys, floats with the Queen and her ladies-in-waiting, a pet parade, and lots of music and dancing in the plaza in front of the Palace of the Governors. People crowd into the plaza to watch the performers and to dance to Latin music. On the stage mariachis play for the dancers of *Los Niños de Santa Fe y Compañía.*

The dance company was begun by Janelle Ayón in 1995. Initially it was only for children, but later on adults began to perform as well. Janelle taught, did the choreography, and danced. Kane's mom started taking lessons with Janelle.

Kane talks about his family's involvement in folk dancing. "Since the whole family would come into town for Mom's lessons, we would watch as she took her classes. Then one day Dad decided he wanted to dance, so he began to take lessons too. He picked it up really fast."

In 2005 Janelle went to live in Mexico. Kane's mom, Antonina, now teaches and directs the company.

Guitarists parade in the Fiesta of Santa Fe.

"My mom started dancing when she was very young," says Kane, "so she's danced all her life." Antonina grew up in Santa Fe. Her family was among the early Spanish settlers in the Southwest. She and her cousins began to dance when they were little girls. Antonina loved Mexican dancing because traditionally the girls wear colorful skirts that they swirl back and forth as they dance.

Kane smiles as he recollects his first experiences with dancing. "I asked my mom if I could take a lesson. When I first started taking classes, I was really shy. I didn't have any friends, and I would stand by myself. I didn't like it, but my mom kept me going. It was hard for me at first, but once I got to know the people of the dance group it became really easy. Since then it's been a hobby for me. Now when I'm in class showing off, my friends come over to compete with me.

"When I dance with my dad," says Kane, "it's a chance to look big and dance away and have fun with each other. It's like when we wrestle. We're trying to throw each other around and have fun."

Friendly competition among the boys and men is a customary practice in Mexican folk dancing.

"There's a lot of competition between me and my dad," says Kane. "We try to see which of us can dance the *zapateado* (sah pah teh AH doh), or footwork, the loudest by pounding the floor with our boots. Or we try to look stronger or look the best. In some dances I have to try hard to keep up with him. We compete with each other big time."

Kane adds, "When I dance with my mom there is no competition. She's very graceful. She has taught me to be a strong partner and leader. When I see someone not in the right place, I try to help out. Sometimes I forget myself and begin to dance loudly. Then she tells me to quiet down.

"When my sister Ariana started classes, she would do the same steps I did. Then we'd go home and be so excited we'd start dancing while watching TV. We wanted to be the best in our group. Mom would watch and correct us, and we'd keep on dancing till we figured out the steps.

"My little sister, Salomé, is big enough to dance too," Kane says proudly. "Now the whole family is dancing."

(left) Kane dancing with his father, mother, and sister Ariana; (right) Kane and his family, including sister Salomé

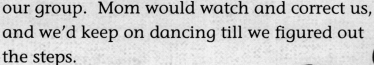

STOP AND THINK
Summarize Summarize Kane's different feelings about dancing, including when he started and when he dances with members of his family.

181

Kane dances the Presumida *from the Huasteca region of northeastern Mexico.*

"The first dance I learned," says Kane, "was called *El Alcarabán* (el ahl kah rah BAHN). It comes from Chiapas (CHYAH pahs) in southern Mexico. It's a dance about chicks dancing around each other in the barnyard. The rooster comes in and shows off in front of them, and they all follow him off the stage.

"We perform dances from different regions of Mexico," Kane adds. "My favorite dances are *La Bamba* from Veracruz, the machete (mah CHEH teh) dance from Nayarit (nah yah REET) and the *Jarabe* (hah RAH beh) from Colima. In *La Bamba* my girl partner unwinds a sash from my waist and we put it on the floor. Then together we dance and kick the sash into a beautiful bow, which we hold up at the end of the dance."

The dances of Mexico reflect the great variety of cultures that make up the country. Over the centuries invaders, slaves, and immigrants settled in Mexico. They came from Europe, Africa, the Middle East, and Asia, bringing their music and dances. In time, these blended with the many indigenous dances to become the multitude of songs and dances in Mexico today.

A Nation of Dances

Many regions in Mexico have at least one special folk dance that helps express its unique culture. Enslaved Africans who were brought to the West Indies contributed their distinctive rhythms to the music of the *Danzón* (dahn SOHN) in the Yucatán (yoo kah TAHN) Peninsula. In Chihuahua (chih WAH wah), in the north, they dance the polka and *Evangelina* (eh vahn heh LEE nah). The heel-stomping footwork comes from Spanish flamenco dances. From Jalisco (hah LEES koh), in the southwest, comes the *Jarabe Tapatio* (tah pah TEE oh), familiar to many as the Mexican hat dance. The *Sones* (SOH nehs), from nearby Michoacán (mee chwah KAHN), have their roots in the indigenous dances of pre-Columbian Mexico. In Chiapas, in the south, they dance *Chiapanecas* (chyah pah NEH kahs) to the music of the marimba. Three other dances are shown below.

Evangelina from Chihuahua

Jarana from Yucatán

La Negra from Jalisco

Chiapanecas from Chiapas

La Botella from Michoacán

MEXICO

Great dancers may make it look easy, but the learning is hard work. Kane and his family spend many hours rehearsing the dances they will perform. They have to master each dance step by step. Putting it all together is the joyful payoff.

"We go to class to learn the basic steps of a dance," Kane explains. "Then we learn the dance. The dances are a whole lot harder because of the choreography, planning the movements of the dancers on the stage. I would learn the steps in class, and then Mom would help me at home so I would get it and go on to the next class.

"It takes a long time to prepare for a performance. We learn how to dance with partners together and apart. We have to learn where to go from place to place on stage. Then we practice the dance over and over in the studio."

Kane continues, "Then there are the rehearsals on stage where we learn where to move on the floor. Finally, at the dress rehearsal we practice with all the props we carry, like jugs or baskets, or machetes for the machete dance.

"At the same time, the mariachis rehearse with us so they can play the music we will dance to. When we rehearse for a performance we run through the entire program on stage."

Kane in rehearsal

Mariachi music is said to have originated in the state of Jalisco. The band includes violins; guitars, including the vihuela (vee HWEHL ah), a small guitar; trumpets; and a large bass guitar called the guitarrón (gee tah ROHN).

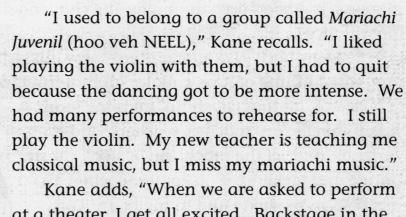

"I used to belong to a group called *Mariachi Juvenil* (hoo veh NEEL)," Kane recalls. "I liked playing the violin with them, but I had to quit because the dancing got to be more intense. We had many performances to rehearse for. I still play the violin. My new teacher is teaching me classical music, but I miss my mariachi music."

Kane adds, "When we are asked to perform at a theater, I get all excited. Backstage in the dressing rooms while everybody gets ready and the girls braid their hair in ribbons and put on makeup, I get butterflies in my stomach big time. Seeing all those people in the audience makes me nervous, but then I go out and have fun."

Kane and a friend waiting before the machete dance

185

Kane likes to dance for many of the same reasons he likes to play sports. The two activities offer similar rewards. They both rely on partners working together, learning through teamwork and coaching. They both develop strength and agility.

"I think dance relates very well to sports," Kane says. "When I play football there's no music, but when you see the ball you're ready to cut and to move. My legs are a whole lot stronger than most kids', so when they give me the ball I put my shoulders down and run right through the defense. I love football. I love running into things. I'll have a football and even run into a wall, spin off it, and keep on going.

"In baseball when I'm in the outfield and I see where the ball is going, my body automatically pulls me there. It knows what it's doing."

That kind of confidence, coming from both dance and sports, is a good preparation for the challenges Kane will face in life.

Kane leans back and after a pause, says, "It's funny, when I think of it nowadays, all that listening and learning, all that coaching, from my mom, my dad, Janelle, my coaches, teachers, and even my friends, and all the practicing of steps, music, running, and tackling, it all comes together. It works both in my head and in my body. Lots of times it's hard, but both on stage and on the field I have fun."

Having fun may be the best reason of all for why Kane likes to dance.

 STOP AND THINK
Persuasion What reasons does the author use to persuade the reader that dancing is a worthwhile activity?

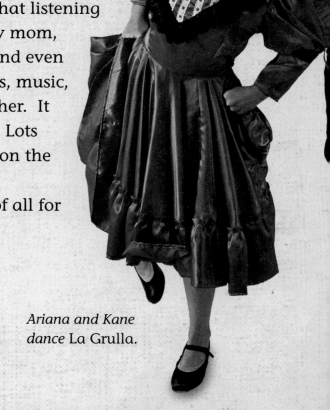

Ariana and Kane dance La Grulla.

Your Turn

What's Important?

Write About Values Folk dancing helps Kane make friends, stay fit, and learn about Mexican culture. What might these activities tell you about what Kane values, or what is important to him? Think about activities in your life, such as sports, hobbies, or family events. Write a paragraph explaining how these activities might show others what you value. PERSONAL RESPONSE

Fast Facts

Make Flash Cards Work with a partner to create flash cards featuring the musical styles, dance groups, and Mexican folk-dancing traditions described in "Dancing Kane." Write the name of each style, group, or tradition on one side of an index card. Then write a brief explanation on the back. Trade cards with other partners, read their explanations, and see how many styles, groups, or traditions you can name. PARTNERS

La Bamba

Presumida

Mariachi

Keep It Going

Turn and Talk Think about why folk dancing is important to Kane's family. Imagine Kane as an adult explaining to his children the importance of carrying on the folk-dancing tradition. What might Kane say to encourage his children to keep Mexican folk dancing in the family?

PERSUASION

Readers' Theater

TIME TREK: MEXICO

by Ann Weil

Cast of Characters
Reporter (Trigon 320)
Aztec Farmer
Ball Player
Craftsperson

Reporter: Welcome to *Time Trek,* the show that commemorates the past! I'm your time-traveler, Trigon 320. As you see on the map, our time trek this week is to Lake Texcoco in Mexico in the early sixteenth century. I'm here talking to an actual Aztec farmer.

Farmer: It is customary to call us the Mexica, not Aztecs. And please stand still. You are rocking the *chinampa.*

Reporter: Sorry. I was just trying to get a better view. These floating gardens are incredible.

Farmer: Yes. Initially this was all swamp. We staked out plots and layered them with mud and vegetation to make little islands for growing our food.

Reporter: Amazing. How do you keep the islands anchored?

Farmer: We plant trees in the corners. The roots grow down below the water and hold the *chinampas* in place.

Reporter: I see a multitude of crops. Exactly what are you growing?

Farmer: We have maize, which you would call corn, as well as chili peppers, squash, tomatoes, and medicinal plants and herbs.

Reporter: And my *Time Trek* producer recollects that *chocolate* originated in Mexico as well! I don't suppose—oops, time to move along!

Lake Texcoco

Tenochtitlán

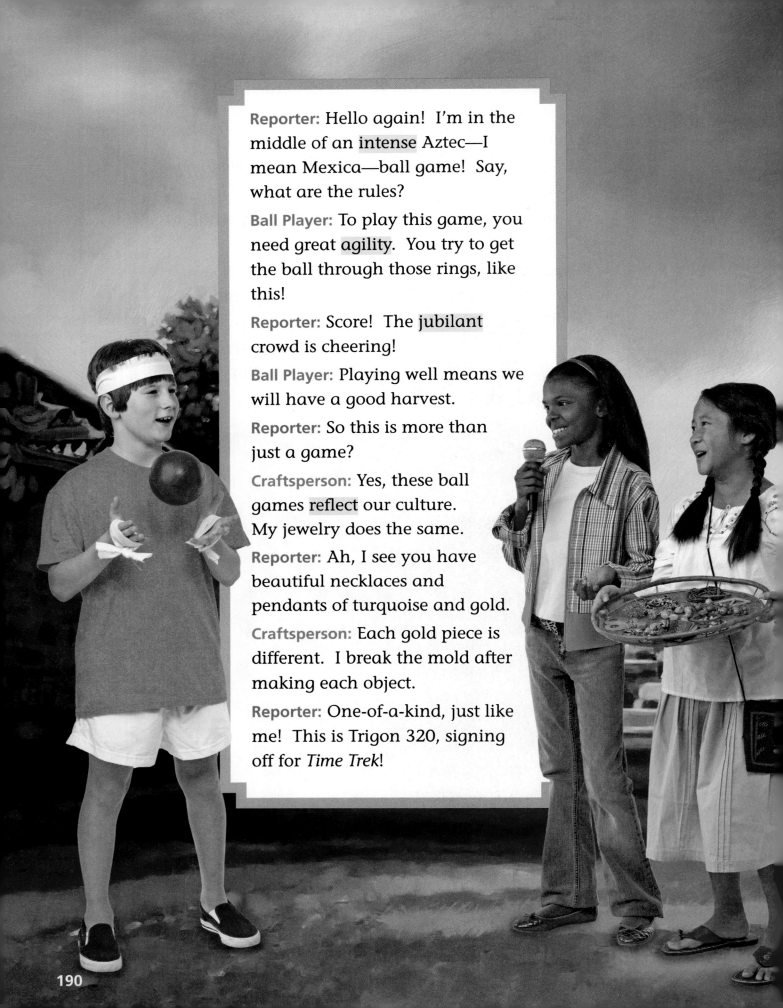

Reporter: Hello again! I'm in the middle of an intense Aztec—I mean Mexica—ball game! Say, what are the rules?

Ball Player: To play this game, you need great agility. You try to get the ball through those rings, like this!

Reporter: Score! The jubilant crowd is cheering!

Ball Player: Playing well means we will have a good harvest.

Reporter: So this is more than just a game?

Craftsperson: Yes, these ball games reflect our culture. My jewelry does the same.

Reporter: Ah, I see you have beautiful necklaces and pendants of turquoise and gold.

Craftsperson: Each gold piece is different. I break the mold after making each object.

Reporter: One-of-a-kind, just like me! This is Trigon 320, signing off for *Time Trek*!

Making Connections

 Text to Self

Express Culture Kane connects with Mexican culture through folk dancing. Demonstrate, illustrate, or describe a way you connect to a culture. Think about such categories as food, art, music, or language.

 Text to Text

Perform a Readers' Theater Bring together the two genres you have been reading. With a partner, choose a passage from "Dancing Kane." Using "Time Trek: Mexico" as a model, rewrite the passage and perform it as a Readers' Theater. Include the roles of Interviewer, Kane, and at least one of Kane's family members.

 Text to World

Connect to Social Studies "Dancing Kane" and "Time Trek: Mexico" teach us about Mexican culture. Before reading the selections, what did you already know about this culture? How can one group of people benefit from studying another culture and its history? Share your thoughts with a small group.

Grammar

What Are Transitive and Intransitive Verbs? A
transitive verb is an action verb that sends its action to a
noun or pronoun that is its **direct object**. When there are
two or more direct objects receiving the action, they make
up a **compound direct object**. An **intransitive verb**
has no direct object. The same verb can be transitive in
one sentence and intransitive in another.

Academic Language

transitive verb
direct object
compound direct object
intransitive verb
indirect object

Transitive and Intransitive Verbs	
transitive verb	direct object The dancers celebrate an important event. *Event* receives the action of *celebrate*.
intransitive verb	Kane Romp dances to mariachi music. *Dances* has no direct object.

An **indirect object** usually tells *who or what was affected by the action.*
The indirect object comes between the transitive verb and the direct object.

transitive verb   indirect object   direct object
Janelle Ayón taught many people the traditional dances.

Try This! **Read the sentences below. On another sheet of
paper, write the verb in each sentence. Label it
transitive or *intransitive*. If it is transitive, write the direct
object and the indirect object, if there is one.**

1 We will attend the next festival in Santa Fe.

2 I have shown my sister an article about it.

3 She teaches young children traditional dances.

4 She performs in a folk dance group.

Sentence Fluency You can vary your sentence structure and make your writing easier to read by combining direct objects from sentences that have related ideas. Using a compound direct object often helps to eliminate repetition.

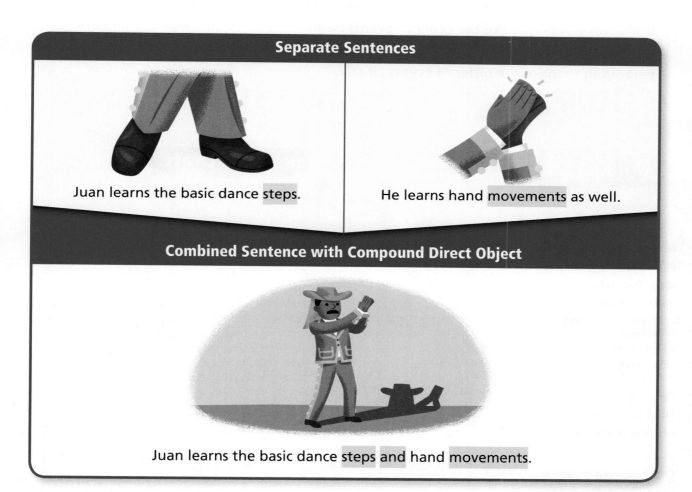

Separate Sentences

Juan learns the basic dance steps.

He learns hand movements as well.

Combined Sentence with Compound Direct Object

Juan learns the basic dance steps and hand movements.

Connect Grammar to Writing

As you revise your summary paragraph, look for sentences that you can combine. Do this by moving direct objects from related sentences to create a single sentence with a compound direct object.

Write to Respond

☑ Organization A **summary** of narrative nonfiction should tell the main events and important details in the selection. A detail is important when it helps make main ideas and events clear to readers. To organize your summary, begin by telling whom or what the selection is about. Then tell the main events in the order in which they take place. Include transition words to make the order of events clear.

Tristan summarized part of "Dancing Kane." Later, he revised his paragraph to make the order of events clearer.

Writing Traits Checklist

☑ Ideas
Did I include only the most important ideas, events, and details?

☑ Organization
Did I put events in the proper order?

☑ Sentence Fluency
Did I use verbs and objects correctly?

☑ Word Choice
Did I use exact words when I summarized?

☑ Voice
Did I summarize in my own words?

☑ Conventions
Did I use correct spelling, grammar, and punctuation?

Revised Draft

Kane's mother was the first family member to become involved in dancing. She began dancing as a little girl. *Then* Kane's father started dancing. ~~His little sisters began dancing, too.~~ *Next,* Kane himself took lessons. He was very shy before, but once he began dancing, he made many friends and came out of his shell. *Finally, Now* The whole family dances.

194

Summary of "Dancing Kane"

by Tristan Marlborough

Kane Romp is a young dancer who lives in Santa Fe, New Mexico. He belongs to a dance company that does traditional dances from Mexico. The company travels to towns throughout the Southwest and performs at special festivals that celebrate each town's history. Kane's mother was the first family member to become involved in dancing. She began dancing as a little girl. Then Kane's father started dancing. Next, Kane himself took lessons. He was very shy before, but once he began dancing, he made many friends and came out of his shell. Finally, his little sisters began dancing, too. Now the whole family dances.

> In my final summary, I moved one sentence that was out of order and added transitions. I also made sure that I used verbs and objects correctly.

Reading as a Writer

What changes did Tristan make to improve his organization? In your summary, are events told in the proper order? Can you add any transitions?

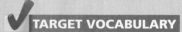

✓ **TARGET VOCABULARY**

principle

elegant

equations

reluctant

detached

decomposition

specimens

complex

compromise

shriveled

Vocabulary
Reader

Context
Cards

Vocabulary in Context

1 principle

A scientific principle, such as Isaac Newton's law of gravity, is an important rule that can guide future research.

2 elegant

This computer processor is an elegant solution to a scientific problem, resolving it in a simple, ingenious way.

3 equations

Much of math and science is working with equations, in which one thing is equal to another.

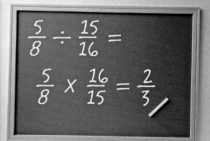

4 reluctant

A scientist would be reluctant, or unwilling, to handle chemicals without taking safety precautions.

- **Study each Context Card.**

- **Discuss one picture. Use a different Vocabulary word from the one on the card.**

5 detached

A scientist may try to be detached, like an outside observer, in order to keep an open mind.

6 decomposition

The decomposition, or rotting, of dead plants returns essential nutrients to the soil.

7 specimens

Geologists collect specimens of rocks and minerals. They carefully study the samples.

8 complex

The science of weather covers both simple and complex ideas that explain natural phenomena.

9 compromise

Lab partners may need to compromise to get along. They may settle on an idea both can agree on.

10 shriveled

Science can explain how a plump grape changes into a shriveled, dried-up raisin.

Background

✔ **TARGET VOCABULARY** **The Science of Teamwork** The selection you are about to read is a bit complex. It is about the sometimes weird science of teamwork. You will meet a team whose members are reluctant to accept the principle that it is important to compromise. The team is a collection of odd specimens.

Do they end up feeling detached and distant? Do they learn the equations of getting over yourself = cooperating, and working together = having fun? Read on to find out if they scowl at each other like a bunch of shriveled prunes or find an elegant solution to their problems. Meanwhile, here's a weird science experiment even they can do. Try it yourself to view the decomposition of food firsthand.

You will need one orange.
1 Put the orange on a shelf.
2 Wait one month.
3 Your orange isn't so orange!

198

Comprehension

✔ **TARGET SKILL** **Sequence of Events**

As you read "Science Friction," pay attention to the order, or sequence, of events. Look for signal words or phrases such as *on the way*, *next week*, and *that afternoon*. You can use a chart like the one below to list the sequence of events in "Science Friction."

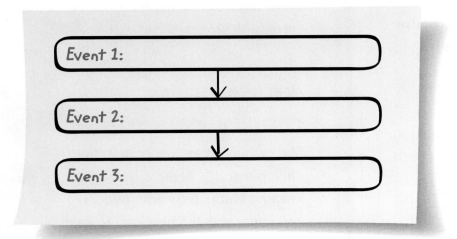

Event 1:

Event 2:

Event 3:

✔ **TARGET STRATEGY** **Infer/Predict**

You can use the sequence of events listed in your chart to help you make inferences about the characters in "Science Friction" and predict what will happen next. Inferring and predicting make a story more enjoyable to read.

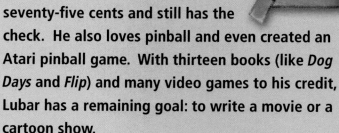

Main Selection

Tripping Over the Lunch Lady and Other School Stories

✔ TARGET VOCABULARY

principle	decomposition
elegant	specimens
equations	complex
reluctant	compromise
detached	shriveled

✔ TARGET SKILL

Sequence of Events Identify the time order in which events take place.

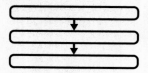

✔ TARGET STRATEGY

Infer/Predict Use text clues to figure out what the author means or what might happen in the future.

GENRE

Realistic fiction has characters and events that are like people and events in real life.

MEET THE AUTHOR

David Lubar

David Lubar originally aspired to be a comedian. He sold a joke for seventy-five cents and still has the check. He also loves pinball and even created an Atari pinball game. With thirteen books (like *Dog Days* and *Flip*) and many video games to his credit, Lubar has a remaining goal: to write a movie or a cartoon show.

MEET THE ILLUSTRATOR

Macky Pamintuan

Macky Pamintuan was born in the Philippines. His parents found that keeping Macky busy with pencils and paper was the best way to keep him happy. As an adult, Pamintuan moved to California. He is the illustrator for the book series *Weird Planet* and *Nancy Drew and the Clue Crew*.

Science Friction

from Tripping Over the Lunch Lady and Other School Stories

by David Lubar
selection illustrated by Macky Pamintuan

Essential Question

How can team members learn to cooperate?

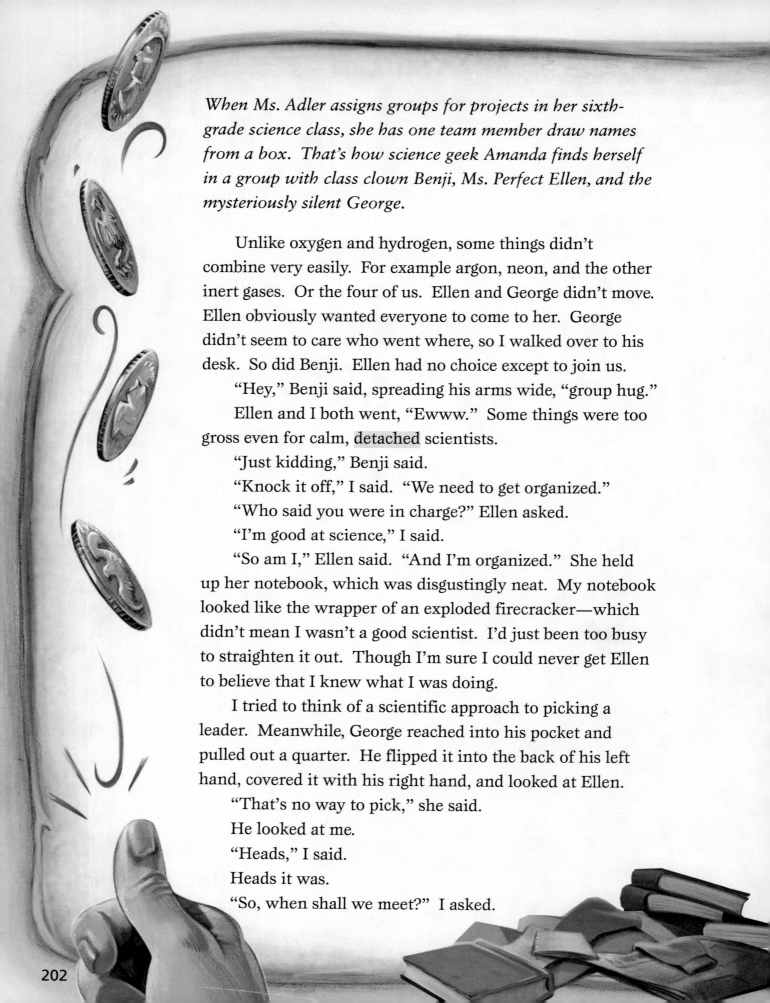

When Ms. Adler assigns groups for projects in her sixth-grade science class, she has one team member draw names from a box. That's how science geek Amanda finds herself in a group with class clown Benji, Ms. Perfect Ellen, and the mysteriously silent George.

Unlike oxygen and hydrogen, some things didn't combine very easily. For example argon, neon, and the other inert gases. Or the four of us. Ellen and George didn't move. Ellen obviously wanted everyone to come to her. George didn't seem to care who went where, so I walked over to his desk. So did Benji. Ellen had no choice except to join us.

"Hey," Benji said, spreading his arms wide, "group hug."

Ellen and I both went, "Ewww." Some things were too gross even for calm, detached scientists.

"Just kidding," Benji said.

"Knock it off," I said. "We need to get organized."

"Who said you were in charge?" Ellen asked.

"I'm good at science," I said.

"So am I," Ellen said. "And I'm organized." She held up her notebook, which was disgustingly neat. My notebook looked like the wrapper of an exploded firecracker—which didn't mean I wasn't a good scientist. I'd just been too busy to straighten it out. Though I'm sure I could never get Ellen to believe that I knew what I was doing.

I tried to think of a scientific approach to picking a leader. Meanwhile, George reached into his pocket and pulled out a quarter. He flipped it into the back of his left hand, covered it with his right hand, and looked at Ellen.

"That's no way to pick," she said.

He looked at me.

"Heads," I said.

Heads it was.

"So, when shall we meet?" I asked.

It turned out that they had stuff going on all week except for today right after school. Three coin tosses and a short argument later, we agreed to meet at my place.

"My room's a little messy," I warned everyone.

"Messy room, messy mind," Ellen said.

"Empty room, empty head," Benji said.

Much as I hated to admit it, I was starting to like him.

We met outside after school and walked to my house. On the way, Ellen mentioned thirty-seven reasons why she was so great and wonderful and perfect, Benji made nineteen jokes, and George kicked a rock.

When we went inside, my mom got all excited. "Oh, you brought friends, Amanda. How nice. I'll make snacks." She seemed to think I spent too much time by myself.

"Watch your step," I warned everyone as we approached my room. I pushed against the door. It didn't move. I leaned into it and gave a hard shove.

"Eeew. You want us to go in there?" Ellen scrunched up her face.

"Hey—it's not dirty. It's just messy." I walked over various piles of clothes, books, magazines, and other essentials, then plopped down on my bed. Okay—actually, I plopped down on the clothes that were on my bed.

Ellen tiptoed in, followed by Benji and George. George sat on my hamper. Ellen perched on the edge of a chair. "You should fire your maid," she said. "Ours would never leave a room like this."

I ignored her.

"Wow. It's sort of like you live inside a laundry basket." Benji walked over to the highest mound of clothes, right near my bookcase, and reached up. "Hey, I can touch the ceiling." He thumped his chest and shouted, "I'm king of the laundry!"

STOP AND THINK

Sequence of Events Summarize the sequence of events on page 202 that results in Amanda's becoming group leader.

"Cut that out," I said. "We have work to do."

"Knock, knock." My mom appeared with a tray stacked full of goodies. Before anyone could speak, she'd handed each of us a plate. Turkey sandwiches, and baby carrots with little dishes of ranch dip. Mom made great sandwiches.

"Okay—back to the project," I said. "What about chemistry?"

"Boring," Benji said.

George nodded.

I took a bite of my sandwich. I really loved chemistry, but I was willing to compromise. "Biology?" I asked.

"Not interesting," Benji said.

George curled his lip.

I took another bite, and tried another field. After getting similar responses from them for everything I could think of, I looked over at Ellen, who'd been sitting quietly, eating her snack. Even there, she was disgustingly neat. I didn't see a crumb on her plate. She'd finished her sandwich and started on the carrot sticks.

"You like chemistry?" I asked her.

"Astronomy," she said, dabbing a speck of mayonnaise from the corner of her lip with her napkin.

That figured. I bet if I'd mentioned astronomy, she'd say she liked chemistry. We kept talking, but got absolutely nowhere. Ellen didn't like any of my ideas. I didn't like any of hers. Benji seemed more interested in touching the ceiling.

And George just sat there. Though, compared to the noise everyone else was making, I had to admit I was beginning to appreciate the value of silence. We only had an hour because Ellen needed to leave for a piano lesson. When it was time to go, we agreed that everyone would think about stuff for a week. Then we'd get back together.

"Nice friends," my mom said after they'd left. "Wouldn't you like to have a neat and tidy room where all of you could hang out?"

"It's fine the way it is," I said. I'd rather spend my time trying to understand the universe than straightening out one little unimportant part of it.

We met the next week. Mom brought snacks again. And once again, we couldn't agree on anything. Finally, I said, "Look, we can't keep going like this. If we don't pick a project now, we're toast."

"Planning is important," Ellen said.

"So is toast," Benji said.

"But we aren't planning, we're arguing," I said.

"We are not," Ellen said.

"We are too," I said.

"Are not."

"Are too."

"R2-D2!" Benji shouted.

"You're the only one who's arguing," Ellen said.

We argued about that until it was time for her to go.

Third week—third meeting. We might as well have been in third grade. Ellen and I argued. Benji seemed fascinated by his ability to touch the ceiling near my bookcase. I actually thought about moving that pile of clothes, but I sort of hated to spoil his fun. George kept his thoughts to himself, though he did seem interested in checking out some of the books I'd stacked up next to the hamper, which surprised me.

We finally agreed that since we couldn't agree on a project, everyone would bring an idea next week and we'd vote for the best one.

Week four. I voted for my project. Ellen voted for hers. Benji voted for Albert Einstein. George didn't vote, but he did offer the use of his quarter.

"Look," I said. "It's obvious we can't agree. So let's each start an actual project. Next week, we'll pick the best one, and everyone will work on it."

STOP AND THINK

Infer/Predict Benji keeps touching the ceiling, and George is very interested in the books next to the hamper. What might explain their behavior?

205

Week five. We each decided we needed another week. Everyone left right after our snack. When Mom came back for the dishes, she sniffed, looked at my piles of clothes, and said, "You really need to think about picking up."

She was right. It was getting a little stuffy. But I couldn't pick things up just then. I needed to think about my project. So I found a more elegant solution. I opened a window.

Week six.

"What's that supposed to be?" I asked Benji when he lugged his project into my room.

He looked down at the pile of ice-cream sticks and coat-hanger wires attached to a board with bits of duct tape, bent nails, and large globs of glue. "It's a roller coaster."

"You're kidding."

He shrugged. "It sort of fell apart. I'm not great with tools."

I figured he'd make a joke about the project, but he just sighed and said, "Sorry I let the group down."

I looked over at Ellen, who hadn't brought anything. "Did you start a project?" I'd expected her to drag in a display charting the life cycle of designer handbags.

"I tried to spot comets," she said. "It would be so great to discover a new one. Dad bought me this excellent telescope last month. But it's been cloudy every night."

I waited for her to say she was sorry, but she didn't. I guess the word wasn't in her vocabulary. I glanced at George. He shook his head and spread his empty hands. Then I looked at my desk, where I'd balanced a large board that contained my experiments. I'd grown crystals in various solutions. "I guess we'll have to use mine," I said. "Notice how the copper sulfate produces a—"

Just then, Mom appeared in the hallway with a tray. She pushed at the door. Then she pushed harder. There still wasn't enough space for her to get in. She gave the door a good, hard shove. I could feel the floor shake.

On my desk, the whole display started to slide. I tried to dash across the room, but I tripped on a pair of jeans. All of my hard work crashed to the floor.

I lay on my stomach, staring at the icky mess. Mom put the tray down in the hall and squeezed through the doorway. "That's it. I've had it. This room is a disgrace." She grabbed a handful of clothes from the floor. I expected her to drop them somewhere, or toss them. Instead, her eyes opened wide. Then she went, "Eeewww."

I looked over. Under the clothes was . . . something. It was dark green and shriveled. *What in the world is that?* I leaned closer. It was some kind of food.

"That does it!" Mom yelled. "You are grounded until this room is clean."

"But—"

"Disgusting." She shook her head and walked out.

I stood there, staring at the *thing*. Whatever it was, I hadn't put it there. I was a slob, but I wasn't a pig.

Behind me, Ellen whispered something.

I spun toward her. "If you mention your maid one more time, I'm going to scream."

Ellen flinched and backed away from me. I realized I was already screaming.

"I just wanted to tell you I was sorry," she said.

"What?"

"I'm sorry. It's my fault."

"Your fault?"

She shrugged. "I'm allergic to wheat."

I let her words roll around in my brain for a second, hoping I'd somehow misunderstood what she meant. But the equations only seemed to have one solution. Ellen didn't eat bread. Ellen's plate was always empty. Ellen had just apologized. "Are you telling me you've been stashing sandwiches in my room?"

"Not sandwiches. Just the bread. The turkey was delicious."

"Why?"

"I didn't want your mom to think I didn't like her food. And I felt kind of funny about mentioning my allergy. I try so hard to fit in, but it's not easy sometimes. I'm not good at it like you are. You're just so comfortable with stuff."

"What?"

"You don't worry about what people think," she said. "I worry so much that I always end up saying the wrong thing. And you're so smart. I have to study so hard. I have to keep everything so carefully organized, or I get lost. But you—you're so good at science."

"Oh." I'd definitely need to think about what she'd just said. I guess I'd been making a lot of assumptions. But at the moment, I had a more urgent issue to deal with. I looked at the moldy slab. "How many?"

"Every week," she said.

"Where?"

She went to various clothes heaps in my room and revealed the slices of bread, which ranged from slightly moldy to totally overgrown.

Benji picked up the pieces and laid them out on my desk. If the bread hadn't been buried in my wardrobe like some sort of ancient Egyptian funeral offering, I probably would have found it pretty fascinating.

"I'm sorry," Ellen said again. "I'll explain to your mom that this was my fault. And I'll help you clean your room. Okay? If there's one thing I'm really good at, it's straightening up." She looked at me like she expected me to turn her down.

STOP AND THINK

Author's Craft In paragraph one, Amanda thinks of the moldy bread mystery as a set of math equations with a logical solution. Why do you think the author uses this **metaphor**, describing one thing in terms of another?

She seemed really sorry. "Sure. You can help. That would be wonderful."

"I'll help too," Benji said.

George nodded.

"Thanks," I said as we tackled the top layer. "This is great. But we still don't have a project."

"Sure we do."

I was so shocked by the voice, I just stared at George.

"We do?" Benji asked.

George nodded and pointed at the bread.

"Mold!" Ellen said. "We have a whole display of the stages of mold growth."

"Yeah," I said. George was right. We had pieces of bread for each week. "But is that enough?" It was hard to imagine a whole project from some slices of moldy bread. Then I realized it wasn't just about mold growth.

"Look," I said, flipping a piece over.

Ellen nodded. "Mayonnaise. It's acidic."

"Yup. We have an example of mold inhibition too. We just have to figure out a way to display it so you can see both sides."

"Great," Ellen said. "But what if it's still not enough?"

"Oh, there might be some more . . ." Benji said.

"What do you mean?" I asked.

"Promise you won't kill me?"

"No."

"Promise you won't make it slow and painful?"

"No."

He shrugged. "I sorta don't like turkey a whole lot."

"Oh, please don't tell me you've been stashing meat in my room."

He nodded.

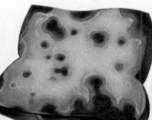

"Where?" I sniffed and looked around.

Benji pointed at the top of my bookcase.

"You slimeball," I said as I climbed a chair to take a look. Oh, yuck. There were five piles of turkey in various stages of decomposition, neatly laid out from left to right. It was absolutely disgusting. It was also pretty fascinating. And I guess I was relieved to know the smell wasn't coming from my clothes.

I looked over at George. "What about you? Is there anything you don't like?"

He lifted a stack of books to reveal baby carrots.

"Good grief. How could all of you just hide food away like that?"

"Well," Ellen said, "the place is kind of a dump. If you don't care, why should we?"

210

"When in Slobovia," Benji said, "do as the Slobs do."

I couldn't argue with them. All they'd done was sink to my level. Maybe this was one area where it wouldn't hurt for me to try to be a bit more like Ellen. But just a bit. No way would my pens ever match my wardrobe.

We got back to work. At five, I asked Ellen, "Don't you have a piano lesson?"

"It won't hurt me to miss one." She flipped open her cell phone and made a call.

Right after that, George left. I figured he had some sort of appointment he couldn't cancel. But I was grateful he'd helped for as long as he could.

There was still plenty to do. The rest of us kept working.

"I found it!" Benji screamed a couple minutes later.

"What?" I asked.

"The floor!"

I stared down at the spot where he pointed. "So that's what it looks like."

"Nice rug," Ellen said.

"Thanks. I forgot I had one."

Just as we were finishing, George returned, holding a beautiful display case with sections for the bread, turkey, and carrots. It even had mirrors in it to show both sides of the specimens.

"Wow," I said, "that's perfect. Did you build it?"

He nodded.

"You're a genius with your hands," I said.

He smiled.

Ellen patted him on the shoulder. "And you don't waste time talking unless you have something to say."

"I'll do the captions," Benji said. He started coming up with these awful puns that made everyone groan, like, "Spore score and seven weeks ago," "Rot and roll," and "Bacterial Girl." But we laughed too. And I knew Ms. Adler had a great sense of humor, so I figured it wouldn't hurt to use Benji's titles.

Ellen, who had beautiful handwriting, lettered the signs. I typed a report to go along with the display. As we all finished up the project together, I realized I'd discovered an important scientific principle. It had nothing to do with mold, but everything to do with chemistry. Some elements combined quickly. Others combined slowly. And some didn't combine at all unless you mixed them together under high heat and intense pressure.

We got an A. Ms. Adler complimented us on our planning. "I'm impressed," she wrote, "that you worked so nicely as a group and immediately got started on a well-planned and complex project. Your use of familiar food items was especially clever."

That afternoon, as I was leaving school, I found Ellen, Benji, and George waiting for me.

"Want to hang out?" Ellen asked.

"Do you?" I asked back.

All three of them nodded. I thought about those reluctant elements again—the ones that didn't want to combine. When you finally got them together, they usually formed incredibly strong bonds.

"Seems a shame not to take advantage of all our work cleaning your room," Ellen said.

"Good point." I didn't have the heart to tell them that half the floor had vanished again. They'd find out for themselves soon enough. On the other hand, it would give us something to do. There was one other thing I had to tell them, though. "This time, I think we should make our own snacks."

They all agreed about that too.

Your Turn

Just Like Me

Find Your Match Which of the four students described in "Science Friction" are you most like? Write a paragraph describing how you are similar to that character. Include story details to make your description clear, and give examples from your own life to show how you are like that character.

PERSONAL RESPONSE

Where and When

Draw a Diagram Work with a partner to draw a diagram of Amanda's bedroom. Show the locations of the hidden food, and include labels that identify each piece of food and the week it was placed there. PARTNERS

It Takes All Kinds

Turn and Talk With a partner, discuss the events that helped Amanda and her classmates learn to cooperate. Talk about the events in the order in which they happened, and think about how each event influenced the next. Then predict what might happen if the students work together again in the future.

SEQUENCE OF EVENTS

GROWING MOLD

by Ed Schuler

You're hungry. You grab some bread. *Ewwww!* It's moldy. This may be a question you're reluctant to ask, but what *is* mold, anyway?

Mold is a type of fungus, a microscopic organism that grows on organic matter such as food. Mold eats bacteria, which, as you'll read, can sometimes be a good thing!

As a detached observer, you can see for yourself how mold grows under different conditions. You might even learn a scientific principle or two while you're at it!

A 300x magnification of the mold fungus Epicoccum purpurascens, often found in decomposing foods

A MOLDY EXPERIMENT

What You Need

- bread (three dry slices)
- cheese (three medium-hard slices)
- tomato (three slices)
- plastic wrap
- plastic knife
- small paper plates

STEP 2

What To Do

1. Make three separate groups, each with a slice of bread, cheese, and tomato. Cut each slice in half. If using three foods is too complex, you can compromise and use one.

2. In Group A, wrap a half-slice of each food in plastic. Leave the rest unwrapped.

3. In Group B, put one set of halves in a dark cupboard. Put the others in an indoor location that has constant light.

STEP 3

4. In Group C, put one set in a warm, dark place. Put the others in a refrigerator.

5. Check your samples daily for a week. Notice how mold forms as food changes (becomes shriveled or fuzzy) through decomposition.

What To Look For

- Which foods grow mold first? Which foods grow the most mold?
- Which food has more mold on it, the wrapped food or the unwrapped food?
- What equations can you make between mold growth and location? Does mold grow better in light or dark? in warm or cool places?

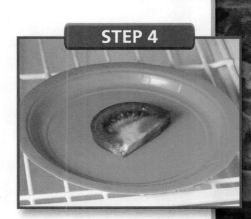
STEP 4

FLEMING'S MIRACLE MOLD

Mold once helped scientists find an elegant solution to a big problem.

In 1928 a Scottish scientist named Alexander Fleming was working in a hospital lab, hoping to find a way to fight bacterial infection. To study bacteria, Fleming grew specimens in dishes. One day, he noticed that a mold had grown on one specimen. Then he discovered that around the mold, bacteria had died.

What had killed them? It was a chemical in the mold!

After years of further research, scientists used the mold, *Penicillium notatum*, to make a drug called penicillin. At first, penicillin was hard to make in large batches. Then scientists found that it grew fast on corn and rotting melon.

By the mid-1940s, the United States was making 650 billion doses of penicillin per month. Infections that once were deadly could now be cured with an antibiotic drug made from a mold!

Alexander Fleming, 1952. The background photo on this page shows spores of the mold used to make penicillin.

Making Connections

217

Text to Self

Write About Groups "Science Friction" shows how a diverse group can work together. Think of a time when you were part of a working group or team. What were some of the challenges of working with the group? What were some of the benefits? What was the result? Write a paragraph that answers these questions.

Text to Text

Compare Texts Fiction and nonfiction present scientific information in different ways. Review "Science Friction" and "Growing Mold" to compare the information in them on how food decomposes. What is the same? What is different?

Text to World

Connect to Science Mold is a type of fungus. So are mushrooms and yeast. Look up *fungus* in a dictionary. What do you think is the value of studying fungi such as mushrooms and yeast? Share your thoughts with a partner.

Grammar

What Is a Coordinating Conjunction? The connecting words *and, or,* and *but* are called **coordinating conjunctions**. You can use these conjunctions to join two simple sentences into a **compound sentence**.

Coordinating Conjunctions in Compound Sentences
The group had its first meeting, and Amanda became the leader.
Would the group cooperate, or would it waste time on squabbles?
Amanda liked chemistry, but Ellen was more interested in astronomy.

In each part of a compound sentence, the subject and verb must agree.

singular subject | singular verb | coordinating conjunction | plural subject | plural verb

Mold grows on bread, and meat and vegetables rot.

Work with a partner. Identify the conjunction in each sentence below. Then explain the subject-verb agreement in each part of the sentence.

1. Ellen puts her clothes away, but other students toss their clothes anywhere.

2. Students pick topics for projects, or teachers assign topics.

3. George says very little, but Ellen and Benji talk a lot.

4. Ellen has the moldy bread, and Benji has the rotting meat.

218

Sentence Fluency Choppy writing does not flow smoothly. It contains too many short sentences, one after the other. You can avoid choppy writing by combining two or more short sentences that have related ideas to form a compound sentence. Remember to use a comma before the conjunction in a compound sentence.

Separate Sentences

Ellen hid her wheat bread.

Benji hid his turkey slices.

Compound Sentence

Ellen hid her wheat bread, and Benji hid his turkey slices.

Connect Grammar to Writing

As you revise your book review, look for short sentences with related ideas that you can combine to make compound sentences. Improve sentences that are too long by breaking them into separate simple or compound sentences.

Write to Respond

In a **book review,** a writer analyzes and evaluates a selection to form an opinion about it. To write a review of realistic fiction, think about the setting, characters, and plot. Ask yourself: *Are the setting and characters well described? Is the plot interesting and easy to follow? Is the story enjoyable to read?* Once you've formed an opinion, support it by using examples from the story.

Amy wrote a book review in which she expressed an opinion about the setting of "Science Friction." Later, she added examples from the story to make her points clear.

Writing Traits Checklist

✔ **Ideas**
Did I state my opinion and support it with examples from the story?

✔ **Organization**
Did I arrange ideas in a logical order?

✔ **Sentence Fluency**
Did I include compound sentences?

✔ **Word Choice**
Did I use specific nouns and vivid verbs?

✔ **Voice**
Did I express an opinion in my own unique way?

✔ **Conventions**
Did I use correct spelling, grammar, and punctuation?

Revised Draft

One of the things I enjoyed about "Science Friction" was the setting. Most of the story takes place in Amanda's room, where she and her classmates meet to plan a science project. Because the room is so messy, Amanda's classmates can hide foods that they don't like.

The room is piled high with books, magazines, and clothes.

220

Setting in "Science Friction"

by Amy Nukaya

One of the things I enjoyed about "Science Friction" was the setting. Most of the story takes place in Amanda's room, where she and her classmates meet to plan a science project. The room is piled high with books, magazines, and clothes. Because the room is so messy, Amanda's classmates can hide foods that they don't like. Ellen hides bread, Benji hides turkey, and George hides baby carrots. After six weeks, the group still hasn't agreed on a science project. Then the food is discovered, and there is their project! The setting is very realistic. Many kids I know have messy rooms. I recommend the story to anyone who isn't disgusted by the idea of moldy food!

In my final book review, I added more examples to support my opinion. I also used coordinating conjunctions to form compound sentences.

Reading as a Writer

What examples did Amy add to support her opinion? In your book review, are there examples you can add to make the support for your opinion stronger?

rudimentary

immaculately

defy

permeated

venture

poised

rigid

consequences

sparsely

array

Vocabulary
Reader

Context
Cards

Vocabulary in Context

1 rudimentary

This picture of a man on a beach gives a rudimentary, or simple, idea of a castaway on an island.

2 immaculately

White sand on a tropical beach seems to sparkle immaculately, as if it were spotless.

3 defy

Only an emergency would force a resident of an island to defy, or challenge, a hurricane.

4 permeated

The sweet smells of tropical flowers have permeated, or spread through, many islands.

- ⬤ Study each **Context Card**.
- ⬤ Ask a question that uses one of the Vocabulary words.

5 venture

Few adult hermit crabs will venture, or dare to go, very far from the safety of their shells.

6 poised

These gulls are poised above the sea. Balanced, they wait for the right moment to snatch a fish.

7 rigid

In time, the trunk of a palm tree grows rigid. It is harder and stiffer than it used to be.

8 consequences

This boy has learned to fish. One of the consequences of his knowledge is that he can catch his own food.

9 sparsely

Only a few people may be found on a beach that is sparsely populated.

10 array

This platter includes an array of tropical fruit. The fruit has been set out in an impressive display.

Background

✔ **TARGET VOCABULARY** **If You Were a Castaway** Imagine the consequences of being a castaway, stranded on an island in the middle of the Pacific Ocean with white sand and blue water stretching immaculately before you. How would you live? Lacking rudimentary items, you might need to venture into the interior of the island, looking for food and water. With luck the island wouldn't be sparsely populated with wildlife but would be permeated with the calls of birds. You would probably need their eggs. You would also need branches and an array of stone tools to make a shelter with a strong, rigid framework. If you were poised to use the resources around you, then you might defy the odds and survive!

Castaway Survival Kit

Shelter	Fresh Water	Food
trees	rain	fruit
bushes	spring	fish
cave	well	coconuts

Comprehension

✔ **TARGET SKILL** **Cause and Effect**

As you read "Kensuke's Kingdom," look for cause-and-effect relationships between events. To identify a cause, ask why an event happens; to identify an effect, ask what happens as a result. You can use a chart like the one below to show each cause and its effect.

Cause	Effect
Examples:	Examples:

✔ **TARGET STRATEGY** **Visualize**

Noting causes and effects can help you visualize what you are reading about Michael and Kensuke. Forming pictures in your mind of the characters and events can help keep you connected to "Kensuke's Kingdom" as you read.

TARGET VOCABULARY

rudimentary	poised
immaculately	rigid
defy	consequences
permeated	sparsely
venture	array

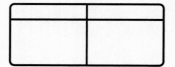

TARGET SKILL

Cause and Effect Tell how events are related and how one event causes another.

TARGET STRATEGY

Visualize Use text details to form pictures in your mind of what you are reading.

GENRE

Realistic fiction has characters and events that are like people and events in real life.

Set a Purpose Before reading, set a purpose for reading based on what you know about the genre and your own experience.

MEET THE AUTHOR

Michael Morpurgo

British author Michael Morpurgo runs Farms for City Children, a program that allows children from British cities to spend time on his own three farms. Many of his books center on an elderly man "giving back to nature more than he takes from it." Author of more than one hundred books, Morpurgo was Britain's Children's Laureate for 2003–2005.

MEET THE ILLUSTRATOR

William Low

Although he paints in a dark basement, William Low is known for his use of light. He once captured a sunset kayaking trip so accurately, viewers assumed he'd been there. Low's other books include *Old Penn Station* and *Chinatown*.

Kensuke's Kingdom

by Michael Morpurgo
selection illustrated by William Low

Essential Question

What causes two castaways to trust each other?

Sailing with his parents around the world, Michael and his dog, Stella, fall overboard during a wild storm. They are washed up on an island in the Pacific. A mysterious old man who has befriended the island's orangutans brings food and water to the boy and dog. But when Michael builds a signal fire to attract a passing ship, the man stomps it out. He draws a line in the sand beyond which Michael is not allowed to go and forbids him to swim in the ocean. Angry, the stranded boy waits for another chance to light a beacon.

With every day that passed, in spite of the fish and fruit and water he continued to bring me, I came to hate the old man more and more. Dejected and depressed I may have been, but I was angry, too, and gradually this anger fueled in me a new determination to escape, and this determination revived my spirits. Once again I went on my daily trek up Watch Hill. I began to collect a fresh cache of dry leaves and twigs from the forest edge and squirreled them away in a deep cleft in the rock so that I would always be sure they were dry when the time came. My beacon had dried out at last. I built it up, higher and higher. When I had done all I could I sat and waited for the time to come, as I knew it must. Day after day, week after week, I sat up on Watch Hill, my fireglass polished in my pocket, my beacon ready and waiting.

As it turned out, when the time did come, I wasn't up on Watch Hill at all. One morning, with sleep still in my head, I emerged from my cave, and there it was. A boat! A boat with strange red-brown sails—I supposed it to be some kind of Chinese junk—and not that far out to sea, either. Excitement got the better of me. I ran helter-skelter down the beach, shouting and screaming for all I was worth. But I could see at once that it was hopeless. The junk was not that far out to sea, but it was still too far for me to be either seen or heard. I tried to calm myself, tried to think . . . the fire! Light the fire!

STOP AND THINK

Author's Craft The phrase "dejected and depressed" in the first paragraph is an example of **alliteration**, the repetition of the beginning consonant sounds of words for emphasis or to create a mood. Find another example of alliteration in that paragraph.

I ran all the way up Watch Hill without once stopping, Stella hard on my heels and barking. All around me the forest was cackling and screeching and whooping in protest at this sudden disturbance. I readied my cache of dry leaves, took my fireglass, and crouched down beside the beacon to light my fire. But I was trembling so much with excitement and exhaustion by now that I could not hold my hand still enough. So I set up a frame of twigs and laid the glass over it, just as I had before. Then I sat over it, willing the leaves to smolder.

Every time I looked out to sea, the junk was still there, moving slowly away, but still there.

It seemed an age, but there was a wisp of smoke, and shortly afterward a glorious, wondrous glow of flame spreading along the edge of one leaf. I bent over it to blow it into life.

That was when I saw his feet. I looked up. The old man was standing over me, his eyes full of rage and hurt. He said not a word, but set about stamping out my embryo fire. He snatched up my fireglass and hurled it at the rock below, where it shattered to pieces. I could only look on and weep as he kicked away my precious pile of dry leaves, as he dismantled my beacon and hurled the sticks and branches one by one down the hill. As he did so the group of orangutans gathered to watch.

Soon nothing whatsoever now remained of my beacon. All about me the rock scree was littered with the scattered ruins of it. I expected him to screech at me, but he didn't. He spoke very quietly, very deliberately. "*Dameda* (dah meh dah)," he said.

"But why?" I cried. "I want to go home. There's a boat, can't you see? I just want to go home, that's all. Why won't you let me? Why?"

He stood and stared at me. For a moment I thought I detected just a flicker of understanding. Then he bowed very stiffly from the waist, and said, "*Gomenasai* (gah meh nah sy). *Gomenasai*. Sorry. Very sorry." And with that he left me there and went off back into the forest, followed by the orangutans.

I sat there watching the junk until it was nothing but a spot on the horizon, until I could not bear to watch anymore. By this time I had already decided how I could best defy him. I was so enraged that consequences didn't matter to me now. Not anymore. With Stella beside me, I headed along the beach, stopped at the boundary line in the sand, and then, very deliberately, I stepped over it. As I did so, I let him know precisely what I was doing.

"Are you watching, old man?" I shouted. "Look! I've crossed over. I've crossed over your silly line. And now I'm going to swim. I don't care what you say. I don't care if you don't feed me. You hear me, old man?" Then I turned and charged down the beach into the sea. I swam furiously, until I was completely exhausted and a long way from the shore. I trod water and thrashed the sea in my fury—making it boil and froth all around me. "It's my sea as much as yours," I cried. "And I'll swim in it when I like."

I saw him then. He appeared suddenly at the edge of the forest. He was shouting something at me, waving his stick. That was the moment I felt it, a searing, stinging pain in the back of my neck, then my back, and my arms, too. A large, translucent white jellyfish was floating right beside me, its tentacles groping at me. I tried to swim away, but it came after me, hunting me. I was stung again, in my foot this time. The agony was immediate and excruciating. It permeated my entire body like one continuous electric shock. I felt my muscles going rigid. I kicked for the shore, but I could not do it. My legs seemed paralyzed, my arms, too. I was sinking, and there was nothing I could do about it. I saw the jellyfish poised for the kill above me now. I screamed, and my mouth filled with water. I was choking. I was going to die, I was going to drown, but I did not care. I just wanted the pain to stop. Death I knew would stop it.

I smelled vinegar, and thought I was at home. My father always brought us back fish and chips for supper on Fridays and he loved to soak his in vinegar—the whole house would stink of it all evening. I opened my eyes. It was dark enough to be evening, but I was not at home. I was in a cave, but not my cave. I could smell smoke, too. I was lying on a sleeping mat covered in a sheet up to my chin. I tried to sit up to look around me, but I could not move. I tried to turn my neck. I couldn't. I could move nothing except my eyes. I could feel, though. My skin, my whole body, throbbed with searing pain, as if I had been scalded all over. I tried to call out, but could barely manage a whisper. Then I remembered the jellyfish. I remembered it all.

The old man was bending over me, his hand soothing on my forehead. "You better now," he said. "My name Kensuke. You better now." I wanted to ask after Stella. She answered for herself by sticking her cold nose into my ear.

I do not know for how many days I lay there, drifting in and out of sleep, only that whenever I woke, Kensuke was always there sitting beside me. He rarely spoke and I could not speak, but the silence between us said more than any words.

✔ STOP AND THINK

Cause and Effect What does Michael do in the fourth paragraph on page 230 that might help explain why he is attacked by a jellyfish?

My erstwhile enemy, my captor, had become my savior. He would lift me to pour fruit juice or warm soup down my throat. He would sponge me down with cooling water, and when the pain was so bad that I cried out, he would hold me and sing me softly back to sleep. It was strange. When he sang to me it was like an echo from the past, of my father's voice, perhaps—I didn't know. Slowly the pain left me. Tenderly he nursed me back to life. The day my fingers first moved was the very first time I ever saw him smile.

When at last I was able to turn my neck I would watch him as he came and went, as he busied himself around the cave. Stella would often come and lie beside me, her eyes following him, too.

Every day now I was able to see more of where I was. In comparison with my cave down by the beach, this place was vast. Apart from the roof of vaulted rock above, you would scarcely have known it was a cave. There was nothing rudimentary about it at all. It looked more like an open-plan house than a cave—kitchen, sitting room, studio, bedroom, all in one space.

He cooked over a small fire that smoked continuously at the back of the cave, the smoke rising through a small cleft high in the rocks above—a possible reason, I thought, why there were no mosquitoes to bother me. There always seemed to be something hanging from a wooden tripod over the fire, either a blackened pot or what looked like and smelled like long strips of smoked fish.

I could see the dark gleam of metal pots and pans lined up on a nearby wooden shelf. There were other shelves, too, lined with tins and jars, dozens of them of all sizes and shapes, and hanging beneath them innumerable bunches of dried herbs and flowers. These he would often be mixing or pounding, but I wasn't sure what for. Sometimes he would bring them over to me so that I could smell them.

The cave house was sparsely furnished. To one side of the cave mouth stood a low wooden table, barely a foot off the ground. Here he kept his paintbrushes, always neatly laid out, and several more jars and bottles, and saucers, too.

Kensuke lived and worked almost entirely near the mouth of the cave house where there was daylight. At night he would roll out his sleeping mat across the cave from me, up against the far wall. I would wake in the early mornings sometimes and just watch him sleeping. He always lay on his back wrapped in his sheet and never moved a muscle.

Kensuke would spend many hours of every day kneeling at the table and painting. He painted on large shells but, much to my disappointment, he never showed me what he had done. Indeed, he rarely seemed pleased with his work, for just as soon as he had finished, he would usually wash off what he had done and start again.

On the far side of the cave mouth was a long workbench and, hanging up above it, an array of tools—saws, hammers, chisels, all sorts. And beyond the workbench were three large wooden chests in which he would frequently rummage around for a shell, perhaps, or a clean sheet. We had clean sheets every night.

Inside the cave he wore a wraparound bathrobe (a kimono, as I later knew it to be). He kept the cave house immaculately clean, sweeping it down once a day at least. There was a large bowl of water just inside the cave mouth. Every time he came in he would wash his feet and dry them before stepping inside.

The floor was entirely covered with mats made of woven rushes, like our sleeping mats. And everywhere, all around the cave, to head height and above, the walls were lined with bamboo. It was simple, but it was a home. There was no clutter. Everything had its place and its purpose.

As I got better, Kensuke would go off, and leave me on my own more and more but, thankfully, never for too long. He'd return later, very often singing, with fish, perhaps fruit, coconuts or herbs, which he'd bring over to show me proudly. The orangutans would sometimes come with him, but only as far as the cave mouth. They'd peer in at me, and at Stella, who always kept her distance from them. Only the young ones ever tried to venture in, and then Kensuke only had to clap at them and they'd soon go scooting off.

During those early days in the cave house I so much wished we could talk. There were a thousand mysteries, a thousand things I wanted to know. But it still hurt me to talk, and besides, I felt he was quite happy with our silence, that he preferred it somehow. He seemed a very private person, and content to be that way.

Then one day, after hours of kneeling hunched over one of his paintings, he came over and gave it to me. It was a picture of a tree, a tree in blossom. His smile said everything. "For you. Japan tree," he said. "I, Japanese person." After that, Kensuke showed me all the paintings he did, even the ones he later washed off. They were all in black-and-white wash, of orangutans, gibbons, butterflies, dolphins, and birds, and fruit. Only very occasionally did he keep one, storing it away carefully in one of his chests. He did keep several of the tree paintings, I noticed, always of a tree in blossom, a "Japan tree" as he called it, and I could see he took particular joy in showing me these. It was clear he was allowing me to share something very dear to him. I felt honored by that.

In the dying light of each day he would sit beside me and watch over me, the last of the evening sun on his face. I felt as if he were healing me with his eyes. At night, I thought often of my mother and my father. I so much wanted to see them again, to let them know I was still alive. But, strangely, I no longer missed them.

> **STOP AND THINK**
> **Visualize** Which descriptive details on this page help you visualize Kensuke's cave and how the old man lives?

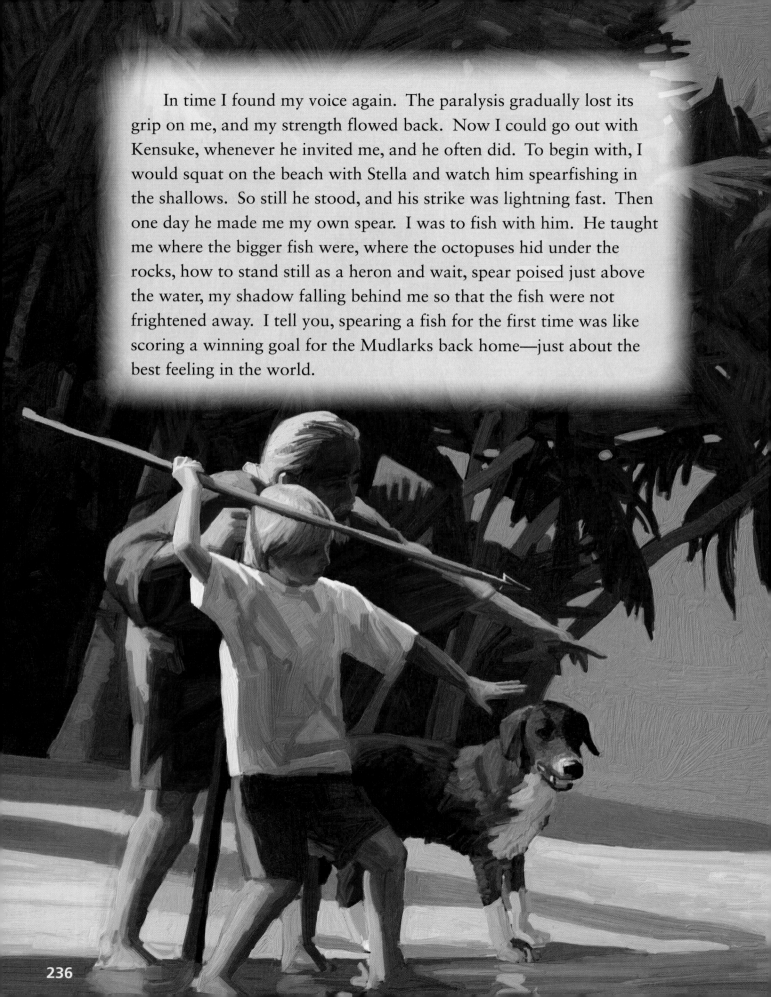

In time I found my voice again. The paralysis gradually lost its grip on me, and my strength flowed back. Now I could go out with Kensuke, whenever he invited me, and he often did. To begin with, I would squat on the beach with Stella and watch him spearfishing in the shallows. So still he stood, and his strike was lightning fast. Then one day he made me my own spear. I was to fish with him. He taught me where the bigger fish were, where the octopuses hid under the rocks, how to stand still as a heron and wait, spear poised just above the water, my shadow falling behind me so that the fish were not frightened away. I tell you, spearing a fish for the first time was like scoring a winning goal for the Mudlarks back home—just about the best feeling in the world.

Your Turn

Have Patience

Write a Paragraph In "Kensuke's Kingdom," Michael shows patience and planning by collecting dry leaves and twigs and waiting for the chance to light his beacon. Write about a time when you had to plan carefully and show patience to accomplish something. How was your experience similar to Michael's?

PERSONAL RESPONSE

In Translation

Conduct an Interview Work with a small group. Have each group member role-play Kensuke, Michael, or a Japanese-English translator. The students playing Kensuke and Michael should write down questions they would like to ask each other. The translator should read the questions in turn for Kensuke or Michael to answer. Use details from the text and your own imagination to think of an answer to each question. SMALL GROUP

Building Trust

Turn and Talk Do you think Kensuke and Michael trust each other more at the end of the selection? With a partner, discuss the events that might have caused each character to place more trust in the other.

CAUSE AND EFFECT

Exploring Islands

by Carole Gerber

Picture an island. What comes to mind? Maybe it's a sparsely inhabited Pacific island with immaculately white sand, where only a few seabirds venture. Maybe it's Greenland, the world's biggest island, at 822,000 square miles. It could be the island nation of Indonesia, home to 211 million people.

Islands come in all varieties. They defy one-size-fits-all descriptions—except for the rudimentary one that applies to all islands: a piece of land completely surrounded by water.

Ancient volcanoes formed the islands of Channel Islands National Park in California.

How Islands Form

There are two main types of island—oceanic and continental. Both types show the consequences of dramatic changes.

Oceanic islands, such as those found along the coast of Southern California, form from the peaks of undersea volcanoes. Some oceanic islands are created when coral reefs, made from rigid coral skeletons, build up around these volcanoes.

Continental islands form when the sea rises and surrounds a section of the mainland of a continent. One kind of continental island is the barrier island. This island forms from the action of water, wind, and tides that shape and move sand and sediment. Many barrier islands are found along the Atlantic coast of North America.

Barrier Island Zones

Barrier islands are always poised for change. A typical barrier island has five zones. Ocean waves bring sand to the beach. Wind forms the sand into dunes that are held in place by plants. Storms push water permeated with sediment over the dunes, forming a mud flat. Ocean tides make an area of salt marsh around the mud flats.

Five Zones of a Barrier Island

1. sea
2. beach
3. dune area
4. overwash area
5. marsh

The Island Ecosystem

The Outer Banks (left) are a chain of barrier islands along the North Carolina coast. This island ecosystem is the home of a rich array of plant and sea life.

Some animals live on the Outer Banks year-round, but others only visit. Often, the sky above the islands is filled with flocks of snow geese and other birds that arrive for the winter. Another visitor, the female loggerhead sea turtle, lives in the ocean but comes ashore in summer to dig a nest and lay her eggs.

To care for this ecosystem and protect its animals and plants, portions of the Outer Banks have been named federal wildlife refuges.

Female loggerhead sea turtles return to the Outer Banks every two to three years to nest.

Making Connections

Text to Self

Describe an Experience In "Kensuke's Kingdom," Michael is often surprised and frustrated by Kensuke's actions. Write a paragraph about a time when someone's actions surprised or frustrated you. What did you learn from this experience?

Text to Text

Compare Texts "Kensuke's Kingdom" and "Exploring Islands" are selections that are both alike and different. Identify the genre of each selection, and then tell what the texts have in common and how they differ. Present your ideas in a Venn diagram or a compare-and-contrast chart.

Text to World

Connect to Social Studies On a world map, find the Hawaiian Islands or another group of islands. Research the different ways people there depend on the sea. Create a list that shows what you find, and add illustrations if you wish. In a small group, share what you learned.

Grammar

What Is a Subordinating Conjunction? Words such as *although, because, if,* and *since* are **subordinating conjunctions**. The part of a sentence that begins with a subordinating conjunction is a **dependent clause**. Dependent clauses are not complete sentences. A **complex sentence** consists of a dependent clause and an **independent clause**. An independent clause can stand alone as a sentence. It is the most important part of a complex sentence. Use a comma after a dependent clause that comes at the beginning of a sentence.

Subordinating Conjunctions in Complex Sentences

dependent clause   independent clause

When Michael built a signal fire, the man stomped it out.

subordinating conjunction

---

independent clause   dependent clause

Michael wept because the man had shattered his fireglass.

subordinating conjunction

Try This! **Write the complex sentences below on a sheet of paper. Circle the subordinating conjunctions. Underline the independent clauses, and draw two lines under the dependent clauses.**

❶ Michael swam furiously until he was exhausted.

❷ After the jellyfish stung him, Michael felt great pain.

❸ Michael could not swim because his muscles had become rigid.

❹ When Michael screamed, his mouth filled with water.

Sentence Fluency You can vary your sentence structure and make your writing smoother by using a subordinating conjunction to combine two related simple sentences to form a complex sentence.

Separate Sentences

The boy lay motionless in bed.

His dog shoved her nose into his ear.

Complex Sentence

As the boy lay motionless in bed, his dog shoved her nose into his ear.

Connect Grammar to Writing

As you write your opinion essay, look for sentences that you can combine by using a subordinating conjunction to form a complex sentence.

Write to Respond

☑ **Ideas** When you plan an **opinion essay** in response to literature, begin by analyzing the story. You can ask yourself questions such as these: *What is unique about the story? Are the characters unusual? Are the plot events believable? What does the story reveal about life?* Once you form an opinion about the story, think of reasons that support your opinion. Use details and examples from the story as well as from your own experience.

May explored a character in "Kensuke's Kingdom." Once she formed an opinion, she listed reasons that supported her opinion. Then she deleted an idea that didn't fit with the others. Later, she organized her ideas in an opinion chart.

Writing Process Checklist

▶ **Prewrite**

☑ Have I identified my opinion?

☑ Do I have enough reasons?

☑ Are my reasons convincing?

☑ Did I find details and examples to support each reason?

☑ Did I organize my ideas in a logical way?

Draft

Revise

Edit

Publish and Share

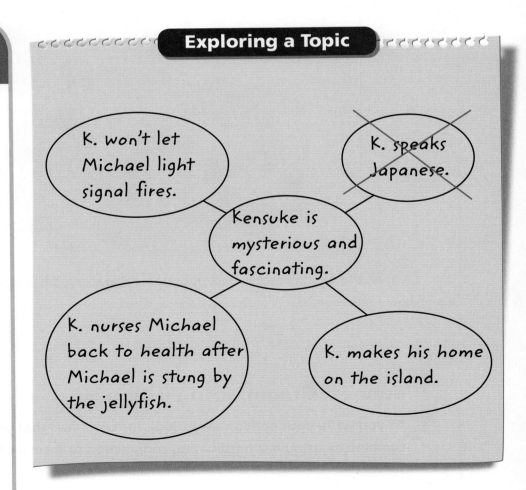

Exploring a Topic

K. won't let Michael light signal fires.

K. speaks Japanese.

Kensuke is mysterious and fascinating.

K. nurses Michael back to health after Michael is stung by the jellyfish.

K. makes his home on the island.

Opinion Chart

Kensuke is a mysterious character. He makes the story enjoyable to read.

Reason: Kensuke won't let Michael light signal fires.	**Detail:** Kensuke stomps out Michael's fire for no clear reason.
Reason: Kensuke helps Michael heal after the jellyfish attack.	**Detail:** Like a friend, Kensuke soothes Michael when he is in pain.
Reason: Kensuke makes his home on the island.	**Detail:** Kensuke's cave includes a kitchen, bedroom, and sitting room.

When I organized my opinion essay, I used details from the story to support each of my reasons.

Reading as a Writer

**How do May's details support her reasons?
Where can you add one or two more supporting
details to your opinion essay?**

✓ **TARGET VOCABULARY**

lore

abundance

altered

sophisticated

cultural

lush

teeming

retains

heritage

concept

Vocabulary
Reader

Context
Cards

Vocabulary in Context

1 lore

A tribe's lore, or collected knowledge, is passed on by adults who teach traditions to new generations.

2 abundance

These fishermen can feed many families with this abundance of salmon.

3 altered

Computers have changed Alaskan schools. They have altered how students learn.

4 sophisticated

This artwork is sophisticated. It shows many complex details.

- **Study each Context Card.**

- **Discuss one picture. Use a different Vocabulary word from the one on the card.**

5 cultural

A totem pole is a cultural work, expressing ideas and customs of the community.

6 lush

Every summer, the valleys of Alaska are lush, full of flowers and green plants.

7 teeming

During the fall, Alaska's sky is teeming with thousands of migrating geese.

8 retains

Though times change, a tribe retains, or keeps, ancient practices such as carving.

9 heritage

Traditional clothes are part of the heritage, or common past, of Native Alaskans.

10 concept

Many ceremonies reflect the concept, or idea, that sharing is important.

Background

✓ TARGET VOCABULARY **What Does It Mean To Be a Tribal Member?**

Think about the concept of a community, a group of people with a common identity. A tribe's identity is not based only on its setting, whether lush valley or desert. It is mainly cultural, built on shared beliefs. The heritage of every tribe and clan, or tribal division, is teeming with traditions in art, music, food, and clothing. Each tribal member shares in this abundance. Some practices have not been altered for centuries. Other ideas change with the times, perhaps becoming more sophisticated. However, each tribe retains the lore, the special knowledge, of its artisans, or craftspeople, and storytellers.

Tlingit and Haida Alaska and Canada

ALASKA
CANADA

Chilkat River

North
West — East
South

• Klukwan

★ Juneau

Gulf of Alaska

Prince of Wales Island
Hydaburg

Key
Tlingit region
Haida region
★ State capital
• Town

Queen Charlotte Island (Canada)

The Haida (HY duh) and Tlingit (KLIHNG it) tribes are neighbors in southeastern Alaska.

Comprehension

✔ **TARGET SKILL** **Compare and Contrast**

As you read "Children of the Midnight Sun," notice similarities and differences between groups of people, settings, or periods of history. Look for clue words, such as *in common*, *similar*, *but*, *all*, *each*, and *better*. You can use a Venn diagram like the one below to show details that describe these similarities and differences.

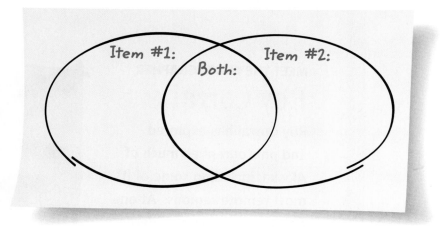

Item #1:   Both: Item #2:

✔ **TARGET STRATEGY** **Question**

Noting similarities and differences with a Venn diagram can help you answer questions about what you are reading. Asking questions and finding the answers help keep you connected with what you read.

Main Selection

✓ TARGET VOCABULARY

lore	lush
abundance	teeming
altered	retains
sophisticated	heritage
cultural	concept

✓ TARGET SKILL

Compare and Contrast Examine how two or more details or ideas are alike and different.

✓ TARGET STRATEGY

Question Ask questions about a selection before you read, as you read, and after you read.

GENRE
Narrative nonfiction gives factual information by telling a true story.

Set a Purpose Before reading, set a purpose for reading based on what you know about the genre and your own experience.

MEET THE AUTHOR
Tricia Brown

Tricia Brown has lived and worked in Alaska since the 1970s. A writer and editor, she has published books on a wide range of topics, including the Iditarod sled dog race, quilt-making, and the Alaska Highway. She has won numerous awards for her writing and continues to write for both adults and children.

MEET THE PHOTOGRAPHER
Roy Corral

Roy Corral has explored and photographed much of Alaska, including some of its most remote regions. At one point, he lived in a wilderness area above the Arctic Circle in a log home he built himself. His photographs have appeared in *National Geographic Magazine*, *Sports Illustrated for Kids*, and many children's books.

Children of the Midnight Sun:
Young Native Voices of Alaska

by Tricia Brown   photographs by Roy Corral

Essential Question

How are two groups' traditions alike and different?

These portraits of two Native American children growing up in Alaska reveal how they each celebrate their culture's ancient traditions in the context of modern life.

Selina Tolson Haida

Belly down on the Hydaburg dock, Selina Tolson, nine, and her cousin Jamie peer into the shadowy water beneath them. The girls identify seaweed, jellyfish, and salmon while they wait for Selina's teenage brother Charles to come with his skiff. Selina's family left earlier on the *Haida* (HY duh) *Girl*, her grandfather's fifty-six-foot commercial seiner, and the girls are anxious to join them at a picnic across the water.

"Look at those fish!" says Selina. "I wish I had my brother's rod." She loves to fish for salmon, although she admits that a brother helps reel them in. Selina has three brothers and two sisters, a cat named Fatso, a pen pal, a treehouse, and a *chanáa* (chah NAH), or grandfather, who tells her wonderful stories.

This late August day is sunny and dry, a rare occasion. Hydaburg, a village of about 400 Haida Indian people, lies in rain forest country on Prince of Wales Island in Southeast Alaska. Each year, the area normally gets about 150 inches of rain and a little snow.

Rows of totem poles stand next to Selina's school. Some are new poles; others are very old, collected from other places on the island.

Minutes pass slowly. The girls roll onto their backs to stare at the clouds. On Selina's wrist are two broad, engraved silver bracelets that tinkle whenever they touch. The Eagle clan symbol adorns one. Selina wears a silver ring too.

"My uncle gave me this ring," Selina says. "This bracelet was my dad's mother's, and when she died, he gave it to me. I don't take them off, ever."

Art and Culture

Artistically, the Haidas have much in common with their neighbors, the Tlingits (KLIHNG its) and Tsimshians (SIHM shee uhns). Their styles vary so slightly that only a clan member or a fellow artist might notice the differences. All three groups carve totem poles and follow similar customs in clan organization. But each group retains its own identity and tribal lore, and each is known for its artistic specialty. Historically, for the Haidas, it was dugout canoes, made from the biggest cedar trees in the region—found about forty miles south on Canada's Queen Charlotte Islands.

In Selina's village there is an abundance of artists. Rosa Alby makes beautiful button blankets. Her brother, Warren, carves Haida-style boats and totems. Viola Burgess teaches Haida art to the children. Selina's mom, Christine, is among those who teach Haida dance.

"Our dance costume is a special blanket with our clan on it," says Selina. "Jamie and I are Eagle. There's Eagle, Frog, Bullhead, and Beaver.

"We don't use the same dance steps for every song," she explains. "We practice what we're going to do. Our teachers teach us Haida words, like *kwáadaa* (KWAH dah). That means 'quarter,' and *dáalaa* (DAH lah) means 'money,' and *dúus* (doos) means 'cat.' *Háw'aa* (huh WAH) means 'thank you.'"

STOP AND THINK

Question What question or questions does the information on this page help you answer?

Selina loves to fish. Although she'd rather have a coho salmon on the end of her line, she'll settle for this rockfish. ▶

Next to Selina's school is a grassy lot lined with totem poles. Life in a rain forest means there are always plenty of large trees for carving. The frequent rain and constant dampness speed the natural decay of these valuable pieces of history and art. Some were moved from other places on Prince of Wales; others were carved here. Historically, the totems served as storytellers, memorials, or signs of clan ownership.

Finally, Selina spots Charles on the horizon and jumps to her feet. Within minutes, he motors in and helps his passengers aboard for a twenty-minute ride.

At the picnic, three generations of adults—Selina's aunts, uncles, grandparents, older cousins, and family friends—sit on driftwood logs, talking, laughing, and feeding a bonfire. Over the flames, they roast hot dogs and marshmallows. Tupperware containers of salads, smoked *chíin* (cheen), or salmon, and desserts are opened. A few grown-ups keep their eyes on the young ones romping in the chilly ocean. Selina can't be tempted to jump in, but wades instead, squealing when the cold water laps against her ankles.

Occasionally, a shivering child runs up to a parent for a rubdown with a towel. A few head into the woods to look for berries. Seated in nearby lawn chairs are Selina's grandparents, Sylvester and Frieda Peele, respected tribal elders who are passing on stories, language, and dance, teaching the Haida ways in daily life and in cultural heritage classes for children.

Selina poses with her mother, Christine, and grandparents Sylvester and Frieda Peele. Because clan membership is passed from mother to child, Frieda, Christine, and Selina are all Eagles.

The third largest American island, Prince of Wales Island lies just across the border from Canada.

Haida History

Sylvester was born in Hydaburg, but his parents were not. His mother came from British Columbia, and his father was from Kilnkwun, a village about ten or twelve miles away from Hydaburg. Kilnkwun and another village were abandoned in 1911 when the government forced the residents to move to Hydaburg.

"It was mostly for school purposes," Sylvester says gently. "But this was a better place to live, with a river and lots of salmon." At one time his ancestors all lived in Canada. Some tribal stories say that about 400 years ago there was a food shortage, and one group came north to Prince of Wales Island.

The Alaska Haidas settled in villages that had been abandoned by Tlingits. However, other storytellers say the new arrivals warred with the Tlingits, driving them to the northern part of the island. Today, an invisible boundary splits the island, with Tlingit country in the north and the Haidas in the south. But wars? None lately.

The Haidas found plentiful food when they arrived: deer, berries, fish eggs, crab, salmon, halibut, and seaweed. And even though Hydaburg's children can walk to the little Do Drop grocery store for candy, pop, crackers, or other snacks, their families still mostly rely on the ocean to feed them.

"I like coho eggs and dog salmon eggs," says Selina. "We dry them and save them for the winter. I help pick the berries, and I help with drying seaweed, too.

"My brothers usually go out on the boat and get seaweed on the beach somewhere. At home, they grind it up in the grinder and lay it out on the roof of the house to dry. Then we seal it in plastic bags."

The picnic is wrapping up, and as mothers and aunties are replacing lids and gathering children, the men fold up chairs and carry supplies to the water's edge.

In the middle of the cove, the beautiful *Haida Girl* waits, anchored in the still, gray water. Charles shuttles the party from the beach to the seiner, a handful at a time. Voyaging home to Hydaburg, Selina turns her face toward the bow of the *Haida Girl*. Her long, black hair flutters in the wind like a flag.

STOP AND THINK
Author's Craft In the last sentence, the author uses a **simile**, a comparison using the word *like*, when she says that Selina's hair "flutters in the wind like a flag." Why do you think she chooses this simile?

A member of the Eagle Clan, Selina models her ceremonial regalia.

Josh Hotch  Tlingit

Josh Hotch doesn't know whom he'll marry when he grows up, but he knows she'll be a Raven, so his children will be Ravens. That's because Josh is a member of the other Tlingit clan—the Eagle clan—just like his mother.

"You are what your mother is," he explains. "An Eagle can't marry an Eagle, and a Raven can't marry a Raven." Marrying within your clan would be like marrying a member of your family.

At ten, Josh may not know the word *moiety* (MOY uh tee), but he understands the concept. Throughout Tlingit territory—nearly all of Alaska's Southeast Panhandle—the Natives historically were born into two moieties, or membership groups, called Eagle and Raven, and further divided into subclans with animal symbols such as Killer Whale, Wolf, or Frog.

The clan shared responsibilities. If one clan organized to build a house, the other clan finished the work. Then the first hosted a potlatch, a ceremonial feast that focused on gift-giving memorials, and displays of wealth. If a clan member died, the other clan prepared the dead for cremation or burial. Later, the deceased's clan would show their thanks by hosting a potlatch. And so it went, back and forth, sharing labor and gifts, with each clan helping and honoring the other.

Josh is robed in a Chilkat blanket, part of his dance regalia.

These customs are among the ancient Tlingit traditions woven into daily life in Klukwan, Josh's home village of 140 people in the northern part of the state's Panhandle. So, too, are practices such as smoking and drying fish, carving totem poles and masks, weaving Raven's Tail robes and Chilkat blankets, dancing and singing, storytelling, and celebrating in potlatches. Nothing is done for the sake of tourists—it's just everyday living. The residents also drive cars and own fax machines in a village that mixes past and present in a postcard setting.

Living with Nature

"Klukwan is a nice place," says Josh. "We have the biggest mountains in the U.S.A. We have evergreen and cottonwood trees and glaciers. Salmon, fish, and deer, too. In the spring, the hooligans are here—they're the teeny fish that you can't catch in salmon fishing nets. We make hooligan oil out of them. We dip dried fish or dried hooligan in it—it's a snack!"

Klukwan is indeed a beautiful, bountiful place to live. That's probably why Chilkat Tlingits have lived in this valley for thousands of years. They were sophisticated artisans who often traded with their Athabascan (ath uh BAS kuhn) neighbors. They also held the rights to the trails later used by the Gold Rush prospectors headed for the Klondike.

At the edge of Josh's backyard, beyond the swing set and the fringe of cottonwoods, beyond the smoke house and the skiff, the Chilkat River rolls by in a broad, braided pattern. In the distance, snow-capped mountains tower above a lush, green valley teeming with fish and wildlife.

The people of Klukwan depend on fish and game as their food staples, and drive twenty-one miles to Haines for any other groceries, to pick up mail, see a movie, or board the ferry on the Inside Passage. The villagers share this valley with the largest gathering of bald eagles in North America. Each October and November, up to 4,000 eagles congregate to glut themselves on late-run salmon in the Chilkat River. "Eagles fight with eagles for fish," Josh says.

Klukwan is so small that there are ten children in Josh's class of second- through fourth-graders.

Josh's village is long and narrow, laid out parallel to the river along one unpaved street with weathered cabins and newer frame homes sprinkled on each side. Near the middle is the community center, used for potlatches and other special events. Josh and his cousins like to explore, run, play hide-and-seek, and go bike riding around town. There's plenty of room and little traffic. And everybody knows everybody else.

Growing Up Tlingit

Even though Josh is still young, he has learned the rules of his society, not from books, but from the Ravens and Eagles around him. And if he'd been born a century ago, he would have practiced another Tlingit tradition, the "avunculate." At about age six, Tlingit boys used to go live with their mother's brother, who taught them as they grew to manhood. It was believed that fathers would be too easy on their sons, but that an uncle was the right combination of softness and strictness.

Josh's dad, Jones, is a tribal government leader who's teaching his son with assistance from a special uncle. Today, Tlingit children don't leave home for the avunculate, but uncles still help to instruct them, and not just the boys in the family. When Josh's mom, Lani, was growing up, she and her brothers learned from their mother's brother, Albert Paddy. And when Josh was born, Lani gave him Uncle Albert's Tlingit name: *Kaan-kai-da* (kahn KY dah).

"He still watches out for us now, even though we're grown," Lani says. "And he's been training Josh on the fishing boat on the river. He also had an important role in showing me how to make dried fish, along with my grandmother, my mom, and my dad."

✔ **STOP AND THINK**
Compare and Contrast What does information on these pages tell you about the differences and similarities between Tlingit traditions now and in the past?

Josh uses a spotting scope to watch for eagles in trees along the river. ▶

Contact with non-Native settlers, gold miners, missionaries, and educators in the last two centuries has altered the ancient ways of the Tlingit people. Especially in the 1900s, the loss of traditional dancing, singing, and weaving was sorely felt.

"Josh's grandparents weren't taught to dance and sing," Lani says. "If they used their language, they were punished." And as old weavers died, few young people were trained to follow. Only in the last decade has Lani's generation learned the songs and dances of their ancestors by listening to old recordings and experimenting with movements. "We had a lot of encouragement from the elders," she says.

From the adults around him, Josh has learned the meaning of the symbols on totem poles and on his special dance clothing. He's learned how to bead, dance, sing, and prepare salmon for smoking.

"You cut off the head, tail, and fins," Josh says. "You use cottonwood to burn in the smokehouse. There's a screen so that no bugs can get in. It's just like how it sounds: dried fish would be dry; smoked fish would taste like smoke. What I like are herring eggs. They're crunchy. They're better than potato chips!"

On his way to becoming a man, Josh is surrounded by a village full of Eagles and Ravens who will make sure he knows who he is: *Kaan-kai-da*, a Tlingit, a son of Klukwan.

Josh and his uncle, Albert Paddy, leave the village for a fish site on the Chilkat River.

Your Turn

Land and Culture

Share a Point of View Both Selina and Josh live in the Pacific Northwest. Write about how that setting shapes the way of life for both the Haida people and the Tlingit people. Then think about the land and climate where you live and write about how they shape your own way of life. SOCIAL STUDIES

Tour Guide

Role-Play Imagine that Josh were to give Selina a tour of his village. What things would he show her and tell her about? How would Selina respond to her tour? With a partner, role-play a meeting between Josh and Selina in which these questions are answered. Include details from the text in your dialogue. PARTNERS

Ties That Bind

Turn and Talk Think about the traditions of the Haida and Tlingit cultures. With a partner, discuss how these traditions are alike and different. What questions would this information lead you to ask about the Haida and Tlingit cultures? COMPARE AND CONTRAST

NATIVE AMERICAN POETRY

The Native American poems in this selection connect to a rich cultural past. The Makah Nation of Washington State retains tribal dancing as an important part of its heritage. "Song" honors that tradition. "Reweaving the World Ohlone" celebrates a craft of the Rumsien Ohlone people in the Monterey Bay area of California. The Maidu of California's Sierra Nevada are represented in "Lesson in Fire," which recalls the lore of making a fire in a poem teeming with dreamlike images.

SONG

Mine is a proud village, such as it is,

We are at our best when dancing.

Makah

REWEAVING THE WORLD OHLONE

by Stephen Meadows

for Linda Yamane

Enmeshing
with bone awl
with curved tooth
with dreaming
Again living patience
the slow walk
and choosing
The arms
and the fingers
of plants
the bent branches
the willow
the cattail
the root
the crisp grasses

The green limb
the gold stem
the soft flesh
the cleansing
the sheer thought
the taut hand
the earth's
whirling music
In your palm
in your lap
in your sphere
in your circle
This basket
this dance
upon the ground

Linda Yamane

Stephen Meadows dedicates his poem to Linda Yamane (yuh MAH nee), a master basketweaver. Yamane traces her ancestry to the Rumsien Ohlone people. She has helped revive the art of Ohlone basket weaving.

Yamane has not altered ancient techniques. She uses traditional tools, such as the bone awl, to weave sophisticated patterns from the roots and shoots of grasses and willows. These plants grow in abundance in the lush Monterey Bay area. Yamane is also a storyteller. Her presentations have included songs she learned from recordings made by elders who remembered these traditional ways.

263

LESSON IN FIRE

by Linda Noel

My father built a good fire
He taught me to tend the fire
How to make it stand
So it could breathe
And how the flames create
Coals that turn into faces
Or eyes
Of fish swimming
Out of flames
Into gray
Rivers of ash

And how the eyes
And faces look out
At us
Burn up for us
To heat the air
That we breathe
And so into us
We swallow
All the shapes
Created in a well-tended fire

Write a Community Poem

The concept of community is an important theme in poetry. Use "Song" as a model to write a short poem about a community you are a member of, such as school, family, a sports team, or any other group. In your poem's first line, describe the community. In the second line, tell when this group is at its best. Here is an example.

Mine is a cool school, full of cool people.
We are at our best when helping each other.

Making Connections

 Text to Self

Describe Favorite Activities Selina and Josh enjoy doing many activities with their families and people from their villages. What activities do you enjoy doing with your own family, friends, or neighbors? Write a paragraph describing those activities.

 Text to Text

Make a List Lore, or special knowledge shared by a particular group of people, plays an important role in Native American life and culture. Review "Children of the Midnight Sun" and "Native American Poetry." Make a list of details that show how tribal lore shapes the lives of various Native American peoples.

 Text to World

Connect to Social Studies Imagine that your class could visit a Native American community anywhere in the United States. Choose a region to visit, and identify one or more native groups in the area. Create a map and an itinerary, or plan, for your trip. List highlights of what you might see and learn. Share this information with a small group.

Grammar

What Is a Compound-Complex Sentence? You have learned that two simple sentences can be joined by a **coordinating conjunction** to form a **compound sentence**. You have also learned that two simple sentences can be joined by a **subordinating conjunction** to form a **complex sentence**. A **compound-complex sentence** is a long sentence created by joining a compound sentence and a related complex sentence.

complex sentence	Although no official dividing line is visible, the people live separately.
compound sentence	The Tlingits live on the northern part of the island, and the Haidas live on the southern part.
compound-complex sentence	Although no official dividing line is visible, the Tlingits live on the northern part of the island, and the Haidas live on the southern part.

Turn and Talk **With a partner, read aloud each sentence below. Identify each sentence as *compound, complex,* or *compound-complex*. Then identify the subordinating and coordinating conjunctions.**

1. Prince of Wales Island is in Alaska, and the Queen Charlotte Islands are in Canada.

2. When the Haidas needed trees for dugout canoes, they traveled to the Queen Charlotte Islands.

3. The Queen Charlotte Islands are far from Prince of Wales Island, but the Haidas traveled there often because the biggest cedar trees in the region grow there.

4. The Haidas carve totem poles, but their specialty is dugout canoes.

Sentence Fluency You can avoid choppy writing and vary your sentence structure by using conjunctions to combine simple sentences into longer sentences. When you create a compound sentence, a complex sentence, or a compound-complex sentence, be sure that your new sentence is clearer than the short sentences you combined. Also, be sure to use commas correctly.

Separate Sentences

The people in Klukwan must work hard.

The village is their home.

Its traditions enrich their lives.

Compound-Complex Sentence

Although the people in Klukwan must work hard, the village is their home, and its traditions enrich their lives.

Connect Grammar to Writing

As you revise your opinion essay, look for sentences that you can combine to form compound, complex, or compound-complex sentences. Check to see that each longer sentence you write is clear and properly punctuated.

Write to Respond

☑ **Sentence Fluency** When you write an **opinion essay**, it is important to make your sentences clear and easy to understand. You also want to show connections between ideas. When revising sentences, look for ways to create compound or complex sentences by using coordinating or subordinating conjunctions.

May drafted an opinion essay in response to "Kensuke's Kingdom." As she revised, she combined sentences to show clear connections between ideas.

Writing Process Checklist

Prewrite

Draft

▶ **Revise**

☑ Did I include a summary of the selection?

☑ Did I state my opinion clearly and support it with specific reasons?

☑ Did I use details and examples to explain each reason?

☑ Did I include compound and complex sentences?

Edit

Publish and Share

Revised Draft

"Kensuke's Kingdom" is a story about a boy named Michael who is stranded on an island. There, Michael meets a mysterious Japanese man named Kensuke. The two cannot speak each other's language, ^but^ Over time, Michael learns more about the old man. ^Because^ Kensuke is a mysterious, complex character, ^He makes the story enjoyable to read.

The Mysterious Kensuke

by May Owens

"Kensuke's Kingdom" is a story about a boy named Michael who is stranded on an island. There, Michael meets a mysterious Japanese man named Kensuke. The two cannot speak each other's language, but over time, Michael learns more about the old man. Because Kensuke is a mysterious, complex character, he makes the story enjoyable to read.

One reason that Kensuke seems mysterious to me is that he won't let Michael light a signal fire. When Michael sees a ship, he tries to start a fire, but Kensuke comes and stomps it out. I don't understand why he does this, unless he is trying to protect Michael. It makes me want to read to find out.

In my opinion essay, I varied the length of my sentences. I also used conjunctions properly to form compound and complex sentences.

Reading as a Writer

What changes did May make to improve her sentence fluency? In your opinion essay, are there ideas that you can join to make longer sentences?

Schooling on the American Frontier

On the frontier, a schoolhouse with just one room was usually large enough for all the children in a district. One-room schoolhouses were used in rural areas from the early 1800s through the 1940s. Only one teacher taught all the children, who were in grades one through eight. Because many families depended on farming, school schedules were structured around the growing season. School might be held for four or five months of the year. For the rest of the year, children were needed at home to help on family farms.

The Schoolhouse

Each community was responsible for creating its school. Sometimes log cabins or barns were used as schools. Often, schools were built and maintained by the people who lived in the area. A one-room schoolhouse was often no larger than a modern classroom. Usually, a wood or coal stove kept it warm in winter. At the back of the room, children's coats hung on pegs and lunch buckets were stored on a shelf. There was also a pail of fresh drinking water with children's cups nearby.

In early days, the children often sat on rows of benches facing the teacher's big desk in the front of the room. Later, students in most schools had wooden desks of their own. Near the teacher's desk was often a "recitation bench." Groups of students came forward to sit there while the teacher drilled them. Other students were expected to work quietly at their desks until it was their turn. Usually, younger children sat near the front of the room and older children at the back. Boys and girls sat on separate sides of the room. At many frontier schoolhouses, boys and girls were separated at recess, too.

Schoolhouses were often used as community buildings. The schoolhouse was a common meeting place for social events. Debates, plays, and lectures were often held for the public at the community schoolhouse.

The Teachers

In the early 1800s, teachers sometimes had very little education themselves. Their teaching consisted of having students memorize and recite facts or whole lessons. Later in the century, teachers went to a "normal school," an early teachers' college, and were given an exam by a local school board. They had to earn a passing score to be hired. Teachers still emphasized memorizing sets of facts, though.

In the early 1800s, most teachers were men. But by the second half of the century, the need for teachers grew quickly, and many women moved to the western frontier regions to become teachers. Female teachers received much lower pay than male teachers.

In general, most teachers were young and not well paid. Families with schoolchildren were expected to arrange for housing and food for their teachers. Sometimes teachers lived in the schoolhouses. Usually, they received meals and a room from a family living near the school or from all the families, with whom they stayed in rotation. Local school boards often had strict rules limiting how teachers could spend their free time.

Challenges of Teaching on the American Frontier

Teachers were expected to arrive at school at 8 A.M. to hoist the flag and bring in drinking water and fuel for the stove. While school was in session, teachers had to keep order in a room full of restless children who preferred to be outdoors. Maintaining that order in a classroom with students of varying ages was a challenge. Often, older children were expected to help the teacher keep control of the class.

Another challenge that teachers on the frontier faced was the lack of supplies. Most schools on the frontier did not have what we now consider to be basic supplies, such as pencils, pens, and maps. Blackboards did not become common in frontier schoolhouses until the end of the 1800s. Textbooks were too expensive to purchase, and students were often sent to school with books from home. Because of this, teachers had to teach lessons to students who had different books—or even no books at all.

Most families believed that education for their children was important. Even though there were many obstacles, communities with one-room schoolhouses worked hard to provide learning for the students. These students would go on to become citizens who shaped American society as the United States grew and developed.

Unit 2 Wrap-Up

The Big Idea

You, Me, and We Think of a person in your life who differs from you in an important way. It may be a close friend or someone you do not know very well. Write a paragraph describing your differences. Then write another paragraph describing what you and that person have in common. How are the things you have in common more important than your differences?

Listening and Speaking

Photos Versus Drawings The selections in Unit 2 have different kinds of illustrations. Some of them have photos. Others have drawings. Work with a partner to analyze and evaluate the kinds of illustrations. Is one kind more helpful than another? Why? Discuss what makes each kind of illustration effective.

272

Going the Distance

Big Idea

Sometimes you need to give it all you've got.

Paired Selections

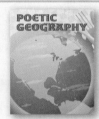

✓ TARGET VOCABULARY

frothing

eerie

receded

collided

desperation

looming

stabilize

dismay

mounting

jutted

Vocabulary
Reader

Context
Cards

Vocabulary in Context

1 frothing

When waves are frothing, churned up by a strong wind, they appear to be white.

2 eerie

A fog in a harbor may create an eerie scene, making things appear strange and scary.

3 receded

After a storm has receded, or gone away, it may take a while before the sea is calm.

4 collided

The *Titanic* collided with an iceberg. The crash caused seawater to pour into the ship.

- **Study each Context Card.**
- **Use two Vocabulary words to tell about an experience you had.**

5 desperation

Many survivors of the *Titanic* disaster felt hopeless. They waited in desperation for rescuers.

6 looming

A lighthouse warns ships of dangerous rocks looming in the darkness.

7 stabilize

Even in choppy waves, a skilled sailor can stabilize a sailboat and keep it from tipping over.

8 dismay

The rocking of a boat may cause dismay for passengers at first. Later they may feel less upset.

9 mounting

Mounting waves rise too high for the comfort and safety of boaters, but surfers like the challenge.

10 jutted

With skill and luck, sailors have steered clear of icebergs that jutted above the horizon.

Background

Newfoundland, 1912 When the *Titanic* collided with an iceberg in April of 1912, the eerie news must have caused particular dismay on the island of Newfoundland. Its shores lay only 450 miles from where the ship went down in the frothing Atlantic Ocean. In 1912 the island of Newfoundland was a territory of Great Britain, though it governed itself. Along its coastline, the docks of many small fishing villages jutted into the cold Atlantic. Fishing could be hard work, and the sea could be dangerous. Often the supply of cod receded. With debts mounting and feelings of desperation looming, villagers had to depend on each other for support. Yet even when the economy began to stabilize, the closeness of neighbors made a hard life easier.

Along with Labrador, its mainland neighbor, Newfoundland became a province of Canada in 1949. Bonnie Bay, the setting of "Star in the Storm," is based on the village of Moreton's Harbour.

Comprehension

Understanding Characters

As you read "Star in the Storm," notice details that tell you more about what a character is like, such as Maggie's thoughts, actions, and words. Make a chart like the one below to keep track of details and what they reveal about the character's personality.

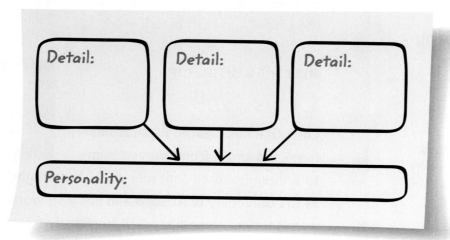

Detail:

Detail:

Detail:

Personality:

✔ **TARGET STRATEGY** **Summarize**

You can use the details in your character chart to help you summarize that character's place and importance in "Star in the Storm." Summarizing helps you remember key events and understand how characters change.

Main Selection

STAR in the STORM

JOAN HIATT HARLOW

✓ **TARGET VOCABULARY**

frothing	looming
eerie	stabilize
receded	dismay
collided	mounting
desperation	jutted

✓ **TARGET SKILL**

Understanding Characters
Use text details to explain why characters act, speak, and think as they do.

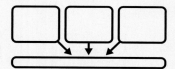

✓ **TARGET STRATEGY**

Summarize Briefly tell the important parts of the text in your own words.

GENRE

Historical fiction is a story whose characters and events are set in a real period of history.

Set a Purpose Before reading, set a purpose for reading based on what you know about the genre and your own experience.

MEET THE AUTHOR

Joan Hiatt Harlow

Joan Hiatt Harlow knows the setting of *Star in the Storm* well. Her mother came from Newfoundland, which the author calls "The Beautiful Rock." Her new novel *Thunder from the Sea* is another exciting story about a Newfoundland dog. Hiatt Harlow explains that there is more to writing than coming up with a good story. "Writing is craft," she says. "And craft means work."

MEET THE ILLUSTRATOR

Chris Gall

Chris Gall has created illustrations large and small, from product logos to a three-hundred-foot mural. He has taught at the University of Arizona and has also worked as a stand-up comedian. Gall frequently travels the country, visiting schools and book fairs.

STAR IN THE STORM

by Joan Hiatt Harlow

selection illustrated by Chris Gall

Essential Question

Why does a character take risks for a friend?

It is the summer of 1912 in Newfoundland. Earlier that year, the Titanic *struck an iceberg in waters not far from Bonnie Bay, the fishing village where twelve-year-old Maggie lives with her family and her Newfoundland dog, Sirius. In fact, another huge iceberg lies just outside the harbor. Bonnie Bay is a close-knit community of neighbors, many of them fishermen like Otto and his assistant, Cliff, and relatives, like Maggie's younger cousin, Vera. Right now, Vera is ill with a high fever. She has asked Maggie to bring her ice. Maggie has promised Vera that she would do so.*

But where could Maggie find ice? Once winter was over, there was no way to keep food or water cold. Meat and fish were preserved by sprinkling them with salt and drying them in the sun.

Maybe freshly drawn well water would be cool enough for Vera. That was the coldest water they had . . . except for the sea. Maggie took the water pail from behind the door and trudged down the hill to the well.

Bonnie Bay lay before her, glittering in the late morning sun. Out by Killock Rock Island, where the rocky cliffs enclosed the harbor like outstretched arms, the great iceberg shimmered, like an uncut blue jewel.

Ice, thought Maggie. Cold, clean, freshwater ice.

> **STOP AND THINK**
> **Author's Craft** In the third paragraph, the author uses a simile, comparing the rocky cliffs to open arms with the word *like*. In the same sentence find another example of **figurative language:** words that create an image by comparing one thing to another.

Maggie ran down the dirt road to the dock where Pa tied up their red dory. She tossed the pail into the flat-bottomed boat and climbed in. The small boat tipped with her weight, and she was suddenly aware of the swells and whitecaps in the harbor. She looked out at the iceberg. Vera wanted ice, and Maggie was going to get it for her.

The boat teetered as Maggie scrambled to the stern. A box containing some of her father's fishing tackle and knives was tucked under the seat. Among the tools Maggie found a small chisel. Good! She would use that to chip the ice from the iceberg.

She untied the ropes that secured the dory to the wharf and settled into the center seat. Maggie took hold of the long, wooden oars and began rowing out into the harbor. I'll have to row gently so I don't disturb the berg, Maggie thought. Sometimes icebergs would turn in the water, or large chunks of ice, called *growlers*, might break off from the mother berg. If either of these things happened, huge waves could swamp boats much larger than her little dory. Maggie shuddered as she thought about what it must have been like for the *Titanic* to have collided with that iceberg.

The harbor waters were like a giant sea monster, whose deep breaths raised and lowered the boat. The waves were heading toward shore, against Maggie, slowing her progress away from the wharves. Gradually, though, the shoreline receded. The sounds of church bells drifted on and off the breeze, and Maggie could make out the distant spire and the figures of the parishioners, some walking, others riding in carriages, as they left Sunday worship.

The waters around her had lost their aqua blue color and were now almost black. Threatening clouds were beginning to darken the sun. Maggie turned to see how far away the iceberg was, and gasped. There it was, looming just ahead, like a giant phantom. If the *Titanic*, as big and powerful as she was, could be destroyed by an iceberg, what chance could her little red dory stand against this massive, monstrous berg? I can't go any farther, Maggie thought with sudden desperation. I shouldn't have come.

But the ice. She had promised Vera she would get ice.

What was that eerie sound? Almost afraid to look, she scanned the choppy water. It was a growler, about the size of a barrel. The smaller iceberg made deep grumbling noises as it bobbed in the waves to the port side of the boat. I'll chip off ice from that, Maggie decided. It's closer and safer! She pulled hard on her right oar, turning the boat to port, then began rowing with all her strength. Waves were hitting the dinghy broadside, and the gunwales dipped into the frothing surf.

I'll be swamped, Maggie thought. But then the growler was alongside, and Maggie managed to pull in the oars and grab the chisel, and she leaned over to the floating mound of ice.

The small iceberg bobbed away each time Maggie stabbed at it. Then, finally, as the dory turned slightly in the mounting surf, the ice stayed close enough for Maggie to proceed.

She chiseled at the ice, grabbing the loose pieces and tossing them into the pail. For one terrifying moment, Maggie almost toppled overboard as the dory rose and dropped in the swells. She shifted her weight to the center of the boat to stabilize it, but it made it harder to chip the precious ice floating alongside. All the while, Maggie tried to ignore the wind that whistled around her and the sound of breaking waves.

Maggie knew she should head back. When her pail was almost full, she set it carefully under the seat and rowed hard on one oar, pointing the bow toward the safe shore of Bonnie Bay.

Maggie had thought that rowing back would be easier since the wind was in her favor. But she had not counted on the turning tide. The harbor waters had become a swift current that tugged against her. Arching her body, she pulled the long oars with all her strength. Slowly, slowly, she moved closer to the village. Her arms felt as if they would break.

I won't look, she thought. I'll just keep rowing until I'm back. One, two, three . . . Maggie counted. When she reached twenty-two, she looked around. To her dismay, she had drifted away from the village and was heading toward the huge rocks that jutted out from the cliffs. Bearing on her right arm, she headed the bow toward the village wharves. She could see several people gesturing to her from the docks.

 **STOP AND THINK**
Understanding Characters What do Maggie's actions while chipping the ice tell you about the kind of person she is?

She could make out Otto and Cliff and a third dark form. Good! They'll help me. Without thinking, she let go of the oars, stood up, and waved desperately at them. Then, suddenly, a huge swell lifted the boat, knocking Maggie into the bottom of the dory. The pail of ice tipped, and Maggie grabbed it, setting it upright again. Nothing could happen to that ice. She had promised Vera. . . .

Maggie reached for the oars. They were gone! She searched the pounding waves and saw them drifting away.

Now what would she do? How stupid! she thought helplessly. Again, she stood up in the boat and screamed, "Help me!" The boat tipped, and she sank down onto the seat again.

Otto and Cliff were climbing into a dory that was even smaller than Maggie's. Could they make it in time to help her? The wind gusted wildly, and clouds gathered and boiled in the sky. Maggie's boat drifted closer to the rocks.

Then Maggie saw the third dark form on the docks leap into the water, making a faint splash.

It was Sirius. He was coming to help her.

"Go back, Sirius," she called. "Go back!"

But the huge dog had disappeared into the tossing waves. Surely he would drown in the wild surf. Ocean spray and salty tears drenched Maggie's face. In her eagerness to help Vera she had risked her own life, and now her dog's and her friends' lives, as well.

She scanned the black water. She could see Sirius's huge head as he rose with the swells. Maybe he *could* help her.

"Come on, Sirius!" she cried.

The dog was approaching the boat, his shoulders heaving as his great paws reached out through the water.

Scrambling to the front of the boat, she gathered the bowline into her arms. "Here, boy," she called. "Take the line and pull me in." Treading water at the side of the boat, Sirius grabbed the length of rope in his mouth and headed toward the shore.

Maggie could feel the boat turn and tug. It had been almost impossible for *her* to row against the strong tide. Could Sirius do it?

Maggie spotted Otto and Cliff's dory bobbing in the waves. She sank to her knees on the floor of the boat and watched as the dog struggled with his heavy load.

Sirius had pulled the boat away from the rocks, and now they were headed in the direction of the wharves.

Finally Otto pulled up to her and grabbed the line from the dog. "Go back," he ordered the panting Sirius, who treaded water, his eyes never leaving Maggie.

"Go!" Maggie yelled. "Good dog!" Sirius turned obediently and swam ahead.

In the stern of Otto's skiff, Cliff took hold of Maggie's bowline while Otto rowed to shore with long, sure strokes.

As they pulled up to the docks, Cliff climbed out and tied the red dory to the wharf while Otto hitched up his own boat. Sirius staggered onto the shore and shook himself, sending off a spray of seawater.

"Come on, Maggie," Cliff said, holding out his hand. "You nearly did yourself in on that trick."

"Don't be tongue-lashing her," said Otto, giving Cliff a stern look. "She's feeling bad enough."

"I'm sorry. I'm *so* sorry," Maggie said as she climbed out of the boat. "Wait!" She turned back to retrieve the pail from under the seat.

Vera would have her precious ice after all.

STOP AND THINK

Summarize Use the events on this page to summarize the ending of the story.

Your Turn

Your Best Friend

Write About Dogs In "Star in the Storm," Sirius leaps into icy waters to rescue Maggie. There are many true tales of dogs helping humans. Write a paragraph explaining why you think dogs behave this way. Include examples from your own life or from stories you have read or heard. PERSONAL RESPONSE

Paint a Picture

Turn Language into Art The author of "Star in the Storm" uses figurative language to help readers imagine what is happening in the story. An iceberg looms in front of Maggie "like a giant phantom." Harbor waters are "like a giant sea monster, whose deep breaths raised and lowered the boat." With a partner, discuss imaginative ways that these similes might be illustrated. Then use your ideas to draw or paint a picture of one or both of them. PARTNERS

Reliable or Reckless?

Turn and Talk With a partner, discuss why Maggie made the trip out to the iceberg. Did her actions show that she was a good friend or simply reckless? What could she have done differently to make the trip safer? Use a situation you or someone you know experienced to discuss why people take risks for friends. UNDERSTANDING CHARACTERS

Finding the Titanic

BY PATRICK SHEA

The story has become the stuff of legend. On the night of April 14, 1912, the supposedly "unsinkable" ship, the *Titanic,* collided with an iceberg. It sank into the frothing Atlantic, some four hundred miles southeast of Newfoundland.

Soon after the tragedy, a group of passengers hired a company to find the *Titanic.* They wanted the company to stabilize the ship and bring it to the surface. To the group's dismay, the company said no. The 46,000-ton ship would be difficult to find. It would have to be raised from a depth of more than two miles. The technology of that time was not up to the task.

The *Titanic* would never be raised. Seventy years later, though, a team of scientists would use their modern technology to find it.

The Search for the *Titanic*

By the 1980s, hope had receded that the *Titanic* would ever be found. By 1983, Texas millionaire Jack Grimm had performed three fruitless searches for the wreck. In desperation, he produced a photograph of a ship's propeller. Was it the *Titanic*'s? No one seemed to think so.

In 1985, marine biologist Robert Ballard began a new search in the area where the ship was believed to have sunk. Ballard had been looking for the *Titanic* since the 1970s. He gathered together a team of French and American scientists. Their search for the *Titanic* would be a test for their newest technology. They wanted to try out a French sonar system known as SAR. They also wanted to try the American sonar and video camera systems known as *Argo* and ANGUS.

Sonar is short for *so(und) na(vigation and) r(anging)*. Sonar equipment sends out sweeps of sound waves. The sound waves are reflected back by objects. By studying prints of these echoes, a scientist could "see" a profile of whatever jutted from the ocean floor.

On the morning of September 1, 1985, *Argo* and ANGUS picked up images of man-made debris. With mounting excitement, the scientists watched a huge object appear on the monitor. It was a ship's boiler. They had found the *Titanic*!

Argo became the eyes of the world when its sonar and camera located the *Titanic* on September 1, 1985.

In 1986, Ballard returned to the *Titanic*. This time he brought a deep-sea submersible craft called *Alvin*. Tethered to it was a remote-controlled robotic camera called *Jason Jr.*, or *JJ*.

The sub descended on July 12. Ballard and two colleagues were inside. It went down thirteen thousand feet, a journey of two and a half hours. Finally, six hundred feet above the seabed, Ballard saw the *Titanic*'s hull looming before him. It made for an eerie and moving sight. The following day, *Alvin* and *JJ* went down again. Ballard would have amazing photographs of the *Titanic* to share with the world.

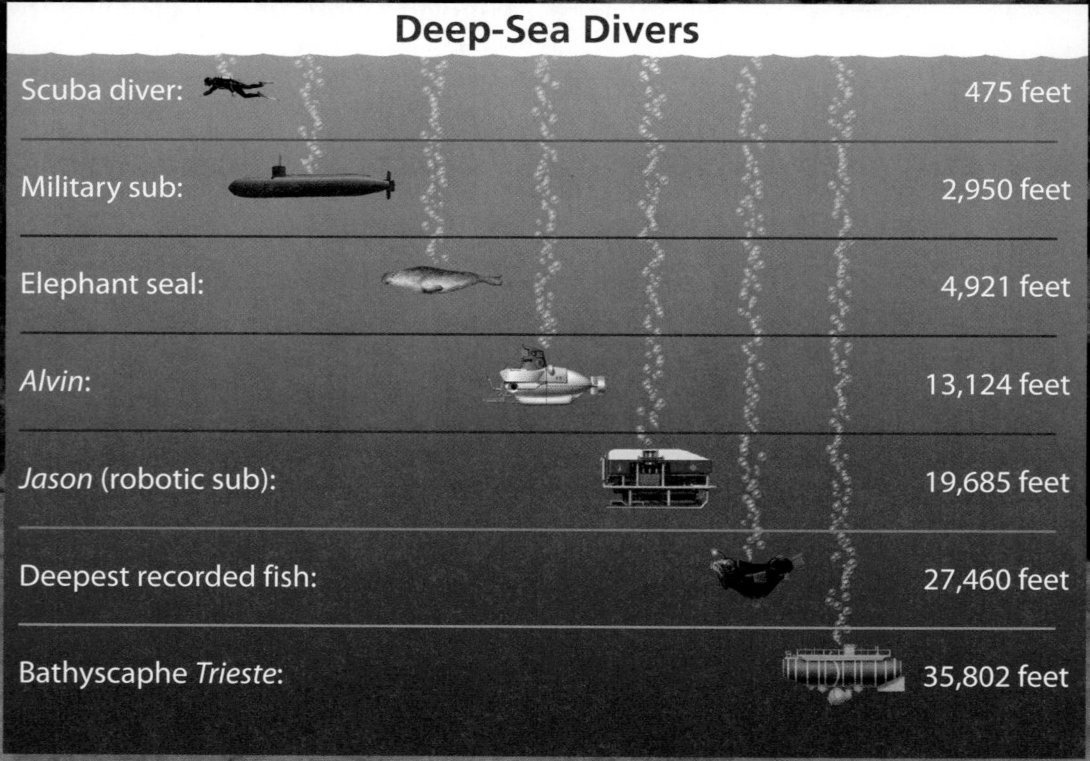

Deep-Sea Divers

Scuba diver:	475 feet
Military sub:	2,950 feet
Elephant seal:	4,921 feet
Alvin:	13,124 feet
Jason (robotic sub):	19,685 feet
Deepest recorded fish:	27,460 feet
Bathyscaphe *Trieste*:	35,802 feet

This graph shows how *Alvin*'s dive of 13,124 feet compares with the depths of other divers, both natural and man-made.

Making Connections

Text to Self

Write a Paragraph Maggie and Robert Ballard both work hard to accomplish what they set out to do. Write about something you would like to accomplish or explore even though it would be a challenge.

Text to Text

Discuss Genres "Star in the Storm" and "Finding the *Titanic*" both give information about the *Titanic*, but one selection is historical fiction and the other is nonfiction. Discuss the two genres. What are the strengths of each one? How do the two genres deal with the same topic differently?

Text to World

Connect to Technology Explorers like Robert Ballard use the latest technology to get a glimpse into the past. How might studying old shipwrecks, such as the *Titanic*, benefit us today? Think of the fields of science, engineering, and public safety. Share your thoughts with a small group.

Grammar

What Are Subject and Object Pronouns? A **pronoun** is a word that can replace a noun. A **subject pronoun** replaces a noun as the subject of a sentence. An **object pronoun** is used in place of a noun after an action verb or after a word such as *to, in, for, by*, or *at*. In compound subjects, use a subject pronoun. Be sure to use an object pronoun in compound direct objects.

---

subject:
subject pronoun

direct object:
object pronoun

Vera was ill. She wanted ice. Maggie would help her.

---

compound subject

compound direct object

Bill and I like sea stories. Those tales excite him and me.

subject
pronoun

object   object
pronoun   pronoun

Work with a partner. Read each sentence below. Tell which pronoun form is correct. Then explain why it is the correct form.

1. My sister Mary and (I, me) own a rowboat.

2. (She, Her) and I use it for fishing.

3. A trip can be planned by her or (I, me).

4. Pa bought fishing rods for Mary and (I, me).

Sentence Fluency If you use the same subject too many times in your sentences, you will bore your reader. When two sentences have the same subject, you can combine them and replace one subject with a pronoun. Sometimes you can use a subordinating conjunction to form a complex sentence.

Repeated Subject

The dog swam to the boat. The dog wanted to rescue Maggie.

Combined Sentences with Pronoun and Subordinating Conjunction

The dog swam to the boat because he wanted to rescue Maggie.

Because the dog wanted to rescue Maggie, he swam to the boat.

Connect Grammar to Writing

As you revise your descriptive paragraph, keep a list of subordinating conjunctions handy. Try to use a subject pronoun and a subordinating conjunction to combine sentences with the same subject.

Write to Narrate

Word Choice In narrative writing, good writers use exact words to make descriptions clearer. For example, the author of "Star in the Storm" writes that Maggie "trudged" rather than "walked" down the hill. As you revise your **descriptive paragraph**, replace vague words with more exact ones.

Ruby drafted a paragraph describing her grandfather, whom she admires. Later, Ruby substituted exact words for vague words.

Writing Traits Checklist

☑ **Ideas**
Did I cover more than one category of personal traits?

☑ **Organization**
Did I organize details in a logical way?

☑ **Sentence Fluency**
Did I vary my writing with pronouns and complex sentences?

☑ **Word Choice**
Did I replace vague descriptive words with exact ones?

☑ **Voice**
Does my voice help to tell the character traits of my subject?

☑ **Conventions**
Did I use correct spelling, grammar, and punctuation?

Revised Draft

Nobody can whistle half as well as my granddad. I love to watch him ~~sit~~ scoot himself forward in his straight-backed porch chair with the unraveling seat. I know Granddad is getting ready to whistle. He sets both of his size-12 feet flat on the porch, just so, and clears his throat as though he were about to perform onstage.

296

Final Copy

My Granddad
by Ruby Garland

Nobody can whistle half as well as my granddad. I love to watch him scoot himself forward in his straight-backed porch chair with the unraveling cane seat. I know Granddad is getting ready to whistle. He sets both of his size-12 feet flat on the porch, just so, and clears his throat as though he were about to perform onstage. Then he puckers his lips, gives me a quick wink, inhales a great breath, and begins to blow. He seems to reach the highest notes of a piccolo and the lowest notes of a trombone. Whether he whistles a familiar song or makes up one that's funny and full of musical surprises, I'm bound to be humming it the rest of the day.

In my final paper, I added exact words. I also combined two sentences into a complex sentence that uses a pronoun in place of a repeated noun.

Reading as a Writer

Which of Ruby's exact words do you think are most descriptive? Where in your descriptive paragraph can you replace vague words with exact words?

297

12

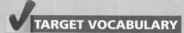

engulf

supple

jostled

taut

careening

frail

undulating

falter

frayed

relishing

Vocabulary Reader

Context Cards

Vocabulary in Context

1 engulf

Clouds will soon engulf, or swallow up, this blimp as it climbs higher into the sky.

2 supple

A hot air balloon is made of supple material that is flexible but strong.

3 jostled

As it flies, an ultralight aircraft may be jostled, or bumped, by the wind.

4 taut

Early gliders were covered with fabric stretched until it was taut, or tight, over a frame.

- **Study each Context Card.**

- **Make up a new context sentence that uses two Vocabulary words.**

5 careening

Caught in a gusty wind, a kite might go careening wildly from side to side.

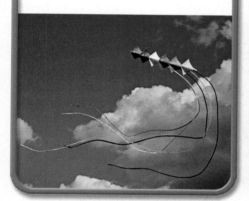

6 frail

A monarch butterfly may look too frail to fly thousands of miles, but it is not as weak as one might think.

7 undulating

Undulating air currents, moving like a roller coaster, can cause clouds to form wavy patterns.

8 falter

A bird seems to falter, or hesitate, as it brakes with its wings when it comes in for a landing.

9 frayed

If the ropes holding down a hot air balloon became frayed, they could break, causing the balloon to escape.

10 relishing

Many people enjoy the hobby of skydiving, relishing the feeling of freedom it brings.

Background

✔ **TARGET VOCABULARY** **Ships of the Air** You may have seen a blimp floating high over a sports event, riding the undulating air currents, barely jostled by the wind. How do blimps work? Unlike a hot air balloon, a blimp is filled with a lighter-than-air gas like helium. Once the blimp's supple envelope becomes taut, an engine powers it skyward. A skilled pilot works to keep the blimp from careening from side to side.

At one time even bigger airships called zeppelins cruised the skies over the Atlantic, their passengers relishing the view from the gondola. However, many zeppelins proved too frail to continue. The hydrogen that filled them could—and did—explode. In 1937 thousands saw the *Hindenburg*, a German zeppelin, falter as it was landing near New York City. In horror, they watched billowing flames engulf the giant ship. The bond between the public and the airship as transportation soon frayed. Today, the blimp is used mainly as a form of advertising.

The air bags inside the blimp
help maintain pressure.

envelope

air valves

gondola

engine

Comprehension

✓ **TARGET SKILL** **Story Structure**

As you read Matt's adventure in "Airborn," note the story elements, including the main conflict, resolution, and events in the plot. Make a story map like this one to identify important story elements in "Airborn."

Characters:	Setting:
Plot:	

✓ **TARGET STRATEGY** **Infer/Predict**

You can use the elements in your story map to help you infer, or figure out, details that the author does not state directly. You can also predict what you think will happen to Matt. Inferring and predicting give you a deeper understanding of characters and events.

tail

Main Selection

✓ TARGET VOCABULARY

engulf	frail
supple	undulating
jostled	falter
taut	frayed
careening	relishing

✓ TARGET SKILL

Story Structure Examine details about characters, setting, and plot.

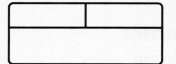

✓ TARGET STRATEGY

Infer/Predict Use text clues to figure out what the author means or what might happen in the future.

GENRE

A **fantasy** is a story with details that could not happen in real life but seem real.

Set a Purpose Before reading, set a purpose for reading based on what you know about the genre and your own experience.

MEET THE AUTHOR
Kenneth Oppel

At age fourteen, Kenneth Oppel wrote a novel that a family friend showed to author Roald Dahl. *Colin's Fantastic Video Adventure* was published a few years later. That experience encouraged Oppel to pursue a career in writing. Oppel's *Silverwing* trilogy has sold over a million copies. He has also published two sequels to *Airborn*, titled *Skybreaker* and *Starclimber*.

MEET THE ILLUSTRATOR
Greg Newbold

Greg Newbold says he "doesn't remember life without art." His parents encouraged his creativity and kept him well stocked with art supplies. Newbold enjoys the outdoor life in Salt Lake City, Utah, and was selected as a torchbearer for the 2002 Winter Olympics there.

AIRBORN

by Kenneth Oppel
selection illustrated by Greg Newbold

Essential Question

How does a sky setting shape a story's events?

Fourteen-year-old Matt Cruse is a cabin boy on the airship Aurora, *on which his father served as a crewman before dying in an accident. As the* Aurora *flies over a vast ocean, Matt, in the crow's nest, spots a hot air balloon drifting dangerously near. When the* Aurora *draws alongside, the crew can see the balloon's pilot lying on the floor of the gondola. The captain decides to attempt a rescue.*

Just then Captain Walken strode in. He was the kind of man everyone felt safer being around. If he'd been wearing a velvet robe and crown, he'd be the very image of a great king; if he were in a doctor's jacket, you'd trust your life to him; if he were in a carpenter's smock, you'd know he'd build you the finest house imaginable. But I preferred him in his blue captain's jacket with the four gold stripes on the sleeve and his cap encircled with thick gold cord. His beard and mustache were trim, and he had steady, kind eyes. He was approaching sixty, with a full head of gray curly hair, and wide in the shoulders. He wasn't a particularly big man or even tall, but when he walked into the room you could almost sense everyone exhaling in relief and thinking, There now, things will work out just fine.

The captain needed only to glance at the situation.

"Mr. Rideau, would you please return to the control car and assume my watch. I'll take over here, thank you."

"Yes, sir," said Mr. Rideau, but I could tell he didn't much like that.

"Ready the davit, please, gentlemen," Captain Walken said.

Centered before the bay doors was a davit, a small crane with an extendible arm that swung out and raised and lowered cargo when we were docked. The crew sprang to it at once, manning the lines and wheeling out the davit's arm to its full length.

"Let's see if she'll reach," the captain said. "Swing her out, please."

Breathless, I watched, wondering if it would be long enough. I knew what the captain had in mind.

I kept looking down at the man on the gondola floor. He was deathly white in the flare of the *Aurora*'s spotlight. But then I saw him stir slightly, a hand twitch.

The davit's arm slowly swung all the way out, as far as it would go.

It was still at least six feet shy of the gondola.

"Pity," said the captain calmly. "Bring her back in, please, gentlemen."

I looked down and saw the water close below us. The captain had vented a little hydrium to keep us level with the balloon, but now we had gone as low as we safely could. Any nearer was foolhardy, for you never knew when a sudden gust or rogue front might clutch the ship and thrust her down into the drink.

"Well, gentlemen, we've not much time," the captain said. "The situation is simple, and our course of action clear. Someone's going to need to hook himself to the end of the davit and swing across to the gondola. It's the only way to get her before she goes down."

He looked across at Mr. Kahlo and Mr. Chen, and the machinists and sailmakers, their faces gray in the starlight, none relishing the idea of careening out over the ocean.

I held my breath, hoping.

The captain stared straight at me and smiled.

"Mr. Cruse, I look at you, and of all the men, you're the one who shows not the slightest hint of fear. Am I right?"

"Yes, sir. I have no fear of heights."

"I know it, Mr. Cruse." And he did, for I'd served aboard his ship for more than two years, and he'd seen the ease with which I moved about the *Aurora*, inside and out.

"Sir," said Mr. Chen, "the lad shouldn't be the one. Let me go."

And all at once the other crewmen were vigorously offering themselves up for the job.

"Very good, gentlemen," said the captain, "but I think Mr. Cruse really is the best suited. If you're still willing, Mr. Cruse?"

"Yes, sir."

"We'll not tell your mother about this. Agreed?"

I smiled and gave a nod.

"Is your harness snug?"

"It is, sir." I was glowing with pride and hoped the others wouldn't see the flush of my cheeks. The captain came and checked my harness himself, his strong hands testing the straps and buckles.

"Be careful, lad," he told me quietly, then stepped back. "All right, Mr. Cruse. Hook yourself up to the davit, and we'll swing you over."

He said it as if he were proposing a stroll up to A-Deck to take in the view. He hadn't chosen me just because he thought I was least fearful. Any of the other crew would have done it. But I was light, too, the lightest here by sixty pounds. The captain was afraid the gondola might be too flimsy to carry her own weight once she was hooked and reeled in, and he didn't want anything heavy added to her. Above all, he needed someone light. But I was still honored he trusted me with the job.

STOP AND THINK

Infer/Predict Captain Walken checks Matt's harness and quietly tells him to be careful. The captain then talks about the dangerous mission casually, as if "proposing a stroll up to A-Deck." What can you infer about the captain's feelings?

The davit's cable ended with a deep hook, and onto this hook I shackled the ends of my two safety lines. They winched me up a little so it was like sitting on a swing. Up close, the davit's arm seemed a frail enough bit of metal to hang your life upon, but I knew she could carry fifty of me.

"I know you'll not falter," the captain told me. "Here. You'll need this to cut the balloon's flight lines." He passed me up his knife. I slid it through a buckle of my harness. "If you're ready, we'll send you over."

"Ready, sir."

With that the crew swung the davit's arm out. I saw the deck
of the cargo bay give way to the ocean's silvered surface, dark and
supple as a snake's skin, four hundred feet below. The arm swung to
its farthest point and stopped. The gondola was still out of reach, its
rim about six feet below me now. Inside, the man shifted again, and
I thought he moaned, but that might have been the wind, or the creak
of the cable unwinding, or maybe some whalesong out to sea.

"Lower me some, please!" I called over my shoulder.

Looking back at the ship did give me a moment's pause. It wasn't
fear—more interest, really. Just the oddness of it. I'd never seen the
Aurora from this angle, me dangling midair, the crewmen standing
on the lip of the deck, staring down at me through the open cargo
bay doors.

They paid out more cable until I was at the same level as the
gondola, not six feet away.

I felt no fear. If someone had put an ear to my chest, he'd find
it beating no faster than it had in the crow's nest. It was not bravery
on my part, simply a fact of nature, for I was born in the air, and so
it seemed the most natural place in the world to me. I was slim as a
sapling and light on my feet. The crew all joked I had seagull bones,
hollow in the center to allow for easy flight. To swing across this little
gap, four hundred feet aloft, was no more to me than skipping a crack
in the pavement. Because deep in my heart, I felt that if I were ever
to fall, the air would support me, hold me aloft, just as surely as it did
a bird with spread wings.

There was a bit of breeze building now, twirling me some at the
end of the cable. I grabbed both my safety lines and started pumping
my legs, a youngster on a playground swing. Back and forth, back
and forth. At the forward end of my arc, when I looked down,
I figured I was almost over the rim of the gondola.
Just a little more. Back I went, legs folded tight.

Then: that moment when you're almost
motionless, just hanging there for a split second
before you start swinging forward again.

"Let run the line!" I shouted. I kicked forward, body flat, legs shooting out, and felt myself drop suddenly—and keep dropping. I sat up quickly as the cable paid out, and I was slanting down toward the gondola fast but—

Falling short.

I flung myself forward, stretching, and just hooked my forearms over the gondola's lip. My body slammed into the side, scratching my face against the wicker and knocking all my breath out. It took a moment to suck some air into me. My arms sang with pain. I heard the crew above in the *Aurora*, cheering me. I heaved myself up, scrabbling with my feet for purchase, and then crashed over into the gondola.

Beside the man.

But there was not time to tend to him. I stood, grabbed hold of the davit's hook, and unshackled my two safety lines. Then I cast about for somewhere secure to attach the hook—it had to be something strong, for it would be bearing the gondola's entire weight once I cut the balloon free. Above my head was a metal frame that supported the burners. The frame had four metal struts that were welded to the gondola's iron rim. It all seemed a little rickety, but it would have to be good enough; I saw nothing better. I curled the hook around the burner frame, as close to its center as I could manage.

"Reel her in!" I bellowed up at the *Aurora*. I saw the line quickly swing up and become taut. The hook grabbed. The gondola shuddered. A long, nasty squeal came from the burner frame. I didn't like the sound of that at all. I stared, breath stoppered in my throat, at those four bits of metal that tethered the burner frame to the gondola. They were never supposed to support the gondola's entire weight. That's what the balloon was meant to do.

But now the balloon was coming down, slowly collapsing toward the gondola—and the burner. The whole lot might go up in flames, with me and the pilot caught beneath.

STOP AND THINK

Author's Craft In the third paragraph the author uses **personification**, giving nonhuman objects human qualities, when he writes that Matt's arms "sang with pain." Find a similar example of personification in paragraph four on page 313.

Flight lines. Flight lines.

I'd never sailed a balloon, and the rigging was unfamiliar to me.

There were eight lines holding the balloon to the gondola, two stretching up from each corner.

"Take care, Mr. Cruse!" I heard the captain shout down at me.

I glanced overhead. Despite being hooked to the davit, the gondola was dragging the great balloon ever closer to the *Aurora*'s hull and engines. In a few minutes, they'd collide. I had to be quicker.

The knife glinted in the starlight as I sawed away at the first flight line. It was thick braid, and my heart sank when I began, but the captain's sharp knife bit deep and kept going. Snap went that first line, and the gondola didn't even shift. I did the line opposite, not wanting the gondola to start hanging crooked.

The balloon was sagging now almost to the burner. I didn't have time to fuss about looking for the gas valve to shut it down, but I was sorely afraid of a fire.

The third and fourth lines went.

At my feet, the man moaned again and his arm twitched and knocked against my boot.

I slashed through the fifth line.

I looked up and saw the balloon slowly billowing down toward me, all but blotting out my view of the *Aurora*. It was awfully close to the engine cars and their propellers.

The sixth line went, and now there were but two lines tethering the balloon to the gondola, attached to opposite corners.

Suddenly the burner came on, triggered by its clockwork timer, and a geyser of blue-hot flame leaped up and scorched the fabric of the balloon. It caught immediately, spreading high. I checked the davit hook, for once I cut these last two lines, the only thing holding us would be that hook and the *Aurora*'s crane.

My wrist throbbed as I began slashing through the seventh line. With a mighty crack the frayed rope snapped high into the air, and the entire gondola slewed over. The unconscious pilot slid toward me and crumpled up against the low side.

Without the crane's cable holding us, we would have been tipped out into the sea. I hauled myself to the high side and the last light flight line. The smell of burning fabric was terrible now, though luckily the smoke and flames were mostly dancing up away from me. But the weight of the blazing balloon was oozing down over the frame now, starting to engulf the gondola.

Frantically I slashed at the last flight line. Something burning hit my shoulder and I struck it off, and then I saw with a panic that a bit of the wicker was alight. I'd deal with it later. That last flight line needed cutting.

Furiously, I attacked it with my knife, severed it, then grabbed hold of the gondola's side as it jerked violently down. The metal burner frame shrieked with stress as it took the full weight. Suspended only on the davit's hook, the gondola swung out from underneath the blazing balloon, and just in time. Aflame, it seeped quickly downward, cut lines trailing, undulating like a giant jellyfish intent on the ocean's bottom. I held my breath as it fell past the gondola.

Fire crackled in the wicker, and I grabbed a blanket from the floor and smothered the flames. There was a sharp tug from the cable, and we were being reeled in, rocking. I made sure the fire was out and then knelt down beside the man. I felt badly that he'd been jostled about so roughly.

Gently I turned him over onto his back and put a blanket beneath his head. He looked to be in his sixties. Through the whiskers, his face had a sharpened look to it, all cheekbones and nose. Lips scabbed over by wind and lack of water. A handsome gentleman. I didn't really know what else to do, so I just held his hand and said,

"There now, we're almost aboard, and Doc Halliday will take a look at you and get you all sorted out." For a moment it looked like his eyes might open, but then he just frowned and shook his head a little, and his lips parted and he mumbled silently for a bit.

Scattered on the floor were all manner of things. Empty water bottles and unopened cans of food. An astrolabe, dividers, a compass, and rolled up charts. From overhead came a terrible shriek, and I looked up to see one of the burner frame's metal struts rip loose from the gondola's rim. We were too heavy. I stared in horror, watching as the frame began twisting from the stress of her load.

"Hurry!" I bellowed up at the *Aurora*. We were getting reeled up fast, but not fast enough, for with a mighty jerk, a second strut ripped clean out. The entire gondola started to slowly keel over as the remaining struts weakened.

We were level with the cargo bay now but still needed to be swung inside, and the gondola was slewing over, about to dump us into the drink. The metal frame was groaning and shrieking. I grabbed hold of the gondola's side with one hand and the man's wrist with the other, knowing I had not the strength to hold us both in if the gondola tried to tip us out.

I looked up and saw the hook screeching along the burner frame, sparking, about to come off the ripped metal strut and we would surely fall—

A violent bump—

And we set down onto the deck of the cargo bay. Inside.

✔ **STOP AND THINK**

Story Structure *Airborn* takes place in or near a huge airship traveling over the ocean. How does the story's setting add to the tension of the events on these pages?

I heard the captain's voice. "Bay doors closed, please! Mr. Kahlo, call the bridge and tell them to take her back to seven hundred feet."

And then everyone was at the side, looking over into the gondola. Doc Halliday was climbing in beside me, and I stepped back to make room for him. A hand clapped me on the shoulder, and I turned to see Captain Walken smiling at me.

"Good work, Mr. Cruse. Very good work, indeed."

I felt terribly thirsty all of a sudden and tired all the way through my bones, and then remembered that I'd been on duty for more than sixteen hours, and normally would have been in my bunk asleep. Instead I'd been swinging across the sky. I started to climb out, but my knees went wobbly, and Captain Walken and Mr. Chen grabbed me under the arms and swung me to the deck.

"You're a brave man, Matt Cruse," Mr. Chen said.

"No, sir. Just light."

"Lighter than air, that's our Mr. Cruse," said one of the sailmakers. "Cloud hopping next, it'll be!"

Hands tousling my hair, clapping me on the back, voices saying, "Well done," and me trying not to smile but smiling and laughing anyway because it felt so good to know I'd brought the gondola in, saved the pilot, and impressed everyone. All these men who had known my father. They would have called him Mr. Cruse too.

Doc Halliday and another crewman were lifting the pilot out of the gondola to a waiting stretcher.

"Is he going to be all right?" I asked the doctor.

"I don't know yet," was all Doc Halliday answered, and his young face looked so grave I felt a queer squeeze in my stomach. The wicker gondola looked odd and out of place in our cargo bay.

"Get some sleep, Mr. Cruse," the captain said to me.

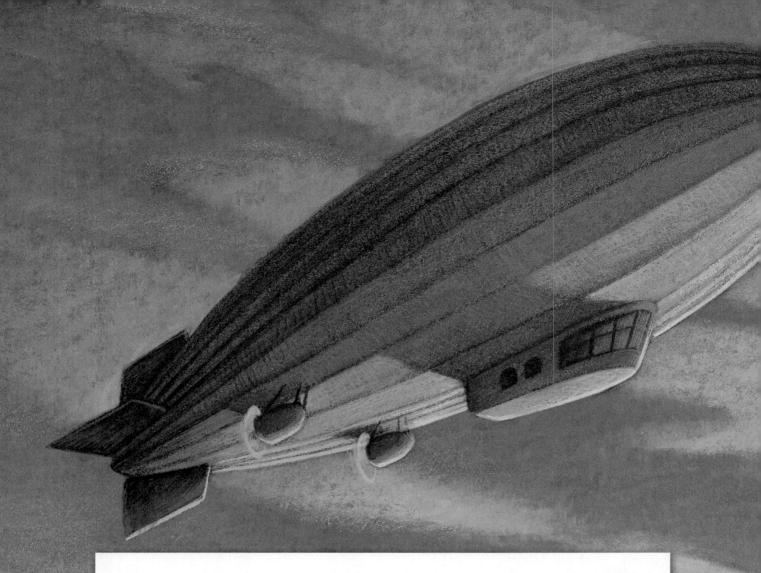

I nodded, but didn't want to go. I watched them take the pilot away on the stretcher. I wondered who he was. I wanted to go through the gondola and find out what had gone wrong.

"Sleep first, Mr. Cruse," said the captain. "Your father would have been very proud of you."

I blinked away the hot tingle behind my eyes. "Thank you, sir."

My legs wobbled as I left the cargo bay and trudged aft along the keel catwalk to the crew quarters. Lighter than air, but I felt heavy as lead. I opened the door to my cabin, caught a glimpse of the clock. Five thirty-nine. I shrugged off my shirt and trousers and climbed into my bunk. And, as so often happened when I slept aloft, I drifted free of my body and glided alongside the *Aurora*, and my father came and joined me, and we flew.

Your Turn

Risk Takers

Explain Why Matt was willing to put himself in danger to help someone. Most people would be fearful, but Matt felt comfortable dangling 400 feet above the sea. Think about something that you can do easily but that other people might fear. Write a paragraph explaining why you feel so comfortable doing this activity.

PERSONAL RESPONSE

Danger...Rescue

Perform a Play The rescue attempt in the sky in "Airborn" is dramatic and risky. Work with a small group to write and perform a short play about a dramatic rescue. Use your imagination or base the action on real events. Rehearse your play and then perform it for classmates.

SMALL GROUP

The Sky's the Limit

Turn and Talk With a partner, discuss the setting of the story. Talk about the ways a story set in the sky is different from one that takes place on land. How does the sky setting affect this story's conflict and resolution? STORY STRUCTURE

Connect to
Science

✓ **TARGET VOCABULARY**

engulf	frail
supple	undulating
jostled	falter
taut	frayed
careening	relishing

GENRE
Informational text, such as this magazine article, gives facts and examples about a topic.

TEXT FOCUS
Headings identify main ideas of text sections, such as chapters, paragraphs, or captions.

Riding on Air

by Victoria Casey

Every year in early October, the sky above Albuquerque, New Mexico, fills with multicolored hot air balloons. The balloons rise by propane-heated air. They are guided—and sometimes jostled—by undulating wind currents. The International Balloon Fiesta is the largest gathering of hot air balloons in the world. In a way, it is also one of the world's biggest science experiments, demonstrating buoyancy, convection (moving heat), and wind power.

The annual Albuquerque International Balloon Fiesta began in 1972 with thirteen balloons launched from a shopping mall parking lot. Today thousands of visitors attend, relishing the sight of hundreds of balloons in the air.

The Rise of Ballooning

Ballooning began in France in 1783. The Montgolfier brothers, paper-makers, had noticed that paper bags rise when they are held over a fire. They experimented and that summer they launched a balloon made of linen and paper. It carried a rooster, a duck, and a sheep. Two months later, two human passengers went up in a Montgolfier balloon. If their nerves were frayed, who can blame them? Today we consider them ballooning pioneers.

Hot Air

How do hot air balloons go up? They rely on the same principle that the Montgolfiers used in 1783: convection, or heat in motion—in this case, hot air filling up a giant bag. Today the bag, or envelope, is made of supple nylon. Beneath it is a basket, the gondola, where the pilot and passengers ride. A frame on the gondola holds one or two burners, which heat liquid propane, turning it to gas. The gas ignites and the air heats up and rises, pulling the lines holding the balloon taut until it is ready to take off.

The Ups and Downs of Navigation

From a distance a hot air balloon might appear as frail as a toy. Clouds seem to engulf it as it climbs. What if the pilot should falter and send the balloon careening in the wrong direction? In fact, a balloon's pilot is controlling forces as much as being controlled by them. After going up, the pilot opens a valve at the top of the balloon, letting hot air escape, in order to go down. Meanwhile, wind currents are traveling crosswise in different directions at different altitudes. The pilot can go up or down to choose the right wind current and travel in the right direction.

To travel horizontally, the pilot of a hot air balloon uses the burner or valve to climb or drop to different altitudes. Air currents at those levels push the balloon in the desired direction.

Making Connections

 Text to Self

Write a Description In "Airborn," the *Aurora* flies over the ocean; in "Riding on Air," balloons fly over land. Imagine you have the chance to ride in a hot air balloon. What scenery do you see below you? Is it a city, the countryside, or some other setting? Write a paragraph describing what you might see from the basket of a hot air balloon.

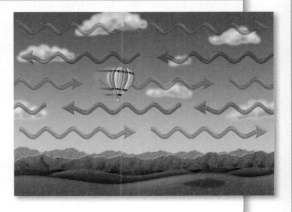

 Text to Text

Role-Play Both Matt Cruse in "Airborn" and the first people to fly in a hot air balloon took risks. Work with a partner. One of you should take the role of Matt Cruse, and the other should take the role of one of the first hot air balloonists. Discuss with each other the risks you took, how you felt, and whether you would take those risks again.

 Text to World

Connect to Science Stretch a balloon over the top of an empty water bottle. Hold the bottle in a bowl of hot tap water. Draw a picture of what happens to the balloon. Tell how this is related to the way a hot air balloon works.

Grammar

What Is a Possessive Pronoun? A **possessive pronoun** shows ownership. It can be used to replace a possessive noun. Some possessive pronouns, such as *my, her,* and *our,* are always used with nouns. Other possessive pronouns, such as *mine, hers,* and *ours,* always stand alone. The pronouns *his* and *its* can be used with nouns or can stand alone.

Possessive Pronouns	
Possessive pronoun used with a noun	possessive noun The captain's jacket has gold stripes on the sleeves. possessive pronoun His jacket has gold stripes on the sleeves.
Possessive pronoun standing alone	possessive noun This picture of an airship is Aunt Faye's. possessive pronoun This picture of an airship is hers.

The **antecedent** of a pronoun is the noun or nouns to which the pronoun refers. A possessive pronoun must agree with its antecedent in number and gender.

singular masculine noun and pronoun

Matt cut the line with his knife.   *His* refers to *Matt.*

Try This! **Write the sentences below on another sheet of paper. Underline each possessive pronoun, and circle its antecedent. Next to each sentence, write *used with a noun* or *stands alone,* depending on how the pronoun is used.**

1. Because Captain Walken is a good leader, his crew respects him.

2. The men on the ship know their jobs.

3. Mr. Chen says that the notebook is his.

4. The sailmakers take good care of their tools.

Sentence Fluency Possessive pronouns can help you avoid awkward use of possessive nouns in your writing. When you use possessive pronouns, make sure they have the same number and gender as their antecedents.

Awkward Possessive Nouns

Karen and Vera flew Karen and Vera's hot air balloon to the island. They repaired the hot air balloon's gondola there. Karen took Karen's turn inflating the balloon, and the friends flew home.

Nouns Replaced with Possessive Pronouns

Karen and Vera flew their hot air balloon to the island.

They repaired its gondola there.

Karen took her turn inflating the balloon, and the friends flew home.

Connect Grammar to Writing

As you revise your personal narrative paragraph, read your sentences aloud. Listen for possessive nouns that sound awkward. Replace some of these with possessive pronouns to make the writing sound smoother.

Write to Narrate

A well-written **personal narrative** reveals the writer's inner thoughts and feelings in interesting, descriptive ways. As you revise your personal narrative, use language that goes beyond just telling the reader what you thought or how you felt.

Eric drafted a personal narrative about a time when something happened that made him afraid. Later, he revised his narrative to reveal his feelings more fully.

Writing Traits Checklist

✔ **Ideas**
Can the reader understand the event from my descriptions?

✔ **Organization**
Did I use elements of story structure?

✔ **Sentence Fluency**
Did I replace overused pronouns with nouns or noun phrases?

✔ **Word Choice**
Did I use exact verbs?

✔ **Voice**
Did I reveal rather than tell my thoughts and feelings?

✔ **Conventions**
Did I use correct spelling, grammar, and punctuation?

Revised Draft

An hour later, my uniform was soaking wet, and I shivered ⋀ , as much from fear as from the rain. I pointed my flashlight beam down one dark street after another, dreading to find our little terrier injured—or worse. Then my phone rang. When Mom said she had found him and he was okay, ~~I was so relieved.~~ ⋀ my shoulders relaxed with relief. He was safe! I ~~ran~~ raced ⋀ home ⋀ , singing .

The Longest Night

by Eric Rodarte

Dad's jokes had the whole family laughing as we pulled in from the baseball field at dusk. When we saw the backyard gate swung wide open, our laughter died. Jupiter had escaped! That night, the night my dog Jupiter ran away, was the longest night of my life. Rain began to fall. An hour later, my uniform was soaking wet, and I shivered, as much from fear as from the rain. I pointed my flashlight beam down one dark street after another, dreading to find our little terrier injured—or worse. Then my phone rang. When Mom said she had found him and he was okay, my shoulders relaxed with relief. He was safe! I raced home, singing.

> In my final paper, I added details that show my thoughts and feelings. I also used pronouns to avoid repetition of nouns.

Reading as a Writer

What kinds of details did Eric add to reveal his thoughts and feelings? What details can you add to your own narrative to accomplish the same thing?

✓ **TARGET VOCABULARY**

expanse

sacrificed

durable

prime

frigid

participants

equivalent

deduced

affirmed

culmination

Vocabulary Reader

Context Cards

Vocabulary in Context

1 expanse
Explorer Matthew Henson sledged across a vast expanse of polar ice. It stretched for miles.

2 sacrificed
Polar explorers gave up many comforts for the sake of adventure. They sacrificed the pleasure of being in a warm home.

3 durable
An explorer's equipment needs to be durable. It has to last a long time and hold up under extreme conditions.

4 prime
Members of a mountain expedition might prime, or prepare, themselves by taking hikes in high elevations.

- **Study each Context Card.**
- **Discuss one picture. Use a different Vocabulary word from the one in the card.**

5 **frigid**

Mountain climbers wear layers of clothing to protect themselves from frigid, or extremely cold, weather.

6 **participants**

The participants in an expedition can be old or young and don't need to travel far from home.

7 **equivalent**

For European explorers, coming to America may have been the equivalent of visiting the moon—equally strange.

8 **deduced**

Henry Stanley deduced, or concluded, that he had found the long-missing British explorer, David Livingstone, in Africa.

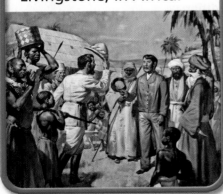

9 **affirmed**

The presence of Native Americans affirmed, or proved, that Europeans were not the first people in the "New World."

10 **culmination**

Reaching the top of a mountain at last may be the culmination of a long, hard climb.

Background

✓ TARGET VOCABULARY **Polar Partners** In 1887, Robert Peary and Matthew Henson met in a hat store in Washington, D.C. Peary, a naval officer, quickly deduced that Henson shared his love of adventure. He hired Henson as his assistant for a project in Central America. It was the start of a long, durable partnership that would move from the tropics to the frigid Arctic. Over a span of fifteen years, the men made six expeditions to Greenland and beyond. Each time, they would prime themselves to reach the North Pole. They sacrificed the comforts of home to cross a vast icy expanse full of deep crevasses. In 1909, new participants signed on for one more try. Peary managed to raise funds equivalent to the supplies he needed. Would his confidence be affirmed? Would the seventh expedition be the culmination of Peary's and Henson's efforts?

Peary and Henson Timeline

1893–1895
Second expedition
to Greenland

1898–1902
Four years
in the Arctic

1909
Seventh Arctic
expedition

1890   1895   1900   1905   1910

1891–1892
First expedition
to Greenland

1896, 1897
Return trips
to the Arctic

1905–1906
Sixth Arctic
expedition

Comprehension

✔ **TARGET SKILL** **Main Ideas and Details**

"Onward" tells about an expedition to the North Pole. The details about each stage of the expedition can help you infer the main ideas as you read. Use a chart like the one below to connect details to main ideas.

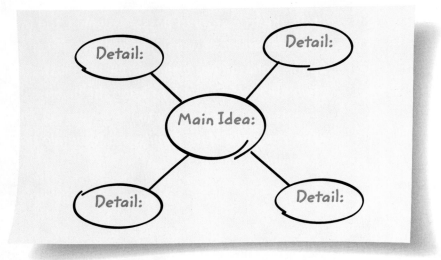

✔ **TARGET STRATEGY** **Monitor/Clarify**

Monitoring your understanding of details in "Onward" and clarifying any parts that are confusing can help you determine the author's main ideas about the expedition.

Main Selection

✓ **TARGET VOCABULARY**

expanse	participants
sacrificed	equivalent
durable	deduced
prime	affirmed
frigid	culmination

✓ **TARGET SKILL**

Main Ideas and Details
Identify a topic's important ideas and supporting details.

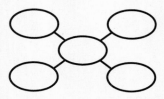

✓ **TARGET STRATEGY**

Monitor/Clarify As you read, see if anything isn't making sense. Find ways to figure out any parts that are confusing.

GENRE

Biography tells about events in a person's life, written by another person.

Set a Purpose Before reading, set a purpose for reading based on what you know about the genre and your own experience.

MEET THE AUTHOR

Dolores Johnson

Dolores Johnson has written several historical books about African Americans. *She Dared to Fly* tells the true story of Bessie Coleman, the first African American woman to become a licensed pilot. Johnson has also written and illustrated two books of fiction that bring the historical events of slavery vividly to life—*Now Let Me Fly: The Story of a Slave Family* and *Seminole Diary: Remembrances of a Slave*.

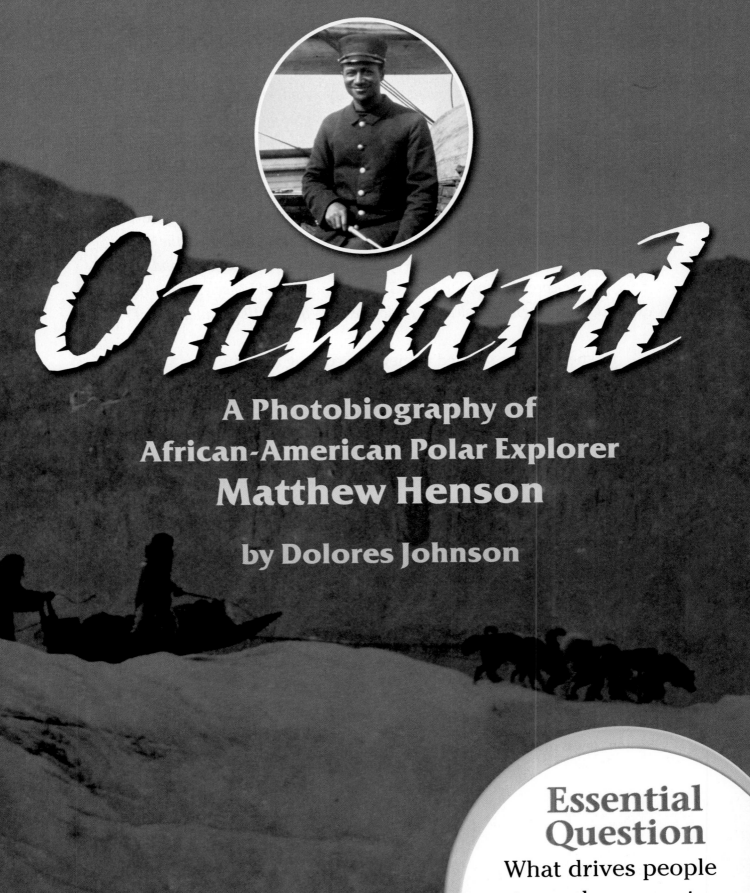

Onward

A Photobiography of African-American Polar Explorer Matthew Henson

by Dolores Johnson

Essential Question

What drives people to explore remote places?

In July of 1908, Matthew Henson and Commander Robert F. Peary set sail from New York City in a heavily fortified ship, the Roosevelt, bound for Ellesmere Island in far northern Canada. Over the past sixteen years, Henson and Peary have made four attempts to cross the Arctic ice and be the first to reach the North Pole. Henson has become good friends with the native Inuit who live nearby, but the explorers have been blocked by stretches of open water called leads, especially one called the Big Lead. Now, with a crew of five—Ross Marvin, Robert Bartlett, and newcomers George Borup, Dr. John Goodsell, and Donald MacMillan—the expedition is bringing its sledges, or dogsleds, to the Arctic for another try.*

The newcomers seemed to view the coming adventure as a sporting event. Henson, who by this time was 42 years old, thought differently. He had devoted practically his whole adult life to the mission. He had teetered close to death. He had lost, and nearly lost, fellow crew members who had fallen into crevasses or the inky black waters of an Arctic Ocean lead. And he had sacrificed a stable family life so that he could be part of history. This was serious business. Yet Henson's mood brightened by the time the ship arrived at Etah, Greenland. He was to be reunited with his Inuit friends once again.

Much of the warm spirit and decent character that endeared him to many of the people he encountered, such as the Inuit and the people who became his benefactors, is shown in this candid photo of Matthew Henson. It was shot on the deck of the Roosevelt.

The specially built ship, the Roosevelt, contributed to the expedition's eventual success because it got the crew members closer to the North Pole than any previous ship. Here the ship is being unloaded of its cargo, after proceeding so far north it became trapped in the ice.

After Henson and Peary persuaded Inuit families to join the expedition, they all sailed to Cape Sheridan in an ice-busting, gut-wrenching voyage that took two weeks. Then the men unloaded the ship and sledged the supplies to Cape Columbia, on Ellesmere, which was only 413 miles south of the Pole.

By February 1909, the entire expedition was prepared to begin the march to the Pole. The novices had practiced their sledging and hunting and had spent enough time outdoors to prime themselves for the frigid Arctic conditions.

Henson supervised the Inuit women in the preparation and sewing of the garments the crew would wear. Each man had a long red flannel shirt and soft bearskin trousers lined with flannel. The soft cloth absorbed sweat and kept the roughness of the fur away from the skin. The pants were wrapped with a band of bearskin that held the legs snugly. A deerskin coat with a hood covered the torso. Bearskin mittens and sealskin boots completed the wardrobe. The outfit was easily transformed into a fur-lined sleeping sack.

On past expeditions, Commander Peary had sent sledges forward to store provisions along the trail. But he realized how unreliable that technique could be if the supplies got buried in deep snow. On this expedition, Peary proposed that a pioneering team would break the trail up ahead. Then six relay teams would follow, each carrying enough food, tools, weapons, and clothes for the whole expedition for five days. The entire expedition would consume supplies from the equivalent of one of the sledges. When those provisions were gone, one team and the weakest dogs would be sent back to headquarters. Until the actual participants of the last relay team were sent back, no one but Commander Peary would know who was to accompany him to the Pole.

Bartlett and Borup were sent out to break the trail. Then Henson and his Inuit team were sent out. Marvin, Goodsell, MacMillan and their teams followed, with Peary trailing. The Commander stayed in touch with the units by leaving notes in igloos for retreating teams so that they could forward information to teams bringing up more supplies.

Men pause while driving a sledge pulled by teams of dogs harnessed in a fan formation.

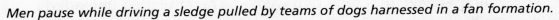

The sledge teams had to confront pressure ridges and steep hummocks of ice, tremendous obstacles in their effort to reach the North Pole. Often they had to lift the sledges and dogs to go forward. Stormy weather, blinding snow, and wide expansive leads would often stop onward progress completely.

The assault began with difficulty. Between March 2nd and 3rd, the temperature fell so low that no one got much sleep. The men had to beat their arms and feet to keep the blood circulating. The next day, the only way the crews could advance was to use their pickaxes to carve through rough ice studded with pressure ridges and sharp hummocks, or projections of ice. Some sledges broke down, and the drivers often had to prod the dogs forward when they balked. Harsh winds stung their faces. Giant fissures in the ice threatened every step.

Henson's party followed Bartlett's tracks as far as the Big Lead. While camped beside the lead, the men woke to the thunderous crack of shifting ice grinding beneath them. At any moment, men, equipment, and dogs could be thrown into the flowing water that was passing below. The crews shifted their campsite.

STOP AND THINK

Author's Craft In the first paragraph, the author refers to pressure ridges. She uses **jargon,** vocabulary that is specific to a profession or field of study. Find another example of jargon in the paragraph.

The team waited six days for the icy path spreading across the lead to freeze solid. They then advanced four days' marches until they caught up with Bartlett, who was stopped again by another wide lead. They had to set up camp and wait.

On March 11, a passable lane across the lead finally formed. But steep, rocky ice ridges studded the trail, and their supply of fuel was dwindling. One by one, the supporting parties and their Inuit crews were sent back to base camp to conserve the remaining fuel and supplies.

First, Dr. Goodsell was sent back with his team, and then MacMillan. Borup was sent back on March 20. The remaining crew crossed plains of deep ice littered with pressure ridges and ice rubble. The temperature rose to 20 degrees below zero; that turned the ice hard and smooth. But the warmer temperature opened up more leads.

Robert Peary, an engineer, used his training to reconfigure the design of the Inuit sledge so that it could carry heavier loads and be more durable. Henson was instrumental in building the sledges that Peary designed, and repairing those that disintegrated in the below-zero temperatures.

Marvin finished five marches, and then Bartlett moved up again as the trail breaker. The temperature dropped. On March 26, a disappointed Marvin was ordered back to land. The expedition had gotten past Peary's record of farthest north. Then on March 30 Bartlett was told to retreat. Bartlett was so frustrated by not being picked to go all the way to the Pole that he walked 5 or 6 miles farther north to reach the 88th parallel, the record up until that date. It was only at Bartlett's departure that Henson knew he would accompany Peary to the North Pole.

The final assault team was made up of Henson, Peary, and the Inuit Ootah, Ooqueah, Egingwah, and Seegloo. Henson, Ootah, and Ooqueah were to break the trail over the last 133 miles. Peary, still crippled by the frostbite that had taken his toes 11 years earlier, took turns riding Egingwah's sledge and walking beside it. The conditions varied from stretches of smooth ice to steep ice ridges. Henson lengthened his marches to a back-breaking 18 to 20 hours a day. Peary caught up to Henson's team at day's end on April 1.

✔ STOP AND THINK

Main Ideas and Details Choose a detail on this page that supports the following main idea: The number of explorers was reduced to help conserve supplies.

On April 5, Peary checked the position of the sun with his sextant. It told him that the Pole was only 35 miles away. The next morning, he alerted Henson to begin the march. Henson's progress was so successful that by the time he had covered 20 miles, he was an hour ahead of Peary. As Henson drove his team across thin ice bridging a lead, the ice suddenly cracked. Henson, along with his dogs and sledge, was plunged into the frigid water. Henson began floundering about, trying to grasp onto jutting ice to save himself. He swallowed frigid water, and his lungs felt like they would burst. Then he found himself being lifted out of the water. It was Ootah who saved him and his sledge and dogs. Ootah slipped off Henson's wet boots and warmed his feet in the Inuit way, against Ootah's bare stomach.

Peary's journals recording the day he and Henson and the four Inuit finally reached their goal. The entry at left says, "The Pole at last!!! The prize of three centuries. My dream and ambition for 20 years. Mine at last!"

They continued the march for four more hours until Henson deduced that they must have reached the North Pole. Henson, who had learned to steer a ship by the stars, had often played a game with Peary that he could estimate their position at the end of marches. "Knowing that we had kept on going in practically a straight line, [I] was sure that we had more than covered the necessary distance to insure our arrival at the top of the earth," wrote Henson later. He, Ooqueah, and Ootah built igloos.

Peary arrived forty-five minutes later. When the clouds parted in the sky, he was able to take a latitude sighting with his sextant that affirmed they were at 89°57'. (The North Pole is at 90°N.) They probably got as close to determining their position as their navigational gear allowed—within five miles of the North Pole. For all intents and purposes, the expedition had reached its goal. It was April 6, 1909. In a whisper, Peary announced his reading to Henson. Then the two explorers, weary with the culmination of so many years of effort, crawled into an igloo, lay down, and went to sleep.

No other but a Peary party would have attempted to travel in such weather. Our breath was frozen to our hoods of fur and our cheeks and noses frozen ...." —Matthew Henson

NORTH POLE
Camp Jesup ▫ Reached on April 6, 1909
89°57'N as recorded by Peary and Henson

88°N

ARCTIC OCEAN

86°N

ARCTIC OCEAN

100°W

Big Lead camp

84°N

Cape Columbia

Cape Sheridan

82°N

90°W

Ellesmere Island
(Canada)

80°N

Greenland
(Denmark)

▫ Etah

78°N

Route of S.S. Roosevelt

76°N

Baffin Bay

	1908–09 Ship route
	1909 North Pole sledge route
	Permanent sea ice
	Seasonal sea ice
	Open water
▫	Camp

Scale varies in this perspective.
Straight-line distance from Cape Columbia
to North Pole is 413 nautical miles
(475 statute miles).

74°N

70°W

60°W

50°W

339

Peary had Matthew Henson and the four Inuit, Seegloo, Egingwah, Ooqueah, and Ootah, pose for photographs holding the four banners he carried to commemorate their reaching the North Pole. The Inuit were amazed that the culmination of so many years of effort was just another expanse of ice. "There is nothing here," Ootah said.

When Peary awoke, he wrote in his diary, "The Pole at last!!!" He unpacked a thin silk American flag he had been carrying with him all of his many years of exploration and planted it on top of his igloo.

Peary, Egingwah, and Seegloo then sledged several miles beyond the camp, covering a rectangular area, to ensure that an inaccurate reading would not spoil their achievement. Peary had Henson thrust an American flag into a large pressure ridge, and he took a photo of the five men holding flags that the Commander had carried with him for the occasion. Henson held an American flag that Josephine Peary had sewn by hand. Ooqueah held a flag of the Navy League. Ootah held a banner from Peary's college fraternity. Seegloo waved a flag of the Red Cross. And Egingwah held a Daughters of the American Revolution peace flag. They all joined in an exhilarated chorus of "Hip, hip, hooray." Then Peary said, "Let us go home, Matt."

STOP AND THINK

Monitor/Clarify Suppose you wondered why sledging in a rectangle ensured greater accuracy. How might rereading paragraph two on page 338 help your understanding?

Your Turn

There at Last!

Write a Journal Entry Robert Peary wrote in a journal to keep a record of his journey. Choose a place you would like to explore, perhaps in space or the ocean depths. Imagine that after a long trip, you have reached your destination. Write a journal entry that describes what you are seeing and feeling. PERSONAL RESPONSE

Raise the Flags!

Create a Flag Work with a partner to reread the descriptions of the flags the team raised when they reached the North Pole. Then work together to design and illustrate a flag especially for the Peary expedition. Include symbols that express the goals and contributions of everyone involved. PARTNERS

The Drive to Explore

Turn and Talk With a partner, discuss the details that show why the final push to reach the North Pole was so challenging. Considering how difficult it was, what do you think drove the explorers to continue? What other reasons drive people to explore remote places? MAIN IDEA AND DETAILS

Poetry

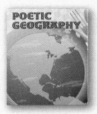

✓ TARGET VOCABULARY

expanse	participants
sacrificed	equivalent
durable	deduced
prime	affirmed
frigid	culmination

GENRE

Poetry uses the sound and rhythm of words in a variety of forms to suggest images and express feelings.

TEXT FOCUS

Rhythm, the regular pattern of stress in words, contributes to the distinctive sound and tone of poems.

POETIC GEOGRAPHY

Few of us have been participants in an expedition to the North Pole. No problem! Even if you haven't sacrificed your comfort to visit a frigid region, you can still go traveling through poetry. Reading a poem about a faraway place is almost the equivalent of going there. So prime yourself for a word voyage. You'll find the first poem to be a durable craft and the second an adventure. As for the third, be careful— geographical puns lie ahead!

LONG TRIP

The sea is a wilderness of waves,
A desert of water.
We dip and dive,
Rise and roll,
Hide and are hidden
On the sea.
　Day, night,
　Night, day,
The sea is a desert of waves,
A wilderness of water.

Langston Hughes

CLOUD FOREST

Mist blows through a gap in the trees,
And mosses hang like ragged beards.

Deep in the shadows, owl eyes peer.
—No, it's only a butterfly.

Fog drifts like curtains of gauze,
And vines creep through twisted trees.

Somewhere a *bonk* like a haunted clock.
—No, it's only a bellbird's cry.

A frog on a leaf, porcelain bright,
Winks its eye and seems to smile.

Shadows and mist, ghosts and fog.
—Real bird, real butterfly, real frog.

Susan Katz

INSTRUCTIONS FOR THE EARTH'S DISHWASHER

Please set the
continental plates
gently on the
continental shelves.
No jostling or scraping.

Please stack the
basins right side up.
No tilting or turning
upside-down.

Please scrape the mud
out of the mud pots.
But watch out!
They're still hot.

As for the forks
in the river,
just let them soak.

Remember,
if anything breaks,
it's your fault.

Lisa Westberg Peters

WRITE A PLACE POEM

By now you may have deduced that there's one more leg to your voyage.
As the culmination of your adventure, write your own geographical poem!
Go anywhere you like—a desert expanse, a rain forest, Antarctica, or around
the world. Your experience as a poet-traveler will be affirmed.

Making Connections

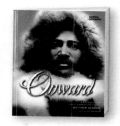 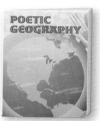

Text to Self

Make a Wish List Henson and Peary traveled to the North Pole. Where in the world would you like to travel? On a sheet of paper, list three places that you would visit if you could. For each destination, note what you would like to see or do there. Post your list in the classroom.

Text to Text

Compare and Contrast Compare the three poems in "Poetic Geography." Identify ways in which two or all three of the poems are alike. Discuss ways in which they are different from one another.

Text to World

Connect to Social Studies Choose one of the places you listed for "Make a Wish List" above. Research information about its landscape, climate, and other geographic features. Write a fact file about it, and add an illustration.

Grammar

What Are the Verb Tenses? The tense of a verb tells when the action or the state of being takes place. The **present tense**, the **past tense**, and the **future tense** are the simple tenses. The **present perfect tense**, the **past perfect tense**, and the **future perfect tense** are the perfect tenses. Each perfect-tense verb is made up of a form of the helping verb *have* and a simple past-tense verb.

Academic Language

present tense
past tense
future tense
present perfect tense
past perfect tense
future perfect tense

Simple Tenses	Perfect Tenses
present tense Explorers seek new discoveries.	present perfect tense Polar explorers have made many discoveries.
past tense Peary and Henson sailed to Greenland.	past perfect tense They first had sailed to Greenland eighteen years before they began this expedition.
future tense Readers will learn about their trek.	future perfect tense Our class will have read two other books about explorers by the end of the year.

 **Find the verb in each sentence. On another sheet of paper, write each verb and name its tense.**

1. Peary chose Henson for this expedition because of his skills and experience.

2. The temperature will drop far below zero.

3. Inuit women sew warm clothes for the explorers.

4. Matthew Henson had become a friend of the Inuit on earlier trips.

Conventions Different tenses of the same verb show when an action or a state of being occurs. As you write, your verb tenses tell your readers when events take place. You may confuse your readers if your verb tenses do not match other time clues in your writing.

Time Clues

Now they stand on the icy expanse.

All last week, they imagined this trek.

Tonight, they will dream of the view of the snowy landscape.

Connect Grammar to Writing

As you edit your letter, examine the verbs. Make sure you used the proper tenses. To determine the correct tense, ask yourself when the action or state of being occurs. Be sure to use the proper verb form for each tense.

Write to Narrate

☑ Organization Good writers pay attention to organizing their writing, even in informal contexts such as a **friendly letter**. As you revise your letter, make sure your ideas are organized in a logical way.

Felice drafted a friendly letter describing her recent visit to a cave at Lava Beds National Monument. Later, she revised her letter so that information about Skull Cave would make sense to her reader.

Writing Traits Checklist

☑ **Ideas**
Did I choose a topic that I could organize well?

☑ **Organization**
Did I organize the ideas logically?

☑ **Sentence Fluency**
Did I use verb tenses correctly?

☑ **Word Choice**
Did I include a suitable greeting and closing?

☑ **Voice**
Did I write in a friendly, informal tone?

☑ **Conventions**
Did I use the correct capitalization and punctuation for a letter?

Revised Draft

This past summer my family had a blast at Skull Cave, part of Lava Beds National Monument. ~~It is one of almost 700 lava tube caves.~~ The cave gets its name because of animal and human bones that were found inside it long ago.
Skull Cave is one of almost 700 lava tube caves at the monument. They
~~The caves~~ were formed over a very long time by lava from eruptions of the Medicine Lake volcano.

Dear Mrs. Wilson,

I'll bet you miss California and having us as your neighbors! This past summer my family had a blast at Skull Cave, part of Lava Beds National Monument. The cave gets its name because of animal and human bones that were found inside it long ago.

Skull Cave is one of almost 700 lava tube caves at the monument. They were formed over a very long time by lava from eruptions of the Medicine Lake volcano. As a lava stream flowed, the outer part cooled and hardened. The inner hot lava finally flowed away, and a tubelike cave was left.

Skull Cave is actually one lava tube on top of another. Winter air is trapped inside all year. I wish I'd followed the park ranger's advice to wear mittens. My favorite part was the lower level, which has an ice floor that never melts.

Missing you,
Felice Amado

In my final paper, I put the different aspects of the cave in a logical order. I also made sure that I used verb tenses correctly.

Reading as a Writer

Do you see how Felice organized her letter according to different aspects of the cave? What is the best organization for your letter topic?

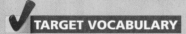

✔ **TARGET VOCABULARY**

emulate

motive

anonymous

bland

skeptical

veered

reception

aim

understatement

fanatic

Vocabulary
Reader

Context
Cards

Vocabulary in Context

1 emulate

A good person can serve as a role model whom others want to emulate. They want to be like that person.

2 motive

The motive of volunteers is not to make money. The reason for their actions is to help those in need.

3 anonymous

When a donation is from someone who wants to remain anonymous, no one knows who gives it.

4 bland

A day without a visit from a friend can be as bland as pasta without sauce.

- **Study each Context Card.**
- **Ask a question that uses one of the Vocabulary words.**

5 skeptical

People who are skeptical about learning a skill may need a friend to help them overcome their doubts.

6 veered

Many people have veered from their normal routine, changing their path to help someone in need.

7 reception

Those who attend a reception, a welcoming gathering, get a chance to meet others whom they admire.

8 aim

The aim, or purpose, of many fundraisers is to raise money to help people in need.

9 understatement

Saying "I helped" after saving someone's life is an understatement. It describes a big event in a few plain words.

10 fanatic

A sports fanatic may act too wild for some in a crowd, but the home team often appreciates the enthusiasm.

Background

✔ **TARGET VOCABULARY** **Good Coaches** Good coaches do not tend to be anonymous. We remember their names. Why does a coach stand out? It's not because he or she yells and cheers like a fanatic. Coaches are often calm, but they're not bland. They know how to spice things up.

Do they like to win? Saying yes is an understatement. But victory is not their chief aim. If a team has veered from its winning ways, good coaches are patient. They are skeptical only about players who aren't trying. They know how to give their players a motive for doing their best. They can make a new kid feel like family instead of an outsider. They can even calm an angry player who has a chip on his or her shoulder.

Is it any wonder that good coaches get a great reception from the crowd, or that their players want to emulate them? You can tell good coaches by the respect they earn.

Coach John Wooden of UCLA and his most famous player, later to be an NBA star, Kareem Abdul-Jabbar

Comprehension

✔ **TARGET SKILL** **Author's Purpose**

As you read "Any Small Goodness," think about the author's purpose for writing the story. An author can have more than one purpose for writing, but often text details support one overall purpose. Make a chart like this one to explain the author's main purpose for writing "Any Small Goodness."

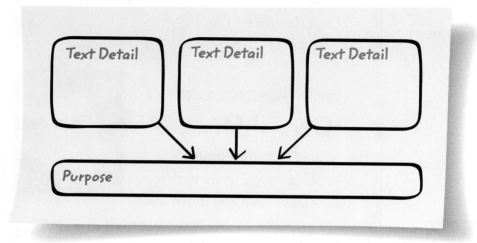

✔ **TARGET STRATEGY** **Visualize**

Keeping track of the details in "Any Small Goodness" can help you visualize events. Picturing those events in your mind can give you a better idea of the author's purpose and keep you connected to the story events.

✔ **TARGET VOCABULARY**

emulate	veered
motive	reception
anonymous	aim
bland	understatement
skeptical	fanatic

✔ **TARGET SKILL**

Author's Purpose Use text details to figure out the author's viewpoint and reasons for writing.

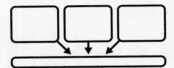

✔ **TARGET STRATEGY**

Visualize Use text details to form pictures in your mind of what you are reading.

GENRE

Realistic fiction has characters and events that are like people and events in real life.

MEET THE AUTHOR

Tony Johnston

Born in California, Tony Johnston spent fifteen years in Mexico. As she traveled, she collected handmade Indian belts. Her notes and stories about the belts became a collection of poems called *My Mexico*. Johnston usually works on several ideas at once and has published more than seventy-five books, including *The Harmonica* and *Uncle Rain Cloud*.

MEET THE ILLUSTRATOR

David Diaz

David Diaz developed his bold art style while making sketches on a trip down the Amazon River. His first illustrated children's book was Gary Soto's *Neighborhood Odes*. Diaz's illustrations for *Smoky Night*, by Eve Bunting, won the 1995 Caldecott Medal.

Any Small Goodness

by Tony Johnston

selection illustrated
by David Diaz

Arturo is a basketball fanatic, just like the rest of his family and everyone else in the barrio, his Spanish-speaking neighborhood in Los Angeles. He gets up at the crack of dawn nearly every morning to attend practice at his school. This day will be a little different.

Ours is a barrio of basketball maniacs. Our fans don't wear cheese hunks on their heads like some of those *idiotas* (ee DYOH tahs) on TV. But they get pretty into the game. When the season approaches, like now, too-worn shoes stop and start, with no squeak. Too-soft balls loft through the air. The whole neighborhood starts dribbling and jumping around. Like a great big popcorn machine. Guess that's another reason I signed up. Like the ad says, "I love this game!"

Now we're in the gym, waiting for Coach. He comes late a lot because he owns a watch as primitive as a sundial and a car that's easily Jurassic.

"I count on every one of you players," Coach pounds into us again and again. "I can't count on my watch; I can't count on my car; I've *got* to count on something."

Everyone's about as zoned-out as me. So there's a spurt of talk now and then, but mostly pretty senseless mumblings. Some kids stretch out on the bleachers for extra z's.

Our school colors are orange and green. Our mascot's the tiger. What *menso*-heads thought these things up? Tigers don't exist in that color combination. Tigers don't exist in L.A.

ANYWAY, dressed like peas and carrots, our basketball class's waiting for Coach, *again*.

Unbelievable! Coach strolls into the gym—in a suit! With a tie! (Off to one side, like a skinny, wind-flopped flag.) He usually wears grey oversized sweats that make him look like a melting elephant. Today he's dressed sharp.

The reason's standing beside him. Seven-foot plus, with the build of a post, and bald as a light bulb. An NBA basketball player once so famous he made Santa Claus seem like a total unknown. He's been out of the game a while, but any true fan knows him. *¡Ay!* The day's shaping up!

What I notice most about this guy is his eyes. Like owls'. It seems there are deep things in them. Deep and mysterious.

What's he doing lost among the Tigers? He must have really veered off the road from Beverly Hills!

"Listen up, everybody," Coach says. As if he needs to grab our attention. We're all gaping like apes.

"You all know who this is, right?" His face looks completely satisfied. Like a cat who's swallowed an entire turkey. Man, do we know this guy.

He's here, says Coach, to hang out with us. Watch our moves. Instruct us. To be our *assistant coach*. Wow! At this news, it's amazing all the Tigers don't swoon to the floor. But we don't. We're too stupefied.

"One thing," Coach adds, "nobody breathes his name, understood? Our new assistant wants to remain anonymous—to keep cameras from snooping around."

Right now nobody can breathe anything. But somehow guys pipe up with "*Yo juro,*" (yoh HOO roh) "Scout's honor"—even though there are no scouts here—and "I swear on the grave of my hamster."

Then Coach Tree (my name for the wandering all-star) steps forward and says, "*Buenos días.*" (BWAY nohs DEE ahs) That snaps the spell. The Tigers can no longer control themselves. They totally swarm the guy. He hugs everyone and they hug him. And he laughs and laughs.

At home we're discussing this coach thing over supper. *Chiles rellenos* (CHEE lehs reh YEH nohs), which Mami and Abuelita prepared together. For this dish you need *poblano* (poh BLAH noh) chilies, the black-green glossy kind. Abuelita says you count the veins to pick the hottest ones. Some people prefer bland, but we want those strong enough to blow your head off. Once the skins are roasted and steamed off, you stuff the rest with meat or cheese and dunk them in flour. Then, with stiff coats of egg whites, they fry in oil, floating like hot islands. Last touch, a drizzle of tomato sauce.

To help out, I usually chop the onions, wearing ski goggles that Abuelita and I got at a yard sale. So my tears don't dilute the sauce. One thing I know, if on my own, *por lo menos* (pohr loh MEH nohs), I could always fix *chiles rellenos*.

Our whole family loves basketball. Even Abuelita. Probably even our cat, who sits in Abue's skimpy lap to watch all games. Especially we love the Lakers. We know the names of all the players, their numbers, their stats. We are wild for their announcers, Chick and Stu, and given the chance, we would vote Chick in for president.

My brother's both excited and skeptical about Coach Tree, the barrio interloper. Luis is three years older than me. Maybe that's why he's untrusting.

"His motive must be money," Luis says, studying his mangled fork, a garbage-disposal victim. But his eyes say no way can that be. The school district's wish list has a focus on *books*, not on NBA coaches.

"Yeah," I say, "like we've got a gushing oil well at school to turn into dollars at will."

Luis burns me a look, so I say, "So cut my heart out and fry it for dinner."

Everyone, including him, laughs at this Aztec humor.

Papi finishes his stuffed chili pepper. "*Ay, qué delicia.*" (KEH deh LEE syah) He almost sings about how delicious it is. Instead, he exclaims, "You are such a good cook, *mi vida* (mee VEE *th*ah)! It's that *mole* (MOH leh) runs in your veins."

All happy, Mami laughs and goes a little red. Then she grows serious and says, "I believe this basketball man has all he will ever need. I believe he is doing this coaching for love only."

That sends Luis' eyes spinning in his skull. I can nearly hear his brain grinding: *Love! Man, don't you know? The world goes on* verde (VEHR deh)—*the green of dollars.* But he says nothing disrespectful. Neither do I. I plan to just dribble my brains loose while this guy's here. To gain every possible tip. Maybe, with buckets of sweat, I'll become *excelente* (ehk seh LEHN teh) at this game.

> **STOP AND THINK**
>
> **Author's Craft** In paragraph four, Papi praises Mami's cooking by saying that she has *mole* in her veins. He is using **hyperbole**: extreme exaggeration. Find another example of hyperbole in paragraph six.

Coach Tree arrives every morning just about before anyone. He slips into the parking lot in some anonymous car and slowly unfolds himself out. Like a giant and rusted pocketknife. I say he's there *before* most everyone. Actually, at first just about the whole school's waiting for a glimpse of him.

He takes that easily. Just strides along, talking to crowding kids and smiling. Like he's found himself a good home. From a distance, where I'm watching, this reception looks like a tall, calm ship riding a choppy sea.

The new basketball program affects everyone. Not just the big kids. From kinder on up, anyone can play. (Our school is so old, kinder to eighth, all grades are there.)

And they do play—if the ball doesn't bog them down. And even if it does. They just keep trying and trying. That's Coach Tree's real aim.

Though everyone gets a shot at basketball, against other schools it's the older kids who suit up. I'm not world-class, but somehow I make the team. For Coach Tree, the Tigers work like crazy. We don't have much height. But speed, we've got *muchísimo* (moo CHEE sih moh). And we're okay shooters, too.

To say Coach Tree helps us a lot is the understatement of the millennium. No whistles. No yells. No heaving of chairs. From steady practice and from his calm voice, the fundamentals sink in.

Once, between classes, he stops me in the hall. My nerves get tangled as a fistful of paper clips.

"You're working hard, Arturo," he says, quiet as ever. "Doing good."

¡Ay! Like a warm look from a girl (rare for me), I can live on these words forever.

Before long we're actually winning some games. That's partly due to one guy. José. A natural, you could say. He can steam past all defenders. Fake one way, stutter-step, elevate, shoot, and *swish*! All day, all night, if he has to. Like breathing. José, he can flat *play*.

José's a smooth player, but a real troublemaker. His family's a mess, so he bears a chip on his shoulder the size of a sequoia stump. He's been kicked out of school more times than there are numbers. He'd as soon spit on you as talk. Has *pleitos* (PLAY tohs), fights, for fun. José's a strong reason why we win. Still, for survival, after practice, wherever he is, our team pretty much vacates the area.

There's a sign on my door: NO SE ACEPTAN CHISMES (noh seh ah SEP tahn CHEES mehs). But, actually, in my room I allow carloads of gossip. *Chismes* bloom at school, too. Soon everyone knows that Coach Tree's losing things. A pen. A handkerchief. A key chain. Once even a tennis shoe! Next thing I hear, the culprit's José. Word is, he's vending Coach Tree-abilia to guys. Wow! Stealing from Coach Tree's like stealing from God. My opinion? José's the undisputed king of the *menso*-heads.

If it's true, we all expect that this is the last of him. He ought to depart the team fast. But, after all, it must be a story invented for excitement, because José keeps playing. Weird thing, though. *Mucho muy* (MOO choh MWEE) strange. Sometimes he asks to shoot hoops with us. Sometimes he says hello.

One night Alicia comes over. To do homework. And snack on Mexican cooking. Crunchy *chicharrón* (chee cha ROHN), with lime juice squeezed on. We gouge it into guacamole, while we're sort of studying.

STOP AND THINK

Visualize How does the author's description of José's movements help the reader visualize how he plays?

"Sort of" because immediately concentration slips away. The air feels crackly as the pork rinds. Like Alicia's got something to say.

I mark my book with a tomato, the only thing around.

From nowhere she plunges in. "Coach Tree caught José stealing his stuff."

"Yeah?" I say, low-key, to see where this's going.

"Yeah. And he's letting it slide."

"¡*Mentirosa!*" (mehn tee ROH sah) She's gotta be lying. Amazement must fill my face like the look of a stuffed deer.

"Well, not exactly letting it slide," she says. "Coach Tree sees promise in José. He's spending free time with him. Making him practice ball. Making him study. Coach Tree says he won't *let* him toss his life into the Dumpster."

So Coach Tree works with José, one-on-one. I let that sink in. "Think it'll work?" I ask.

"Yeah, I do."

"Why?"

"Because for the first time in forever, José trusts someone."

After Alicia goes, I'm in my room thinking. About Coach Tree and José. Coach doesn't have to do this. He's lost by choice in our nothing barrio, helping a kid with not many chances.

Even though he's a hardcase, I have hope if Alicia does. And she ought to know. José's her brother.

My grandmother takes a decision. "I prepare *chiles rellenos* for this Coach man."

That said, there's no stopping her. I'm ordered to tell him (*tell* the ex-NBA champ!) that the peppers will arrive today after school— along with my whole family. And they do. In a see-through tub. (Not my family, the chilies.)

Coach Tree's waiting in the lunch court with a mob of curious kids when Abuelita gets there. Like a little broom, she sweeps right up and says, "I am happy to meet. You play basket real good. *Chiles muy excelentes*. Eat."

"Yes, ma'am."

He samples a *chile relleno* with Abuelita cheerfully breathing down his neck and prodding, "*¿Excelente? ¿Excelente?*"

Suddenly, Coach Tree's like some cartoon character, steam puffing from his ears, strangling out words in speech balloons: "Agh! Agh!" I say, "Agh!" too, casting an arrowy stare at Abuelita. She's brought the hottest chilies in the universe! Man. My basketball days are over. Probably my life's over.

"CPR!" some kid shouts. What a *menso*-head! There's no CPR for peppers.

Abuelita turns away, totally mortified. I take that back. She's giggling. We all hold our breath. Then—"*Graa-ci-us, Sonora. Ex-ell-en-tees,*" Coach Tree gasps.

Everyone loses it, *muriendo de la risa* (moo RYEN doh deh lah REE sah). Then Coach Tree wipes tears from his face and bows and shakes Abuelita's hand. He shakes hands with everybody in my family. He laughs and laughs. And over the haze of the hot blacktop, carrying the leftover chili peppers, he walks to his car. Slowly, a tall ship of (smoking) calm.

Luis's right. I find out from Alicia, Coach Tree *is* coaching for money. His relative's a teacher here, so he said he'd help out our school—for the salary-shattering price of one dollar.

I know my limits. In pickup games I hold my own, but I'm not NBA-bound. Still, maybe I could do something like Coach Tree. Something for love. Something that's mine. Though right now, I've got zero idea what. To use one of Papi's favorite words, Coach Tree's a person to emulate.

> ✔ **STOP AND THINK**
> **Author's Purpose** Think about the last paragraph. What does it tell you about the author's possible purpose for writing this selection?

Your Turn

You Said It!

Notable Quotes Coach Tree unfolds himself "like a giant and rusted pocketknife." Arturo eats chilies "strong enough to blow your head off." Think about the effects that similes and hyperboles have on the story. Then make up three of your own hyperboles or similes. Use them in a paragraph describing a character from your imagination. AUTHOR'S CRAFT

Winning Ways

Be a Coach Coach Tree taught his team basketball skills *and* life skills. With a partner, choose a sport, game, or physical activity you both enjoy. Together, make a poster or prepare a short demonstration about the skills needed for the activity. Be sure to include tips on how to improve the skills. PARTNERS

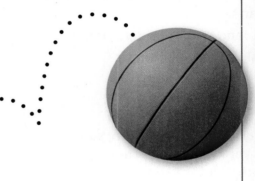

It's Time to Take Action

Turn and Talk With a partner, discuss what actions Coach Tree took after he caught José stealing from him. How did his actions bring out the best in both José and Arturo? What message do you think the author wants readers to understand from this? Then discuss leaders who have inspired you with their words and actions. AUTHOR'S PURPOSE

The Ball Is in Their Court

✓ TARGET VOCABULARY

emulate	veered
motive	reception
anonymous	aim
bland	understatement
skeptical	fanatic

GENRE

Narrative nonfiction, such as this newspaper article, gives factual information by telling a true story.

TEXT FOCUS

Primary Sources Nonfiction may include a primary source, an original document such as a quote or photo, from the time of the topic.

TODAY'S

MONDAY, SEPTEMBER 16

The Ball Is in Their Court

by Jeff Morse

What would you do if you became rich and famous? Would you choose to keep your wealth to yourself, or would you use your resources to help others?

Many players from the National Basketball Association (NBA) have chosen the second path. They give time and money to community outreach programs like *Es Tu Cancha* (It's Your Court) that help young people. A skeptical observer might wonder if athletes just want to polish their image. In fact, most have found that doing good means feeling good. Their motive is to give back to the communities they play for.

A young athlete has almost veered around the Lakers' Andrew Bynum.

The Lakers hold court at the Nueva Maravilla Housing Development.

The NBA founded *Es Tu Cancha* (It's Your Court) in 2004. The program's aim is to build or renovate basketball courts in Latino communities across the country.

How do basketball courts help kids? If you're a young hoops fanatic, it helps to have a place to emulate your favorite stars. But playing sports is also a great way for kids to get in shape. Los Angeles Lakers' player Andrew Bynum says that *Es Tu Cancha* is "an initiative we hope will encourage kids to get up and get moving in a local environment that is both safe and fun."

So far, *Es Tu Cancha* has opened more than a dozen courts in cities across the nation. On September 26, 2006, the Lakers helped open a new court in the Nueva Maravilla Housing Development in Los Angeles.

Perhaps the best part of the event was when Bynum and coach Craig Hodges hosted a passing and shooting clinic for local kids.

COMMUNITY

To say that the kids are excited at these court-opening ceremonies is an understatement. But athletes also say that being part of *Es Tu Cancha* helps to keep their lives from becoming bland. Rather than be anonymous donors, many stars are proud to show up at the neighborhood courts.

"It is an honor for us to contribute to such a great cause," says former Women's NBA (WNBA) player Sheila Lambert.

Former New York Knicks' guard John Starks agrees. "It's a great feeling to be a part of something that's so positive," he says.

A ribbon-cutting ceremony at the opening reception for a new basketball court in Mexico

Making Connections

Text to Self

Make an Activity List Coach Tree in "Any Small Goodness" and the NBA players in "The Ball Is in Their Court" give back to their communities. How can you give back to your own community? Make a list of volunteer activities you already do or would like to do. Choose one, and tell why the activity is a good match for your talents or strengths.

Text to Text

Hoop Art Think about what you have read in "Any Small Goodness" and "The Ball Is in Their Court." Create a picture that could be an illustration for one or both selections. Include a caption.

¡Es tu cancha!

Text to World

Connect to Social Studies Write a short summary of what you have learned about Arturo's family life, neighborhood, and culture. Include a list of Spanish words and phrases, and give their definitions.

Grammar

What Is the Active Voice? What Is the Passive Voice? A verb in the **active voice** puts the focus on the subject, the doer of the action. A verb in the **passive voice** tells what was done to, or what happened to, the subject. The doer of the action becomes not as important as the receiver of the action. Passive voice combines a form of the verb *be* and a simple past-tense verb.

Academic Language

active voice

passive voice

Verbs in the Active and Passive Voice	
active-voice verb The players notice a tall visitor. doers of the action	passive-voice verb A tall visitor is noticed by the players. receiver of the action

A passive-voice verb, like an active-voice verb, must agree with the subject. If the subject is a personal pronoun, a special verb form may be required.

plural   plural form of
subject   helping verb

Decisions are made by the coach.

singular subject: helping verb: special
personal pronoun   form used with *you*

You were elected captain by your teammates.

Turn and Talk

With a partner, read aloud each sentence below. Identify each verb, and say whether it is in the active or passive voice. Then explain how the subject and verb agree.

❶ You are applauded by the fans often.

❷ Spectators appreciate your skill and hustle.

❸ I am feared by our opponents.

❹ They are intimidated by my strength.

370

Conventions When a personal pronoun is the subject of a sentence, be sure to use the correct verb form with it.

Correct Subject-Verb Agreement with Personal Pronouns

Active-Voice Verbs	Passive-Voice Verbs
A local sportswriter mentions you in this week's sports section. She praises you for your footwork.	I am included in the article, too. We are called a "dynamic duo."

Connect Grammar to Writing

As you write your personal narrative, remember to use the correct verb form when the subject of a sentence is a personal pronoun.

Write to Narrate

☑ Ideas As they plan to write a **personal narrative**, good writers explore their ideas. They think carefully about the events they will include and the order, or sequence, in which the events happened.

Ashley thought about what took place on his first horseback ride. He listed events in time order. Later, he put the events into a flow chart and added important, interesting details.

Writing Process Checklist

▶ **Prewrite**

☑ **Did I choose a topic I remember well?**

☑ **Will this topic interest my readers?**

☑ **Did I focus on the main events?**

☑ **Did I organize the events in time order?**

☑ **Did I include a variety of interesting, important details about the events?**

Draft

Revise

Edit

Publish and Share

Exploring a Topic

woke up early

didn't sleep much

~~remembered to set new alarm clock~~

nervous

got picked up at seven

saw Abacus

tall with huge head

shiny coat — copper color
made snorting noises
got up courage to ride

Aunt Chloe gave me a boost

moved smoothly

walked in a circle

Flow Chart

> **Event:** Woke up early
>
> **Details:** Didn't sleep much the night before; nervous Aunt & Marissa picked me up at seven

> **Event:** We drove to the farm
>
> **Details:** Wondered whether I would ride the horse

> **Event:** Saw Abacus—wow
>
> **Details:** Tall, with a big head, and shiny copper hair; he made snorting sounds

> **Event:** Got up the courage to ride him
>
> **Details:** Chloe helped me up. Walked in a circle; Abacus moved smoothly

> **Event:** Decided I like riding horses
>
> **Details:** Gone back almost every weekend Can go over jumps now

As I organized my personal narrative, I kept adding to my chart. For each main event, I listed details.

Reading as a Writer

Which of Ashley's details show how he felt? What important details could you add to your own chart to show how you felt?

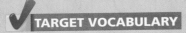

ascent

perilous

unpredictability

lunar

likelihood

hovering

impending

presumably

option

random

Vocabulary
Reader

Context
Cards

Vocabulary in Context

1 ascent
A rocket's ascent stage, or climb into space, begins with a powerful, fiery liftoff.

2 perilous
Movies and comic books often portray outer space as perilous, or full of danger.

3 unpredictability
Even though astronauts are well prepared, there is always unpredictability about a mission. No one knows what will happen.

4 lunar
Astronauts have brought back moon rocks that they gathered from the lunar surface.

- **Study each Context Card.**

- **Tell a story about two or more pictures, using Vocabulary words of your choice.**

5 likelihood

After animals successfully traveled in space, there was a strong likelihood, or probability, that people would be next.

6 hovering

This lunar module seems to be hovering over the surface of the moon. It looks as though it is hanging in space.

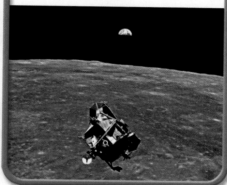

7 impending

Impending bad weather may threaten to delay the launch of a space shuttle flight.

8 presumably

Presumably, people knew the moon was not made of green cheese before *Apollo 11* landed there. That is a safe guess.

9 option

In the future, space travelers may have the option of a window or an aisle seat. Which would you choose?

10 random

Because of dust in the atmosphere, stars twinkle in a random order, not following a pattern.

Background

Flying to the Moon Before 1969 there were no lunar landings, but the scientists of NASA—the National Aeronautics and Space Administration—had been getting astronauts ready. The NASA team knew that space travel could be perilous and full of unpredictability. Through simulations and actual flights orbiting Earth and the Moon, they tried to plan for impending problems. Presumably, planning would increase the likelihood of success. Finally, on July 16, 1969, the *Apollo 11* rocket made its ascent. The mission would take eight days. One astronaut would orbit the Moon in a command module, and two others would land the lunar module (LM) on the Moon. Back in Houston, the NASA scientists were hovering over their computers, reviewing every option. This was no time for random decisions. Both teams needed be focused on the goal!

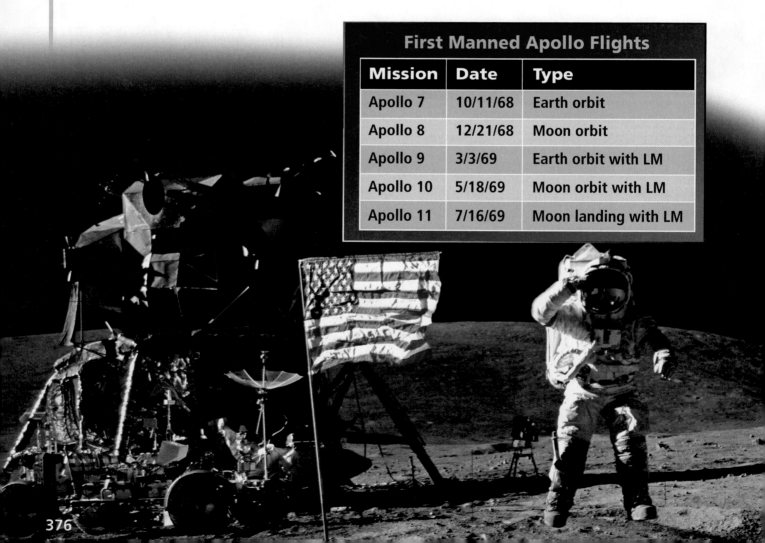

First Manned Apollo Flights

Mission	Date	Type
Apollo 7	10/11/68	Earth orbit
Apollo 8	12/21/68	Moon orbit
Apollo 9	3/3/69	Earth orbit with LM
Apollo 10	5/18/69	Moon orbit with LM
Apollo 11	7/16/69	Moon landing with LM

Comprehension

✔ **TARGET SKILL** **Text and Graphic Features**

Graphics such as photos or drawings illustrate what is happening in "Team Moon." As you read, pay attention to text and graphic features such as captions, quotations, and photos. Make a chart like the one below to note examples of these features and the purpose each one serves.

Text or Graphic Feature	Page Number	Purpose
Examples:		

✔ **TARGET STRATEGY** **Analyze/Evaluate**

Use your chart to analyze and evaluate each text or graphic feature in the selection and to decide how well it fills its role. Analyzing and evaluating gives you a critic's-eye view of what you are reading.

Main Selection

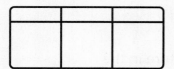

MEET THE AUTHOR

CATHERINE THIMMESH

Catherine Thimmesh is a big fan of space exploration. While researching *Team Moon*, she regretted having been born too late to see the Apollo missions in person. However, Thimmesh is saving money to go up as a space tourist (estimated cost: $98,000). Thimmesh's other books include *Madam President: The Extraordinary, True (and Evolving) Story of Women in Politics* and *Girls Think of Everything: Stories of Ingenious Inventions by Women*.

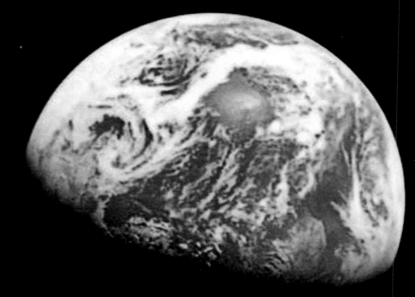

TEAM MOON

How 400,000 People Landed
Apollo 11 on the Moon

BY CATHERINE THIMMESH

Essential Question

How do text and graphics show a crisis in space?

*The year is 1969. After years of preparation, Apollo 11 is minutes away from being the first space expedition to land a man on the moon. With only 3,000 feet to go, a software alarm from **Eagle**, the* **lunar** *module* **(LM)**, *puts astronauts Neil Armstrong and Buzz Aldrin and Mission Control on high alert.*

Their voices were rapid-fire. Crisp. Assured. There was no hesitation. But you could practically hear the adrenaline rushing in their vocal tones, practically hear the thumping of their hearts as the alarms continued to pop up.

Then the *Eagle* was down to 2,000 feet. Another alarm! 1202. Mission Control snapped, "Roger, no sweat." And again, a 1202! Then the *Eagle* was down to 700 feet, then 500. Now, they were hovering— helicopter-like—presumably scouting a landing spot.

In hundreds of practice simulations, they would have landed by now. But Mission Control couldn't see the perilous crater and boulder field confronting Neil and Buzz. Those things, coupled with the distraction of the alarms, had slowed them down.

More than eleven minutes had passed since they started down to the moon. There was only twelve minutes' worth of fuel in the descent stage.

Telescopic views showing the

✔ **STOP AND THINK**

Text and Graphic Features How does the close-up photo of the moon on page 380 contribute to your understanding of the moon expedition?

An interior view of the LM cockpit, showing the 16 mm film camera out Buzz's window

Almost Empty

"Sixty seconds!"

Not sixty-one. No wiggle room. No "just a couple more seconds—we're almost there." And no second chances. They had just sixty seconds to land on the moon.

Absolutely no one expected it to happen. They painstakingly planned so it absolutely wouldn't-couldn't happen. But here they were, less than 500 feet from the moon, and just about plumb out of fuel.

Robert Carlton, the CONTROL position in Mission Control, who was in charge of monitoring fuel consumption among other things, had just sent the shocking sixty-second notice through the voice chain up to the astronauts. Both Neil and Buzz knew when they heard the words "sixty seconds," that was how much time remained until they *had* to abort. Until they *had* to push the button, fling themselves away from the moon, never to land. Or else, they could possibly die.

"We wanted to give him [Neil] every chance to land," explained Robert Carlton. "So we wanted it [the LM] to be as near empty as it could possibly get, but on the other hand, we didn't want him to run out of gas ten feet from the surface. That would have been a bad thing to do, you know. So you had to hit both. You wanted to make the mission, but you didn't want to jeopardize your crew, and you wanted to play it just as tight as you could safely."

The heavier the spacecraft, the harder it is to launch. And fuel is heavy. So it was critical to pinpoint the fuel needed, add a cushion, then take no more than necessary. But now, because the landing was taking far longer than planned, the fuel was almost gone. Mission Control wanted Neil to take as much time as he needed and fly the LM as near empty as possible *only* because they wanted him to make the landing. But if he ran out of fuel above the surface, in all likelihood, the LM would crash onto the moon. So they were trying to time it to the last possible second before calling an abort—calling off the landing.

If they aborted, if they flung themselves away from the moon (never to land), they would be slung into lunar orbit, where they would meet up with Mike Collins in the command module and head home to Earth. If they landed, though, leaving the moon wouldn't be a problem because there was a full tank of fuel in the ascent stage for liftoff (an abort also used the ascent stage). But the ascent and descent stages were completely separate. When the supply for the descent stage was empty, that was it. Sharing fuel was not an option.

In every simulation, the LM had been landed well before the low-level sensor was tripped, indicating 120 seconds of fuel left. Bob Nance, backroom support for CONTROL, was calculating the seconds of fuel remaining on his paper strip chart. (Flight Director Gene Kranz would write in his memoir, "I never dreamed we would still be flying this close to empty and depending on Nance's eyeballs.") Bob Carlton backed up the backup with a stopwatch.

Thirty seconds!

Now would not be the time for the two Bobs to miscalculate, miscount, or lose their superhuman powers of concentration. They could not afford to be wrong.

"When we tripped low level, things really got quiet in that control center," recalled Bob Carlton. "We were nervous, sweating. Came to sixty seconds, came to thirty seconds, and my eyes were just glued on the stopwatch. I didn't see [the control center as a whole]. The system could have [fallen] apart at that instant, and I wouldn't have [known] it. I was just watching the stopwatch."

Eighteen seconds!

Click.

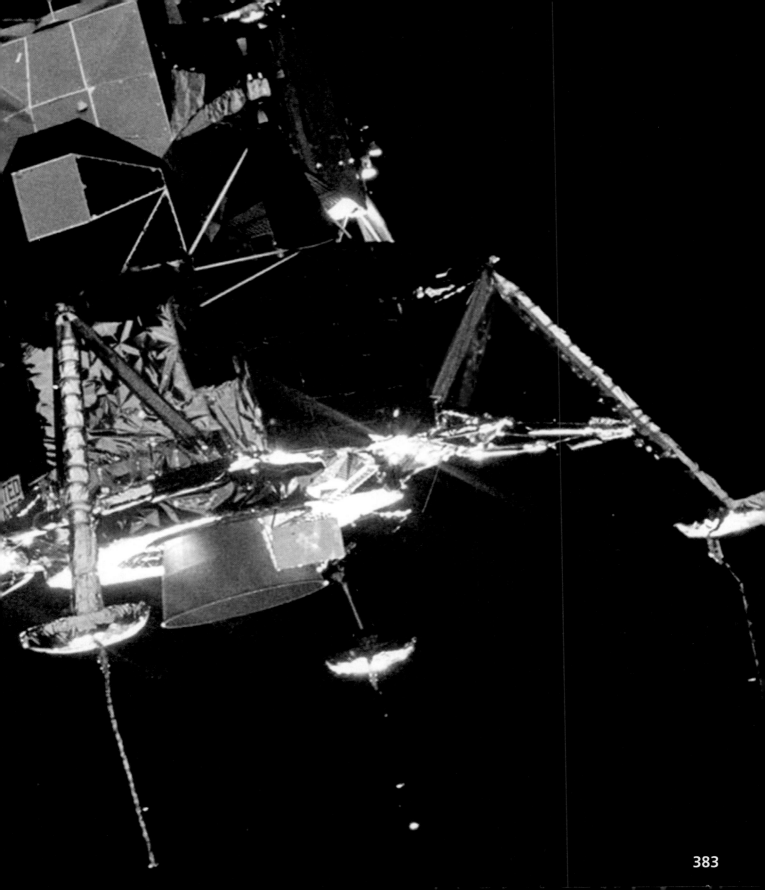

People [were] concerned about the amount of fuel you had left, the master alarms. . . . I don't believe anybody in the room breathed for the last five minutes. We were just hanging on every word. And trying to force the vehicle down by sheer willpower. Get down! Get down! *Neil, get down. Turn off that engine.*"

— *Charlie Mars, chief lunar module project engineer; listening in on a headset in one of the backrooms at the Mission Control complex*

"*Forty feet, down two and a half, picking up some dust...*"
— **Apollo 11** *astronaut Buzz Aldrin, from the LM*

STOP AND THINK

Analyze/Evaluate On these pages, the author shows quotes only from the astronauts and the control room personnel. Why do you think the author has chosen to do that?

You know it's real when you walk in [to the Mission Control building]. Then you sit down and start doing what you've done a hundred times and it becomes surreal—you don't know or care if it's real, you're just doing your thing. And then all of a sudden it doesn't go quite the same. Somebody calls out something that brings you . . . wakes you up—and says . . . 'It is real!' And that was what happened when he said 'We've got some dust.' We'd never heard that before."

— AGC Jack Garman, in Mission Control

"Houston, Tranquility *Base here. The* Eagle *has landed."*
—Apollo 11 *commander Neil Armstrong, from the LM*

"Roger, Tranquility. *We copy you on the ground. You got a bunch of guys about to turn blue. We're breathing again. Thanks a lot."* ("I was so excited," Duke later said. "I couldn't get out Tranquility Base. It came out sort of like Twangquility.")
—CapCom (and astronaut) Charlie Duke, in Mission Control

Frozen Slug

After eight challenging years and countless hours, man was finally on the moon. Flight Director Gene Kranz would soon "go around the horn" for the very first Stay/No Stay decision.

"You know, they landed, and everybody's cheering and everything and then all of a sudden somebody notices that something's gone wrong. Temperature's building up. Uh-oh! It shouldn't be like that," explained Grumman engineering manager John Coursen.

Up, up, up went the temperature in a fuel line on the descent engine. Up, up went the pressure. Rocket science rule number one? Do *not* allow the fuel to become unstable. Instability equals unpredictability—and unpredictability is just another word for random explosions and all sorts of unwanted chaos.

Engineers John Coursen, Manning Dandridge, and a whole lot of others sprang into action. Back at the Grumman plant in Bethpage, New York (where Coursen was stationed), there was a frenetic burst of engineering pandemonium:

from table to table, rushing;

blueprints and schematics, unfurling;

telephones, dialing;

telephones, ringing . . .

Do you remember that one test? What about when such and such happened? Remember when so-and-so talked about . . . Any ideas? . . .

At 300 degrees, the fuel was quickly approaching its 400-degree instability rating. Engineers at Grumman, and their counterparts at NASA in Houston (like Grumman manager Tom Kelly), simultaneously deduced the likely culprit: a slug. A solid slug of frozen fuel had trapped a small amount of the descent fuel in the line. This caused the temperature and pressure in the line to rise rapidly—and dangerously.

"First thing we did was get the drawings out so you could see," recalled John Coursen. "All kinds of functional diagrams, say of the heat exchanger; the line that runs from there to the valve of the tank. . . . You want to get all of the data before you that you can; and that's the purpose for having a good call room back at the plant—because there's more data there that the people didn't take with them [to Houston]."

Up went the pressure; the temperature—now 350 degrees. Terrified of an impending explosion (even a small blast could damage vital engines or components), Coursen and the Grumman engineers argued their options. They could (1) abort now and leave the problem on the moon. (The slug was isolated in the descent stage—and liftoff relied on the separate ascent stage. The descent stage—no longer necessary—would be left behind.) Or they could (2) try to "burp" the engine—give the valve a quick open-close to release the built-up pressure.

The trouble with option 2 was that venting might push the fuel to an unstable condition. Or, another possible outcome of the "burping": what if the landing gear hadn't deployed correctly? Could any movement, or any resulting burst—no matter how small—tip the LM over? Many a voice in the debate thought the safest option was to abort—now! But that opinion was quickly overruled by the Grumman and NASA leadership (who were confident of the landing gear), and the consensus of the leaders was that it would be safe to gently, *gently* burp the engine.

> *"I'm going to step off the LM now."*
> —Neil Armstrong, from the moon

> *"That's one small step for man,*
> *one giant leap for mankind."*
> —Neil Armstrong, first man on
> the moon

Suddenly, though, just as the procedure was about to be relayed to the astronauts, the pressure . . . the temperature . . . dropped! And . . . stayed down. The frozen slug, apparently, had melted! (Probably due to the extreme heat in the fuel line.) Problem solved. And only now—a solid, panic-stricken, gut-wrenching, heart-palpitating ten minutes by clock but feeling like an eternity later—did it sink in for John Coursen, Tom Kelly, and a lot of the other Grumman folks who had poured years of their lives into building the lunar module: Their baby was on the moon. Let the cheering begin!

STOP AND THINK

Author's Craft In the passage above, the author uses sensory words such as *gut-wrenching* and *heart-palpitating.* How do these add to the **mood** of the selection?

Your Turn

What's Your Job?

Write About Careers Review "Team Moon," and list the job titles of all the people involved in the moon landing. Choose one job, and list its required skills. Where else might a person with these skills be able to work? Write a short paragraph explaining which of the jobs you might want and why. SCIENCE

Measuring Up

By the Numbers Feet, minutes, seconds, years: "Team Moon" is filled with units of measurement. With a partner, scan the selection and make a list of the measurement words you find. Create a word search using the terms. Trade with another pair of partners, and complete their word search. Did all pairs find the same units of measurement? PARTNERS

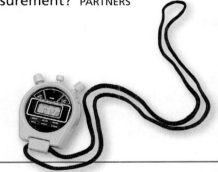

Teamwork!

Turn and Talk With a partner, review and discuss the selection's photos, captions, and quotations. Which of those three features do you think shows best how the team worked together in a crisis? Explain how that feature highlights teamwork.

TEXT AND GRAPHIC FEATURES

Traditional Tales

The Woman in the Moon

✔ **TARGET VOCABULARY**

ascent	hovering
perilous	impending
unpredictability	presumably
lunar	option
likelihood	random

GENRE

A **folktale** is a story that the people of a country tell to explain or to entertain.

TEXT FOCUS

Origins Many folktales and myths explain the origin of a feature or phenomenon in nature.

Readers' Theater

The Woman in the Moon

retold by Cynthia Benjamin

Cast of Characters
Narrator
Chang E
Hou Yi
Emperor
Hare

Setting: Ancient China

Narrator: The moon is a popular subject in folktales. In China, the tale of Chang E is a central part of the Moon Festival, or Mid-Autumn Festival, which takes place on the fifteenth day of the eighth lunar month. Here is one version of the tale.

According to legend, long ago ten suns circled Earth, threatening to destroy all living things with their perilous heat. A frightened emperor called Hou Yi to the palace.

Emperor: Ooh, it is hot! These ten suns are hovering in the sky, cooking us alive. Hou Yi, you are a famous archer. What do you think is the best option for beating the heat?

Hou Yi: I could try to shoot the suns down, Emperor.

Emperor: What is the likelihood *that* would work?

Hou Yi: Well, it's worth a try.

Emperor: Then do it and save us from impending doom.

Hou Yi: May I leave one sun so we can still see what we're doing?

Emperor: Yes, good point.

Narrator: Hou Yi completed his mission. The Emperor rewarded him with a potion that gave eternal life.

Emperor: But be careful. This bottle contains enough potion for two people. Do not drink more than half of it.

Narrator: Hou Yi rushed home and began to tell his wife, Chang E, about their good fortune. But before he could finish explaining, Chang E grabbed the bottle and drank it all. Immediately, she began to float toward the sky.

Chang E: What's happening? Hou Yi, help me!

Hou Yi: You weren't supposed to drink the entire bottle!

Narrator: Chang E flew out the door and began an ascent to the heavens, never to return. Her journey took her to the moon, where her only companion was a hare.

Hare: I wasn't expecting company.

Chang E: I wasn't expecting to end up on the moon.

Hare: Ah, the unpredictability of life!

Narrator: Back on Earth, Hou Yi gazed up at the full moon.

Hou Yi: What are those shadowy shapes on the lunar surface? One of them looks like Chang E, and the other looks a lot like a hare!

Narrator: For generations, the tale of Chang E has explained why there is only one sun and why people see shapes on the lunar surface.

Emperor: Presumably, they are not just random patterns.

Narrator: Meanwhile, it is said that once a year, on the fifteenth day of the eighth lunar month, Hou Yi is able to fly to the moon and visit his wife.

Hou Yi: I'm coming, Chang E!

Making Connections

 Text to Self

Conduct Interviews Older people you know may remember the moon landing in 1969. Make a list of interview questions, and set up an interview with one of those people. Write down or make a recording of that person's memories of the landing and feelings about it at the time. Share your interview with the class.

 Text to Text

Moon Web Write *moon* at the center of a word web. Complete the web with a partner by brainstorming a list of movies, stories, articles, myths (including "Team Moon" and "The Woman in the Moon"), computer and video games, songs, and other works you know of that focus on the moon. Discuss how they present the moon in different ways.

 Text to World

Connect to Science Imagine that in the future, it becomes common for ordinary people to travel to and live on the moon. Think about the positive and negative effects this might have on both our planet and the moon. Share your thoughts with a small group.

Grammar

What Are Regular and Irregular Verbs? A **regular verb** adds *ed* to its present form to show action that happened in the past. A regular verb also adds *ed* when it is used with the helping verb *has, have,* or *had.* An **irregular verb** does not add *ed* in these situations. It changes in other ways. You must memorize the spellings of irregular verbs.

Academic Language

regular verb

irregular verb

Regular and Irregular Verbs Showing Past Action	
regular verbs	The lunar module *approached* the moon. A difficult situation *had developed*. The astronauts *had* not *identified* a landing site.
irregular verbs	The lunar module *had* little fuel in its tank. An engineer *had sent* the "sixty seconds" message. The astronauts still *had* not *found* a suitable landing spot.

With a partner, read aloud each sentence below. Find the verb or main verb in each sentence. Say whether it is regular or irregular.

1. The astronauts chose a landing site just in time.

2. Soon they had become the first humans on the moon!

3. A few minutes later, another problem arose.

4. The temperature in a fuel line increased steadily.

Word Choice When you write, use vivid verbs and consistent tenses to communicate action precisely. Vivid verbs help to make your writing more lively, and consistent tenses eliminate confusion for your audience.

Vague Verbs, Confusing Tenses	Vivid Verbs, Consistent Tenses

The lunar module is over the surface of the moon. While the fuel level was falling, Neil and Buzz will make a difficult landing.	The lunar module hovered over the surface of the moon. While the fuel level plunged, Neil and Buzz tackled a difficult landing.

Connect Grammar to Writing

As you revise your personal narrative, look for vague verbs that you can replace with vivid verbs in the correct tense. Use these verbs to create clear pictures in your writing.

Write to Narrate

✔ **Voice** Good narrative writing connects with readers because it expresses honest feelings. The writer's personality comes through in a strong writing voice. As you revise your **personal narrative**, think about what details you can add to express your feelings honestly.

Ashley drafted a personal narrative about achieving a goal that was important to him. Later he added sentences to express his strong writing voice.

Writing Process Checklist

Prewrite

Draft

▶ **Revise**

☑ Does my beginning grab readers' attention?

☑ Did I present important events in a logical order?

☑ Did I use descriptive details and dialogue?

☑ Did I use figurative language?

☑ Does my writing show my personality?

☑ Is my ending satisfying?

Edit

Publish and Share

Revised Draft

At exactly seven o'clock, their car pulled up. Excited to get going and show me the barn, Marissa yelled, "Hurry up!" She'd been riding horses for years and had even competed in equestrian events. I liked observing her skill, but I was afraid of
her horse. ∧ *He was huge!* As I got into the car, I didn't know if I could go through with it. ∧ *I wasn't even sure I wanted to.*

Learning from Abacus

Ashley Barnes

I was nervously waiting for my Aunt Chloe and my cousin Marissa to arrive. They were picking me up at seven, but I'd been awake for hours. We were heading to Stonewell Farm, where I was going to ride a horse for the first time.

At exactly seven o'clock, their car pulled up. Excited to get going and show me the barn, Marissa yelled, "Hurry up!" She'd been riding horses for years and had even competed in equestrian events. I liked observing her skill, but I was afraid of her horse. He was huge! As I got into the car, I didn't know if I could go through with it. I wasn't even sure I wanted to.

Before long, we got to the farm. We walked into the barn, and I saw Abacus. His coat was the color of a new penny, and he snorted softly.

> In my final paper, I added sentences to show readers what I was feeling. I also used verb tenses consistently.

Reading as a Writer

Where did Ashley use words and sentences to show his personality? What can you add to your narrative to show a strong writing voice?

Read the next selection. Think about how the setting affects the plot events.

The Record-Setting Popcorn String

The idea began with a gift Chima had received for her birthday. It was *The Guinness Book of World Records*. She read the book and became absorbed in the facts and records involving nature, the universe, sports, and all kinds of other topics. She learned about the fastest animals, the tallest buildings, and unusual records set by people. Chima could hardly believe that someone had actually balanced on one foot for almost seventy-seven hours. She thought *The Guinness Book of World Records* was the most fascinating book she had seen in a long time, and she wanted to share it with her friends. At first, Mei-Mei and Max weren't very interested. Then Chima found something to appeal to each of them. She pointed Mei-Mei to the section about nature and animals. Max, who loved sports, was amazed that someone had once run a mile with a pint of milk balanced on his head.

One morning the three friends were quizzing each other about world-record trivia. They were especially interested in the records set by friends working together, such as a group that made the longest paper chain. Chima suggested that it would be fun to try to set a Guinness record. She challenged her friends to help her. Mei-Mei became excited and agreed at once. Max was hesitant, saying he thought it might be too difficult and take too much time.

Chima and Mei-Mei began to talk about records that they might attempt to break. Chima mentioned that maybe they could break the record for hopping the longest distance. Mei-Mei looked up the record for the tallest sand castle, thinking that perhaps they could top that record. Then Chima had a thought. She had often made strings of popcorn to hang from trees to feed the birds. Why not try to make the world's longest string of popcorn? Even Max now agreed that this was something they could do, and that it would be fun, too.

For the remainder of the day, the friends mapped out a plan and bought the supplies for their challenge. They finally parted, enthusiastic about setting a new world record and eventually seeing their names in the book.

Over the next month, the friends spent weekend mornings popping popcorn. Long afternoons spent in Chima's garage were devoted to stringing the popped kernels. At times, the project became tedious. Mei-Mei complained that the stringing was boring. Max said he detested the smell of popcorn and never wanted to eat it again. Chima agreed.

Finally, one Saturday afternoon, the friends realized they had finished stringing 5,280 feet of popcorn. They had tracked the length of the string by recording how many spools of thread they had bought and tied together. They called their families to look at the long string of popcorn and to share in the proud moment. Everyone was impressed.

The next morning, Chima was awakened by a clatter near the garage. As she walked toward the garage, she recognized the noise of squawking birds. With a sinking feeling, Chima remembered how she had gotten the idea for the popcorn string in the first place. The flock of birds scattered when Chima walked into the garage. All that remained of the record-setting popcorn string were long threads and popcorn strewn around the garage. Chima realized that she was the one who had left the garage door open the night before. She wished she could fix her mistake, but all she could do now was call Max and Mei-Mei and share the news.

When Max and Mei-Mei saw the bits of popcorn and the lengths of exposed string, they knew the possibility of setting a world record had disappeared. Chima explained her mistake and apologized. After a while, the friends began talking about the experience of trying to set a world record. They were disappointed by the accident, but they had enjoyed setting a goal and trying to achieve it. In their own minds they had set a world record, even if this feat would never make it into *The Guinness Book of World Records*. The friends even talked about other records they could try to set. They agreed, however, that any future record-setting challenges would not involve popcorn!

Unit **3** Wrap-Up

The Big Idea

Givers in Your World In Unit 3 you read about people who gave their all to help others or to accomplish a goal. Think of a person you know who gave his or her all in a crisis or for a cause. Draw a picture of this person in action. Write an extended caption explaining this person's efforts.

Listening and Speaking

Newsmakers Read a recent issue of a local newspaper. Choose an article that you think describes a person or group that has "gone the distance" in your community. Summarize the article for a partner, and explain why you chose it.

Treasures
of the
Ancient World

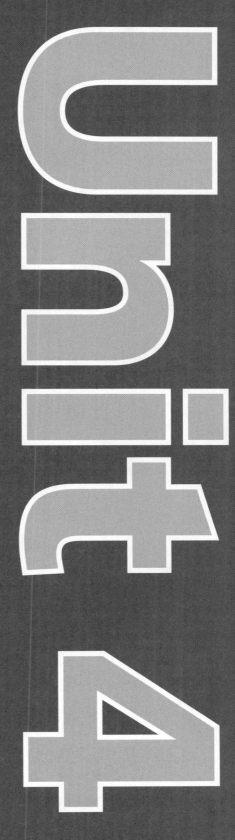

Unit 4

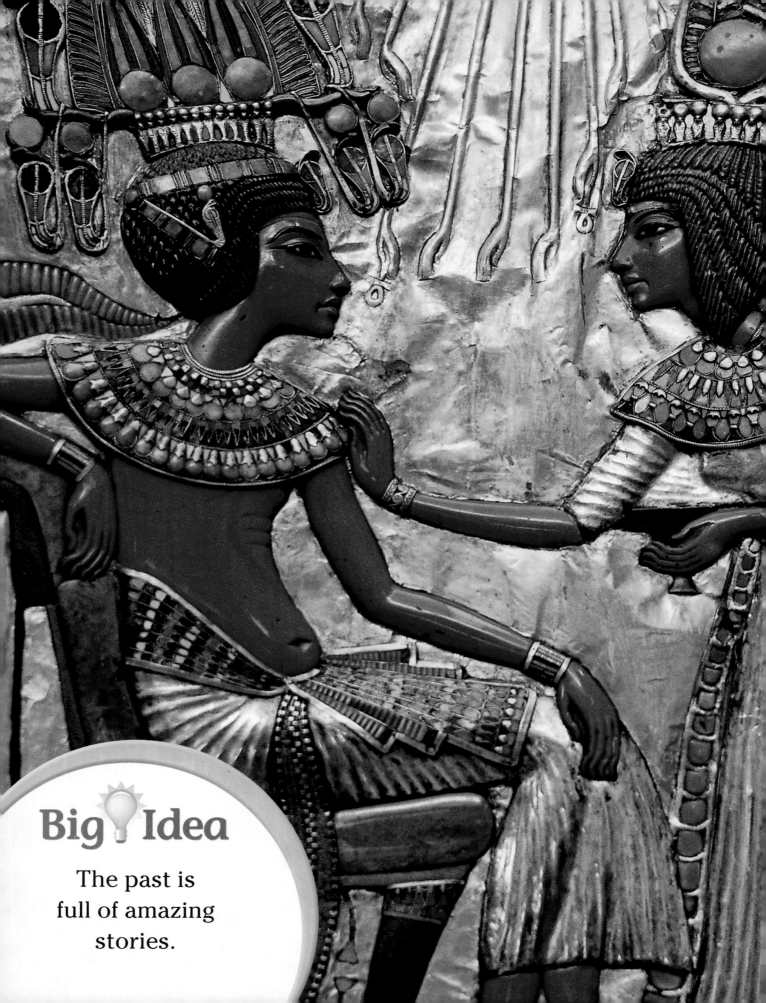

Big Idea

The past is
full of amazing
stories.

Paired Selections

ruthless

unearthed

ancestral

forge

embodied

artistry

recreational

saga

majestic

destiny

Vocabulary
Reader

Context
Cards

Vocabulary in Context

1 **ruthless**

During raids, Vikings sometimes acted in a ruthless fashion. At other times, they were peaceful.

2 **unearthed**

Remains of Viking settlements have been unearthed, or dug up, in Greenland.

3 **ancestral**

The descendants of this lord lived on ancestral land that he had owned many generations ago.

4 **forge**

Viking friends worked to forge, or build, a strong bond by helping each other through hard times.

- **Study each** Context Card.
- **Make up a new context sentence that uses two Vocabulary words.**

5 **embodied**

Viking ships had dragon heads carved into their prows. These embodied, or gave form to, the Vikings' warrior spirit.

6 **artistry**

Early books had decorated pages that showed the artistry of the illustrator who created them.

7 **recreational**

This early chess piece shows that games were one type of recreational activity that Vikings found relaxing.

8 **saga**

The poem *Beowulf* tells the saga of a hero. It is a tale of his great deeds.

9 **majestic**

The mountains and inlets of former Viking lands are still a majestic, or impressive, sight.

10 **destiny**

This stone shows Vikings in Valhalla, a paradise they saw as their destiny, where they would go, if they died in battle.

Background

Artifacts: Windows into the Past

Archaeologists have unearthed many artifacts that shed new light on old cultures. For example, objects found in Scandinavia—Norway, Sweden, and Denmark—show that the Vikings were much more complex than a stereotype of ruthless people whose destiny was to raid and loot.

Majestic jewelry shows the artistry of Viking crafts. Molds, holders of molten metal, were used to forge objects of silver and gold. Chess pieces reveal how Vikings spent their recreational time.

The Vikings also wrote down stories in letters called runes. A saga might tell ancestral histories or a tale of heroes. Embodied in these pieces of the past, cultures such as the Vikings' have come vividly to life.

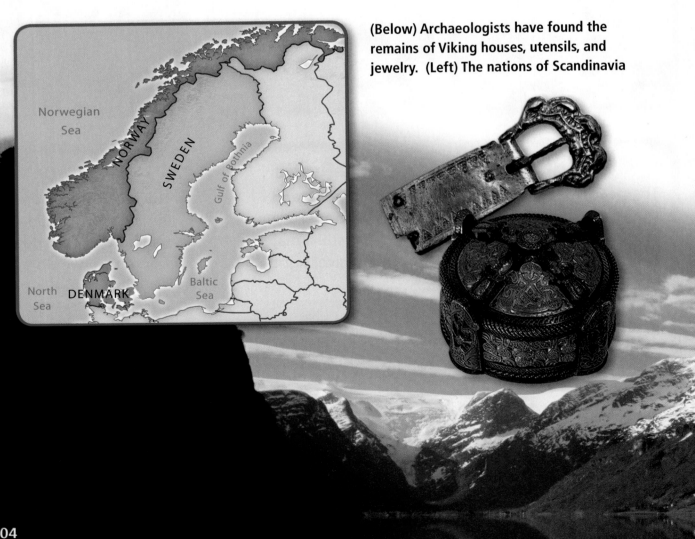

(Below) Archaeologists have found the remains of Viking houses, utensils, and jewelry. (Left) The nations of Scandinavia

Norwegian Sea

NORWAY

SWEDEN

Gulf of Bothnia

North Sea

DENMARK

Baltic Sea

Comprehension

As you read "The Real Vikings," notice how categories of people, settings, and objects are alike and different. Look for clue words, such as *also*, *as well*, and *similar to*. You can make a Venn diagram like the one below to compare and contrast people, settings, and other details.

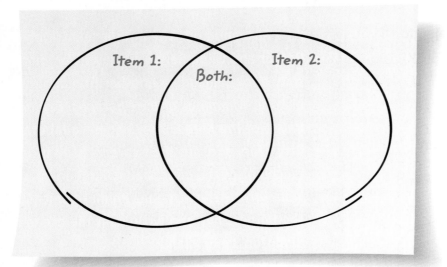

Item 1:

Both:

Item 2:

✔ **TARGET STRATEGY** **Summarize**

Using your Venn diagram to compare and contrast can help you summarize how ideas in "The Real Vikings" are alike and different. Summarizing helps you focus on the topic you are reading about.

THE REAL VIKINGS

✔ TARGET VOCABULARY

ruthless	artistry
unearthed	recreational
ancestral	saga
forge	majestic
embodied	destiny

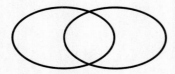

✔ TARGET SKILL

Compare and Contrast
Examine how two or more details or ideas are alike and different.

✔ TARGET STRATEGY

Summarize Briefly tell the important parts of the text in your own words.

GENRE

Informational text gives facts and examples about a topic.

Set a Purpose Before reading, set a purpose for reading based on what you know about the genre and your own experience.

MEET THE AUTHORS

Melvin Berger and Gilda Berger

As a husband-and-wife author team, Melvin Berger and Gilda Berger have written more than sixty books, including another title about early history: *Mummies of the Pharaohs: Exploring the Valley of the Kings.* They began collaborating fifty years ago, but their careers have included teaching special education (Gilda) and playing viola for the New Orleans Philharmonic (Melvin). The Bergers live and write near the ocean in East Hampton, Long Island.

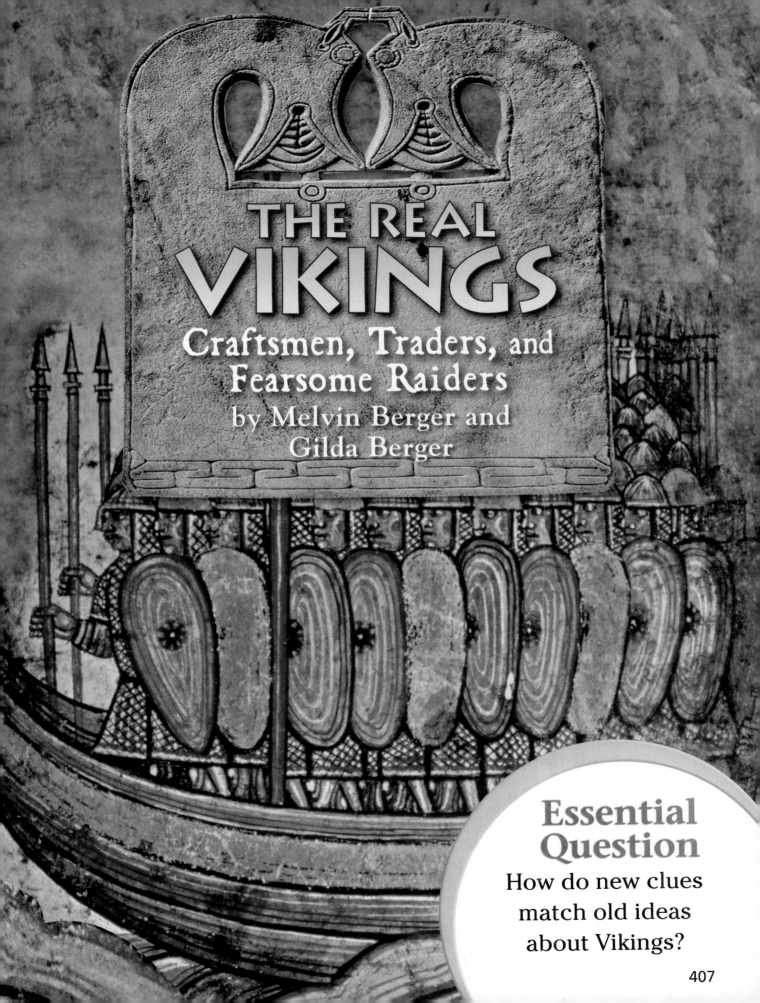

THE REAL VIKINGS

Craftsmen, Traders, and Fearsome Raiders

by Melvin Berger and
Gilda Berger

Essential Question

How do new clues
match old ideas
about Vikings?

The Vikings often sailed their majestic longships from Scandinavia and swarmed ashore to rob their neighbors—including the monks of Lindisfarne, England, in 793 C.E. Raiding, however, does not tell the whole story of the Vikings.

Who Were the Vikings?

From the Lindisfarne attack and the many other attacks that followed arose the popular—though now disputed—belief that all Vikings were cruel, ruthless pirates and murderers.

Archaeologists have recently uncovered many remains from the Viking Age, the period from around 800 to 1100, that give a more balanced view of Viking life than previously held. As experts dig in the places where Vikings lived, they are finding many everyday objects preserved in the soil. These include coins and silver jewelry, carved animal bones, furniture, clothing, boots, and weapons. Archaeologists are also uncovering the foundations of buildings and the remains of large ships.

From studies of these finds, scholars have learned that the majority of Viking Age Scandinavians did not go out raiding. Instead, most of them stayed home, where they farmed, raised cattle, and hunted and fished. Some built ships. Viking craftsmen produced a variety of goods in their workshops. Viking merchants traveled widely, trading these goods for materials from other lands.

Egil (AY gihl) Skallagrimsson, the hero of Egil's Saga, embodied both sides of the Viking character. According to the saga, he was tough and cruel, but at the same time he won fame as a merchant, farmer, and great poet.

A dig in what is now Dublin, Ireland, revealed the wooden planks of a Viking road and the remains of houses and shops.

Evidence from Viking graves tells us about everyday life. Some men and women were buried with their most valuable possessions and occasionally with their horses and dogs. Some people were buried in fine wooden ships or within enclosures of stones arranged in boat shapes. The ship settings suggest that the Vikings thought that death was followed by a voyage to the next world.

Clues to Viking life and beliefs also come from their ancestral histories and heroic legends, which families once passed on by word of mouth. On long, dark, cold winter evenings in Viking lands, family elders repeated these stories, sometimes known as sagas, again and again. Later, long after the end of the Viking Age, scribes wrote down the sagas. Among the most famous tales are *Egil's Saga*, *Erik the Red's Saga*, and *The Greenlanders' Saga*, all of which people still enjoy reading.

The few written records left by the Vikings consist of inscriptions on gravestones, road markers, weapons, and jewelry. The Vikings wrote in letters called runes, which also served as magic symbols. The 16 letters of the runic alphabet were angular in shape, which made them easy to carve into hard surfaces, such as stone or metal. Although many runic stones were memorials to dead relatives, other inscriptions marked property boundaries, noted important events, or offered thanks to a god.

From archaeological excavations, sagas, runes, and the writings of their enemies and victims, we've learned much about the Vikings, a people who triumphed over the cold and isolation of their homelands to forge a distinctive culture and destiny.

At Home in Scandinavia

Hedeby, a large, important town in Viking times, is the most thoroughly explored of all Viking sites. From remains that archaeologists have uncovered there, we have a fairly good idea of what a Viking town looked like and of how ordinary people lived there.

Both a fort and a trading center, Hedeby is located at the southeast corner of Denmark, facing the Baltic Sea. In Viking times, a high wall of earth surrounded the town. In some places the wall was 40 feet tall—the height of a four-story building. People had to walk through tunnels in the wall to get in or out of Hedeby. A small brook ran through the center of the town, providing the residents with water for drinking and washing.

Hedeby had at least two main streets, both paved with planks of wood. Most houses were built of wattle and daub—flexible willow branches threaded in and out of posts and covered with mud and cow dung. Wealthy people lived in wooden houses built from tree trunks, which were split lengthwise and placed upright in the ground to form a continuous wall. Other houses were made with wooden planks placed horizontally. Covering the houses were roofs of reed thatching or sod—thick, matted grass growing in a thin layer of earth. Behind each house was an outhouse, a well, a cesspool, and a pit for garbage.

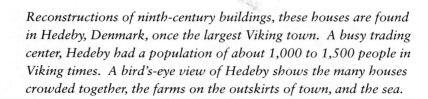

Reconstructions of ninth-century buildings, these houses are found in Hedeby, Denmark, once the largest Viking town. A busy trading center, Hedeby had a population of about 1,000 to 1,500 people in Viking times. A bird's-eye view of Hedeby shows the many houses crowded together, the farms on the outskirts of town, and the sea.

Perched amid metalworking tools, a delicate animal ornament reflects the artistry of a Viking jeweler. Viking craftsmen used molds, such as the dragon's head mold at left, to produce a variety of metal objects.

Rich merchants and craftsmen in Hedeby lived in large wooden houses that measured about 16 by 40 feet. The living room had a central fireplace with a cooking pot hanging over the hearth. The fireplace provided both heat and light. A small hole in the roof let the smoke out. Low earth platforms, built up on both sides of the fireplace, served as benches for sitting and sleeping.

The houses had no windows. Light came from the fireplace or from lamps, which were small iron or soapstone bowls holding wicks, probably made of plant fibers, for burning oil. Still, it must have been dark indoors—as well as smelly and smoky—so many tasks were probably done outside.

The wattle-and-daub huts of the poorer people of Hedeby were about 9 by 12 feet. They had a fireplace in one corner and earthen benches along the walls.

From objects found at Hedeby, it appears that many of the townspeople worked as merchants and craftsmen. Some of the craftsmen made jewelry. Others were expert glassblowers, who produced everything from glass beads for necklaces to drinking cups. Some craftsmen carved objects of horn or bone. Still others made their living weaving and sewing cloth.

Archaeologists have found two important tools that Viking craftsmen used to make marvelous objects from metal: the crucible and the mold. The crucible, a pot of hard-fired clay, allowed workers to melt metal at very high temperatures before shaping it. Molds, also made of clay, made it possible to easily produce a great many objects, from pots to rings to battle-axes to statues.

STOP AND THINK

Compare and Contrast Use information on these pages to compare and contrast the houses of poorer and wealthier people in Hedeby.

Viking merchants brought fine goods from Germany, France, England, Constantinople, and Persia to trade in Hedeby. Indeed, people from all over Scandinavia visited the town's bustling market to buy jewelry, silk, lace, and other luxuries. Slaves captured on raids were also traded at Hedeby.

While some Vikings lived in towns such as Hedeby, most people were farmers in the countryside. A typical farm contained the family house, stables and barns for the farm animals, a workshop to make metal tools, and small huts for slaves. Farms on the coast usually had a shed to hold the farmer's boat during the winter months.

Farmers raised mainly corn, peas, cabbage, barley, and oats. They kept cattle both for meat and for milk. The farmers' wives churned the milk into butter or made cheese, which they kept in cold storerooms, using the winter snow as a kind of deep freeze. They also pickled and smoked meat and stored dried peas and beans. Without these preserved foods, the people would have had nothing to eat during the winter.

Every member of a farm family shared in the work. Men worked in the fields, hunted and fished, and looked after the livestock. Women preserved and cooked the food, cared for the children and the sick, spun and wove wool, and sewed, embroidered, and washed clothes. They ran the farm while their husbands and sons were away fishing or on trading or raiding voyages—sometimes for months or years at a time. Children helped their parents around the house and farm. Even the youngest ones contributed by feeding the animals or gathering firewood.

Viking family groups were large. A man and his wife, their children—including older sons with their wives and children—and the grandparents all lived together on the family farm. When a daughter married, she usually left home to join her husband's family.

Vikings ate two main meals a day. The women served the first meal at about eight or nine o'clock in the morning, which was after the farmers had already worked in the fields for about two hours. The other meal, which they ate at about seven or eight o'clock in the evening, marked the end of the day's work.

At dinner, members of the family sat around the table, sometimes on the same benches they slept on at night. They ate off rectangular

In this scene of a Viking home, a woman stirs a cooking pot over a hearth. The fire provides both heat and light. The hole in the roof allows smoke to escape and serves as another source of light for the windowless house.

wooden platters or from soapstone bowls, using only spoons and knives, which they carried in their belts. Forks were a later invention.

In good times, Viking families supped on soups and stews of beef or mutton or on fish from the sea. Women roasted meat on huge spits over the hearth and cooked vegetables in big iron cauldrons. They baked bread in stone ovens or on long-handled flat metal griddles placed on the ashes of the fire.

When not working, Vikings played games such as chess and went swimming and skiing. A board game called *merils*, which is similar to checkers, has been found in Viking graves. Other recreational activities included fencing, running, and wrestling, as well as training falcons to hunt wild birds and animals.

Winter sports included racing on snowshoes and ice-skating. Skates were made of sharpened animal bones attached to shoes with leather straps. Skaters used long, sharpened poles to push themselves on the ice. In warmer weather, ball games were popular.

> **STOP AND THINK**
> **Summarize** Use facts on this page to summarize a typical Viking dinner.

413

The Vikings were fond of music. They celebrated victories and festivals in song, which might be accompanied by harps or lyres. From findings at various archaeological sites, we know that the Vikings also had simple wind instruments. Pipes unearthed in Sweden were made of hollowed-out animal bones, with holes drilled along the length to produce the different tones.

If a girl wanted to marry into a good family, she had to be able to sing and play an instrument. Boys also had to be musical, but they needed to master other skills as well, especially the use of weapons. One young Viking man boasted:

"There are nine skills known to me—

> At the chessboard I am skillful,
> Runic writing I know well,
> Books I like; with tools am handy,
> Good with snowshoes,
> Rowing, and shooting,
> And expert with harp and verse."

Life was hard in Viking times—but there was obviously still time to relax and have fun.

STOP AND THINK
Author's Craft The author changes to first person **point of view** by using the exact words of a Viking man. How does this enrich the selection?

Carved from walrus tusks, these ivory chess pieces date back to 12th-century Norway.

Your Turn

Then and Now

A Voice from the Past Imagine that "The Real Vikings" had been written from a Viking's point of view. Write a paragraph explaining how the selection would be different. POINT OF VIEW

On the Record

Hold a Press Conference Role-play a press conference in which Vikings explain why their reputation as fierce raiders is unfair. Have group members choose roles as reporters or Vikings. Before the performance, write some possible questions and responses. SMALL GROUP

Changing Views

Turn and Talk With a partner, discuss the types of things that might change our ideas about people in history. Then talk about what clues tell us that some ideas about Vikings turned out to be true. What might cause our view of Vikings to change in the future?

COMPARE AND CONTRAST

✔ **TARGET VOCABULARY**

ruthless	unearthed
ancestral	forge
embodied	artistry
recreational	saga
majestic	destiny

GENRE
Poetry uses the sound and rhythm of words in a variety of forms to show images and express feelings.

TEXT FOCUS
Imagery Poetry often creates a vivid description by using exact words that appeal to the senses.

POEMS THAT BOAST

The poet at the end of "The Real Vikings" doesn't brag that he is a ruthless raider. Instead, he boasts about his artistry with words and how well he plays chess. These poems also boast. "A Mighty Fine Fella" and "Super Samson Simpson" have embodied the idea of bigness in majestic images. In "A Song of Greatness," the narrator honors the sagas of her ancestral heritage. She is confident about her destiny.

A MIGHTY FINE FELLA

by Eloise Greenfield

I don't want to be
Mr. Big
with a hundred different suits
counting my money in public
and showing off
in my new sports car
I'm a mighty fine fella
And I don't need things
to prove it

SUPER SAMSON SIMPSON

by Jack Prelutsky

I am Super Samson Simpson,
I'm superlatively strong,
I like to carry elephants,
I do it all day long,
I pick up half a dozen
and hoist them in the air,
it's really somewhat simple,
for I have strength to spare.

My muscles are enormous,
they bulge from top to toe,
and when I carry elephants,
they ripple to and fro,
but I am not the strongest
in the Simpson family,
for when I carry elephants,
my grandma carries me.

A SONG OF GREATNESS
CHIPPEWA TRADITIONAL

by Mary Austin

When I hear the old men
Telling of heroes,
Telling of great deeds
Of ancient days,
When I hear that telling
Then I think within me
I too am one of these.

When I hear the people
Praising great ones,
Then I know that I too
Shall be esteemed,
I too when my time comes
Shall do mightily.

POEM OF CELEBRATION

Use a poem in this selection as a model to help you write a poem celebrating yourself. Think about your talents. Maybe one is recreational, such as a sport. Once you have unearthed your skills, forge them into a poem that celebrates you!

Making Connections

Text to Self

Write a Description Archaeologists use objects as clues to Viking daily life. Imagine that two of *your* possessions are dug up a thousand years from now. Write a description an archaeologist might write for each object, explaining its use in your society.

Text to Text

Connect to Poetry Compare two of the poems from "Poems That Boast." How are they alike and different? Think about the character narrating each poem, the tone of the poem, and the poet's purpose in writing it. List your ideas in a chart or Venn diagram.

Text to World

Trading Places Most young people in the Viking culture lived with their families on farms. Think about how a typical young person would spend his or her day on the farm. What might young people in the modern world enjoy about the Viking way of life? What about that way of life might be difficult for them? Share your thoughts with a partner.

Grammar

What Are the Four Principal Parts of Verbs? Every verb has four basic forms called **principal parts**. You use the principal parts to form all verb tenses. You use some of these principal parts in other ways, too. For example, you use the **present participle** and **past participle** forms of verbs as describing words. The chart below shows the four principal parts of some regular and some irregular verbs.

Principal Parts of Regular Verbs			
Present	**Present Participle**	**Past**	**Past Participle**
learn	(is) learning	learned	(has) learned
stay	(is) staying	stayed	(has) stayed
raise	(is) raising	raised	(has) raised

Principal Parts of Irregular Verbs			
Present	**Present Participle**	**Past**	**Past Participle**
dig	(is) digging	dug	(has) dug
come	(is) coming	came	(has) come
know	(is) knowing	knew	(has) known

 **Copy the chart below onto another sheet of paper. Fill in the missing principal parts.**

	Present	**Present Participle**	**Past**	**Past Participle**
1	uncover	(is) _____	uncovered	(has) _____
2	run	(is) running	_____	(has) _____
3	build	(is) _____	_____	(has) built
4	carve	(is) carving	_____	(has) _____

Sentence Fluency Present participles and past participles can be used to describe nouns. Sometimes you can combine two sentences into one by using a participle to describe a noun.

Two Sentences

Quite a few remains have been uncovered in the town of Hedeby.

These remains give us a good idea of what ancient Viking towns were like.

Sentences Combined by Using a Participle

Uncovered remains in the town of Hedeby give us a good idea of what ancient Viking towns were like.

Connect Grammar to Writing

As you revise your compare-contrast paragraph, look for sentences that you can combine by using participles to modify nouns.

Write to Inform

☑ **Ideas** One way to write to inform is to compose a **compare-contrast paragraph**. A compare-contrast paragraph tells how two things are alike and how they are different. It starts with a topic sentence introducing the two things that are focused on. It includes supporting sentences that describe similarities and differences in a clear and organized way.

   Whitney drafted a compare-contrast paragraph about the types of work Viking men and women did on a farm. Then she added details and examples to make the similarities and differences clearer.

Writing Traits Checklist

☑ **Ideas**

   Did I include enough examples to make the similarities and differences clear?

☑ **Organization**
   Does my organization follow the structure of a compare-contrast paragraph?

☑ **Sentence Fluency**
   Did I form and use verbs properly?

☑ **Word Choice**
   Did I use specific nouns and verbs to show differences and similarities?

☑ **Voice**
   Is my writing clear and informative?

☑ **Conventions**
   Did I use correct spelling, grammar, and punctuation?

Revised Draft

Most Vikings lived on farms, and men and women alike worked to provide food and clothing for their families. Their jobs were similar in that both men and women did chores that required physical strength and endurance. However, the particular jobs that they did were very different. Men hunted, fished, and took care of cattle.

Both men and women were busy from dawn until dark.

Men's Work, Women's Work
by Whitney Viers

Most Vikings lived on farms, and men and women alike worked to provide food and clothing for their families. Their jobs were similar in that both men and women did chores that required physical strength and endurance. Both men and women were busy from dawn until dark. However, the particular jobs that they did were very different. Men hunted, fished, and took care of cattle. They tended fields of many different crops. Women, on the other hand, cooked and served two meals a day. They made butter and cheese, preserved meat, and dried peas and beans for the family to eat in the winter. They also took care of the children and spun and wove wool to make clothes for the family. By doing these different jobs, both men and women were able to support their families.

> In my final paper, I added details to make the similarities and differences clearer. I also made sure that I formed verbs properly.

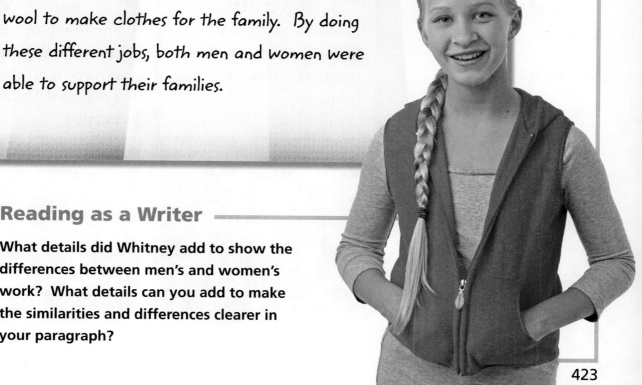

Reading as a Writer

What details did Whitney add to show the differences between men's and women's work? What details can you add to make the similarities and differences clearer in your paragraph?

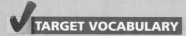

archaeologists

replicas

lustrous

elaborate

excavate

distinct

dignified

mythical

temperaments

precede

Vocabulary
Reader

Context
Cards

Vocabulary in Context

1 archaeologists

Archaeologists are scientists who study items left behind by cultures from the past.

2 replicas

Replicas, or copies, have been made of ancient Chinese pottery and statues.

3 lustrous

Chinese royalty wore lustrous silk robes. The material seemed to shine or gleam.

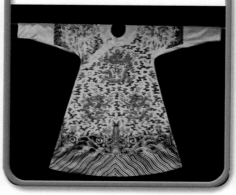

4 elaborate

The Great Wall of China was an elaborate building project. It involved a great deal of careful detail.

- **Study each Context Card.**

- **Ask a question that uses one of the Vocabulary words.**

5 excavate

To learn about ancient China, men and women excavate artifacts that have been buried for centuries.

6 distinct

The Chinese writing system has hundreds of distinct, or different, characters.

7 dignified

Members of the emperor's court acted in a manner that was dignified, or worthy of honor.

8 mythical

The Chinese dragon is a mythical creature, one that exists only in the imagination.

9 temperaments

According to Chinese astrology, people born in certain years have similar temperaments, or personalities.

10 precede

A horseman might precede, or go ahead of, the emperor during his travels.

Background

✔ TARGET VOCABULARY **Introducing the Emperor** An emperor is a powerful figure, ruling over many distinct kingdoms, not just one. While commanding millions, an emperor may show as many different temperaments as his subjects. He may appear serene and dignified in a lustrous silk robe, or fierce and warlike at the head of a vast army. Some emperors see themselves as almost mythical, craving immortality, or eternal life. For others, the goal is to precede a long line of future emperors. In life, they may be surrounded by elaborate monuments and replicas created by artisans, makers of art and crafts. When archaeologists excavate the tomb of an emperor, however, what evidence will they find of all that power?

CHINA

PACIFIC OCEAN

Key

◼ Qin Dynasty
— Present-day borders

(Left) Qin Shihuang (259–210 B.C.E.) was China's first emperor. Qin's empire united seven kingdoms. One of the achievements of his reign was beginning China's Great Wall.

Comprehension

✔ **TARGET SKILL** **Fact and Opinion**

As you read "The Emperor's Silent Army," look for facts—ideas that can be proven—and opinions—ideas that cannot be proven. Signal words such as *may*, *probably*, or *is considered* often point to opinions. You can make a graphic organizer like the one below to keep track of facts and opinions as you read.

Fact	Opinion
Example:	Example:

✔ **TARGET STRATEGY** **Question**

Identifying facts and opinions in your graphic organizer can help you ask further questions about "The Emperor's Silent Army." Asking questions and finding the answers help to keep you focused on what you read.

Main Selection

✓ TARGET VOCABULARY

archaeologists	distinct
replicas	dignified
lustrous	mythical
elaborate	temperaments
excavate	precede

✓ TARGET SKILL

Fact and Opinion Decide whether an idea can be proved or is a feeling or belief.

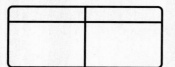

✓ TARGET STRATEGY

Question Ask questions about a selection before you read, as you read, and after you read.

GENRE

Informational text gives facts and examples about a topic.

Set a Purpose Before reading, set a purpose for reading based on what you know about the genre and your own experience.

MEET THE AUTHOR
Jane O'Connor

Jane O'Connor is the author of more than thirty books for all age groups. Writing runs in O'Connor's family. Her younger son, Tim, is an author; she has collaborated with her husband, Jim (*The Magic Top Mystery*, *Slime Time*); and when her older son, Robert, was in sixth grade, the two of them wrote the book *Super Cluck*, about a chicken from outer space. O'Connor's nonfiction includes books on art, movie special effects, and the White House.

THE EMPEROR'S SILENT ARMY

Terracotta Warriors of Ancient China

by Jane O'Connor

Essential Question

What can we prove about China's first emperor?

A STRANGE DISCOVERY
LINTONG COUNTY, PEOPLE'S REPUBLIC OF CHINA, MARCH 1974

It's just an ordinary day in early spring, or so three farmers think as they trudge across a field in northern China. They are looking for a good place to dig a well. There has been a drought, and they must find water or risk losing their crops later in the year.

The farmers choose a spot near a grove of persimmon trees. Down they dig, five feet, ten feet. Still no water. They decide to keep on digging a little deeper. All of a sudden, one of the farmers feels his shovel strike against something hard. Is it a rock? It's difficult to see at the bottom of a dark hole, so the farmer kneels down for a closer look. No, it isn't a rock. It seems to be clay, and not raw clay but clay that has been baked and made into something. But what?

Now, more carefully, the men dig around the something. Perhaps it is a pot or a vase. However, what slowly reveals itself is the pottery head of a man who stares back at them, open-eyed and amazingly real looking. The farmers have never seen anything like it before. But they do remember stories that some of the old people in their village have told, stories of a "pottery man" found many years ago not far from where they are now. The villagers had been scared that the pottery man would bring bad luck so they broke it to bits, which were then reburied and forgotten.

The terracotta figures were discovered in the countryside of northern China.

STOP AND THINK

Author's Craft The author begins the selection with a **flashback**, telling about an earlier event as if it were happening now. Why do you think she chose to use this technique?

The terracotta army was discovered when well-diggers found the head of a "pottery man" like this one. No photographs were taken that day.

The three well-diggers are not so superstitious. They report their discovery to a local official. Soon a group of archaeologists arrives to search the area more closely. Maybe they will find pieces of a clay body to go with the clay head.

In fact, they find much more.

During the weeks and months that follow, the archaeologists dig out more pottery men, which now are called by a more dignified term—terracotta figurines. The figurines are soldiers. That much is clear. But they come from a time long ago, when Chinese warriors wore knee-length robes, armor made from small iron "fish scales," and elaborate topknot hairdos. All of the soldiers are life-size or a little bigger and weigh as much as four hundred pounds. They stand at attention as if waiting for the command to charge into battle. The only thing missing is their weapons. And those are found too—hundreds of real bronze swords, daggers, and battle-axes as well as thousands of scattered arrowheads—all so perfectly made that, after cleaning, their ancient tips are still sharp enough to split a hair!

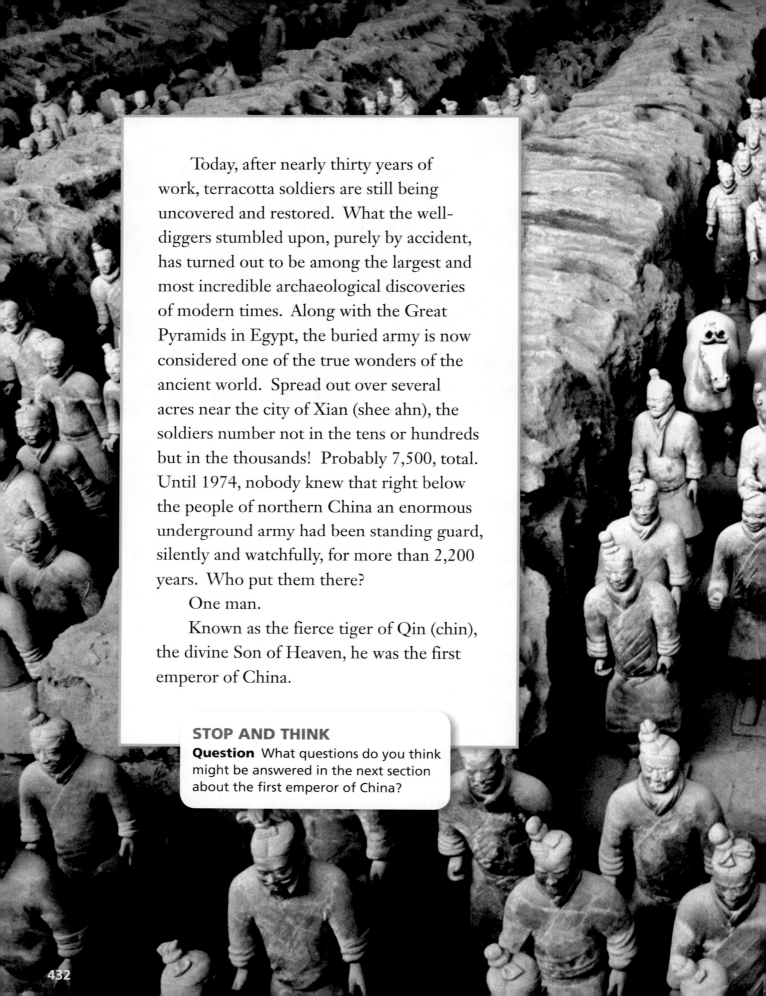

Today, after nearly thirty years of work, terracotta soldiers are still being uncovered and restored. What the well-diggers stumbled upon, purely by accident, has turned out to be among the largest and most incredible archaeological discoveries of modern times. Along with the Great Pyramids in Egypt, the buried army is now considered one of the true wonders of the ancient world. Spread out over several acres near the city of Xian (shee ahn), the soldiers number not in the tens or hundreds but in the thousands! Probably 7,500, total. Until 1974, nobody knew that right below the people of northern China an enormous underground army had been standing guard, silently and watchfully, for more than 2,200 years. Who put them there?

One man.

Known as the fierce tiger of Qin (chin), the divine Son of Heaven, he was the first emperor of China.

STOP AND THINK

Question What questions do you think might be answered in the next section about the first emperor of China?

Although more than seven thousand strong, the terracotta army is small compared to the emperor's real army.

THE QUEST FOR IMMORTALITY

Before the time of Qin Shihuang (chin shir hwong), who lived from 259 to 210 B.C.E., there was no China. Instead there were seven separate kingdoms, each with its own language, currency, and ruler. For hundreds of years they had been fighting one another. The kingdom of Qin was the fiercest; soldiers received their pay only after they had presented their generals with the cut-off heads of enemy warriors. By 221 B.C.E. the ruler of the Qin kingdom had "eaten up his neighbors like a silkworm devouring a leaf," according to an ancient historian. The name China comes from Qin.

The king of Qin now ruled over an immense empire—around one million square miles that stretched north and west to the Gobi (GOH bee) desert, south to present-day Vietnam, and east to the Yellow Sea. To the people of the time, this was the entire civilized world. Not for another hundred years would the Chinese know that empires existed beyond their boundaries. To the ruler of Qin, being called king was no longer grand enough. He wanted a title that no one else had ever had before. What he chose was Qin Shihuang. This means "first emperor, God in Heaven, and Almighty of the Universe" all rolled into one.

No paintings exist of the emperor done in his lifetime, so there is no way to know how faithful this portrait is.

434

But no title, however superhuman it sounded, could protect him from what he feared most—dying. More than anything, the emperor wanted to live forever. According to legend, a magic elixir had granted eternal life to the people of the mythical Eastern Islands. Over the years, the emperor sent expeditions out to sea in search of the islands and the magic potion. But each time they came back empty-handed.

If he couldn't live forever, then Qin Shihuang was determined to live as long as possible. He ate powdered jade and drank mercury in the belief that they would prolong his life. In fact, these "medicines" were poison and may have caused the emperor to fall sick and die while on a tour of the easternmost outposts of his empire. He was forty-nine years old.

If word of Qin Shihuang's death got out while he was away from the capital, there might be a revolt. So his ministers kept the news a secret. With the emperor's body inside his chariot, the entire party traveled back to the capital city. Meals were brought into the emperor's chariot; daily reports on affairs were delivered as usual— all to keep up the appearance that the emperor was alive and well. However, it was summer, and a terrible smell began to come from the chariot. But the clever ministers found a way to account for the stench. A cart was loaded with smelly salted fish and made to precede the chariot, overpowering and masking any foul odors coming from the dead emperor. And so Qin Shihuang returned to the capital for burial.

The tomb of Qin Shihuang had been under construction for more than thirty years. It was begun when he was a young boy of thirteen and was still not finished when he died. Even incomplete, the emperor's tomb was enormous, larger than his largest palace. According to legend, it had a domed ceiling inlaid with clusters of pearls to represent the sun, moon, and stars. Below was a gigantic relief map of the world, made from bronze. Bronze hills and mountains rose up from the floor, with rivers of mercury flowing into a mercury sea. Along the banks of the rivers were models of the emperor's palaces and cities, all exact replicas of the real ones.

This detail of a silk robe shows an embroidered dragon, the symbol of Chinese emperors.

In ancient times, the Chinese believed that life after death was not so very different from life on earth. The soul of a dead person could continue to enjoy all the pleasures of everyday life. So people who were rich enough constructed elaborate underground tombs filled with silk robes, jewelry with precious stones, furniture, games, boats, chariots—everything the dead person could possibly need or want.

Qin Shihuang knew that grave robbers would try their best to loot the treasures in the tomb. So he had machines put inside the tomb that produced the rumble of thunder to scare off intruders, and mechanical crossbows at the entrance were set to fire arrows automatically should anyone dare trespass. The emperor also made certain that the workers who carried his coffin to its final resting place never revealed its exact whereabouts. As the men worked their way back through the tunnels to the tomb's entrance, a stone door came crashing down, and they were left to die, sealed inside the tomb along with the body of the emperor.

Even all these measures, however, were not enough to satisfy the emperor. And so, less than a mile from the tomb, in underground trenches, the terracotta warriors were stationed. Just as flesh-and-blood troops had protected him during his lifetime, the terracotta troops were there to protect their ruler against any enemy for all eternity.

THE FACES OF ANCIENT CHINA

About two thousand soldiers have been unearthed, yet, amazingly, so far no two are the same. The army includes men of all different ages, from different parts of China, with different temperaments. A young soldier looks both excited and nervous; an older officer, perhaps a veteran of many wars, appears tired, resigned. Some soldiers seem lost in thought, possibly dreaming of their return home; others look proud and confident. Although from a distance the figures appear almost identical, like giant-size toy soldiers, each is a distinct work of art.

Did real-life models pose for the figures? Probably not. But hundreds of craftsmen from all over the empire spent more than ten years in workshops set up near the pits creating the warriors. It is likely that they made the faces of the soldiers look like the faces of people that they knew from home.

The uniforms of the terracotta figures are exact copies in clay of what real soldiers of the day wore. The soldier's uniform tells his rank in the army. The lowest-ranking soldiers are bareheaded and wear heavy knee-length tunics but no armor. Often their legs are wrapped in cloth shin guards for protection.

The generals' uniforms are the most elegant. Their caps sometimes sport a pheasant feather; their fancy shoes curl up at the toes; and their fine armor is made from small iron fish scales. Tassels on their armor are also a mark of their high rank.

The terracotta soldiers are now the ghostly grayish color of baked clay, clay that came from nearby Mount Li. Originally the soldiers were all brightly colored. Tiny bits of paint can still be seen on many of the figures and are proof that uniforms came in a blaze of colors—purple, blue, green, yellow, red, and orange. The colors of each soldier's uniform indicated not only which part of the army he belonged to—cavalry or infantry, for example—but also what his particular rank was. The terracotta horses were fully painted, too, in brown with pink ears, nostrils, and mouths. Unfortunately, when figures are dug out of the ground, most of the paint on them peels off and sticks to the surrounding earth. Also, when exposed to air, the paint tends to crumble into dust.

The colored computer image shows how the general would have looked originally.

Today groups of artisans in workshops near the three pits make replicas of the soldiers, following the techniques used 2,200 years ago. Their work helps archaeologists learn more about how the original figures were created. Even though the workers today have the advantages of modern kilns that register temperatures exactly, no copies have ever come out as hard or as lustrous as the ancient originals. (The workers of today are also not under the same kind of pressure as the emperor's potters—if they made a mistake, they were killed!)

Who were the potters who made the original soldiers? For the most part, they have remained anonymous. In ancient times, being a craftsman was considered lowly work. However, some soldiers are signed, probably by the master potter in charge of a workshop. The signature is like a stamp of approval, a sign of quality control.

Of course, the creators of the terracotta warriors never intended their work to be seen by anyone other than the emperor. That is a strange notion for twenty-first-century minds to accept. Artists today want their work to be seen, enjoyed, admired. But as soon as the emperor's army was completed, it was buried. Pits were dug twenty feet deep. Green-tiled floors were laid down. Dirt walls were constructed, creating tunnels in which the soldiers and horses and chariots were placed. A wooden roof was built overhead, and then ten feet of dirt was shoveled on top of the army. It was supposed to remain undisturbed for all eternity, but it did not turn out that way. How surprised the Qin sculptors would be by the crowds of people from all over the world who come to see their creations!

This cross-section drawing shows how soldiers in Pit 1 were placed in underground tunnels, which were separated by earthen walls and covered by a wooden roof.

✔️ **STOP AND THINK**

Fact and Opinion In the second paragraph, find one fact and one opinion about the potters and their work.

INSIDE THE EMPEROR'S TOMB

What exactly is the terracotta army guarding so steadfastly? What, besides the body of the dead emperor, is inside the tomb? The answer is that nobody knows. And the government of China has no plans to excavate and find out.

In ancient China it was the custom to build a natural-looking hill on top of a person's tomb. The more important a person was, the bigger the hill. Thousands of years of harsh weather have worn down the emperor's mound; originally it was four hundred feet high, almost as high as the biggest of the three Great Pyramids in Egypt.

Like the ancient Egyptians, the ancient Chinese believed that the body of a dead person should be preserved as a "home" for the soul. However, the Chinese did not make a person's body into a mummy. They believed that jade had magic powers, among them the ability to keep a dead body from decaying. In Chinese tombs from the first century B.C.E., bodies of noblemen and princesses have been found wearing entire suits of jade. It is believed that Qin Shihuang is buried in just such a suit, the thousands of small tiles all beautifully carved and sewn together with gold thread. And over this jade burial outfit, his body is supposedly covered in a blanket of pearls.

As for all the things placed with the emperor, certainly they must be grand beyond imagining—silk robes embroidered with dragons, gem-encrusted crowns and jewelry, musical instruments, hand-carved furniture, lamps, beautiful dishes, cooking pots, and golden utensils. Like the pharaohs of ancient Egypt, the first emperor would have made certain that he had everything he might possibly want in the afterlife. But unless his tomb is excavated, what these treasures look like will remain a mystery.

The body of the emperor, which has never been recovered, may wear a jade funeral suit like this one found in the tomb of a Chinese princess from the late second century.

Your Turn

Express Yourself

Write an Opinion Paragraph
Think about Qin Shihuang and life in ancient China. Would Qin Shihuang make a good leader today? Write a paragraph in which you express your opinion and support it with facts from the selection. SOCIAL STUDIES

Everyday Life

Favorite Things Imagine that Qin Shihuang lived in modern times. What kinds of things might he want placed in his tomb? With a partner, make a list of items a modern emperor might want placed in his or her tomb. Create a poster with photographs or other illustrations of the items, and present the poster to another pair of students.

PARTNERS

Facts and Artifacts

Turn and Talk Review the selection with a partner, and read about the artifacts that have been found in China. Discuss what facts we can learn about Qin Shihuang and his time in power by studying such artifacts. Then discuss the opinions people might form based on those discoveries.

FACT AND OPINION

✓ **TARGET VOCABULARY**

archaeologists	replicas
lustrous	elaborate
excavate	distinct
dignified	mythical
temperaments	precede

GENRE
Informational text, such as this encyclopedia article, gives facts about a topic and is usually organized around main ideas and supporting details.

TEXT FOCUS
Headings identify the main ideas of sections of a text, such as chapters, paragraphs, or captions.

Ancient China
Visual Arts

Chinese civilization began about seven thousand years ago near a river, the Huang He. Over time, ruling families known as dynasties came to power. People skilled in calligraphy, pottery, carving, and bronzeworking created works of art. Archaeologists today continue to excavate burial sites and buildings. They are finding treasures that give us many details about ancient Chinese culture.

This 56-foot-tall statue of Buddha in northern China seems both powerful and dignified.

Shang Dynasty: 1650–1050 B.C.E.

Calligraphy, or the art of writing, developed during China's first recorded dynasty, the Shang. Chinese pictographs were engraved into bones or written on bamboo. Other artists from this time formed glazed pottery and bronze figures.

Shang leaders read cracks in oracle bones as answers to important questions. Spoken answers would precede the written ones. Then calligraphers would engrave the answers on the bones.

Han Dynasty: 202 B.C.E.–220 C.E.

Artists of the Han Dynasty created elaborate items from bronze and jade. Chinese crafts and silk fabrics traveled west on the trade route known as the Silk Road. Western ideas began to enter Chinese thought and art at this time.

The artist who created this bronze figure may have been inspired by mythical flying horses.

Tang Dynasty: 618–906 C.E.

During the Tang dynasty, the art of making porcelain was perfected. A white clay called kaolin was baked at high temperatures, creating a lustrous material like glass.

Buddhism became China's official religion at this time. Artwork reflected Buddhist ideas, and artists painted the life of the Buddha in colorful natural settings.

This glazed porcelain Tang vase comes from Henan province.

Song Dynasty: 960–1279 C.E.

The Song Dynasty emphasized the ideas of the philosopher Confucius. He taught that there should be harmony between individuals and society. Artists painted everyday pictures that showed people's temperaments. Landscape paintings reflected the ideas of Daoism, a religion that stressed balance between humans and nature.

(background) More than just replicas of nature, *shanshui* (mountain-water) landscapes show nature's distinct beauty.

The Qingming scroll is ten inches high and almost six yards long. Details in the scroll show parts of city life during the Song Dynasty.

Making Connections

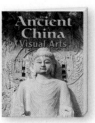

Text to Self

Share Your Views Would you want to trade places with Qin Shihuang or another emperor? Why or why not? If you did trade places, how would you use your powers? Jot down your thoughts and then discuss them with a partner.

Text to Text

Connect to Social Studies Share your knowledge of Chinese history. Construct a timeline of dynasties. Research the Qin Dynasty (221–206 B.C.E.), as well as other dynasties referred to in "The Emperor's Silent Army" and "Ancient China: Visual Arts." In your timeline, include labels and captions that briefly describe some of the remarkable features of each time period.

Text to World

Locate Dig Sites There are archaeological digs taking place all over the world. Choose a country or continent. Use the Internet to find the location of any digs taking place there. Share your findings with the class. Tell where the digs are located and what scientists have discovered.

Grammar

What Are Some Other Kinds of Pronouns? Words like *someone* and *something* are **indefinite pronouns**. They refer to an unidentified person or thing. The words *this, that, these,* and *those* are called **demonstrative pronouns** when they are subjects or objects in a sentence. Words like *himself* and *itself* that refer back to the subject of a sentence are called **reflexive pronouns**. When words such as *who, what,* and *which* begin questions, they are called **interrogative pronouns**.

Academic Language

indefinite pronoun
demonstrative pronoun
reflexive pronoun
interrogative pronoun

Kinds of Pronouns
indefinite pronoun The farmer's shovel strikes something.
reflexive pronoun He asks himself what the object might be.
demonstrative pronoun This could be an important discovery.
interrogative pronoun What will he and the other farmers find?

Turn and Talk **With a partner, read aloud each sentence below. Tell whether the word in bold type is an indefinite, a demonstrative, a reflexive, or an interrogative pronoun.**

1 The farmers found **themselves** staring at a pottery head.

2 **Someone** remembered stories about discoveries of pottery men long ago.

3 **What** would the farmers do next?

4 **That** was the reason archaeologists came to the area to dig.

Sentence Fluency Repeating words or phrases in one sentence after another can make your writing seem dull and boring. To fix this, sometimes you can join sentences by replacing a word or phrase with a pronoun.

Repetitive Sentences

Emperor Qin Shihuang had a strong desire to become immortal. The emperor's strong desire to become immortal caused him to send explorers in search of a legendary potion.

Smoother Combined Sentence

Emperor Qin Shihuang had a strong desire to become immortal, and that caused him to send explorers in search of a legendary potion.

Connect Grammar to Writing

As you revise your problem-solution paragraph, look for sentences that you can combine by replacing a word or phrase with a pronoun.

Write to Inform

✓ Organization A **problem-solution paragraph** is a paragraph that explains a problem and suggests a possible solution. Begin your paragraph by writing a topic sentence that states the problem. Provide enough facts and details to make the problem clear. Once you have described the problem, explain how the problem should be solved. End your paragraph with a concluding sentence.

Warren felt that his community wasn't bicycle-friendly, so he drafted a problem-solution paragraph about it. To improve his organization, he moved a sentence that was out of order and added a transition word.

Writing Traits Checklist

✓ **Ideas**
Did I include enough facts and details to make the problem and solution clear?

✓ **Organization**
Did I explain the problem first and then the solution?

✓ **Sentence Fluency**
Did I form and use pronouns properly?

✓ **Word Choice**
Did I use transition words to signal each solution?

✓ **Voice**
Did I sound interested in my topic?

✓ **Conventions**
Did I use correct spelling, grammar, and punctuation?

Revised Draft

Maplewood is a great community to live in, but it has a problem: it's not bicycle-friendly. Bicycling is dangerous here! First, ^ The city should add striped bike lanes to major streets. When my friends and I ride our bikes to school, we have to travel along busy streets with no bike lanes. To get downtown, we have to cross three major intersections. I have a few solutions. ^

Making Maplewood Bicycle-Friendly

by Warren Brown

Maplewood is a great community to live in, but it has a problem: it's not bicycle-friendly. Bicycling is dangerous here! When my friends and I ride our bikes to school, we have to travel along busy streets with no bike lanes. To get downtown, we have to cross three major intersections. I have a few solutions. First, the city should add striped bike lanes to major streets. Studies show that both bicyclists and car drivers are more comfortable when there are bike lanes. Bike lanes only have to be four feet wide, so there is plenty of room for that here. My second suggestion is to put up bike signs at busy intersections. They would remind people to share the road. Finally, the city should install bicycle racks downtown. These improvements would make Maplewood a great bicycle town!

In my final paper, I moved a sentence that was out of order and added transitions. I also made sure that I used pronouns properly.

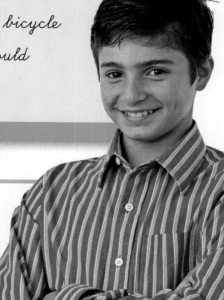

Reading as a Writer

Which sentence did Warren move? What transition did he add? Can you move any sentences or add transitions to improve the organization of your own paragraph?

steadfast

rash

bitterly

unravels

labyrinth

fury

embrace

abandon

massive

somber

Vocabulary
Reader

Context
Cards

Vocabulary in Context

1 **steadfast**

The Greek hero Odysseus is steadfast. He stays true to his goal of returning home.

2 **rash**

Icarus acts in a rash, or foolish, manner when he chooses to fly close to the sun. The heat melts his wings, and he falls.

3 **bitterly**

The hero Heracles fights bitterly, in anger, with a fierce wild boar before he defeats it.

4 **unravels**

Each day, Penelope weaves a cloth while waiting for Odysseus to return. Each night, she unravels it again.

450

- **Study each Context Card.**
- **Tell a story about two or more pictures, using Vocabulary words of your choice.**

5   labyrinth

King Minos of Crete has a twisting labyrinth built. The maze is home for the Minotaur, a monster.

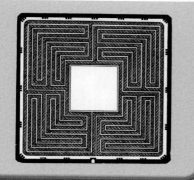

6   fury

The warrior Achilles fights bravely during the fury, or violence, of the Trojan War.

7   embrace

When Odysseus finally returns home, he hugs his wife, greeting her with a warm embrace.

8   abandon

A god or other character in a myth might help a person in need or abandon her to her fate.

9   massive

During the Trojan War, Greek soldiers slip into Troy by hiding in a massive wooden horse.

10   somber

In a Greek myth, the somber, or gloomy, boatman, Charon, takes Psyche to the underworld.

Background

✓ **TARGET VOCABULARY** **What Is Greek Mythology?** Greek mythology is a massive collection of stories from ancient Greece. The plots of the tales deal with both fury and love, and their characters often act in a rash, unthinking fashion. Many myths feature monsters, such as the one-eyed colossus, or giant, Cyclops. Gods and goddesses may arrive to help steadfast heroes who embrace danger, as Theseus does when he tracks down a dreadful beast in a confusing labyrinth. Some myths recount somber events, such as when the goddess Demeter must abandon her daughter in the underworld. Others tell about long battles. In the bitterly fought Trojan War, the city of Troy nearly unravels during a Greek siege.

Poseidon, the god of the sea, could use his powers to make voyages safe or disastrous.

Theseus sailed from Athens to Crete to defeat the Minotaur. (Below) The Parthenon in Athens was built as a temple to the goddess Athena.

Comprehension

✔ **TARGET SKILL** **Story Structure**

As you read "The Hero and the Minotaur," pay attention to the elements
that make up the story structure, including the characters, the settings,
and the story's plot—including conflict and resolution. You can make a
story map like the one below to keep track of story elements as you read.

Characters:	Settings:
Plot:	

✔ **TARGET STRATEGY** **Infer/Predict**

You can use your story map to help you figure out details that
the author doesn't directly state or to predict what will happen
next in "The Hero and the Minotaur." Making inferences and
predictions helps you connect with a story's characters and plot.

✔ **TARGET VOCABULARY**

steadfast	fury
rash	embrace
bitterly	abandon
unravels	massive
labyrinth	somber

 **TARGET SKILL**

Story Structure Examine details about characters, setting, and plot.

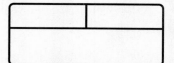

✔ **TARGET STRATEGY**

Infer/Predict Use text clues to figure out what the author means or what might happen in the future.

GENRE

A **myth** is a story that tells what a group of people believes about the world.

Set a Purpose Before reading, set a purpose for reading based on what you know about the genre and your own experience.

MEET THE AUTHOR AND ILLUSTRATOR

Robert Byrd

Robert Byrd's work combines simple storytelling with highly detailed illustrations. In this story he uses pen-and-ink and watercolor to bring ancient Crete to life. He says, "The most important thing is to have the small world I create in a picture perfectly match the words of the story, so that even if it is a make-believe world in the eyes and minds of the readers, everything you see is real." Byrd studies objects from the settings of his books, whether Crete or Leonardo da Vinci's Italy (*Leonardo: Beautiful Dreamer*), to make his illustrations as accurate as possible.

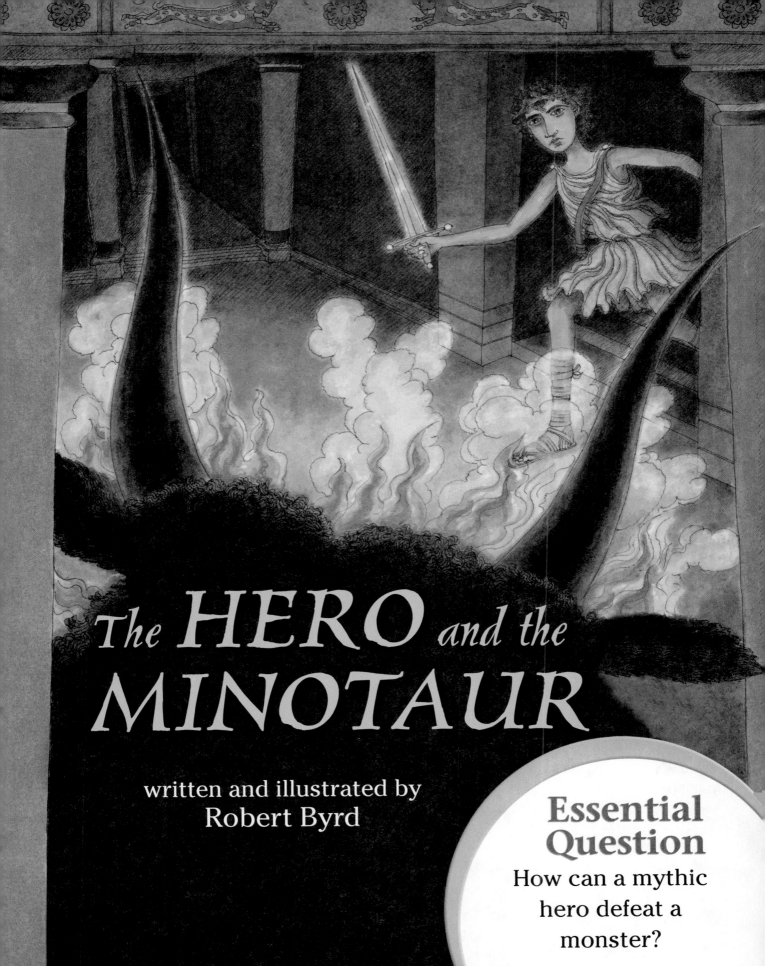

The HERO and the MINOTAUR

written and illustrated by
Robert Byrd

Essential Question

How can a mythic hero defeat a monster?

A Greek youth, Theseus, lifts a huge boulder, revealing a golden sword and sandals that were left for him by his father, King Aegeus. It is a sign that he is ready to join the king in Athens. On his journey, Theseus gains fame by killing three terrible giants who have been preying on travelers.

Word of Theseus' adventures soon reached Athens. As Theseus approached the city, crowds came out to greet him.

"Who performs these daring deeds?" Aegeus asked. "Let me meet the valiant champion." Aegeus decided to honor the stranger's bravery with a magnificent banquet in the Temple of Dolphins. When the prince stepped forward to present himself, the old king recognized the sandals and the golden sword, and he knew the youth before him was his son. He welcomed Theseus with a cry of wonder and a loving embrace. The sight of their happy reunion filled everyone with joy, and the people feasted, danced, and lit altars in every temple in Athens.

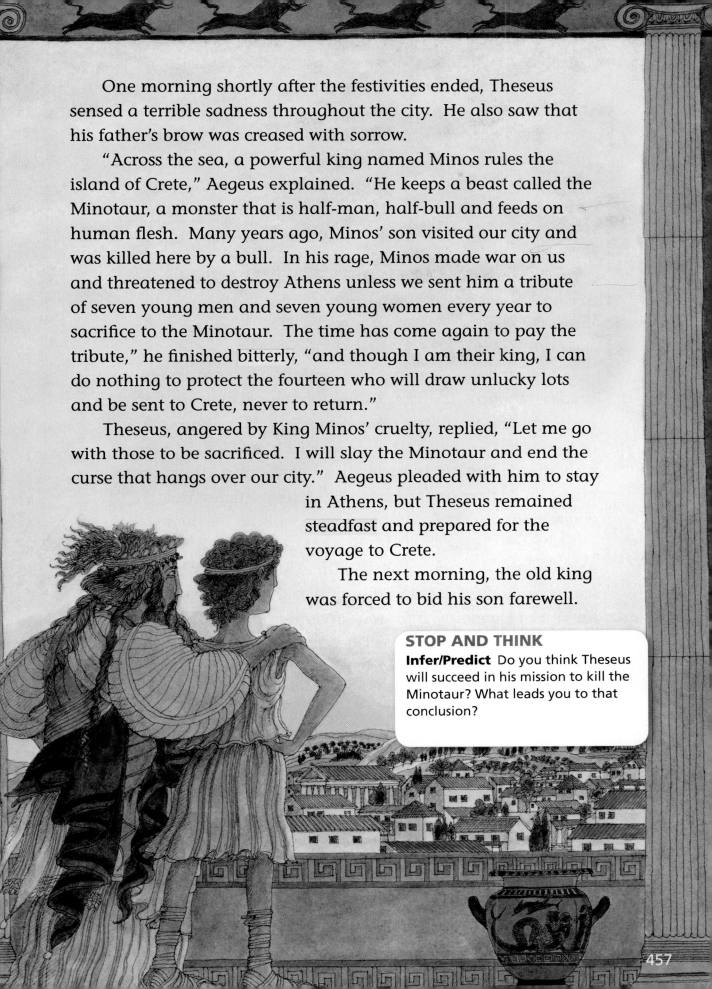

One morning shortly after the festivities ended, Theseus sensed a terrible sadness throughout the city. He also saw that his father's brow was creased with sorrow.

"Across the sea, a powerful king named Minos rules the island of Crete," Aegeus explained. "He keeps a beast called the Minotaur, a monster that is half-man, half-bull and feeds on human flesh. Many years ago, Minos' son visited our city and was killed here by a bull. In his rage, Minos made war on us and threatened to destroy Athens unless we sent him a tribute of seven young men and seven young women every year to sacrifice to the Minotaur. The time has come again to pay the tribute," he finished bitterly, "and though I am their king, I can do nothing to protect the fourteen who will draw unlucky lots and be sent to Crete, never to return."

Theseus, angered by King Minos' cruelty, replied, "Let me go with those to be sacrificed. I will slay the Minotaur and end the curse that hangs over our city." Aegeus pleaded with him to stay in Athens, but Theseus remained steadfast and prepared for the voyage to Crete.

The next morning, the old king was forced to bid his son farewell.

STOP AND THINK

Infer/Predict Do you think Theseus will succeed in his mission to kill the Minotaur? What leads you to that conclusion?

"In mourning for those to be sacrificed," said Aegeus, "your ship has a black sail. If the gods grant you the power to kill the Minotaur, hoist this white sail on your return. I will see it far out on the horizon and rejoice that you are safe." Theseus promised his father he would remember, then eagerly boarded the vessel. Many around him wept at the sad departure, but Theseus could think only of the thrilling adventure before him.

The ship sailed south and soon approached the shores of Crete. A towering figure ran back and forth across the harbor entrance.

"What is this marvel?" cried Theseus in wonder.

"That is Talus," replied the captain. "A senseless giant made of bronze. It moves as though it were alive and guards the harbor against King Minos' enemies. He would smash us to bits if it were not for our black sail, which even he can recognize." The mechanical man allowed the Athenians to pass him as they approached the king's immense palace, where Minos and the Minotaur were waiting for them.

Not only Talus watched the ship arrive. From a bluff, Ariadne, the daughter of King Minos, stood with her friend Icarus and gazed down at the somber ship. Icarus was the son of Daedalus, a famous inventor. Long ago at the king's command, it was Daedalus who built a labyrinth beneath the palace as a cage to hold the Minotaur.

"Who is that who stands so tall and unafraid on the Athenian ship?" Ariadne asked. She was impressed by the stranger's confidence.

"That must be Theseus, son of Aegeus," Icarus replied. He was pleased to be able to show off his knowledge to the beautiful princess, but he wondered at her admiration of Theseus. "I have heard he freely chose to come here and face the Minotaur."

Ariadne knew very well that no one had ever escaped the circling passages and corridors of her father's enormous stone maze. Gazing at the prince, she made up her mind to save him from the king's rash cruelty. "We must go to your father and ask for his advice," she said to Icarus. "If anyone knows the secrets of the maze and can help us rescue Theseus, it is Daedalus." The bold princess was right, for the brilliant inventor revealed to her a clever plan.

That night, while the others slept, Ariadne secretly entered the king's chamber, gathered up the palace keys and Theseus' sword, and crept down to the prisoner's cell. "Theseus," she whispered to him, "I am Ariadne. I have heard tales of your many good deeds. I can show you how to escape the labyrinth, but in return I ask that you help me to escape this island and my father, King Minos, who has grown wicked and pitiless."

Theseus agreed to help her, and so Ariadne explained Daedalus' secret. "You must secure one end of this ball of thread to the entrance of the labyrinth," she said, "and keep hold of the rest of the ball as the string unravels behind you. If you defeat the Minotaur, the thread's path will lead you back out of the labyrinth." Praying that the gods would help him, she led Theseus to the maze and watched as he descended the heavy stone steps. Then she returned to the prison hold to free the other captives.

describes setting when Theseus meets minotaur makes reader feel terror

In the corridors of the labyrinth, the odor was foul, the light dim. Theseus gripped his father's sword in one hand, and in the other he held the unraveling thread. The passages twisted and turned, leading him first one way and then another, winding around and around. Down, down he went, searching for the beast hidden deep in the black abyss. Finally he came to an open space where the Minotaur lay sleeping on the rough stone floor. Its hot breath shook the cavern walls. The creature had the chest and arms of a powerful man, but the rest of its body had the shape of a bull, and two great horns grew out of its head.

Then the Minotaur opened one glowing red eye and fixed it on Theseus. Its snore died away, and the chamber grew deathly still.

creates mood of tension

STOP AND THINK

Author's Craft In the second paragraph, the author uses details about smell and sight to create a dark **mood**. What detail of sound on this page adds to that sense of danger?

With a thunderous bellow, the Minotaur rose to its feet and charged. Theseus leapt aside, but the deadly horns grazed his tunic. The Minotaur spun around, furious, and charged again. As the beast descended upon him, Theseus steadied himself, raised his golden sword, and with a great heave drove the blade through the Minotaur's heart. The monster dropped to the cold stone floor, silenced forever.

Shaken by the **fury** of the struggle, Theseus had dropped the ball of thread. Anxious to escape the gloomy maze, he picked it up again and followed the thread out of the labyrinth and into the cool night air.

Ariadne and Icarus were waiting for him. The princess cried out with delight to see Theseus unharmed.

"Let us waste no time in leaving. The king is sure to come after us," urged Ariadne. Theseus and the freed Athenians boarded the ship, but Icarus stepped back.

"Minos will blame Daedalus for your escape. I cannot abandon my father to the king's wrath," he explained, though it pained Icarus to see Theseus leave with Ariadne. "Daedalus and I will flee Minos together," he vowed. "Then we will join you in Athens."

 **STOP AND THINK**

Story Structure Do you think that the story's main problem is resolved by the Minotaur's death or by the escape of the Athenians? Explain your reasons.

Icarus watched from the bluffs as the ship set a course for Athens, but he was not the only one who followed the black sail in the breaking dawn. At the harbor entrance Talus spied the ship and raised his heavy club high to strike the boat. Theseus stepped forward with his sword, prepared to fight. But Poseidon, ever watchful, sent a massive wave smashing into the bronze giant. The Athenians watched in awe as the shining colossus, crushed into a heap of broken metal, sank to the bottom of the sea.

On his voyage to Athens, Theseus forgets to change the sails of his ship from black to white. Believing that his son is dead, King Aegeus throws himself into the sea. Theseus becomes the next king of Athens and names the surrounding waters the Aegean Sea, in honor of his father.

Your Turn

Noble Qualities

Write About Values Myths often reveal the values of the people who created them. Based on what you read in "The Hero and the Minotaur," what values do you think were important to the ancient Greeks? Are those values still important today? Explain your answer in a paragraph that includes details from the selection and your own knowledge. SOCIAL STUDIES

Hollywood Heroes

Produce a Movie Work in small groups. Imagine that you are producing a movie version of "The Hero and the Minotaur." Write a list of ideas for how you would update the story to modern times. How would the characters, setting, and plot events change? What would stay the same? SMALL GROUP

Recipe for a Winner

Turn and Talk Theseus is a brave hero, but he needs help from other story characters to defeat the Minotaur. With a partner, discuss how Theseus' character traits and the story's plot events work together to lead to the Minotaur's defeat. STORY STRUCTURE

Connect to
Math

The Amazing Algorithm

✓ TARGET VOCABULARY

steadfast	rash
bitterly	unravels
labyrinth	fury
embrace	abandon
massive	somber

GENRE

Readers' theater is a text that has been formatted for readers to read aloud.

TEXT FOCUS

Dialogue is text that stands for the words spoken by the characters.

The Amazing Algorithm

by Matt Carroll

Cast of Characters

Narrator

Tony

Sam, Tony's younger brother

Narrator: Tony and Sam are on vacation in Colorado. One day, they visit a maze.

Tony: Hey, little brother. Why the somber face? We're supposed to be having fun.

Sam: Another dead end. I think we're lost.

Tony: Lost? No way—not with my sense of direction. Don't abandon hope!

Narrator: Knowing the paths would be paved, Sam pulls two pieces of chalk out of his backpack.

Sam: Luckily, I remember this algorithm from math.

Tony: Algo rhythm? Is that a crazy dance? Don't do anything rash, little bro! Senseless fury won't solve anything.

Sam: An algorithm is just a problem-solving process. You mark the dead-end path with a blue chalk back to the choice point. Then you try a different path...

Narrator: After two more wrong paths, Tony begins to panic. Bitterly, he wishes they had never entered the maze.

Tony: This was a massive mistake! We should have brought string, like the one Theseus unravels in Daedalus' labyrinth.

Sam: Be steadfast, big bro. Have faith in the algorithm.

Tony: Oh, no! Another blue line! What if every path out of this maze is a dead end?

Sam: Then we just take a path we've been on. This time, we also mark it in yellow. We'll know we used it twice. And we won't use any path more than twice.

Tony: I just hope there's no Minotaur lurking around the corner.

Narrator: It took some time, but Sam's algorithm worked. The brothers found the path out!

Tony: Little brother, let me embrace you! You're smarter than Daedalus.

Sam: Don't thank me. Thank the amazing algorithm.

Making Connections

 Text to Self

Write a Paragraph Theseus could not have escaped the labyrinth without the help of Ariadne and Icarus. Think of a time when friends helped you face a challenge or when you helped someone else do so. Write a paragraph describing the experience.

 Text to Text

Replay as a Myth How would "The Amazing Algorithm" be different if it were an ancient Greek myth like "The Hero and the Minotaur"? Find out by writing or performing a Greek myth version with classmates. Add new characters or events if you wish.

 Text to World

Connect to Math Each labyrinth in the two selections you have read can be seen as a pattern, a form of visual math. Look for patterns in nature, such as in shells, feathers, leaves, or bark. Use their patterns to design a maze of your own. Share your creation with a partner.

Grammar

What Are Adjectives and Adverbs? An **adjective** gives information about a noun. Some adjectives are **descriptive adjectives** that tell *what kind*. One type of descriptive adjective, a **proper adjective**, is formed from a proper noun and is capitalized. Adjectives such as *this, that, these,* and *those* tell *which one* and are called **demonstrative adjectives**. An **adverb** is a word that modifies a verb, an adjective, or another adverb.

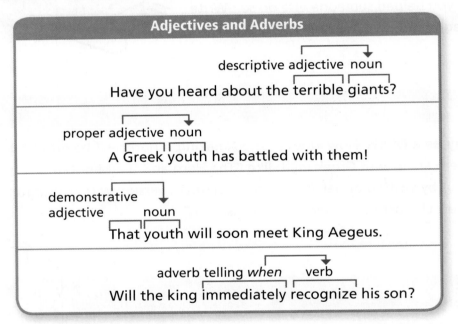

Adverbs that modify verbs answer these questions: *How? Where? When?*

Try This! **Read the sentences below. List the adjectives and adverbs on another sheet of paper. Label each adjective *descriptive, proper,* or *demonstrative,* and write the noun it modifies. Then write the verb each adverb modifies.**

1. Theseus freely chose a difficult task.

2. He stood on the deck of the Athenian ship.

3. A fearsome beast lived in a maze on Crete.

4. This beast leapt savagely at Theseus.

Word Choice When you write, use precise adjectives and adverbs to create clear and vivid pictures for your readers. Also, be careful not to use the same adjectives or adverbs over and over.

Less Precise Adjectives and Adverb

Ancient myths tell good stories about characters who behave badly.

More Precise Adjectives and Adverb

Greek myths tell cautionary stories about characters who behave foolishly.

Connect Grammar to Writing

As you revise your cause-effect paragraph, look for opportunities to use precise adjectives and adverbs. Use those words to create clear pictures for your readers.

Write to Inform

A **cause** is an event or action that makes something happen, and an **effect** is the result. A cause can have more than one effect, and an effect can then be the cause of another effect. A good **cause-effect paragraph** includes transition words such as *therefore, so, because, since,* and *as a result* to connect ideas and sentences.

Michael explained the chain of events that led to Theseus' journey to Crete. Then he added transition words to make the relationships between the causes and the effects clear.

Writing Traits Checklist

✔ **Ideas**
Did I support my ideas with details from the text?

✔ **Organization**
Are the events in a logical order?

✔ **Sentence Fluency**
Did I use transition words to signal causes and effects?

✔ **Word Choice**
Did I use vivid adjectives and adverbs?

✔ **Voice**
Did I describe causes and effects in a way that sounds like me?

✔ **Conventions**
Did I use correct spelling, grammar, and punctuation?

Revised Draft

In "The Hero and the Minotaur," the death of Minos' son causes a tragic chain of events. A bull in Athens had killed Minos' son, so Minos declared war on Athens. His rage caused him to demand a terrible price: a yearly human sacrifice to the Minotaur. As a result, Fourteen people traveled from Athens to Crete every year to die.

One Bad Thing Leads to Another

by Michael Wu

In "The Hero and the Minotaur," the death of Minos' son causes a tragic chain of events. A bull in Athens had killed Minos' son, so Minos declared war on Athens. His rage caused him to demand a terrible price: a yearly human sacrifice to the Minotaur. As a result, fourteen people traveled from Athens to Crete every year to die. Theseus was horrified when he heard about the cruel practice. Therefore, he was determined to go to Crete, kill the Minotaur, and put an end to the senseless killings.

> In my final paper, I added transition words to connect ideas and sentences. I also made sure that I used adjectives and adverbs properly.

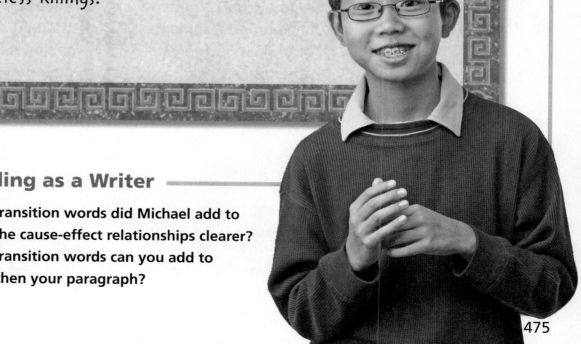

Reading as a Writer

What transition words did Michael add to make the cause-effect relationships clearer? What transition words can you add to strengthen your paragraph?

✓ **TARGET VOCABULARY**

divine
ceremonial
fragments
pondered
supportive
erected
mission
prosperity
emerge
depicted

Vocabulary
Reader

Context
Cards

Vocabulary in Context

1 divine

Pharaohs ruled Egypt by divine right. They claimed their power came from the gods.

2 ceremonial

Pharaohs wore special ceremonial robes when attending important events in their temples and palaces.

3 fragments

Digging in ancient ruins, archaeologists have found fragments of broken pottery and other objects.

4 pondered

For centuries people have pondered, or thought deeply about, the mystery of the Egyptian pyramids.

- **Study each Context Card.**
- **Use two Vocabulary words to tell about an experience you had.**

5 supportive

Hatshepsut was supportive of her husband, Thutmose II, and helped him rule Egypt wisely.

6 erected

Several impressive stone monuments were erected, or built, when Hatshepsut ruled Egypt.

7 mission

Hatshepsut sent traders on a mission. She asked them to bring goods back from the land of Punt.

8 prosperity

Crops flourished in the rich soil around the Nile River, making ancient Egypt a land of prosperity.

9 emerge

When historians learned to read ancient Egyptian hieroglyphics, new information about Egypt began to emerge.

10 depicted

In Egyptian art, the god Thoth is often depicted with the head of a bird—the ibis.

Background

✓ TARGET VOCABULARY **A Great Civilization** In 3100 B.C.E., King Menes (MEE neez) united the lands of Upper and Lower Egypt into a single kingdom. This marked the beginning of a civilization of great prosperity and achievement. Over the next several thousand years, Egypt would emerge as one of the ancient world's most powerful nations.

The pharaohs, or Egyptian kings, erected magnificent pyramids, temples, and palaces. Some of these structures, such as the Great Pyramid of Giza, still stand. Others have crumbled into small fragments. These pieces provide clues to scholars who have pondered Egypt's history and culture. Pharaohs were also supportive of trade. They sent traders on missions to other countries to trade items including ivory, cattle, and gold.

Besides governing the country, the pharaohs played an important ceremonial role. The Egyptians believed their rulers were living gods whose presence protected the kingdom. In most ancient Egyptian art, the pharaohs are depicted as divine beings.

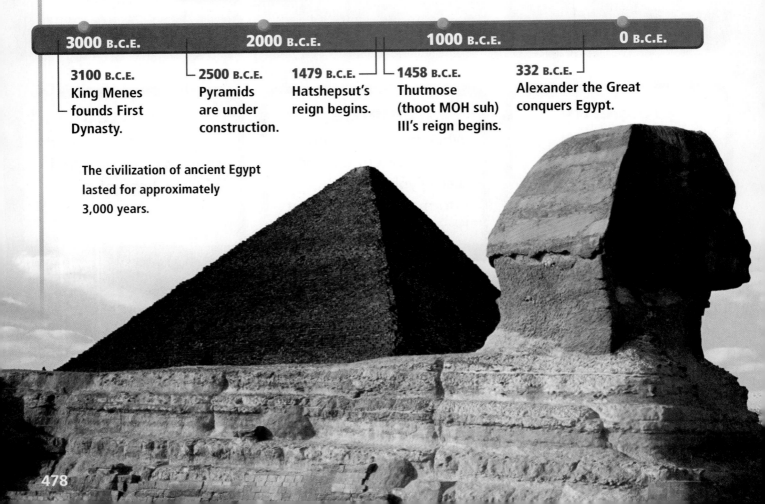

| 3000 B.C.E. | 2000 B.C.E. | | 1000 B.C.E. | 0 B.C.E. |

3100 B.C.E.
King Menes
founds First
Dynasty.

2500 B.C.E.
Pyramids
are under
construction.

1479 B.C.E.
Hatshepsut's
reign begins.

1458 B.C.E.
Thutmose
(thoot MOH suh)
III's reign begins.

332 B.C.E.
Alexander the Great
conquers Egypt.

The civilization of ancient Egypt
lasted for approximately
3,000 years.

Comprehension

✔ TARGET SKILL **Cause and Effect**

As you read "The Princess Who Became a King," notice the causes, or reasons things happen, and their effects, or results. Look for clue words such as *because* and *when* to help you identify causes and effects. You can make a chart like the one below to keep track of these relationships.

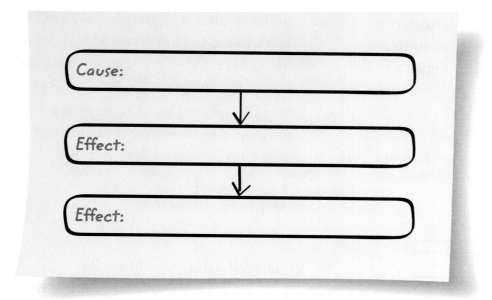

Cause:

↓

Effect:

↓

Effect:

✔ TARGET STRATEGY **Monitor/Clarify**

Keeping track of causes and effects can help you monitor and clarify your understanding of "The Princess Who Became a King." Checking your comprehension as you read helps you clear up any confusing ideas.

African Princess

✔ TARGET VOCABULARY

divine	erected
ceremonial	mission
fragments	prosperity
pondered	emerge
supportive	depicted

✔ TARGET SKILL

Cause and Effect Tell how events are related and how one event causes another.

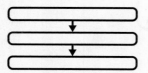

✔ TARGET STRATEGY

Monitor/Clarify As you read, see if anything isn't making sense. Find ways to figure out any parts that are confusing.

GENRE

Informational text gives facts and examples about a topic.

Set a Purpose Before reading, set a purpose for reading based on what you know about the genre and your own experience.

MEET THE AUTHOR

Joyce Hansen

Joyce Hansen's career as an author spans three decades. As her many titles show, she is equally at home writing realistic fiction *(The Gift-Giver)*, historical fiction *(I Thought My Soul Would Rise and Fly)*, and nonfiction *(Women of Hope)*. A former teacher, Hansen is currently at work on a five-book series about a family of African Americans living in pre-Civil War New York City. Hansen has said, "Real success for me is when young people tell me that they were encouraged and helped by something I've written."

MEET THE ILLUSTRATOR

Laurie McGaw

A portrait painter and illustrator, Laurie McGaw lives and works in Ontario, Canada. She has illustrated many books for young people, including *To Be a Princess: The Fascinating Lives of Real Princesses* and *The Secrets of Vesuvius: Exploring the Mysteries of an Ancient Buried City*.

The Princess Who Became a King

from *African Princess: The Amazing Lives of Africa's Royal Women*

by Joyce Hansen   illustrated by Laurie McGaw

Essential Question

How did a pharaoh's daughter become a pharaoh?

This limestone bust of Hatshepsut (hat SHEHP soot) wearing a pharaoh's beard was once part of an eighteen-foot statue that stood in the temple at Deir el-Bahri (dair ehl BAH ree), where her tomb was housed.

On a hot day in 1922, there was great excitement at a dig site in what had once been the Egyptian city of Thebes (theebz). The archaeologists had stumbled upon a pit containing hundreds of pieces of ancient granite statues. Some of the pieces were as small as fine gravel; others were so huge that a crane was needed to lift them. (The head archaeologist, Herbert E. Winlock, said later that putting the fragments together was like working on one hundred jigsaw puzzles, each one with pieces missing.) The statues were of a pharaoh wearing the traditional kilt and crown—as well as the beard—of an Egyptian ruler. But the pharaoh's face was that of a woman!

STOP AND THINK

Author's Craft Sometimes authors use **foreshadowing** to give hints about future events. Where does the author use foreshadowing on these two pages? How does this hint at what readers will learn about Hatshepsut?

On some of the broken columns, the dig team found the name *Hatshepsut* written in hieroglyphs. Was this the same Hatshepsut who had reigned over Egypt around 1479–1457 B.C.E.? Herbert Winlock knew that her empty burial tomb had been found a few years earlier at Deir el-Bahri but that her mummy had yet to be discovered. If this was the same Hatshepsut, he wondered, why had so many statues of her been destroyed? As the archaeologists studied and pondered, the story of an extraordinary woman began to emerge after thousands of years of silence.

This set of Egyptian hieroglyphs represents the pharaoh Hatshepsut. The symbols are enclosed in an oval, called a cartouche (kahr TOOSH).

Statues of Hatshepsut stand at her Mortuary Temple in Deir el-Bahri. It was traditional to show a deceased pharaoh holding a shepherd's crook and flail (a rod with three strands of beads attached). These objects were symbols of a pharaoh's power and responsibilities.

The crowds on the banks of the river cheered wildly as the gilded royal barge came into view. Standing next to the pharaoh was a lovely young girl in white linen robes—his eldest daughter, the Royal Princess Hatshepsut. For Pharaoh Thutmose (thoot MOH suh) I, these trips along the Nile from Thebes to Memphis gave him an opportunity to inspect his kingdom and see his people. We can imagine him pointing out to his daughter the great monuments and temples, teaching her about the world they lived in. With Hatshepsut's mother, the Royal Wife Ahmose (AH mohs), and other members of the royal family, they would stay in temporary palaces called the "Mooring Places of Pharaoh."

The Nile River and its fertile valley (background) helped develop farming in Egypt. Along the Nile grew the royal cities of Memphis in the north of Egypt and Thebes in the south.

MEDITERRANEAN SEA

Giza

Memphis

Nile River

RED SEA

Deir el-Bahri

Thebes

Temple of Karnak

EGYPT

Throughout her childhood, Hatshepsut had a very close relationship with her father. She was the only surviving child of Ahmose. Sadly, with the exception of Hatshepsut's half brother, Thutmose II, all of the pharaoh's other children had died. Hatshepsut and Thutmose II, who would someday marry and rule Egypt together, must have been a great comfort to the pharaoh. Egyptian royalty married close family members in order to keep the royal blood "pure" and to keep wealth and power within the ruling family.

Hatshepsut's carefree days and nights spent in the palace at Thebes ended when she became a teenager. Her beloved father died, and her life changed completely. Historians are not certain whether Hatshepsut was older or younger than Thutmose II, but either way she could not become the new pharaoh because she was a woman. Pharaohs were not only supreme rulers; they were also divine. Their right to rule came directly from the gods. The pharaoh was the head of all the priests (a very powerful group of men) and was the only person who was allowed to communicate directly with the gods. Next in line to be the new pharaoh was Hatshepsut's half brother, Thutmose II. Princess Hatshepsut became his Royal Wife.

The goddess Mut (moot), shown here, was known as Mother of the Gods. Mut's crown often depicted a vulture, which was revered as a fierce protector of its young.

Ancient Egyptians worshiped the god Amun (AH moon) as the king of all gods.

Hatshepsut probably accepted her marriage to Thutmose II as her duty. If she refused to marry him, the Theban royal family would be weakened, and other people would try to claim the throne. She was only fourteen or fifteen years old when she married, but like her father, Hatshepsut had a deep sense of responsibility. Childhood things were put aside, and she gracefully stepped into her role as the "King's Great Wife," although she preferred the title "God's Wife of Amun." The title of God's Wife of Amun was politically important, as it gave Hatshepsut influence over the powerful priests and allowed the royal family to control the vast wealth and property of the Amun temples.

In the years that followed her marriage, the young queen had a daughter, Neferure (neh feh ROO ray), whom she loved very much. As well as being a mother, Hatshepsut seems to have been a supportive queen and wife. She might even have shared power with her husband.

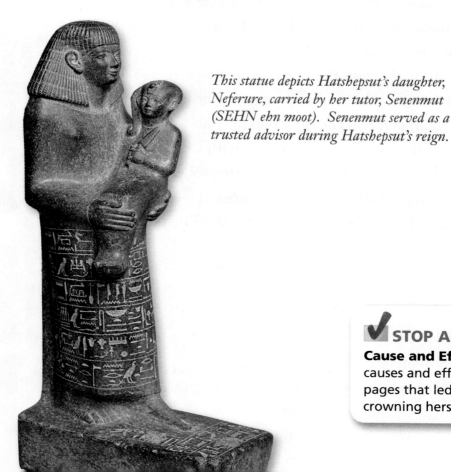

This statue depicts Hatshepsut's daughter, Neferure, carried by her tutor, Senenmut (SEHN ehn moot). Senenmut served as a trusted advisor during Hatshepsut's reign.

STOP AND THINK
Cause and Effect Identify the causes and effects on these two pages that led to Hatshepsut's crowning herself pharaoh.

Almost every pharaoh from the 16th century B.C.E. to 30 B.C.E. added buildings, walls, or monuments to the Karnak temple complex, a religious site at Thebes.

Unfortunately, after a short reign of three years, Thutmose II died, and his son by a lesser wife, Thutmose III, became the new pharaoh. There was one serious problem—he was a small child. Hatshepsut was appointed Queen Regent. This was not an unusual situation. In the past, Egyptian queens had acted as regents, governing for their young sons or other male relatives.

But Hatshepsut was different. She had learned how to rule from her father and had taken on some of her husband's royal duties. For her, it must have seemed as though the gods had intervened in her life. She was finally going to be given a chance to rule on her own, at least until the young pharaoh was old enough to govern.

Although she was only seventeen or eighteen years old when her husband died, Hatshepsut was a successful ruler. She knew from her years at court how to deal with the important priests and nobles who helped run the country. Maybe it was a sign of things to come, but she had two obelisks built while she was Queen Regent. When these massive columns were completed seven years later, she did something that had never been done before. Hatshepsut had herself crowned as pharaoh!

Hatshepsut's Obelisks

Towering almost a hundred feet into the sky, one of two massive granite obelisks (AH buh lihsks) that Hatshepsut erected at the temple of Amun in Karnak still stands (at right, in photo) beside one built by her father. They were carved without any iron tools, and no one knows for certain how the Egyptians managed to raise them. Egyptian obelisks have been the model for many other structures, including the Washington Monument, which is almost six times taller than Hatshepsut's obelisk.

Hatshepsut became one of only a few female pharaohs to rule Egypt in three thousand years of history. She must have been confident, smart, and fearless to take such a bold step. She also must have had supporters among the powerful nobles and priests at court. Hatshepsut had obviously earned their respect and confidence. This would not have been an easy thing to do. She would have had to convince them that a female pharaoh would not anger the gods and bring terrible hardship to the Egyptian people.

Hatshepsut's reign did not bring down the fury of the gods. Historians believe she ruled for fifteen years, bringing peace and prosperity to her people. As a pharaoh, she is best known for her monuments at Karnak and Deir el-Bahri.

Hatshepsut was a builder. From the time she sat at her father's side gazing at the pyramids of Giza or visiting the temple complex at Karnak, she understood the importance of building monuments and temples to the gods. For the ancient Egyptians, life was a preparation for death, leading to eternal life in heaven. However, the Egyptians did not want to be forgotten on earth. They left grand monuments behind so that they would be remembered forever.

The three Pyramids of Giza are located near the modern capital of Cairo (KY roh). They were built, seven to ten centuries before Hatshepsut's reign, to house the mummies of Egyptian rulers.

STOP AND THINK

Monitor/Clarify If you need to clarify the time when Hatshepsut viewed the temples and pyramids with her father, reread the text on page 484.

The Expedition to Punt

Hatshepsut understood the importance of building strong trade relationships with other countries. She sent a mission to the fabled land of Punt, thought to be located in present-day Ethiopia or Somalia. The expedition returned from Punt with valuable goods such as gold, ebony, ivory, and myrrh (mur) trees (used for making incense). Hatshepsut was so proud of the successful mission that she had the entire story of the voyage carved on the walls of her mortuary temple.

This carving from Hatshepsut's temple shows the voyage to Punt. The land of Punt may have been located in one of several places on the Red Sea or on the Arabian Sea south of the Horn of Africa.

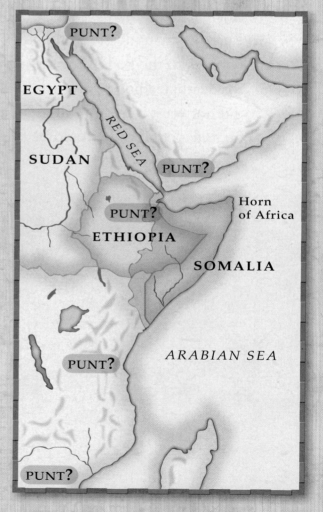

Hatshepsut's splendid mortuary temple at Deir el-Bahri

Hatshepsut asked her loyal and trusted adviser, Senenmut, to plan and build her mortuary temple at Deir el-Bahri. She named it Djeser-Djeseru (JEH sur jeh SEH roo), meaning "Holy of Holies." Nestled near her father's burial tomb, it was an elegant building. It was also very different from other styles of architecture at that time, just as Hatshepsut was so different from other women.

Fifteen years into her reign, Hatshepsut again broke with tradition. She celebrated her jubilee. Normally, a jubilee was held thirty years into a successful reign. After the celebration Hatshepsut followed in her father's footsteps and had two more obelisks built and placed in front of the temple at Karnak. One still stands there today.

Hatshepsut may have been in her forties when she died—an old woman in those days. For years, scholars believed that Thutmose III was so angry at his aunt for crowning herself pharaoh that he knocked down her statues. But the time Hatshepsut spent training her nephew to become a successful ruler suggests that she was a loving woman, not a power-hungry one. And Hatshepsut's monuments were destroyed twenty years after her death. If Thutmose III had been angry with Hatshepsut, why did he wait so long to erase her memory? And why didn't he destroy the images and statues that showed her as a princess and a queen?

Perhaps Thutmose III was having political problems and his throne was threatened. Maybe he destroyed anything that depicted Hatshepsut as pharaoh in order to show that there was a direct line of kings from Thutmose I and II to himself, with no Hatshepsut in between.

We will probably never know who destroyed her statues or why. What we do know is that Pharaoh Hatshepsut can now take her place among the great kings and builders of Egypt.

The mortuary at Deir el-Bahri honors both Hatshepsut and the goddess Hathor, shown here. Ceremonial occasions celebrated Hathor as a joyful, loving protector of women.

Your Turn

Powerful Women

Short Response Think of women leaders in today's world. How might their experiences be similar to or different from Hatshepsut's? Write a paragraph explaining your ideas. Use details from the selection and your own knowledge to support your answer. SOCIAL STUDIES

In Her Honor

Design a Monument Imagine that Hatshepsut built another monument during her lifetime. Picture what the monument might have looked like. What would it have represented? With a partner, design and draw the monument. Then write captions to explain its various features. PARTNERS

Fit to Be Pharaoh

Turn and Talk Consider Hatshepsut's rise to power. With a partner, discuss how earlier events in her life led to the moment when she crowned herself pharaoh. How many of these important events had to do with choices she made? How many seem to have been beyond her control? CAUSE AND EFFECT

Social Studies

✔ TARGET VOCABULARY

divine	erected
ceremonial	mission
fragments	prosperity
pondered	emerge
supportive	depicted

GENRE

Informational text, such as the article on these Web pages, gives facts and examples about a topic.

TEXT FOCUS

Map Informational text may include a map, a detailed drawing that shows a place and its surroundings.

KUSH
LAND AND CLIMATE

Seven thousand years ago, a great society arose along the middle of the Nile River: the kingdom of Kush, also known as Nubia. Kush's civilization was as advanced as that of its neighbor, Egypt.

Hills separated Kush from Egypt and the Red Sea. To the south were the tropical forests of central Africa, but much of Kush had a desert climate. However, the yearly flooding of the Nile River provided fertile soil for animals and crops. In ancient times, Kush was actually wetter than Egypt is today. Huge herds of cattle grazed along the river.

Kush and the lands around it are in northeastern Africa. (See also page 495.)

AFRICA

QUEENS AND PHARAOHS

Kush began as a farming community, but over time, it gained in prosperity. The queens of Kush would emerge as powerful and supportive rulers. They shared the throne, and with the kings, they pondered problems facing the kingdom. A queen was known as a *kandake* (kahn DAH kee), or "strong woman."

The armies of Egypt wanted the gold and copper found in Kush. They conquered the kingdom during the reign of Thutmose (thoot MOH suh) I, around 1500 B.C.E. Then, after hundreds of years, Egypt's power began to decline. During the 700s B.C.E., the Kushite king Piankhi (PYAHNG kee) conquered Egypt. He began a line of Kushite pharaohs who used many Egyptian ceremonial rituals. Later, forced out of Egypt by the Assyrians, the Kushite kings erected a capital farther south, in Meroë (MEHR oh ee).

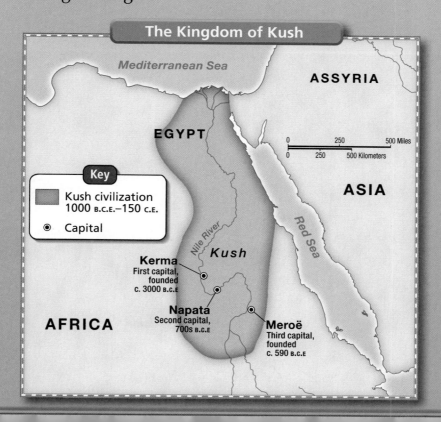

The Kingdom of Kush

Mediterranean Sea

ASSYRIA

EGYPT

0   250   500 Miles
0   250   500 Kilometers

ASIA

Key

Kush civilization 1000 B.C.E.–150 C.E.

⦿ Capital

Nile River

Kush

Red Sea

Kerma
First capital, founded c. 3000 B.C.E.

AFRICA

Napata
Second capital, 700s B.C.E.

Meroë
Third capital, founded c. 590 B.C.E.

TRADE AND CULTURE

The kingdom of Kush carried on a busy trade in gold, ebony, and ivory. Traders on a mission to Egypt could exchange fabric, jewelry, and metal objects for Egyptian goods, such as glass. Kushites also melted down fragments of iron ore to make tools and weapons. Kush's achievements in art, technology, and trade helped it stay in power for nearly a thousand years.

Kushites borrowed many customs from Egypt. They accepted Egyptian ideas of divine figures, worshiping the god Amun. They also adapted what they took to create their own culture. At first, the people of Kush carved Egyptian hieroglyphics into the stone of their buildings. By the Meroitic period, they had begun to change the hieroglyphs to create different symbols and a cursive script that depicted their language. This script reduced the large number of Egyptian symbols to twenty-three signs—an alphabet.

Meroitic cursive script

Making Connections

Text to Self

Describe an Experience Hatshepsut made many decisions while she ruled Egypt. Think of a time when it was your responsibility to be in charge. Describe how you decided what to do, or what you would do if you were in charge of a group.

Text to Text

Make a Travel Poster What information in "The Princess Who Became a King" and "Kush" might be useful to someone who is planning a vacation to Egypt? Create a poster that shows this information.

Text to World

Connect to Social Studies With a partner, look at a map of present-day Africa. Identify the countries that now lie along the Nile River, including those in the region once known as Kush.

Grammar

What Is a Preposition? What Is a Prepositional Phrase? A **preposition** is a word that shows a relationship between a noun or pronoun and another word in the sentence. That noun or pronoun is the **object of the preposition**. A **prepositional phrase** includes the preposition, the object of the preposition, and the modifiers of the object.

Prepositions and Prepositional Phrases

preposition   object of the preposition

Hatshepsut wore a man's kilt in ceremonies.

prepositional phrase

preposition   object of the preposition

She fastened a golden beard to her chin.

prepositional phrase

preposition   object of the preposition

The reign of this female pharaoh was mostly peaceful.

prepositional phrase

Try This! **Copy the sentences onto another sheet of paper. Circle each preposition, underline each prepositional phrase, and draw a box around each object of the preposition.**

1 Hatshepsut's biography is carved inside this temple.

2 The story on its walls is fascinating.

3 Was Hatshepsut really supported by the powerful priests?

4 The walls also feature pictures of the Egyptian gods.

Sentence Fluency To vary sentence structure and to make your writing smoother, you can combine related ideas from separate sentences by using a prepositional phrase from one of them.

Separate Sentences

Pharaoh Hatshepsut prepared for death by selecting a burial place.

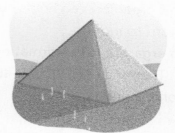

This place was in the Valley of the Kings.

Combined Sentence

Pharaoh Hatshepsut prepared for death by selecting a burial place in the Valley of the Kings.

Connect Grammar to Writing

As you revise your informational essay next week, look for sentences that you can combine by using prepositional phrases. Make sure your meaning is clear in the combined sentences.

Write to Inform

☑ **Organization** When you write an **informational essay**, you write to inform readers about a topic. An informational essay includes an introduction, a body, and a conclusion. Each paragraph in the body of an informational essay should give a main idea about the topic. Using a graphic organizer can help you organize the main ideas and details that you want to include.

To organize her informational essay, McKenna first clustered her facts. Then she used an idea-support map to identify the main ideas and supporting details.

Writing Process Checklist

▶ **Prewrite**

☑ Did I identify my topic?

☑ Did I identify main ideas about the topic?

☑ Did I include details to support the main ideas?

☑ Did I organize my ideas in a logical way?

Draft

Revise

Edit

Publish and Share

Exploring a Topic

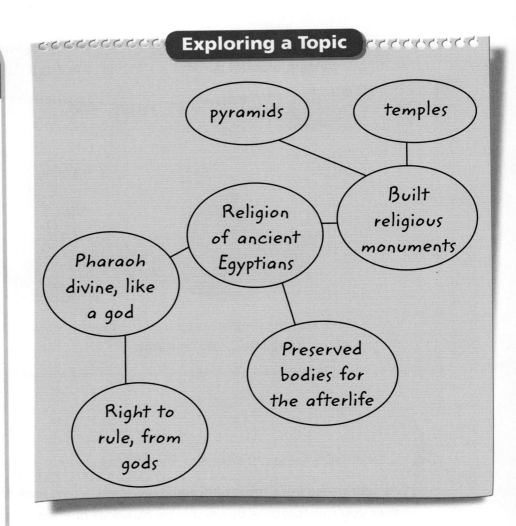

- pyramids
- temples
- Built religious monuments
- Religion of ancient Egyptians
- Pharaoh divine, like a god
- Preserved bodies for the afterlife
- Right to rule, from gods

Idea-Support Map

The Egyptians believed that the pharaoh was not only a ruler but also a divine being, like a god.

The pharaoh's right to rule came from the gods.

The pharaoh communicated with the gods directly.

The pharaoh was the leader of all the priests.

The Egyptians built monuments and temples to the gods.

Hatshepsut had two obelisks built at the temple of Amun at Karnak.

Many pharaohs built pyramids and tombs so that their bodies could be placed there when they died.

To organize my informational essay, I began by clustering. This helped me identify the main ideas and supporting details for my idea-support map.

Reading as a Writer

How can McKenna's map help her develop paragraphs? How might you use an idea-support map for your own informational essay?

✓ **TARGET VOCABULARY**

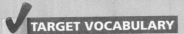

unaffected

dormant

subjected

salvage

outlying

opulent

tremors

imprints

luxurious

meager

Vocabulary Reader

A City Buried in Time

Context Cards

Vocabulary in Context

1 unaffected

Many of Rome's ancient buildings have changed little over the years. They seem to be unaffected by time.

2 dormant

After centuries of being dormant, or inactive, the volcano Mt. Vesuvius awoke with a bang.

3 subjected

The city of Pompeii was subjected to, or made to experience, severe damage from the volcano.

4 salvage

Archaeologists have worked to salvage, or save, relics such as this head from a Roman statue.

- **Study each Context Card.**

- **Discuss one picture. Use a different Vocabulary word from the one in the card.**

5 outlying

Outside Rome's city gates were roads that carried people to outlying areas, away from the city center.

6 opulent

Some bathhouses in ancient Rome were opulent, or richly decorated.

7 tremors

Tremors from earthquakes have damaged important buildings in Rome, such as the Colosseum.

8 imprints

The imprints, or evidence, of the Roman Empire can be seen here, in England. Hadrian's Wall stretches for miles.

9 luxurious

Hadrian's Villa near Rome was luxurious, with expensive, comfortable furnishings and decorations.

10 meager

These bronze coins had a low value. A Roman citizen could buy only a meager amount of goods with them.

Background

✔ **TARGET VOCABULARY** **The City of Pompeii** In the year 79 C.E., the Roman port of Pompeii was one of the largest cities in the Roman Empire, home to approximately twenty thousand people. Years earlier, Pompeii had been subjected to a strong earthquake. The years since then had been quiet, and Pompeii had been mostly unaffected by its neighbor—the volcano Mount Vesuvius. In fact, Pompeii was a popular vacation spot, with luxurious public baths and fountains. Pipes distributed water to both opulent villas and meager homes in outlying areas. Then, one August day, new tremors signaled that dormant Vesuvius was waking up. Hundreds of years later, by examining such clues as dug-up debris and the imprints of chariot wheels on narrow streets, historians would salvage Pompeii's past.

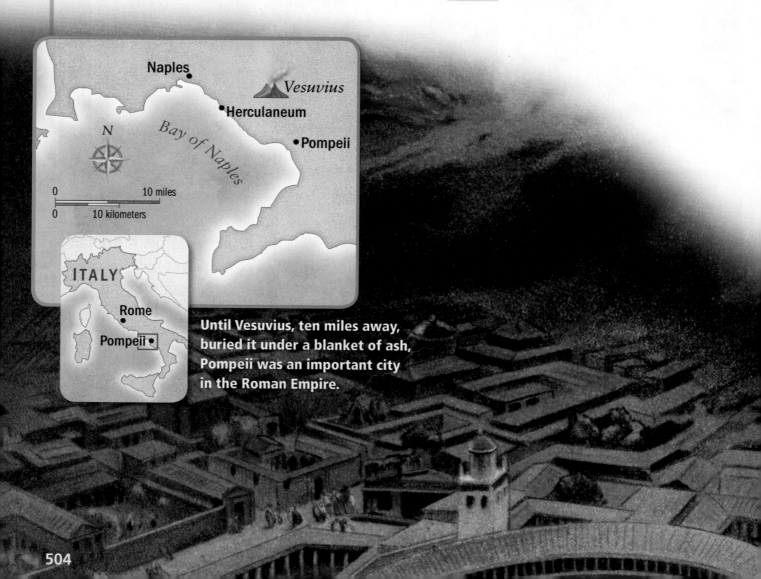

Until Vesuvius, ten miles away, buried it under a blanket of ash, Pompeii was an important city in the Roman Empire.

Comprehension

✔ **TARGET SKILL** **Main Ideas and Details**

As you read "Bodies from the Ash," notice that some sentences present main ideas and some present supporting details. Look for statements that express the most important points of the selection. A graphic organizer like the one below can help you keep track of main ideas and the details that provide more information about them.

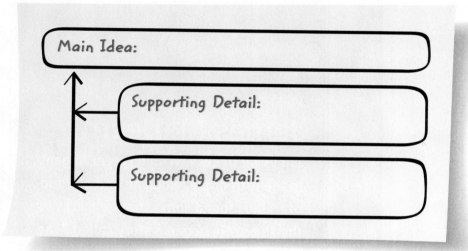

Main Idea:

Supporting Detail:

Supporting Detail:

✔ **TARGET STRATEGY** **Visualize**

You can use the main ideas and details noted in your graphic organizer to help you visualize, or create a mental image of, people, settings, objects, and events described in the text. Visualizing helps you form a deeper understanding of what you read.

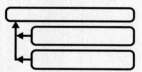

MEET THE AUTHOR

James M. Deem

James M. Deem's writing career began
in the fifth grade, when he and a group
of friends found some strange tracks in
the snow. He began a story called "The
Strange Tracks Mystery," which stopped
after the first page. However, it led to
future books about such subjects as
buried treasure, American presidents,
and the Vikings. Like *Bodies from the
Ash*, Deem's books *Bodies from the
Bog* and *How to Make a Mummy Talk*
explore the secrets that history has to
tell us.

Bodies from the Ash

LIFE AND DEATH IN ANCIENT POMPEII

BY JAMES M. DEEM

August 24 and 25, 79 C.E.

On August 24, the last Tuesday that they would live in their town, the people of ancient Pompeii awoke to a typical hot summer's morning. Four days earlier, a series of small tremors had begun to shake the area, but people were not very concerned. The region had been subjected to so many earthquakes over the years that residents had grown accustomed to them.

What they didn't know is that the region's frequent earthquakes had been caused by nearby Mount Vesuvius. Roman writers had commented on the mountain's strange appearance; one had compared it to Mount Etna, an active volcano in Sicily. A writer named Strabo even concluded that Vesuvius had once "held craters of fire." But because Mount Vesuvius had been dormant, or sleeping, for more than eight hundred years, no one realized that it still had deadly power. What's more, no one understood that the region's frequent earthquakes were actually signs that Vesuvius was building up pressure and getting ready to erupt.

That morning, Vesuvius provided a clearer warning that an eruption was beginning. Between nine and ten o'clock, the volcano shot a small explosion of tiny ash particles into the air. To the residents of Pompeii, ten miles southeast of the volcano, this may have felt like a minor earthquake, but to the people living in the immediate vicinity of Vesuvius, it was terrifying. The ash streamed up and fell like fine mist on the eastern slope of Vesuvius. A woman named Rectina who lived at the foot of the volcano was so alarmed that she quickly sent a letter with a servant to Elder Pliny, the commander of the Roman naval fleet stationed some eighteen miles away, urging him to rescue her.

People in Pompeii might have noticed the small cloud that morning and may have felt tremors, but they continued with their daily activities until early that afternoon. At one o'clock, eighty-one loaves of bread were baking in the ovens of the Modestus bakery, and vendors were selling fruit and other products in the macellum, or marketplace. The priests in the Temple of Isis were preparing to eat an afternoon meal of eggs and fish. It was then that Vesuvius finally awoke with a massive explosion.

This cloud blasted from Vesuvius during its last eruption in 1944, but the cloud from the 79 C.E. eruption was much larger. Since 79 C.E., Vesuvius erupted thirty times before becoming dormant again.

An enormous pine-tree-shaped cloud of ash, pumice, and larger rock fragments blasted into the air. Within a half-hour, the cloud had risen over ten miles high, and winds had blown it toward the southeast—in the direction of Pompeii. The cloud blocked the sun and turned the sky over Pompeii to night. Then it began to release a deluge of ash, lightweight white pumice stones, and some larger, heavier volcanic rocks on Pompeii. At the same time, earth tremors continued to shake the town.

At first, most people would have taken shelter in their homes or other buildings. But as the volcanic fallout began to accumulate at the rate of five or six inches per hour and the pumice grew to an inch in size, many decided to escape. Protecting themselves as best as they could from the falling stones, they headed down the narrow city streets, stepping on the accumulated fallout, toward one of the city gates. Some people used pillows and blankets tied to their heads; others shielded themselves with pans or even baskets. After reaching the gates, many took the coast road; others tried to escape by sea. But the buoyant pumice floated in the water, filling the harbor and making a seagoing escape more difficult. During this time, some were killed on their way out of the city, hit by larger rocks falling from the eruption cloud.

STOP AND THINK

Author's Craft The author makes careful use of **word choice** to describe Vesuvius's eruption. What contrasting words or phrases on these pages show how the eruption started small and grew in force?

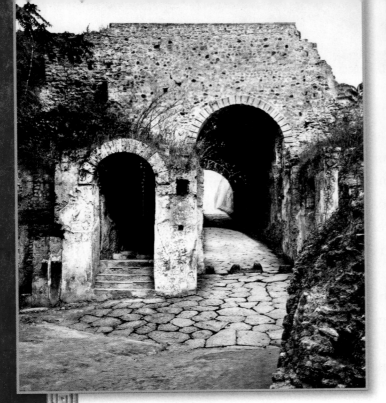

(left) As the fallout continued, Pompeians made their way to one of the eight city gates, hoping to escape the deadly rain of Vesuvius. (right) Most Pompeii streets were narrow and paved with stones. They quickly filled with pumice and ash as the eruption progressed.

By five-thirty that afternoon, two feet of ash and stones had accumulated in the streets, on roofs, and in open areas such as the courtyards of houses and gardens. In fact, so much pumice had built up on roofs that some buildings began to collapse, especially when the loose pumice was shaken by strong earth tremors. Many Pompeians were crushed in their houses when the roofs caved in on them.

As the evening progressed, the raining pumice turned from white to gray and grew bigger, some pieces almost three inches in size. By midnight, first-story doors and windows were completely blocked by fallout. Anyone who had delayed escape would have had to use a second-floor window to reach the street and then walk atop five feet or more of collected stones and ash. Fires were burning on the slopes of Vesuvius. Lightning filled the sky around it, and the eruption cloud had risen almost twenty miles high. But no one in Pompeii would have been able to see this.

STOP AND THINK

Visualize A good way of helping a reader visualize an event is to provide vivid examples. Which examples on this page create a vivid picture of the eruption for you?

At about one o'clock on the morning of August 25, twelve hours after the first major explosion, the eruption shifted to its second—and deadlier—phase. Vesuvius was losing strength and its eruption cloud was beginning to weaken. As the cloud collapsed completely over the next seven hours, it would fall in six separate stages, each one producing a *pyroclastic surge and flow*. With each partial collapse, a surge of superhot gas and ash blew down the slopes of Vesuvius at speeds between 60 and 180 miles per hour and at temperatures ranging between 350 and 650 degrees Fahrenheit, each surge larger than the last, each one spreading farther. The surge cloud destroyed everything in its path, leaving behind a layer of ash. This was quickly followed by a very rapid pyroclastic flow of volcanic debris that covered the area like a hot avalanche. The flow itself was not lava (that is, a melted rock that would have moved slowly and burned everything it touched); rather, it was a mixture of rock fragments and gas that rolled over the ground at temperatures up to 400 degrees Fahrenheit. This combination of surge and flow is sometimes referred to as *nuée ardente,* or glowing cloud; it is the most deadly type of volcanic activity because of its high temperature and speed.

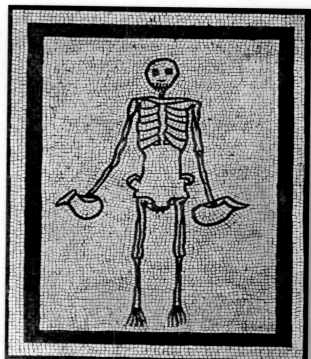

Skeleton images were frequently found in floor mosaics, wall paintings, and even on drinking cups in Pompeii. Such designs served as a reminder that life was short.

The first and second surges in the early morning hours did not reach as far as Pompeii, but they did destroy other towns closer to Vesuvius. At about six-thirty, a third surge ended at the northern edge of Pompeii, destroying some of the walls surrounding the city and suffocating anyone who had taken shelter in any of the outlying buildings.

This calix, a silver two-handled cup, was recovered by archaeologists from the ruins of Pompeii.

By morning, nine feet of pumice and other volcanic debris had accumulated, but the estimated two thousand people in and around Pompeii who had survived the night might have thought that they still had an opportunity to escape. By then, the rain of pumice had lessened so noticeably that many residents took to the streets, which were still darkened by the volcanic cloud, trying to get out of town. Many were carrying lanterns to help them see in the darkness.

But they were cut down around seven-thirty, when a fourth surge engulfed the city and the area beyond it, immediately killing everyone still alive, whether they were inside or out. Some fifteen minutes later, a fifth surge exploded through. Both of these surges deposited a layer of hot ash and a larger amount of pyroclastic flow.

Finally, at about eight o'clock that morning, a final surge—the largest and most violent—shook the area as the remainder of the volcanic cloud collapsed, crushing the top stories of buildings. Bricks, tiles, stones, and other debris were blown through the town. The last surge deposited two more feet of ash and debris on top of the town. But by then there was no one left alive to notice what had happened.

When the eruption ended, Pompeii was covered with more than twelve feet of volcanic debris. Only the very tops of a few ruined buildings were visible; most of the higher stories had been blown down during the pyroclastic surges.

In the days that followed, residents who returned hoping to find their city would have been lost in an unfamiliar landscape. Valleys were filled in; new hills had grown; and the course of the nearby river Sarno had changed. Even Vesuvius had a new look. The volcano's conelike top had collapsed, leaving a gaping crater.

And everywhere they would have looked, the landscape was blanketed by a ghostly covering of ash.

Rediscovering Pompeii

No one knows what happened to the residents of Pompeii who managed to escape, since no written record from any survivor of the town has ever been found. Some people may have left the area; others may have relocated to nearby towns unaffected by the tragedy. Some researchers believe that a few people returned and tunneled into the ruins, trying to salvage what they could, since tunnels have been found during excavations within the ruins. But no one tried to rebuild the city.

By the fourth century C.E., some 220 years after Vesuvius erupted, Pompeii's name no longer appeared on maps. Instead, the area was called Civitas. The volcanic ash that buried the town became fertile soil, and farmers planted olive trees and grapevines there. Sometimes they would come across bricks and other building materials that poked out of the ground. On rare occasions, a farmer might even find a statue hidden in the undergrowth. In 1594 an attempt to build an underground canal brought workers tantalizingly close to the ancient city. They found pieces of marble, parts of painted walls, and statues. But no one realized that the discoveries might lead to the site of the long-buried town.

In 1865 the artist Edouard Sain painted an imaginary version of the excavations at Pompeii. In reality, slaves and convicts were often used to excavate the ruins during the early years that it was explored.

This model depicts the theater in Herculaneum before early excavators looking for treasure plundered it.

Pompeii and its secrets remained hidden for centuries. It was only after the town of Herculaneum, which was also buried by Vesuvius in 79 C.E., was discovered that excavators began digging for Pompeii. In 1709, a group of well diggers came across some beautiful marble. Since the prince in charge of the region was building a new villa nearby, he was told of the discovery. No one knew that the marble was part of a theater or that it was situated in the ancient town of Herculaneum. Instead, the prince ordered an excavation, hoping to find even more marble for his house. Seven years later, when the prince's opulent villa was completed, he ordered workers to stop digging. During that time, they had stripped the theater of its statues and marble façade, without even knowing what they had found.

In 1738, after the Bourbon king Charles III took control of the region, he was eager to find more buried treasures from the same site, so he hired a Spanish military engineer named Alcubierre (al koo BYEH reh). In short order, Alcubierre widened the entrance to the site, quickly discovering that the treasure was part of a theater. He also found an inscription that finally identified the location as Herculaneum. But in his haste to please Charles, Alcubierre essentially turned the site into a tunnel-filled coal mine. Soon, workers were hauling beautiful statues and other treasures out of the tunnels and sending them to the palace of Charles III.

After fourteen years, workers began to find fewer objects, but Alcubierre was not about to give up. Instead, he planned to try another site: the underground canal that had been attempted in the late 1500s. He hoped that it might lead to the ruins of Pompeii—and further favor from Charles III.

On March 30, 1748, a small crew of twenty-four men, twelve of them convicts, began work. Digging was easier at the canal site, but it was filled with areas of firedamp—that is, toxic gasses trapped in the layers being excavated. Every time a pocket of firedamp was exposed, the diggers would have to run away to escape breathing the poisonous gas, and their work could be interrupted for many days.

Twenty days later, the workers discovered something unexpected: the skeleton of a man who had died during the eruption. The excavation report for that day read only: "Found a skeleton and 18 coins." Although this was the first recorded sign of the human tragedy at Pompeii, Alcubierre was more interested in the coins than the man. A few days later, another entry read: "Nothing was found, and only ruined structures were uncovered." Eventually, he became so disappointed with the meager discoveries that he returned to the excavations at Herculaneum, leaving only a small crew to work at the canal site. No more than fifty men—some of them Algerian and Tunisian slaves, chained together in pairs—seemed to have been used at any time, even after the site was finally identified as Pompeii in 1763.

But Pompeii was about to get much more attention. In 1771 excavators made a dramatic find: a large, luxurious house, now called the Villa of Diomedes (dy uh MEE deez), complete with two skeletons near the garden. These skeletons were of much greater interest, thanks to the riches found with them. Next to one man, who held a key and wore a gold ring, was a hoard of coins wrapped in a cloth: ten gold, eighty-eight silver, and nine bronze. This turned out to be one of the largest collections of money found at Pompeii and certainly a dazzling find in 1771.

The next year, as excavations of the house continued, workers discovered twenty more skeletons (eighteen adults and two children) piled together in a nearby underground room. The volcanic debris that had oozed into the room during the pyroclastic flows had hardened around the bodies and created imprints of the people, their clothing, and even their hair. Excavators studied the impressions and concluded that they had found a family and its servants. The woman of the house wore beautifully woven clothing and was adorned with a great deal of jewelry (multiple necklaces, armbands, bracelets, and rings).

This early photo shows the Villa of Diomedes after it was excavated.

She carried a young boy in her arms. A young girl wearing golden jewelry accompanied her; as the fourth surge hit, she had covered her face with her clothing, gasping for breath.

The rest of the victims were dressed quite differently. Most wore canvas or cloth socks that were more like leggings; many had no shoes. The excavators concluded that they were slaves or servants. They also came to believe that the two skeletons found the previous year were the male head of the family, who carried the family's most valuable possessions, and another slave.

Word of this discovery and others traveled around the world. Pompeii and its Villa of Diomedes became part of the grand tour for wealthy American and English travelers. As a result, many tourists flocked to the ruins, not only to watch the excavators, but also to see the skeletons. They would wander through the ruins to encounter tableaux; that is, little scenes arranged by excavators that featured skeletons and objects found at the site. Two victims that fascinated early visitors to the site, according to the writer Jennifer Wallace, were found in the Gladiator's Barracks in 1766. These two men, either prisoners or gladiators, were said to have still been in shackles and chained to the wall when they died in the eruption. Excavators placed their skulls on shelves for all visitors to see.

Unfortunately, some tourists stole bones from the skeletons and other artifacts as souvenirs, since the large site was poorly guarded. It is not surprising, therefore, that of all the coins and jewelry found at the Villa of Diomedes, only two items have been preserved to this day: a necklace and a gemstone. The rest have disappeared without a trace.

 **STOP AND THINK**

Main Ideas and Details What details help support the main idea that the Villa of Diomedes attracted new attention to Pompeii?

Your Turn

Are You Curious?

Plan of Action If you were an archaeologist working on the excavation of an ancient city, what questions would you have about everyday life there? List several questions. Then write a paragraph that explains how you would go about looking for clues to find answers to your questions.

SOCIAL STUDIES

Can You Dig It?

Archaeological Records With a partner, choose two or three classroom objects and treat them as artifacts. Without naming the objects, record details about them, such as their height, length, width, and weight. Then give a description of where they were found in the classroom. Trade information with another pair, and see if you can identify their artifacts. PARTNERS

All of a Sudden

Turn and Talk Some historic changes occur slowly, over time, and others occur suddenly. With a partner, discuss how you think Pompeii would have changed through the years if Vesuvius had not erupted. Would we know as much about everyday life there if the disaster had not happened? Point out details in the selection that support your responses.

MAIN IDEA AND DETAILS

✓ **TARGET VOCABULARY**

unaffected	opulent
dormant	tremors
subjected	imprints
salvage	luxurious
outlying	meager

GENRE

Informational text, such as this science article, gives facts and examples about a topic.

TEXT FOCUS

Diagram Informational text may include a diagram, a drawing that explains how something works or how parts relate to each other.

SINCE VESUVIUS

Since the middle of March of 1980, Mount St. Helens in southern Washington State had been producing steam explosions and tremors. Scientists feared that an eruption was coming—and soon.

On May 18, Mount St. Helens did erupt. The volcano spewed ash and pumice over a 22,000-square-mile area. People who lived nearby had already moved to outlying areas. They were not able to salvage their homes, but most escaped with their lives.

The citizens of ancient Pompeii were not as lucky. Vesuvius's ashes buried both luxurious homes and meager dwellings. We have learned from their experience. Scientists today closely study active volcanoes to learn more about why and when they erupt.

Mount St. Helens: May 18, 1980

OUR FLUID EARTH

Today we know what the Pompeiians didn't: that Earth's interior is always in motion. The theory of plate tectonics tells us that Earth's outermost layer, or *crust*, is made of huge slabs of rock called *plates*. These plates fit together like puzzle pieces. They are thousands of miles across and about fifty miles thick. They float on a bed of molten rock, or *magma*. Magma is part of Earth's *mantle*, the layer that surrounds its core.

The plates don't fit together exactly. They push against each other and slip past each other. This movement can create volcanoes.

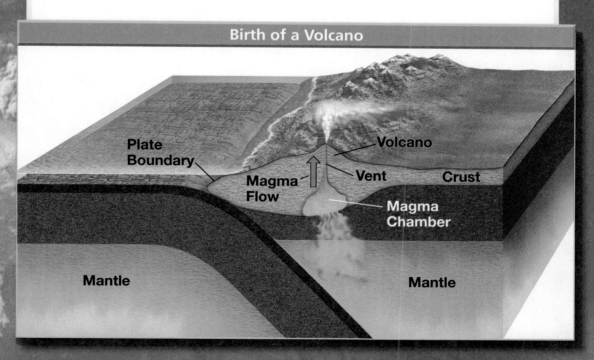

Birth of a Volcano

Plate Boundary · Volcano · Magma Flow · Vent · Crust · Magma Chamber · Mantle · Mantle

When two plates crash into each other, a chain reaction may begin that melts rock in the mantle. The liquid magma can rise through a surface opening called a *vent*. Lava, rocks, and ash build up around the vent, and a new volcano is born.

VOLCANO SPOTTING

No part of Earth is unaffected by plate movement. However, volcanoes usually leave their imprints at or near the edges of tectonic plates. These areas are subjected to more volcanic activity and earthquakes than other areas are. The edges of the plates surrounding the Pacific Ocean are especially active. Scientists call this area the "Ring of Fire."

LESSONS LEARNED

Scientists can now recognize some volcano warning signs, such as groups of small earthquakes. Lassen Peak, a volcano in northern California, erupted in 1915, a year after steam blasted through the ground near its summit.

We will probably never be able to predict the exact time of a volcanic eruption. Volcanoes can remain dormant for hundreds of years. Lassen Peak was quiet for 27,000 years before erupting! Still, because we know some of the warning signs, we are much safer than the people who lived in Pompeii's opulent villas.

One of the active volcanoes (red triangles) in the Ring of Fire is Lassen Peak. Lassen's boiling mud pots show its volcanic activity.

Making Connections

Text to Self

Talk About Preparedness Earthquakes and volcanic eruptions happen in many parts of the world. What types of natural disasters happen in the state or region in which you live? With a partner, discuss what you have done or could do to prepare for a disaster. Then write a list of instructions to follow in case of an emergency.

Text to Text

Connect to Science Draw a diagram of an eruption, based on what you have learned about volcanoes in "Bodies from the Ash" and "Since Vesuvius." Show one or more of the events in the eruption of Vesuvius or Mount St. Helens. Make more than one drawing if necessary.

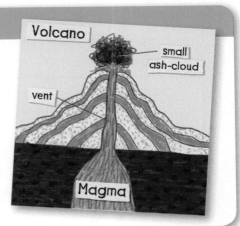

Text to World

Discuss Technology The people of ancient Pompeii had no time to escape the dangerous eruption of Vesuvius. Think about advances in technology since the time of ancient Pompeii. What are some ways that technology keeps people safe during natural disasters today? Share your thoughts with a small group.

Grammar

What Is an Adjective Phrase? What Is an Adverb Phrase? An **adjective** is a word that describes a noun or a pronoun. **Prepositional phrases** can also describe nouns and pronouns. When they do, they are called **adjective phrases**. An **adverb** is a word that modifies a verb, an adjective, or another adverb. Prepositional phrases can also modify verbs, adjectives, and adverbs. When they do, they are called **adverb phrases**.

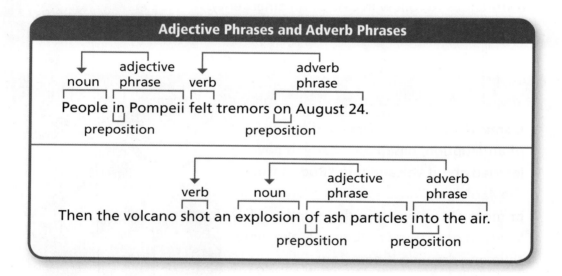

Adjective Phrases and Adverb Phrases

noun — adjective phrase   verb — adverb phrase

People in Pompeii felt tremors on August 24.

preposition   preposition

verb   noun — adjective phrase — adverb phrase

Then the volcano shot an explosion of ash particles into the air.

preposition   preposition

Turn and Talk With a partner, read aloud each sentence below. Tell whether each prepositional phrase in bold type is an adjective phrase or an adverb phrase. Then say which noun or verb it modifies.

1. **Throughout the morning**, most people ignored the warnings **from the volcano**.

2. **At one o'clock**, bakers were baking loaves **of bread**.

3. Then suddenly the volcano erupted **with a massive explosion**.

4. A thick cloud **of ash and rock** rose **from Vesuvius**.

Word Choice When you write, you can use prepositional phrases as modifiers to communicate details to your audience. Use adjective phrases to tell *what kind* or *which one* about nouns. Use adverb phrases to tell *how, where,* or *when* about verbs.

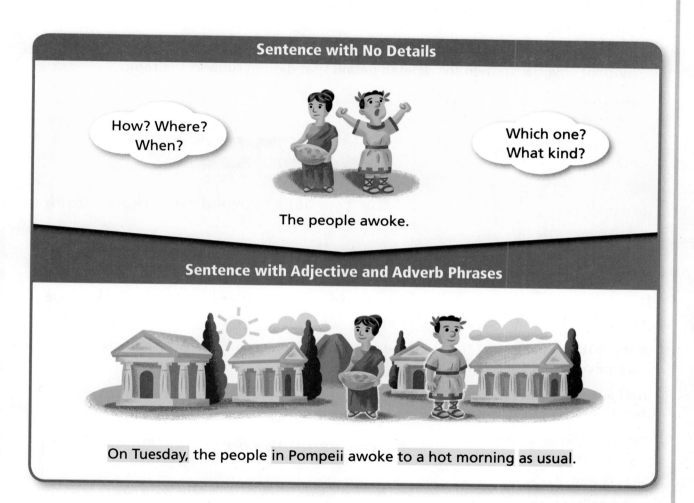

Sentence with No Details

How? Where? When?

Which one? What kind?

The people awoke.

Sentence with Adjective and Adverb Phrases

On Tuesday, the people in Pompeii awoke to a hot morning as usual.

Connect Grammar to Writing

As you revise your informational essay, look for sentences that can be improved by adding adjective phrases to tell about nouns or by adding adverb phrases to tell about verbs. Make sure that the meaning is clear in your new sentences.

Write to Inform

✔️ **Ideas** In an **informational essay** each body paragraph should give a main idea and details about the topic. The details you include should be facts and examples that support your topic and make your main ideas clear to readers.

McKenna drafted an informational essay about the beliefs of the ancient Egyptians. Then she deleted details that did not support the topic.

Writing Process Checklist

Prewrite

Draft

▶ **Revise**

✔️ In the first paragraph, did I introduce the topic?

✔️ Did I include specific facts?

✔️ Did I paraphrase using my own words?

✔️ Did I include a main idea and details in each body paragraph?

✔️ Did I write a conclusion?

Edit

Publish and Share

Revised Draft

The Egyptians believed that the pharaoh was not only a ruler but also a divine being, like a god. ~~The ancient Greeks also believed in gods and goddesses.~~ The pharaoh was given the right to rule from the gods. Only the pharaoh was allowed to communicate with the gods directly. The pharaoh was the leader of all the priests in Egypt. ~~The most famous pharaoh is King Tutankhamen.~~

Religious Beliefs of the Ancient Egyptians

by McKenna Mares

Archaeologists sift through ruins like detectives looking for clues. As they piece together bits of broken pottery or parts of statues, they also piece together facts. Archaeologists have pieced together many fascinating facts about Egyptian religious beliefs. The ancient Egyptians believed in gods and the afterlife, and this shaped the way they lived.

The Egyptians believed that the pharaoh was not only a ruler but also a divine being, like a god. The pharaoh was given the right to rule from the gods. Only the pharaoh was allowed to communicate with the gods directly. The pharaoh was the leader of all the priests in Egypt.

> In my final paper, I deleted details that did not support the topic. I also used prepositional phrases to make my writing more descriptive.

Reading as a Writer

What details did McKenna delete from her draft? Does your essay include any details that do not support your topic?

525

Rave Reviews About Rice

Risotto. Dolma. Biryani. Sushi. These words are from different languages, but they all name foods made with rice. Risotto is a rice dish from Italy that is made by cooking rice with butter, broth, and cheese. Dolma, popular in Greece and Turkey, is a mixture of rice and meat wrapped in grape leaves. Biryani is a dish made in India. It is cooked with highly seasoned basmati rice and meat or vegetables. Sushi is a traditional Japanese dish consisting of cooked rice wrapped in seaweed and topped with small pieces of fish or vegetables. The list goes on—fried rice, curried rice, Spanish rice, rice pudding. It may seem that people can't get enough rice, and in some ways that is true.

Facts About Rice

Rice is grown all over the world, on every continent except Antarctica. China and India are the top two leading producers of rice. About 90 percent of the world's rice crop is eaten in Asian countries. There, people usually eat rice two or three times daily.

In the United States, rice is grown in seven states—Arkansas, California, Florida, Louisiana, Mississippi, Missouri, and Texas. On average, a person in the United States eats 25 pounds of rice every year. When rice is cooked, it expands to three times its original weight. Fortunately, the people who eat the cooked rice don't grow quite as much! A half-cup serving of white rice contains only 103 calories, and a half-cup serving of brown rice contains only 108 calories.

Why Rice Is Popular

There are several reasons for rice's popularity. First, it's an excellent source of vitamins, minerals, and protein. Also, while it provides these important nutrients, it contains practically no fat, is low in sodium, and is cholesterol-free. Rice is inexpensive, requires no special storage conditions, and is easy to prepare. In addition, it can be grown in a variety of climates. Finally, there are many interesting and delicious ways to prepare and eat rice. Rice may be one of the world's perfect foods!

The Legend of the Rice

Ajay Dutt sat at the kitchen table doing his homework. His mother was making vegetable biryani for dinner. The fragrant basmati rice was cooking. Ajay's mother often said, "Grains of rice should be like two brothers: close, but not stuck together." Mrs. Dutt had moved to Washington from India before Ajay was born. Ajay liked to hear the old sayings and eat the foods of his mother's native land.

Now Mrs. Dutt cut potatoes, carrots, green beans, and cauliflower into small thin pieces for frying. She put oil into a pan and added mustard seeds, chili, cinnamon, and other seasonings. A wonderful smell filled the room as she asked, "Ajay, have I ever told you the Indian legend of the rice?"

Ajay set aside his homework and prepared to listen.

Mrs. Dutt continued to cook as she began the ancient tale. "Long ago, the Earth was young, and life was better in every way. Women and men were stronger and more beautiful. Trees were taller, and the fruit they bore was sweet beyond belief. Even the rice was larger. All a person needed for a meal was one grain of rice."

Ajay thought about how odd it would be to eat one grain of rice for a meal.

Mrs. Dutt put some yogurt in a blender and flipped the switch. Then she heated the yogurt and added the fried vegetables. "The people did not even have to gather the rice," she continued. "When it was ripe, it simply fell from the stalks and rolled directly into the village storehouses."

Ajay set the table while his mother added the cooked rice to the vegetables.

"One year there was so much rice growing in the fields that a widow said to her daughter, 'Our storehouse is too small. We must build a larger one.' They demolished the old storehouse. But the rice began rolling into the village before the new storehouse was ready. The widow became angry and struck a grain. 'Couldn't you have waited? We are not ready for you!' she shouted."

Mrs. Dutt put the biryani into a nice dish and garnished it with dried fruits and green coriander leaves. She carried it to the table. As he took a bite of the delicious food, Ajay asked, "What did the rice do?"

"It broke into a thousand pieces," Mrs. Dutt answered. "It said, 'From now on, we will wait in the fields!' And from that day forth, rice has been a small grain, and people must toil in the fields to harvest it."

Unit 4 Wrap-Up

The Big Idea

Choose Your Culture The selections in Unit 4 described Vikings and Romans, ancient Egypt, Greece, and China. If you could be a member of one of these ancient cultures, which would it be? Draw a picture of the location. If you want, put yourself in the scene. Write an extended caption for the picture, explaining why the culture interests you.

Listening and Speaking

Interview a Favorite Were you impressed by Hatshepsut? What could you learn from Theseus? With a partner, make up interview questions for a person from one of the civilizations you read about in Unit 4. Then conduct the interview, taking the roles of that person and a reporter.

Taking Charge of Change

Unit 5

Big Idea

Changing things for the better is worth the challenge.

Paired Selections

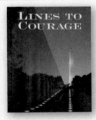

jeopardy

stable

blurted

eventually

scrounged

spiteful

comprehension

abrupt

exhilaration

oracle

Vocabulary
Reader

Context
Cards

Vocabulary in Context

1 jeopardy
If two friends can't talk about problems, their friendship may be in jeopardy. It may be in danger of ending.

2 stable
In a stable relationship, family members stick together through good times and bad.

3 blurted
A friend who has blurted a remark, saying it without thinking, may regret it afterwards.

4 eventually
On a relay race team, the last runner has to wait but eventually receives the baton from a teammate.

- **Study each Context Card.**
- **Use two Vocabulary words to tell about an experience you had.**

5 scrounged

When friends drop in unexpectedly, someone might serve a meal scrounged together from leftovers.

6 spiteful

Spiteful words are spoken or written for the purpose of hurting or angering someone.

7 comprehension

In a classroom, a teacher might feel relieved when a smile of comprehension shows that a pupil understands.

8 abrupt

A bus driver who has to come to an abrupt, or sudden, stop might call out a warning to the passengers.

9 exhilaration

A volunteer might feel a lift of exhilaration, or joy, after finishing a job that others appreciate.

10 oracle

You wouldn't need the Greek oracle at Delphi to predict that being kind and attentive will keep a friendship going.

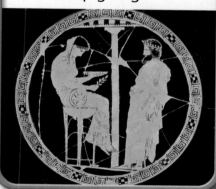

Background

The Ups and Downs of Friendship An oracle could tell you that even the best of friendships will eventually go through difficult times. A crisis may start with something as simple as an abrupt reply or a spiteful remark blurted out in the heat of the moment. Suddenly, the friendship may seem in jeopardy of ending. These challenges are a good test of a friendship. If it is stable, friends will work through the crisis. If they can't, then it may be time to decide whether to continue as friends. A friendship isn't something to be scrounged from good times here and there. It needs to be built on trust, kindness, and the comprehension of who each person really is.

There is nothing like the exhilaration of a close friendship, whether it is made up of two friends or more.

Comprehension

✔ **TARGET SKILL** **Compare and Contrast**

As you read "All Alone in the Universe," think about how elements of the story are alike and different. Compare and contrast characters, settings, and events, or show how attitudes of a single character, such as Debbie, change or remain the same through the story. A Venn diagram like the one below can help you show differences and similarities.

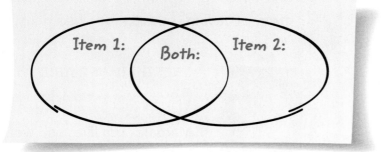

Item 1:   Both: Item 2:

✔ **TARGET STRATEGY** **Infer/Predict**

When you compare and contrast, you may need to make inferences—ideas only hinted at—from text clues or think about how characters might be changing. Making inferences deepens your understanding of the story.

✔ TARGET VOCABULARY

jeopardy	spiteful
stable	comprehension
blurted	abrupt
eventually	exhilaration
scrounged	oracle

✔ TARGET SKILL

Compare and Contrast
Examine how two or more details or ideas are alike and different.

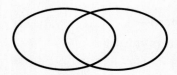

✔ TARGET STRATEGY

Infer/Predict Use text clues to figure out what the author means or what might happen.

GENRE

Realistic fiction has characters and events that are like people and events in real life.

Set a Purpose Before reading, set a purpose for reading based on what you know about the genre and your own experience.

MEET THE AUTHOR
Lynne Rae Perkins

Lynne Rae Perkins grew up in Cheswick, Pennsylvania—in her words, "a paradise of uninterrupted backyards with unlimited playmates." It forms the setting of both this selection and *Criss Cross*, which won the 2006 Newbery Award. The book uses haiku, song lyrics, and other techniques to tell the story of a group of friends. Says Perkins, "I think making books is a way of having conversations with people."

MEET THE ILLUSTRATOR
Margaret Lee

Margaret Lee lives and works in Toronto, Canada. To create an illustration, she often photographs a subject and then creates a new image using computer and collage. She has also worked in animation and created title sequences for movies.

All Alone in the Universe

by Lynne Rae Perkins   selection illustrated by Margaret Lee

Essential Question

How does a new friendship affect an old one?

Debbie and her best friend, Maureen Berck, have grown up together in the same small town, and it seems as if they will be inseparable forever. One summer, though, Maureen's new relationship with classmate Glenna Flaiber puts their friendship in jeopardy. The day after Debbie returns from a family vacation, the three girls go to a carnival.

Three is a lousy number in a lot of ways. One of those ways is that carnivals always have rides with seats that hold two people, so one person has to act as if she doesn't mind waiting by the fence or riding in a seat by herself or with some other leftover. This is why the Three Musketeers became friends with D'Artagnan. Not because of carnivals but because the number three is not a happy number. I know that in geometry the triangle is supposed to be an extremely stable shape, as in the pyramids, but in real life triangles are almost never equilateral. There are always two corners that are closer together, while the third is off a little ways by itself.

I was off a little ways eating some french fries from a paper boat, watching Glenna and Maureen ride the Calypso, when the idea first came to me that Maureen actually liked Glenna. Glenna was shouting over the noise and music of the ride. Whatever she shouted, it made Maureen laugh, and Glenna was laughing, too. They were spinning around together and laughing, their hands up in the air, slammed together by centrifugal force against the painted metal shell of their twirling car. I was in some other not-laughing universe, leaning on a fence that was standing perfectly still. The ride ended, and they tumbled and spun, still laughing, out of the car and through the gate. It seemed as if they might tumble right past me then, and I blurted out, "Anyone want a french fry?"

Maureen spun my way and said, "Oh, yum!"

Glenna said, "No, thanks, I don't like greasy food."

STOP AND THINK
Author's Craft In paragraph one the author creates a **symbol**, a visual image representing an idea, when she compares the girls' relationship to a triangle with "two corners that are closer together." Why is this an effective symbol in the story?

This was wise, because I was planning to put a curse on her french fry that would make her throw up on the next ride.

"Oh, well." I shrugged. "More for us."

Then I said, "I love greasy food."

"Especially when it's salty," added Maureen.

We gobbled up the french fries, and now it was Maureen and I who were together while Glenna remained on her greaseless, unsalted planet.

"Let's go on the Zipper," I said to Maureen.

"Okay," she said.

So we did, and then we all played a game of tossing quarters onto plates balanced on bottle tops. I won a lime green cross-eyed bunny, which I gave to Maureen. I said, "Here, I want you to have this because you mean so much to me. And because I don't want to carry it around."

She grinned and said, "Oh, wow. Thanks a lot."

She glanced down at the bunny as she took it, then held it up to Glenna and said, "Does this remind you of anything?" Glenna crossed her eyes, they both laughed, and that was one for Glenna. Then it was her turn to ride with Maureen, and that was two. Glenna and I weren't taking any turns together, but no one mentioned that.

537

Maureen was too busy having a great time to notice. Glenna was having a great time, too. I wasn't exactly having a great time. I felt off-balance, as if someone kept borrowing my right foot for a few minutes. As if someone were moving into my house while I still lived there.

The three of us wobbled around the dinky midway like a triangle trying to walk. I could see the grass already turning yellow under the parked trailers and their thick, tangled piles of extension cords. I could feel some odd new feelings—uneasy, spiteful, shapeless ones—creeping in.

I hate this stupid carnival, I thought, sitting on a bench across from the Ferris wheel as the other two points of the triangle rose up into the blue sky.

When we had spent all the money Mrs. Berck was willing to throw down the drain, we walked back to the car, where she was waiting, reading a book. It made sense geographically for me to be dropped off first. I got out and watched the car pull away. It was no different from a million times before. Through the rear window, beyond the collapsed tissue box and the green bunny, I saw Maureen's and Glenna's heads turn toward each other, and I felt myself falling away behind. But what could I do? I lived here; it was where I had to get out.

I walked over to rinse my feet off under the spigot. I didn't know how to wash away a crumminess that seemed to be swimming around in my heart. The garage door opened, and my dad pushed the lawn mower out from inside. He put a pretend surprised look on his face.

"Why, hello there, long-lost daughter," he said. "How's every little thing?"

"Okay," I said. I mustered up a smile from somewhere, mostly from his words and the sound of his voice. His words and his voice and my scrounged-up smile pushed the crummy feeling a little way off to the side, and I thought, Probably it was all in my mind.

It's because I was on vacation, I thought. I'm back now.
Don't be a dope, I thought. Maureen is your best friend.

But something was happening; something I couldn't see was shifting. When Maureen and I were together without Glenna, everything seemed fine. Almost. We had fun. We still laughed a lot. But before, when we laughed, we were just laughing. We couldn't help it; it just happened. Laughing and other kinds of thoughts or feelings traveled between us like breathing. Now I found myself holding on to good moments as if I could save them up and prove something to somebody.

It was getting hard even to *be* with Maureen without Glenna because Glenna was there so much. When I called Maureen on the phone, Glenna had already called. Or Maureen wasn't at home because she was sleeping over at Glenna's. Or I could hear Glenna's dippy voice in the background. Maureen always invited me to come along. And I would go, even though being together with Maureen *and* Glenna was not that much fun.

I couldn't figure out how Glenna managed to make so many plans so far ahead all the time.

On summer mornings, when you first wake up, you hear the birds chirping, and a shady green light filters through the leaves, and a coolness in the air means it still feels good to have at least a sheet pulled up over your shoulders. Maybe there is the faint whining and clanking of a garbage truck on a nearby street. For a minute or two you don't even think of any personal facts, like what your name is, or what town you live in, or what kind of life you might be having. Then you hear your mother outside talking to a neighbor or banging around in the kitchen, or you roll over and see your sister, still asleep in the other bed. You know who you are now, and your mind eventually gets around to what you might be doing that day. Which is when your heart feels light or sinks a little bit, depending.

From the backseat of the Flaibers' car, Glenna asked her mother what day they would be leaving for their vacation. My ears pricked up. An unexpected ray of hope lit up little dioramas in my head: happy pictures of a week (or two?) without Glenna. A scrap of song from a passing radio furled through the open window.

Finally, I thought. Finally.

Trying to keep my face calm, I waited for Mrs. Flaiber's answer.

"Saturday," she said. "But early. So probably Maureen should stay over Friday night."

What for? I thought giddily. So she can wave good-bye?

"That way she'll be sure to get up in time," Mrs. Flaiber went on. She threw a quick grin over her shoulder at Maureen. Maureen and Glenna grinned at each other. "We'll just roll you out of bed and into the car, Maureen!" said Mrs. Flaiber in a jolly way.

A tide of comprehension rushed in all around me, separating my little island from the shore where the three of them stood, getting into the car to drive away.

"Where are you going?" I couldn't help asking.

Apparently they could still hear my voice, although it sounded far away, even to me. At least Mrs. Flaiber could.

STOP AND THINK

Compare and Contrast What details on these pages show the difference between Debbie's emotions and her outward behavior?

540

"Borth Lake!" she answered. "We have a camp up there! We decided to let Glenna take along a friend this year! We'll be sitting on each other's laps, but we figure, the more the merrier!"

I don't know what else she said, but all the sentences had exclamation points at the end. The water rose over my island and lapped around my ankles. I pressed my fingers into my knees, then lifted them and watched the yellow-white spots disappear. Maureen's knees were right next to mine. There was her hand on the car seat, with the fingernails bitten down below the nubs, as familiar to me as my own. I looked out the window at whatever was passing by. I felt mean and small, like something wadded up. Weightless, like something that doesn't even matter.

Mrs. Flaiber's voice chorbled merrily away, cramming the air with colorful pictures of capsizing rowboats and dinners of fish fried with their heads still on and the eyeballs looking right at you. I could hear Glenna telling Maureen that Borth Lake was the seventh largest man-made lake in the state.

"Really?" I heard myself say. "That is so interesting."

Suddenly it seemed to me that if I didn't get out of the car, I might completely disappear, and I said, "Mrs. Flaiber, can you let me off here?"

All three heads turned my way, and the abrupt quiet told me that I had probably interrupted someone.

541

"I just remembered," I said. "There's something I have to do. For my mom. I have to pick something up for her."

"Where do you need to go?" she asked. "We can take you there and wait while you run inside."

"No, no—that's okay," I said. "Actually I feel like walking."

"Are you sure?" she said, pulling adroitly over to the curb.

"Yep," I said. "Thanks. See you guys later. Have fun on your vacation."

Then, looking right into Maureen's eyes, I said, "Call me when you get back."

I tried to keep my voice steady, but my eyes were shooting out messages and questions and SOSs. I saw them reach her eyes and spark there in a flash of surprise. She turned to Mrs. Flaiber and Glenna and said, "I'm going to get out here, too."

She was out of the car and closing the door before Glenna could follow. She leaned her head inside to say good-bye. Glenna and her mother wore the startled expression of fish twitching in the bottom of a rowboat or fried on plates. Mrs. Flaiber turned forward, and the car moved slowly back into traffic, crunching pebbles and grit musically beneath its tires.

I was surprised, too. A rush of exhilaration went through me. Maybe Maureen just hadn't seen what was happening, what Glenna was doing. Maybe I just needed to tell her. She dropped her beat-up tennis shoes onto the sidewalk and slid her toes inside.

"Are you mad?" she asked.

I just needed to explain it to her. Make her see. That was all. "Not mad," I said. Then I said it, what was in my heart:

"I just miss when we were friends."

I waited for her to get it.

"We're still friends," she said, standing on one foot to pull the back of her shoe up over her heel. She looked at me as if I had said something really humorous. "You goof," she said. "Hey, let's go down by the river."

She started off across the spongy, shimmering parking lot of the Seldem Plaza, leading the way through the canyons of wavy heat made by the parked cars. I followed her, like maybe I had my whole life. But wanting only to keep on doing that.

"You know what I mean," I said. A few shades less certain, though, that she would. "I miss the way we used to be friends. Before Glenna."

It crossed my mind that to anyone who happened to see us there, we would look the same as we always had. Debbie and Maureen. There they are. "Frick and Frack," my dad said. We would look the same. Did that mean something?

"You should give Glenna a chance," said Maureen. "She tries to be nice to you."

We moved through a short tent of shade next to the supermarket and then the scrubby weeds that are the native flora of Seldem, the kind that can grow up through concrete as long as it's not the middle part that cars drive over all the time. The kinds of scratchy weeds that grow about ten inches high, then branch out and blossom forth in stiff, itchy exploded seedpods.

"Glenna doesn't want to be my friend," I said. "Glenna wants to be *your* friend. Glenna would be happy if I disappeared from the face of the earth in a puff of smoke."

We looked at each other. We both knew it was sort of true, and we smiled a little bit the way you can smile at something that is true when it is said out loud for the first time. It was a relief, in a way, to know that Maureen saw that part of it.

STOP AND THINK
Infer/Predict What can you guess about Debbie's friendship with Maureen from the sentence, "I followed her, like maybe I had my whole life"?

For the moment that seemed enough. Going further seemed dangerous, like stepping off a cliff. Because I could also tell that Maureen wasn't going to be deciding right then and there to dump Glenna. She didn't see why she should.

I realize now that Maureen saw something in Glenna that I could not see. (I leave it to her biographers, or maybe to microbiologists, to discover what that is.) Not that I was trying too hard.

Anyhow, it felt safer then to leave that topic behind and take this bit of time with Maureen any way I could get it. To add it to the little pile of proofs that I hoped would add up to some charm that could eventually ward off Glenna.

So we squeezed between the dusty bushes to get to the riverbank, where we sank our feet into the silty mud, and sat on the low, bouncing branch of a big old tree that leaned out over the water. We crossed our legs like yogis and tried to balance there with our eyes closed. The shallow part of the river flowed along steadily, but in no hurry, about a foot below our branch, greenish brown, the color of a dollar bill. We opened our eyes and dangled our feet, making whirls and eddies form around them, talking about whatever, one thing or another. The sun must have been moving along up above the trees because the patches of sunlight shifted bit by bit over the moving surface of the water, lighting up patches of our shoulders and legs and the tops of our heads. In a way it was the best afternoon of the summer. But it was also like a prediction from the oracle at Delphi; it could mean practically anything.

Your Turn

Coming to Life

Write a Paragraph The author of "All Alone in the Universe" allows readers to infer Debbie's feelings through descriptions instead of simply telling readers how she feels. Write a paragraph in which you evaluate how well this method works. Use examples from the story to support your opinion.

AUTHOR'S CRAFT

Three's a Crowd

Write a Poem With a partner, brainstorm groups of three people or things that go together, such as the Three Musketeers or the Three Little Pigs. Choose one trio, and imagine that one of the three members feels left out, as Debbie often did. Write a poem about his or her problem. PARTNERS

Friends Forever

Turn and Talk With a partner, discuss the reasons why friendships change. Compare and contrast your own experiences in which new friendships changed your old ones. How can you keep old friendships strong while still building new friendships?

COMPARE AND CONTRAST

DNA
DETECTIVES

BY DOLORES HURLEY

In the 1950s, a race was taking place in England. Two teams of scientists, including one researcher who worked alone, were on their way to making one of the most important discoveries of the century: the structure of the DNA molecule. DNA carries the chemical code that determines the characteristics of all living things.

At Cambridge University, James Watson, an American, and Francis Crick, an Englishman, were friends and partners. Watson and Crick knew what DNA was, but they didn't know how its parts were connected. They built models of the molecule, using materials scrounged around their lab, but they couldn't make all the pieces fit.

Francis Crick

THE TWISTED LADDER

Meanwhile, at King's College in London, Rosalind Franklin was using x-rays to try to photograph a DNA molecule. Unlike Watson and Crick, Franklin did not have a friendly, stable relationship with her colleague, Maurice Wilkins. Wilkins had an abrupt manner and often treated Franklin like an assistant.

Despite the tension, Franklin continued to work. It took one hundred tries, but eventually, in 1952, she was able to create a clear photograph of DNA. Without her knowledge, however, Wilkins showed the photo to Watson. Some believe that Wilkins did this to be spiteful because of his dislike for Franklin.

Franklin's photo showed a blurry "X." It was a moment of exhilaration for Watson. "The instant I saw the picture my mouth fell open," he said. The photo led Watson and Crick to a new comprehension. It helped them build a twisting, ladder-shaped model of the DNA molecule. On February 28, 1953, Crick walked into a Cambridge restaurant and blurted that he and Watson "had found the secret of life."

James Watson

Rosalind Franklin's famous x-ray, "Photograph 51," of a DNA molecule

THE MISSING NOBELIST

In 1962 a Nobel Prize in Medicine was awarded to James Watson, Francis Crick, and Maurice Wilkins for their work on DNA. Sadly, the woman whose photo was important to their success was not awarded the prize. Rosalind Franklin had died of cancer in 1958, and the Nobel Prize is given only to living recipients. Some people think that Franklin's work with x-rays put her health in jeopardy. Crick has said that, had she been alive, Franklin should have received the prize because "she did the key experimental work."

Rosalind Franklin

WHAT IS DNA?

DNA is like an instruction book for creating living things. DNA molecules contain four chemicals that attach to each other across the twisted-ladder shape known as a double helix. The pairs of chemicals are the "steps" on the "ladder," and the chemicals can pair up in different patterns. Each pattern is a kind of oracle, predicting what many of the features of a plant or animal will be.

The double helix structure of a DNA molecule

Making Connections

Text to Self

Write a Letter Maureen seems not to notice that she is ignoring Debbie. Think of or imagine a time when you ignored someone, even if by accident. Write a letter to this person, explaining the situation from your viewpoint.

Text to Text

Draw Parallels "DNA Detectives" explains that "DNA is like an instruction book for creating living things." Think about how "All Alone in the Universe" might be an instruction book for friendships. Could a friendship be considered a living thing? Share your ideas with a partner. Then, work together to create a table of contents for a friendship instruction book.

Text to World

Connect to Science DNA supplies the code for plant cells as well as animal cells. Research and draw a plant cell, including the nucleus and chloroplasts. Show how the cell is involved in the process of photosynthesis. Share your project with a small group.

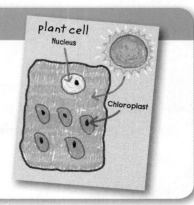

Grammar

What Are Progressive Forms of Verbs? Verb phrases such as *is running* and *has been sleeping* tell about action that is continuing, or *in progress*. These verb phrases are called **progressive forms**. Each of the six verb tenses has a progressive form.

Academic Language

present progressive

past progressive

future progressive

present perfect progressive

past perfect progressive

future perfect progressive

Present Progressive	I <u>am talking</u> with my friend about summer vacation.
Past Progressive	I <u>was talking</u> with her about it yesterday.
Future Progressive	I <u>will be talking</u> with her again later today.
Present Perfect Progressive	I <u>have been talking</u> with her for two hours.
Past Perfect Progressive	I <u>had been talking</u> with her only a few minutes when we had to leave.
Future Perfect Progressive	I <u>will have been talking</u> with her for three weeks by the time vacation starts.

Turn and Talk **With a partner, read each sentence below aloud. Then tell how you would change the verb or verb phrase to the form shown in parentheses.**

1 My friend and I walked to school. (past progressive)

2 I had told her about a cute dog on this street. (past perfect progressive)

3 She has taken photos of dogs. (present perfect progressive)

4 We will look at the photos together. (future progressive)

Conventions Using verb tenses and forms correctly will help you communicate clearly in your writing. If you are writing about events that are occurring at the same time or that are ongoing, use the same tense. Change from one tense to another only if events happen at different points in time.

Inconsistent Tenses	Consistent Tenses
My friends and I **have wanted** to go to the carnival for ages. We **had waited** for this day for weeks! After much discussion, we **are agreeing** on which rides we will try.	My friends and I **have wanted** to go to the carnival for ages. We **have waited** for this day for weeks! After much discussion, we **have agreed** on which rides we will try.

Connect Grammar to Writing

As you edit your opinion paragraph, look for verbs whose tenses should be changed to make your meaning clear.

Write to Persuade

☑ **Voice** Strong writers who intend to persuade readers find ways to show their feelings about their topic, rather than simply stating them. As you write your **opinion paragraph**, choose words and give examples that clearly show your feelings.

Oliver drafted a paragraph on the best things about having close friends. Later, he added strong reasons and examples to support his opinions and to show his feelings.

Writing Traits Checklist

☑ **Ideas**
Did I give reasons to support my opinions?

☑ **Organization**
Did I address my reasons one at a time?

☑ **Sentence Fluency**
Did I combine sentences to vary their structure?

☑ **Word Choice**
Did I use verb tenses correctly?

☑ **Voice**
Did I show my feelings instead of telling them?

☑ **Conventions**
Did I use correct spelling, grammar, and punctuation?

Revised Draft

Another great thing about having close friends is that they can cheer you up. They try to do this whenever you're down. ∧My friends kn~~o~~ew just the kinds of jokes that would ∧make me laugh. Nothing beats having close friends.

Last week, when I got a disappointing grade on a math test, my

Nothing Beats Having Close Friends

by Oliver Drummond

One of the best things about having close friends is that their way of thinking can be similar to yours. For instance, sometimes my friends and I make up songs. One of us thinks of a line of lyrics or the start of a tune. Someone else jumps in to add another line or part of the tune. Before long, we've written a song. Another great thing about having close friends is that they can cheer you up. They try to do this whenever you're down. Last week, when I got a disappointing grade on a math test, my friends knew just the kinds of jokes that would make me laugh. Nothing beats having close friends.

In my final paper, I showed how I feel about my topic. I also used verb tenses correctly.

Reading as a Writer

How did Oliver make his ideas more persuasive? What revisions can you make to reveal your own feelings in your opinion paragraph?

✓ **TARGET VOCABULARY**

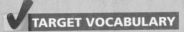

elusive

frustration

instinct

conditions

barren

harsh

decrepit

arose

vertical

lurched

Vocabulary
Reader

Context
Cards

Vocabulary
in Context

1 elusive

The "aha!" moment that leads to an invention may be elusive. It may not be easy to achieve.

2 frustration

Inventors may feel frustration, or angry impatience, at their slow pace of progress.

3 instinct

Thomas Edison and other inventors relied on instinct, a natural sense of what to do, to solve problems.

4 conditions

At Kitty Hawk the Wright brothers found the ideal conditions of wind and landscape to test their airplane.

- **Study each Context Card.**
- **Make up a new context sentence that uses two vocabulary words.**

5 barren

This jet-powered car achieved a speed of 763 miles per hour on an empty, barren desert in Nevada.

6 harsh

Firefighters' equipment was invented to protect them from the harsh, brutal heat of a blaze.

7 decrepit

After a car becomes old and decrepit, its owner might replace it with a newer, stronger model.

8 arose

When a storm suddenly arose, Benjamin Franklin flew a kite and proved that lightning is a form of electricity.

9 vertical

Communications devices, such as cell phones, require tall vertical towers to pick up signals in the air.

10 lurched

The cars of this early locomotive have lurched forward with a sudden burst of steam power.

Background

Early Aviators One windy December day on a barren beach in North Carolina, two brothers achieved an ancient and elusive goal: self-powered flight. For many centuries, people had envied the flying instinct of birds and tried to copy their ability. There were some successes. In 1783, French spectators marveled at the vertical lift-off of a hot-air balloon and its flight over Paris. Meanwhile, determined dreamers strapped themselves into makeshift wings and decrepit flying machines. Even in perfect conditions, when no gust of wind arose, most of these contraptions lurched and plummeted to a harsh landing.

The Wright brothers, two bicycle mechanics from Ohio, studied the attempts of the German aviator Otto Lilienthal, who had been experimenting with the glider. They also learned from their own mistakes. In 1903, they saw their frustration end and a new era of flight begin.

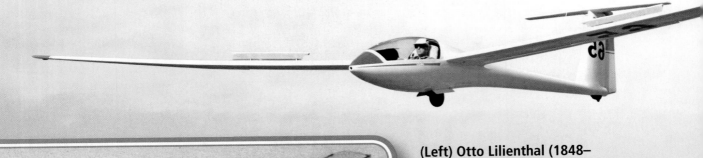

(Left) Otto Lilienthal (1848–1896) inspired the Wright brothers with his early glider flights. (Above) Gliders, which soar without the power of an engine, are still popular today.

556

Comprehension

✔ **TARGET SKILL** **Conclusions and Generalizations**

As you read "First to Fly," use details from the text to draw conclusions or make generalizations about the Wright brothers. Conclusions are judgments you make based on details. Generalizations are broad statements that say something true about a range of facts. Use the chart below to list details that support one conclusion or generalization.

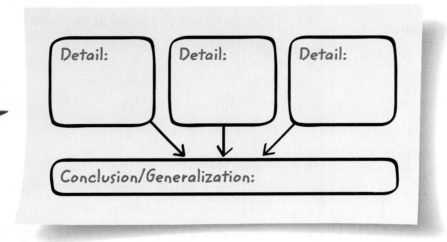

Detail:

Detail:

Detail:

Conclusion/Generalization:

✔ **TARGET STRATEGY** **Monitor/Clarify**

When you draw conclusions or make generalizations about "First to Fly," monitor your reading to make sure the details support your judgment. If you are uncertain, reread to clarify your understanding of the text.

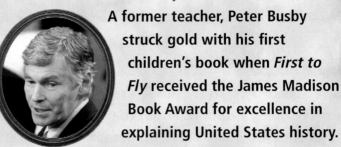

A former teacher, Peter Busby struck gold with his first children's book when *First to Fly* received the James Madison Book Award for excellence in explaining United States history. Busby, from Vancouver, British Columbia, and artist David Craig received the honor while standing beneath the 1903 Wright *Flyer*, which is displayed in the Smithsonian National Air and Space Museum.

TARGET VOCABULARY

elusive	harsh
frustration	decrepit
instinct	arose
conditions	vertical
barren	lurched

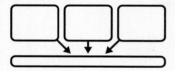

TARGET SKILL

Conclusions and Generalizations Use details to explain ideas that aren't stated or are generally true.

TARGET STRATEGY

Monitor/Clarify As you read, notice what isn't making sense. Find ways to figure out the parts that are confusing.

GENRE

Narrative nonfiction gives factual information by telling a true story.

Set a Purpose Before reading, set a purpose for reading based on what you know about the genre and your own experience.

MEET THE ILLUSTRATOR
David Craig

David Craig grew up in Ottawa, Ontario, the capital of Canada. A keen student of Canadian and United States history, he has designed coins for the Canadian Mint and has illustrated books about the Alamo, World War II, the Battle of Gettysburg, and the 1906 San Francisco earthquake.

FIRST TO FLY

How Wilbur & Orville Wright Invented the Airplane

by Peter Busby • paintings by David Craig

It's the spring of 1900, and brothers Wilbur and Orville Wright have traded bicycle making for the elusive dream of building a piloted aircraft. They're setting up camp to test their latest glider at Kitty Hawk, on a barren, windswept island in North Carolina.

It was far from perfect, but the brothers would learn to love it. There were two lifesaving stations, a weather bureau, a post office, and about twenty little houses among the sand dunes—but not much else. Wilbur's trip to Kitty Hawk, with the glider packed in a crate, was an incredible journey, by train, ferry, then fishing boat. The last part of Wilbur's trip, in a decrepit, flat-bottomed fishing schooner, was a nightmare. It started off calm enough, but when they reached the open sea, a storm arose. The cabin was so filthy that Wilbur spent the whole night on deck. Soaked to the skin, shivering cold, and ravenously hungry, with nothing to eat but a jar of jam, Wilbur wondered if he'd ever set foot on land again. Finally they docked at Kitty Hawk just before dawn. His hosts—the local postmaster Bill Tate and his wife—greeted him with a splendid breakfast of ham and eggs.

Orville arrived two weeks later, bringing supplies of tea and coffee, and they pitched their tent on the sand dunes, close to where they would fly the glider. Their mechanic, Charles Taylor, was left in charge of the bicycle shop back home.

"We certainly can't complain of the place," Orville wrote to his sister, Katharine. "We came down here for wind and sand, and we have got them." Some nights, when the wind came in from the Atlantic, they would have to jump out of their cots and hold the tent to keep it from blowing away, with sand stinging their hands and faces.

Wilbur and Orville pitched a tent on the dunes.

Wilbur and Orville carry the 1900 glider back to camp.

The brothers started off cautiously, flying the glider as a kite. They simply held it up off the sand and let the wind take it, then they played out ropes attached to the struts (the parts between the wings). They pulled on other ropes that moved the wing-warping (side to side movement) and elevator (upward and downward movement) controls, practicing keeping the craft level and bringing it safely down to land, learning the skills of a pilot from the ground.

Each flight brought the moment closer when Wilbur would take his life in his hands and pilot the glider himself.

One day in early October, he was ready. He positioned himself in the cockpit of the glider with his hands on the elevator controls and his feet against the wing-warping controls. Orville grasped one wing tip, and Bill Tate the other, and the two hoisted Wilbur and the glider into the air. Wilbur heard a dry crack as the twenty-five-mile (40 km) per hour wind filled the fabric of the wings, and then he felt a sudden weightlessness. Orville and Bill played out the ropes, letting Wilbur soar higher and higher.

> **STOP AND THINK**
> **Monitor/Clarify** If after reading page 561 you're confused about why the brothers need to test the glider from the ground first, what can you do to better understand their thinking?

The next few seconds passed in a blur. He'd thought there would be all the time in the world to plan his moves, to look around him, and to experience life from the air. Instead he found himself functioning on pure instinct as the plane lurched up and down, one moment plunging straight for the ground, the next nosing upward, threatening to stall and fall over on its back. "Let me down!" he shouted.

Orville and Bill pulled on the ropes and brought the glider safely down onto the sand. Wilbur had done it. He had flown. But he was not intending to risk it again, not until he understood the plane a lot better. For the next two weeks, they went back to testing the craft as a kite, using weights instead of a pilot, noting how it behaved in different wind conditions, and measuring everything: drag, lift, wind speed, and the angle at which the glider kite flew. They even tried turning the glider around, with the elevator in the rear.

In the final week, Wilbur had the confidence to fly again and this time he would try free flight, without the ropes. Altogether, he made about a dozen glides between 200 feet (61 m) and 300 feet (91 m) in length. On October 23, they went home, leaving the glider behind on the dunes. During the winter, it would be destroyed by the savage Atlantic gales—all except for the sateen wing covering. A few days after they left, Mrs. Tate removed the material and made it into dresses for her daughters.

Next July, the brothers were back in Kitty Hawk with a new glider, twice as big as the 1900 model. They made camp at the foot of Kill Devil Hills, a group of huge sand dunes four miles (6.5 km) to the south of Kitty Hawk. They built a shed for the glider, where they could sleep at night and be sheltered from the punishing weather— either the pounding rain or the scorching sun.

With Wilbur at the controls, Bill and Dan Tate let the wind lift the new glider off the top of the dunes.

Then there were the mosquitoes. "The sand and grass and trees and hills and everything were covered with them," Orville wrote to Katharine. "They chewed us right through our underwear and socks. Lumps began swelling all over my body like hen's eggs." They tried everything to protect themselves—blankets, netting, and finally smoking the mosquitoes out by burning old tree stumps.

At first the glider performed poorly, but after making adjustments to the elevator and the camber (the upward curve from the front to the rear of the wings), the brothers started doing better. Their friend Octave Chanute was present for their best glide—390 feet (119 m) in 17 seconds. He was impressed, but the brothers were dissatisfied. The glider's lift was not much better than last year, and the controls seemed worse.

On August 9, when Wilbur tried to turn the glider, he crashed nose-first into the ground, banging his head against a wooden strut.

The accident was not serious, but it added to the brothers' frustration, and they left Kitty Hawk earlier than planned. On the train home, Orville said what both of them were feeling: "Not within a thousand years will man ever fly."

The brothers did not stay depressed for long. Instead they decided to go back to the beginning and think through everything they had done. If size alone hadn't improved their performance, then maybe the secret was the shape of the glider and the wings. To research this, they built a wind tunnel in the workshop. For the next few months, there would be no camping on the dunes and gliding in the open air. Instead they were indoors, testing almost two hundred wing shapes. Every day, they made new discoveries about how the wings of a plane behave in the air. At the end of their research, they had the design of a new glider that was very different from the ones they had made before.

In the first three days back at Kitty Hawk, they made more than fifty flights in the 1902 glider. Already they were staying in the air longer than they had before. Orville had begun to fly a little in the previous year, and now he was making half the flights. One day, as he took the plane higher, the glider nosed upward at a dangerous angle. Orville pushed on the elevator, struggling to get the plane level again. To his horror, he found himself slipping backward, tail-first, toward the ground. There was a crash of splintering timber as the tail pounded into the sand.

Orville stepped out of the glider without a scratch. The tail could soon be mended, but it was obvious that there was something wrong with its design. The 1902 glider was their first one to have a tail, which was fixed in a vertical position. The tail was supposed to give the plane more control, but Orville felt it wasn't doing that. He had an idea. What if they put a hinge on the tail, so that the pilot could move it at the same time as he warped the wings to make a turn?

Orville suggested this to Wilbur, then waited for his brother's reaction. He expected an argument, because that was the way the

The 1902 glider was their first one with a fixed tail. After problems during early trials, Orville suggested a movable tail or rudder. With a rudder, they could keep the glider pointed in the proper direction as they rolled into a turn.

brothers worked out their ideas. "Both boys had tempers," Charles Taylor later recalled. "They would shout at one another something terrible. I don't think they really got mad, but they sure got awfully hot." Instead, on this occasion, Wilbur said nothing for a while, then told Orville he agreed about hinging the rudder but he had a better idea. Instead of having a separate control, they should connect the wing-warping controls and the rudder, so the pilot could use the hip cradle to move both at the same time.

That's what they did, and it worked perfectly. They started doing longer glides, and the control problem was solved.

That year, the Wright brothers made almost a thousand flights. On their final day of gliding, they broke their record again with a glide of 622 feet (190 m), lasting 26 seconds. Wilbur and Orville went home happy. They had achieved their first goal, designing a glider that could be controlled in the air. Now they were ready to build a plane with an engine and propellers.

 STOP AND THINK

Conclusions/Generalizations What evidence on pages 564–565 supports the conclusion that the Wright brothers are determined inventors who learn from their mistakes?

Twelve Magic Seconds

On the morning of December 17, 1903, Wilbur and Orville Wright stepped out of their shack and looked around them. Ice had formed in puddles between the sand dunes from the heavy rain overnight, but the sky was now clear. The weather was almost perfect—except for the wind.

The winds were stiff today—thirty knots. The brothers were cautious men. Any other day, they would have waited for calmer conditions, but they had lost enough time already in the two months they'd spent at Kitty Hawk. There had been problems tuning the engine, making it run smoothly, and cranking up the power, and twice they had had to send the propeller shafts back to Dayton for repairs. Soon it would be winter, the weather would be too harsh, and they'd have to get back to the bicycle shop.

They decided to risk it. Today was the day. They were going to attempt to fly their plane.

Orville hoisted a large red flag on the roof of the shack. The flag was a signal to the men of the Kill Devil Life Saving Station, a mile (1.6 km) away, to come and lend a hand. The over 700-pound (318-kg) *Flyer* was too heavy for two men to carry by themselves. And the brothers had another reason for inviting people to join them. If the world was going to believe them, they had to have witnesses.

A short distance from the house, Wilbur and Orville started laying a line of wooden beams. The machine would move along this track until the propellers pushed the wings through the air fast enough to lift the plane off the ground. By the time they'd finished, the lifesaving crew had arrived.

Once the *Flyer* was in position, Wilbur and Orville took hold of the blades of the two propellers and pulled hard to give them a spin. The engine sputtered and coughed into life.

STOP AND THINK

Author's Craft The author uses the phrase "coughed into life" on page 566 to describe how the plane's engine turns on reluctantly. Why do you think he chooses this **personification**, giving a nonhuman object human qualities?

Wilbur and Orville start their engine by spinning the blades of the two propellers.

Wilbur took aside one of the lifesavers, John Daniels, and showed him the camera placed on a tripod near the ramp. There was a cord attached to it with a rubber ball at the end. When the *Flyer* leaves the ground, Wilbur explained, you squeeze this ball. Daniels looked worried. He had never used a camera before.

The two brothers walked away from the others for a quiet moment. They had spent five years on this project, designing a series of gliders, learning how to control them in the air, and finally, because no one else could make an engine light enough and powerful enough, they had built one themselves in the bicycle workshop.

They had made their first attempt with the Wright *Flyer* three days earlier, on December 14. The track was laid down the side of a hill; then the brothers tossed a coin to decide who would be the pilot. Wilbur won. He climbed into the plane. The *Flyer* rattled down the ramp and lifted off. Wilbur was in the air—but soon he was in trouble. He rose no higher than fifteen feet (4.6 m), then lost height, landing awkwardly with the left wing plowing into the sand. Some might call this a flight, but not the Wrights. A flight for them had to be controlled.

The *Flyer* was soon repaired. It was a mistake, the brothers decided, to take off going downhill. Today they had laid the track on a flat piece of sand.

Now it was Orville's turn to be the pilot. He climbed into the hip cradle on the bottom wing and lay flat on his stomach, settling his hips into the cradle that controlled the wing-warping and rudder, and grasping the lever that controlled the elevator.

"Orville's going to be nervous," Wilbur said to the men watching. "Let's try and cheer him on. Holler and clap."

He turned back to his brother and they clasped hands as if, one of the lifesavers said later, "they weren't sure they'd ever see each other again."

Wilbur took his place at the wing tip as his brother released the wire holding the straining plane in place. The propellers began to move the plane faster and faster along the track.

Wilbur was running next to him, shouting encouragement, ready to let go of the wing.

Then, forty feet (12 m) down the track, the *Flyer* lifted into the air. Wilbur clicked on his stopwatch.

Orville pulled up on the elevator. The *Flyer* started up at a dangerous angle, about to stall and fall back on its tail. Orville reacted,

At Kill Devil Hills, at 10:35 A.M., December 17, 1903, Orville takes off on the first-ever manned and powered flight. Wilbur, who steadied the plane while it moved down the launching rail, is still half-running. This famous photograph was taken with Orville's camera by John Daniels, one of the lifesaving station crew.

throwing the elevator lever down. Now the *Flyer* was heading for the ground. Another touch on the elevator pulled the plane up again. Then down, and the *Flyer* pancaked into the ground. It was a hard landing, but both the plane and the pilot were in one piece.

Wilbur stopped his watch. The *Flyer* had been in the air for twelve seconds. He turned to John Daniels. "Did you get it?"

He had. His picture of the *Flyer* three feet (.9 m) off the ground, with Orville on board and Wilbur running beside him, is one of the most famous photographs ever taken.

Orville had flown 120 feet (36.5 m). Both of them thought they could do better. At 11:20 A.M., Wilbur made a flight of 175 feet (53 m). Then it was Orville's turn again. He managed 200 feet (61 m). At noon, Wilbur climbed into the pilot's cradle.

For the first 300 feet (91 m), it was like the other flights, with the plane bouncing up and down. Then Wilbur managed to keep it level for another 500 feet (152 m) until a sudden gust of wind caught it, sending it diving toward the ground.

Wilbur stepped out of the cradle, unhurt. He had flown for 59 seconds, traveling 852 feet (260 m).

The brothers made several successful flights at Kitty Hawk before moving their base to Huffman Prairie, near Dayton.

Once again, the seven men started back to the track carrying the plane. Just as they reached the track and set the machine down, the wind rose suddenly and caught the *Flyer*. Everyone jumped for it, John Daniels getting tangled in the wires as the plane rolled over and over. When it finally came to rest, the others rushed up and cut him free, snapping a few more wires and wooden ribs as they did so. He was lifted out uninjured.

The *Flyer* was smashed to pieces—but no matter. The Wrights were already thinking ahead, to their next and even *better* plane.

One of the young men dashed all the way to the post office at Kitty Hawk to deliver the news. For the Wright family it took a while longer, until the telegram arrived at 5:30 that evening. "Success four flights Thursday morning," it read. "All against twenty-one-mile wind started from level with engine power alone, average speed through air thirty-one miles, longest 59 seconds. Inform press. Home Christmas. Orville Wright."

Your Turn

Successful Duo

Write a Paragraph The Wright brothers had determination, patience, and the ability to solve problems. Which of these traits do you think was the most important? Write a paragraph that explains your answer. Then write about how this trait can be important to someone your age. PERSONAL RESPONSE

Flight Paths

Design a Feature With a partner, design an illustration or a graph to show the distances the Wright brothers flew at different times during their work at Kitty Hawk. Use a ruler or another measuring device to make sure that the distances are shown in correct proportion to each other. PARTNERS

It's a Small World

Turn and Talk With a partner, talk about the different ways in which airplanes have helped to bring together people around the world. As air travel continues to change and improve, what effect might airplanes have on the world? CONCLUSIONS AND GENERALIZATIONS

TODAY'S

MONDAY, MARCH 16

Young Pilot Sets Records

by Linda Cave

On July 1, 2006, a helicopter pilot named Jonathan Strickland landed his helicopter in Compton, California. Other pilots had done so before him, but this landing was special. It meant a vertical move to the top of an aviation record. Strickland's flight to Canada and back made him, at age fourteen, the youngest African American to fly a helicopter on an international roundtrip.

Jonathan Strickland, fourteen-year-old helicopter and airplane pilot

Jonathan with his flight teacher, Robin Petgrave

A Record-Breaking Flight

Jonathan's flight had begun nine days earlier, on June 22. Because he was too young to fly alone in the United States, his flight teacher, Robin Petgrave, accompanied him. Flying over lush Pacific rainforests and barren fields, Jonathan arrived in British Columbia, where he took tests to fly solo. For many young aviators, flying solo is an elusive goal, calling on instinct and practice. Jonathan's dream was to fly solo in an airplane and in a helicopter on the same day. On June 28, he became the youngest person to do so.

On Jonathan's return flight, rough weather conditions arose. The helicopter lurched at times, but it was not decrepit when it landed in Compton. Jonathan's friends and family greeted him, as did members of the Tuskegee Airmen. This African American squadron of the Army Air Corps endured the frustration of harsh racism at home while becoming one of the most successful fighter groups of World War II.

PEOPLE

Tomorrow's Aviators

Jonathan Strickland was eleven when he began his flight training at Tomorrow's Aeronautical Museum in Compton, California. The museum and its Aviation Explorer Program for teaching young people to fly were founded by Robin Petgrave. In return for their lessons, the students perform community service.

Strickland's goals for the future include a lot more flying. He wants to attend the U.S. Air Force Academy, and he hopes to become a test pilot and an airline pilot. "Taking this trip," he said, "gave me the opportunity to see a whole new world and to discover that there is so much more out there for me."

Aviation Explorer pilots Richard Olmos, Diamond Hooper, and Kenny Roy

Tomorrow's Aeronautical Museum Record-Holders

Name	Record	Age
Breean Farfan	Youngest Latina to fly roundtrip across the country	13
Jimmy Haywood	Youngest African American to fly an airplane on an international roundtrip flight	11
Kenny Roy	Youngest African American to fly solo in an airplane	14

Making Connections

Text to Self

Connect to Technology The airplane and other forms of transportation have made travel quicker and easier. Think of a typical day in your life. Write about how you depend on different forms of transportation to travel and how trains, planes, boats, bikes, buses, or cars affect your daily life. Add illustrations to your writing if you wish.

Text to Text

Interview Trailblazers Think about the character traits that helped Jonathan Strickland and Orville and Wilbur Wright meet their aviation challenges. Write a mock interview in which you ask them about their character traits. Have them explain how each trait helped them succeed.

Text to World

Make a Timeline The Wright brothers were the first to begin developing what would become a very complicated piece of machinery. How has the airplane evolved over the years? Research and create a timeline of significant events in the development of airplanes. Share your discoveries with the class.

Grammar

How Are Direct Quotations Written? A **direct quotation** gives a speaker's exact words. Direct quotations are set off in writing with **quotation marks**. Capitalize the first word and use a comma to set off a direct quotation from the other words in a sentence. In most cases, end punctuation, such as a question mark, a period, or an exclamation point, should go inside the closing quotation mark. If two or more speakers are having a conversation, write the words of each new speaker as a new paragraph.

"Which one of the Wright brothers arrived at Kitty Hawk first?" Rogelio asked his brother Teo.

"Wilbur arrived first," responded Teo. He paused, and then he added, "Orville joined him two weeks later."

Rogelio asked, "Why did they choose Kitty Hawk?"

Try This! **Rewrite each sentence on another sheet of paper. Use quotation marks, spacing, capitalization, and punctuation marks correctly.**

1. When did Wilbur first fly in the glider asked Loreen.

2. Teo paused and then said Wilbur first flew in the glider in October of 1900.

3. Then Loreen asked can you tell me who helped launch the glider?

4. Bill Tate and Orville Wright hoisted the glider into the air replied Teo.

Conventions Use quotation marks in your writing to let readers know which words are a speaker's exact words. When writing quotations, make sure quotation marks, commas, and end punctuation are placed correctly.

Incorrect	Correct
"I want to be a pilot" said Margo.	"I want to be a pilot," said Margo.
"What kinds of planes would you like to fly"? asked Raul.	"What kinds of planes would you like to fly?" asked Raul.
Margo quickly answered "I want to fly jets!	Margo quickly answered, "I want to fly jets!"

Connect Grammar to Writing

As you edit your problem-solution paragraph, make sure you have written any direct quotations correctly. Correct any capitalization and punctuation errors you find.

Write to Persuade

Skilled writers who persuade by proposing a solution to a problem choose words with specific positive or negative connotations. As you revise your **problem-solution paragraph,** change the connotations of your words so that your argument is stronger.

Anna drafted a paragraph proposing a solution to traffic congestion. Later, she added negative connotations to describe the problem and positive connotations to stress the advantages of her solution.

Writing Traits Checklist

✔ **Ideas**
Did I include clear details to explain the problem and the solution?

✔ **Organization**
Did I organize the paragraph clearly?

✔ **Sentence Fluency**
Did I vary the adjectives I used to describe the problem and solution?

✔ **Word Choice**
Did I use words with clear connotations?

✔ **Voice**
Do the connotations of my words show how I feel about my subject?

✔ **Conventions**
Did I use correct spelling, grammar, and punctuation?

Revised Draft

Horns honk. Drivers yell, "Let's go!"

Today, traffic congestion ~~affects~~ *frustrates* travelers

in nearly every city, whether large or small.

One solution is to make *smart* vehicles that

self-adjust their size according to the number

of people traveling in them. I call this *stylish*

invention a Trans-Cell.

The Trans-Cell
by Anna Sung

Horns honk. Drivers yell, "Let's go!" Today, traffic congestion frustrates travelers in nearly every city, whether large or small. One solution is to make smart vehicles that self-adjust their size according to the number of people traveling in them. I call this stylish invention a Trans-Cell. If only one person were in the Trans-Cell, it would shrink to a small yet cozy size. This means that, during commuting hours, the many gas-guzzlers that now carry only the driver would be replaced with much smaller—and cuter—Trans-Cells. Even a Trans-Cell holding two or three people would be smaller than a car is now. Thousands of trendsetters occupying much smaller vehicles on the roads would result in significantly less congestion.

In my final paper, I used words with clear connotations. I also edited my paper and used correct punctuation in my dialogue.

Reading as a Writer

How do the connotations of Anna's words influence your feelings about her invention? Where can you use words with connotations in your own problem-solution paragraph?

✓ **TARGET VOCABULARY**

occupying
confronting
implored
exasperated
contempt
strident
warily
intently
scornfully
subsided

Vocabulary
Reader

Context
Cards

Vocabulary in Context

1 occupying

The Danish people needed to be brave when German soldiers invaded and stayed, occupying their nation.

2 confronting

Confronting, or facing, an enemy in battle requires a great deal of courage.

3 implored

During World War II, posters implored, or urged, people to conserve materials and food.

CAN ALL YOU CAN

IT'S A REAL WAR JOB!

4 exasperated

Some people were exasperated with wartime shortages. Others accepted the lack of supplies calmly.

● **Study each** Context Card.

● **Discuss one picture. Use a different Vocabulary word from the one in the card.**

5 contempt

People who sold scarce items illegally, or on the "black market," were viewed with contempt, or disgust.

6 strident

Dictators might speak to citizens in harsh, strident tones in an effort to intimidate them.

7 warily

During the war, people greeted hopeful news warily, or cautiously. They tried to focus on helping the troops.

8 intently

A general focusing on a battleground often peers intently through a pair of binoculars.

9 scornfully

People who talked about war plans in public were referred to scornfully, with disgust, in World War II posters.

10 subsided

When victory came to Europe in World War II, tension subsided and people began to relax.

Background

✔ **TARGET VOCABULARY** **Denmark and Germany** When Germany went to war in 1939, the king of Denmark, Germany's northern neighbor, was intently aware of the danger to his small nation. He tried to stay out of the war. However, in 1940, the Germans invaded Denmark. Germany's Nazi (NAHT zee) leaders explained that they wanted to protect Denmark by occupying it until the fighting subsided.

Denmark's population included 7,500 Jews. The Nazis wanted to send them to death camps. Danes were exasperated with the inaction of their government. They showed their contempt through demonstrations. Protesters grew strident as they scornfully criticized the Nazis and implored their government to take a stand. In 1943, the Danish government began confronting the occupiers. The Germans took over the government in Copenhagen. Now it was up to the Danish people to act—warily, but bravely—and help Jews escape to nearby Sweden.

Denmark in World War II

0   50   100 Miles
0   50   100 Kilometers

North Sea

SWEDEN
(neutral)

DENMARK
(occupied)   Gilleleje

Copenhagen

Baltic Sea

Key
⊛ Capital
• Town
➤ Escape route

GERMANY

(Left) Sweden was a short boat trip from Copenhagen and other Danish ports such as Gilleleje (gihl eh LY uh). It meant hope for Danish Jews. (Below) German troops in Copenhagen, 1943

Comprehension

✔ **TARGET SKILL** **Cause and Effect**

As you read "Number the Stars," notice the cause-and-effect relationship between events. Sometimes the effect, or result, of one event will be the cause of another event. Key words or phrases, such as *because, that,* and *so,* can signal an effect. A chart like the one below can help you connect causes and effects as you read.

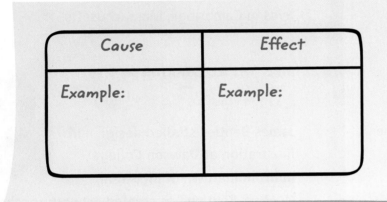

Cause	Effect
Example:	Example:

✔ **TARGET STRATEGY** **Analyze/Evaluate**

Understanding the relationship between causes and effects will help you analyze how the events of "Number the Stars" are connected. You can then evaluate how well the plot of the story works. Analyzing and evaluating helps you stay focused on what you are reading.

✔ TARGET VOCABULARY

occupying	strident
confronting	warily
implored	intently
exasperated	scornfully
contempt	subsided

✔ TARGET SKILL

Cause and Effect Tell how events are related and how one event causes another.

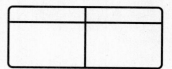

✔ TARGET STRATEGY

Analyze/Evaluate Think carefully about the text, and form an opinion about it.

GENRE

Historical fiction is a story whose characters and events are set in a real period of history.

Set a Purpose Before reading, set a purpose for reading based on what you know about the genre and your own experience.

MEET THE AUTHOR

Lois Lowry

Twice a winner of the Newbery Award for *Number the Stars* and *The Giver,* Lois Lowry has published over forty novels for young people, including nine about the energetic Anastasia Krupnik. "My books have varied in content and style," says Lowry. "Yet it seems that all of them deal, essentially, with the same general theme: the importance of human connections." Lowry lives in Cambridge, Massachusetts.

MEET THE ILLUSTRATOR

James Bentley

James Bentley studied design and illustration at Dawson College in his hometown of Montreal, Quebec. Bentley has created artwork for theater posters, advertisements, book covers, and magazines, as well as for private collectors.

Number the Stars

by Lois Lowry
selection illustrated by James Bentley

Essential Question

How does courage make a difference?

With Nazi soldiers occupying Copenhagen, Denmark, in 1943, Annemarie Johansen travels with her mother and younger sister Kirsti to her Uncle Henrik's house on the Danish coast. Uncle Henrik and Peter Neilsen, the fiancé of Annemarie's older sister, are helping Danish Jews escape in Henrik's boat to safety in Sweden. Among them is the family of Ellen Rosen, Annemarie's best friend. After helping escort a group of escapees to the harbor, Annemarie's mother trips on the way home and breaks her ankle. In the house she discovers that an important packet was not delivered. In alarm, Mrs. Johansen directs Annemarie to place the packet at the bottom of a lunch basket and hurry to the harbor before Uncle Henrik departs. On the way, Nazi soldiers stop Annemarie. They roughly search the contents of the basket.

Annemarie gave an exasperated sigh. "Could I go now, please?" she asked impatiently.

The soldier reached for the apple. He noted its brown spots, and made a face of disgust.

"No meat?" he asked, glancing at the basket and the napkin that lay in its bottom.

Annemarie gave him a withering look. "You know we have no meat," she said insolently. "Your army eats all of Denmark's meat."

Please, please, she implored in her mind. Don't lift the napkin.

The soldier laughed. He dropped the bruised apple on the ground. One of the dogs leaned forward, pulling at his leash, sniffed the apple, and stepped back. But both dogs still looked intently at the basket, their ears alert, their mouths open. Saliva glistened on their smooth pink gums.

"My dogs smell meat," the soldier said.

"They smell squirrels in the woods," Annemarie responded. "You should take them hunting."

The soldier reached forward with the cheese in one hand, as if he were going to return it to the basket. But he didn't. Instead, he pulled out the flowered cotton napkin.

STOP AND THINK

Author's Craft Annemarie gives the soldier a "withering look," a look so scornful it could make him dry up. Such **figurative language** helps a reader imagine one thing in terms of another. Find two other examples in the first five lines of page 587.

Annemarie froze.

"Your uncle has a pretty little lunch," the soldier said scornfully, crumpling the napkin around the cheese in his hand. "Like a woman," he added with contempt.

Then his eyes locked on the basket. He handed the cheese and napkin to the soldier beside him.

"What's that? There, in the bottom?" he asked in a different, tenser voice.

What would Kirsti do? Annemarie stamped her foot. Suddenly, to her own surprise, she began to cry. "I don't know!" she said, her voice choked. "My mother's going to be angry that you stopped me and made me late. And you've completely ruined Uncle Henrik's lunch, so now *he'll* be mad at me, too!"

The dogs whined and struggled against the leashes, nosing forward to the basket. One of the other soldiers muttered something in German.

The soldier took out the packet. "Why was this so carefully hidden?" he snapped.

Annemarie wiped her eyes on the sleeve of her sweater. "It wasn't hidden, any more than the napkin was. I don't know what it is." That, she realized, was true. She had no idea what was in the packet.

The soldier tore the paper open while below him, on the ground, the dogs strained and snarled, pulling against their leashes. Their muscles were visible beneath the sleek, short-haired flesh.

He looked inside, then glared at Annemarie. "Stop crying, you idiot girl," he said harshly. "Your stupid mother has sent your uncle a handkerchief. In Germany the women have better things to do. They don't stay at home hemming handkerchiefs for their men."

He gestured with the folded white cloth and gave a short, caustic laugh. "At least she didn't stitch flowers on it."

He flung it to the ground, still half wrapped in the paper, beside the apple. The dogs lunged, sniffed at it eagerly, then subsided, disappointed again.

"Go on," the soldier said. He dropped the cheese and the napkin back into her basket. "Go on to your uncle and tell him the German dogs enjoyed his bread."

All of the soldiers pushed past her. One of them laughed, and they spoke to each other in their own language. In a moment they had disappeared down the path, in the direction from which Annemarie had just come.

Quickly she picked up the apple and the opened packet with the white handkerchief inside. She put them into the basket and ran around

the bend toward the harbor, where the morning sky was now bright with early sun and some of the boat engines were starting their strident din.

The *Ingeborg* (EENG uh bawrg) was still there, by the dock, and Uncle Henrik was there, his light hair windblown and bright as he knelt by the nets. Annemarie called to him and he came to the side, his face worried when he recognized her on the dock.

She handed the basket across. "Mama sent your lunch," she said, her voice quavering. "But soldiers stopped me, and they took your bread." She didn't dare to tell him more.

Henrik glanced quickly into the basket. She could see the look of relief on his face, and knew that it was because he saw that the packet was there, even though it was torn open.

"Thank you," he said, and the relief was evident in his voice.

Annemarie looked quickly around the familiar small boat. She could see down the passageway into the empty cabin. There was no sign of the Rosens or the others. Uncle Henrik followed her eyes and her puzzled look.

"All is well," he said softly. "Don't worry. Everything is all right."

"I wasn't sure," he said. "But now"—he eyed the basket in his hands—"because of you, Annemarie, everything is all right.

"You run home now, and tell your mama not to worry. I will see you this evening."

He grinned at her suddenly. "They took my bread, eh?" he said. "I hope they choke on it."

"Poor Blossom!" Uncle Henrik said, laughing, after dinner that evening. "It was bad enough that your mother was going to milk her, after all these years of city life. But Annemarie! To do it for the very first time! I'm surprised Blossom didn't kick you!"

STOP AND THINK

Analyze/Evaluate How well does the author show Uncle Henrik's mood on page 589?

Mama laughed, too. She sat in a comfortable chair that Uncle Henrik had moved from the living room and placed in a corner of the kitchen. Her leg, in a clean white cast to the knee, was on a footstool.

Annemarie didn't mind their laughing. It *had* been funny. When she had arrived back at the farmhouse—she had run along the road to avoid the soldiers who might still be in the woods; now, carrying nothing, she was in no danger—Mama and Kirsti were gone. There was a note, hastily written, from Mama, that the doctor was taking her in his car to the local hospital, that they would be back soon.

But the noise from Blossom, forgotten, unmilked, uncomfortable, in the barn, had sent Annemarie warily out with the milking bucket. She had done her best, trying to ignore Blossom's irritated snorts and tossing head, remembering how Uncle Henrik's hands had worked with a firm, rhythmic, pulling motion. And she had milked.

"I could have done it," Kirsti announced. "You only have to pull and it squirts out. I could do it *easily*."

Annemarie rolled her eyes. I'd like to see you try, she thought.

"Is Ellen coming back?" Kirsti asked, forgetting the cow after a moment. "She said she'd make a dress for my doll."

"Annemarie and I will help you make a dress," Mama told her. "Ellen had to go with her parents. Wasn't that a nice surprise, that the Rosens came last night to get her?"

"She should have waked me up to say goodbye," Kirsti grumbled, spooning some imaginary food into the painted mouth of the doll she had propped in a chair beside her.

"Annemarie," Uncle Henrik said, getting up from the table and pushing back his chair, "if you come with me now to the barn, I'll give you a milking lesson. Wash your hands first."

"Me too," said Kirsti.

"Not you too," Mama said. "Not this time. I need your help here, since I can't walk very well. You'll have to be my nurse."

Kirsti hesitated, deciding whether to argue. Then she said, "I'm going to be a nurse when I grow up. Not a cow milker. So I have to stay here and take care of Mama."

Followed as usual by the kitten, Annemarie walked with Uncle Henrik to the barn through a fine misty rain that had begun to fall. It seemed to her that Blossom shook her head happily when she saw Henrik and knew that she would be in good hands again.

She sat on the stacked hay and watched while he milked. But her mind was not on the milking.

"Uncle Henrik," she asked, "where are the Rosens and the others? I thought you were taking them to Sweden on your boat. But they weren't there."

"They were there," he told her, leaning forward against the cow's broad side. "You shouldn't know this. You remember that I told you it was safer not to know.

"But," he went on, as his hands moved with their sure and practiced motion, "I will tell you just a little, because you were so very brave."

"Brave?" Annemarie asked, surprised. "No, I wasn't. I was very frightened."

"You risked your life."

"But I didn't even think about that! I was only thinking of—"

He interrupted her, smiling. "That's all that *brave* means—not thinking about the dangers. Just thinking about what you must do. Of course you were frightened. I was too, today. But you kept your mind on what you had to do. So did I. Now let me tell you about the Rosens.

"Many of the fishermen have built hidden places in their boats. I have, too. Down underneath. I have only to lift the boards in the right place, and there is room to hide a few people. Peter, and others in the Resistance who work with him, bring them to me, and to the other fishermen as well. There are people who hide them and help them, along the way to Gilleleje."

Annemarie was startled. "Peter is in the Resistance? Of course! I should have known! He brings Mama and Papa the secret newspaper, *De Frie Danske* (dee free DAN skee). And he always seems to be on the move. I should have figured it out myself!"

"He is a very, very brave young man," Uncle Henrik said. "They all are."

Annemarie frowned, remembering the empty boat that morning. "Were the Rosens and others there, then, underneath, when I brought the basket?"

Uncle Henrik nodded.

"I heard nothing," Annemarie said.

"Of course not. They had to be absolutely quiet for many hours. The baby was drugged so that it wouldn't wake and cry."

"Could they hear me when I talked to you?"

"Yes. Your friend Ellen told me, later, that they heard you. And they heard the soldiers who came to search the boat."

Annemarie's eyes widened. "Soldiers came?" she asked. "I thought they went the other way after they stopped me."

"There are many soldiers in Gilleleje and all along the coast. They are searching all the boats now. They know that the Jews are escaping, but they are not sure how, and they rarely find them. The hiding places are carefully concealed, and often we pile dead fish on the deck as well. They hate getting their shiny boots dirtied!"

He turned his head toward her and grinned.

Annemarie remembered the shiny boots confronting her on the dark path.

"Uncle Henrik," she said, "I'm sure you are right, that I shouldn't know everything. But, please, would you tell me about the handkerchief? I knew it was important, the

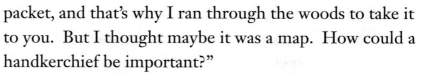

packet, and that's why I ran through the woods to take it to you. But I thought maybe it was a map. How could a handkerchief be important?"

He set the filled pail aside and began to wash the cow's udder with the damp cloth. "Very few people know about this, Annemarie," he said with a serious look. "But the soldiers are so angry about the escaping Jews—and the fact that they can't find them—that they have just started using trained dogs."

"They had dogs! The ones who stopped me on the path!"

Uncle Henrik nodded. "The dogs are trained to sniff about and find where people are hidden. It happened just yesterday on two boats. Those dogs, they go right through dead fish to the human scent.

"We were all very, very worried. We thought it meant the end of the escape to Sweden by boat.

"It was Peter who took the problem to scientists and doctors. Some very fine minds have worked night and day, trying to find a solution.

"And they have created a special drug. I don't know what it is. But it was in the handkerchief. It attracts the dogs, but when they sniff at it, it ruins their sense of smell. Imagine that!"

Annemarie remembered how the dogs had lunged at the handkerchief, smelled it, and then turned away.

"Now, thanks to Peter, we will each have such a handkerchief, each boat captain. When the soldiers board our boats, we will simply pull the handkerchiefs out of our pockets. The Germans will probably think we all have bad colds! The dogs will sniff about, sniff the handkerchiefs we are holding, and then roam the boat and find nothing. They will smell nothing."

"Did they bring dogs to your boat this morning?"

"Yes. Not twenty minutes after you had gone. I was about to pull away from the dock when the soldiers appeared and ordered me to halt. They came aboard, searched, found nothing. By then, of course, I had the handkerchief. If I had not, well—" His voice trailed off, and he didn't finish the sentence. He didn't need to.

If she had not found the packet where Mr. Rosen had dropped it. If she had not run through the woods. If the soldiers had taken the basket. If she had not reached the boat in time. All of the ifs whirled in Annemarie's head.

"They are safe in Sweden now?" she asked. "You're sure?"

Uncle Henrik stood, and patted the cow's head. "I saw them ashore. There were people waiting to take them to shelter. They are quite safe there."

"But what if the Nazis invade Sweden? Will the Rosens have to run away again?"

"That won't happen. For reasons of their own, the Nazis want Sweden to remain free. It is very complicated."

Annemarie's thoughts turned to her friends, hiding under the deck of the *Ingeborg*. "It must have been awful for them, so many hours there," she murmured. "Was it dark in the hiding place?"

"Dark, and cold, and very cramped. And Mrs. Rosen was seasick, even though we were not on the water very long—it is a short distance, as you know. But they are courageous people. And none of that mattered when they stepped ashore. The air was fresh and cool in Sweden; the wind was blowing. The baby was beginning to wake as I said goodbye to them."

"I wonder if I will ever see Ellen again," Annemarie said sadly.

"You will, little one. You saved her life, after all. Someday you will find her again. Someday the war will end," Uncle Henrik said. "All wars do."

"Now then," he added, stretching, "that was quite a milking lesson, was it not?"

STOP AND THINK

Cause and Effect What would have happened if Annemarie had not delivered the handkerchief to Uncle Henrik in time?

Your Turn

Out on a Limb

Write About Risks Write a paragraph that explains the risks Annemarie, her mother, and Uncle Henrik took in "Number the Stars" and why they were willing to take those risks. In a second paragraph, tell what you think the world would be like if people weren't willing to take those kinds of risks.

SOCIAL STUDIES

Secret Agent

Write a Code Work in a group. Have each group member create a secret code for these ideas in "Number the Stars": A boat is leaving for Sweden; German soldiers are approaching; this boat has a secret compartment. (For example, "The wind is blowing north today" could be a secret code for "A boat is leaving for Sweden.") Read the codes aloud, and have group members guess their meanings.

SMALL GROUP

The Effects of Courage

Turn and Talk With a partner, discuss the effects Annemarie's courage had on the Rosens. What might have happened if Annemarie had panicked? Then discuss what effect the events in the story will have on Annemarie's future, and how she might show her courage as an adult. CAUSE AND EFFECT

BOOK REVIEW

NUMBER THE STARS

by Carl Wallach

The award-winning novel *Number the Stars*, by Lois Lowry, is a story about danger, bravery, and friendship. It is set in Copenhagen and Gilleleje, Denmark, in 1943, during World War II. With German Nazi troops occupying Denmark, life is hard for Annemarie Johansen and her family.

Life is even harder for the family of Annemarie's friend Ellen, who is Jewish. The Nazis are planning to move the Jews from Denmark to concentration camps. Feeling contempt for the German soldiers, Annemarie's family resolves to help Ellen's family.

In the course of the novel, Annemarie finds her courage by confronting her fears. In a tense scene, she is delivering a mysterious package to her Uncle Henrik when she crosses paths with a group of German soldiers. In strident voices, they demand to know where she is going. They search intently through her possessions and warily interrogate her. After her panic has subsided, Annemarie responds scornfully. She acts exasperated and begins to cry. Implored by the sobbing girl that they leave her alone, the soldiers finally move on.

Just as memorable as the exciting action are the characters' relationships. The friendship between Annemarie and Ellen is the heart of this book. It makes personal an amazing event in history: the heroic actions of Danish citizens in smuggling some seven thousand Danish Jews to safety in Sweden.

Number the Stars is one of Lois Lowry's most powerful novels. Lowry has tackled a difficult subject with sensitivity. Readers who enjoy history as well as action will appreciate the historical details and the suspenseful plot. All readers will relate to Annemarie and Ellen's friendship and the moving examples of the strength of the human spirit.

(Left) Danish fishermen ferry Jewish passengers to safety in Sweden during World War II. (Above) Jewish refugees arrive safely in Sweden, October 1943.

An Interview with Lois Lowry

What led you to write about the topic of Denmark during World War II?

I think every piece of human history has fascinating individual stories connected to it. I just happened to have a Danish friend who told me of her own childhood in Copenhagen during the Nazi occupation there. With that personal connection, I was able to research the greater historical significance of the events in Denmark. But I tried to tell them on a personal scale, one child's story.

What are the challenges and rewards of writing historical fiction?

The challenge is to get it right. There had been some misinformation about the occupation of Denmark—people are still telling the (false) story that the king wore a yellow star in sympathy with the Jews. It didn't happen. I didn't want to be guilty of repeating myth. So I read a lot of history, talked to real people who had been there then, and tried to write the truth.

The reward was making an important story available and interesting to a young audience. There are countless children now who know about the integrity of the Danish people during that time, and who have been inspired by it. It's my hope that it has affected the thinking of young people about issues of prejudice.

Making Connections

Text to Self

Starting Fresh During World War II, many people were forced to flee their homelands. If you had to pick up and start life somewhere else, what aspects of your old life would you miss most? What would you do differently in your new home? Make two lists.

Text to Text

Evaluate a Review Think about the book review of "Number the Stars." Do you think Carl Wallach's review is accurate and complete? What would you add to the review if you could? Rewrite one part of the review with any changes or additions you see fit to make.

Text to World

Connect to Social Studies Lois Lowry hopes that readers of "Number the Stars" will think about issues of prejudice. Compare the Danes' fight against prejudice with other examples of people who fought or are fighting against prejudice. Share your thoughts with a small group.

Grammar

Academic Language

contraction

apostrophe

What Is a Contraction? A **contraction** is a word formed by combining two words and shortening one of them. An **apostrophe** takes the place of the letter or letters left out of the combined word. You can combine personal pronouns with verbs such as *is, are, have, had,* and *will* to make contractions. You can also combine some verbs with the word *not* to make contractions.

Contractions	
pronoun plus verb	<u>She's</u> my best friend. (She is)
pronoun plus verb	<u>They've</u> gone to the boat already. (They have)
verb plus *not*	Annemarie <u>hasn't</u> delivered the packet yet. (has not)
verb plus *not*	The soldiers <u>aren't</u> letting her go. (are not)

When you use a contraction with *not,* make sure you are not creating a double negative. Avoid using *ain't,* which looks like a contraction but is usually not accepted as a word.

 **Rewrite each sentence below on another sheet of paper, replacing the words in bold type with a contraction.**

❶ **I am** worried about Annemarie.

❷ That young girl **is not** acting politely.

❸ If she angers the soldiers, **they will** probably arrest her.

❹ She **will not** say anything about the boat or the Rosen family.

Conventions A single punctuation error can confuse your reader, so edit your writing carefully. When you write contractions, be sure to set the apostrophe in the correct place.

Incorrect	Correct
There are'nt any papers in the envelope.	There aren't any papers in the envelope.
Its empty except for a handkerchief.	It's empty except for a handkerchief.
The soldier does'nt expect this.	The soldier doesn't expect this.
Hes tossing the handkerchief to the dogs.	He's tossing the handkerchief to the dogs.

Connect Grammar to Writing

As you edit your persuasive letter, look for any contractions and make sure you have used and written them correctly.

Write to Persuade

✓ **Ideas** Successful persuasive writers use more than one approach in their arguments to appeal to their readers. As you revise your **persuasive letter**, use additional approaches to be more convincing.

John drafted a letter that the king of Denmark might have written to persuade the German government to remove its troops from Denmark during World War II. Later, he added a third approach to his argument.

Writing Traits Checklist

✓ **Ideas**
Did I use a variety of approaches to my argument?

✓ **Organization**
Is the body of my letter clearly organized?

✓ **Sentence Fluency**
Did I try combining sentences by changing words to adjectives?

✓ **Word Choice**
Did I use an appropriate greeting and closing?

✓ **Voice**
Did I consider my audience in my wording and reasoning?

✓ **Conventions**
Did I use correct spelling, grammar, and punctuation?

Revised Draft

I urge you to withdraw your troops from Denmark immediately. ^This withdrawal It is in your best interests for ~~two~~ ^three reasons.

First, you're upsetting the population.

The soldiers' practice of searching Danish citizens on the street frightens them.

Government of Germany,

I urge you to withdraw your troops from Denmark immediately. This withdrawal is in your best interests for three reasons. First, you're upsetting the population. The soldiers' practice of searching Danish citizens on the street frightens them.

Second, as long as you keep troops in Denmark, your reputation as a bullying nation grows. Surely, you must care what the world thinks.

Third, like Germany, Denmark is an independent country with the right to govern itself. We simply cannot tolerate uninvited foreign troops in our midst any longer. I'm certain your country would feel the same way if the situation were reversed.

Sincerely,
King of Denmark

My final paper includes three approaches to my argument. I also proofread my letter for correct use of contractions.

Reading as a Writer

How does John's third approach strengthen his argument? What additional approaches might you use in your own persuasive letter?

✓ **TARGET VOCABULARY**

conceive

controversy

distinguished

inclined

agitation

prejudice

significance

ecstasy

regal

serene

Vocabulary
Reader

Context
Cards

Vocabulary in Context

1 conceive

It took many people to conceive of the civil rights movement, just as it did to form the idea of the United States.

2 controversy

In the 1950s, sit-ins at lunch counters created controversy. People argued about civil rights.

3 distinguished

Martin Luther King Jr. was a distinguished leader. He was widely honored and respected.

4 inclined

Americans in 1964 were inclined, or likely, to vote for Lyndon Johnson, who supported a national civil rights law.

- **Study each Context Card.**
- **Ask a question that uses one of the Vocabulary words.**

---

5 agitation

During the civil rights movement, many people felt an agitation, or stirring up of feelings, for change.

---

6 prejudice

Civil rights leaders spoke out against the prejudice of judging people because of the color of their skin.

---

7 significance

Rosa Parks's refusal to give up her bus seat had great significance, or importance. It led to the end of racist laws.

---

8 ecstasy

Americans felt ecstasy, or great joy, when Jackie Robinson joined Major League baseball in 1947.

---

9 regal

Marian Anderson had a regal, dignified quality that impressed thousands who heard her sing.

---

10 serene

During his "I have a dream" speech in 1963, Martin Luther King Jr. spoke in a serene tone—full of calm hope.

Background

Meet Marian Anderson "I have lived in a time of change," wrote Marian Anderson. She became part of that change through both her talent as a singer and her serene courage. Anderson was born in Philadelphia in 1897, when prejudice limited opportunities for African Americans. A local music school refused to accept her as a student, so friends paid for private lessons in New York.

It was in Europe that Anderson became known as a distinguished artist. Her voice moved legendary conductor Arturo Toscanini to ecstasy. However, her appearances caused controversy in her own country. Some people could not conceive that an African American woman could win such fame. Anderson kept her regal dignity and displayed little agitation. She was not inclined to bitterness, believing that "you lose a lot of time hating people." What mattered more was the significance of being the first African American soloist at the Metropolitan Opera and of singing for thousands in Washington, D.C.

(Right) Marian Anderson at the Metropolitan Opera. (Below) In 1939, First Lady Eleanor Roosevelt presented Anderson with the NAACP Spingarn Medal for achievement by an African American.

Comprehension

✔ **TARGET SKILL** **Author's Purpose**

As you read "The Voice That Challenged a Nation," think about the author's purpose in writing about Marian Anderson's 1939 concert. Look for details in the text that reveal the author's feelings or point of view. Use a chart like the one below to keep track of the details throughout the selection that show the author's purpose.

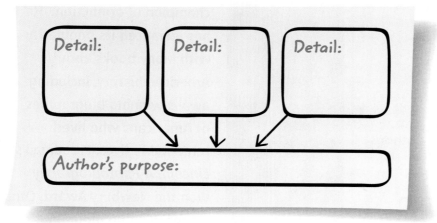

Detail: Detail: Detail:

Author's purpose:

✔ **TARGET STRATEGY** **Question**

You can use the Question strategy to help you identify the author's purpose as you read. Ask yourself, "Why did the author include this information?" Asking questions helps you to better understand what you are reading.

conceive	prejudice
controversy	significance
distinguished	ecstasy
inclined	regal
agitation	serene

Author's Purpose Use text details to figure out the author's viewpoint and reasons for writing.

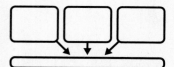

Question Ask questions about a selection before you read, as you read, and after you read.

GENRE

Narrative nonfiction gives factual information by telling a true story.

MEET THE AUTHOR

Russell Freedman

Russell Freedman is a strong champion of nonfiction. He has advanced its popularity with many books about American history, including award-winning biographies of Americans who lived remarkable lives. Freedman's *Lincoln: A Photobiography* won the Newbery Award. Other award-winning biographies he has written include books about the Wright brothers and about an important player in the Marian Anderson story, Eleanor Roosevelt.

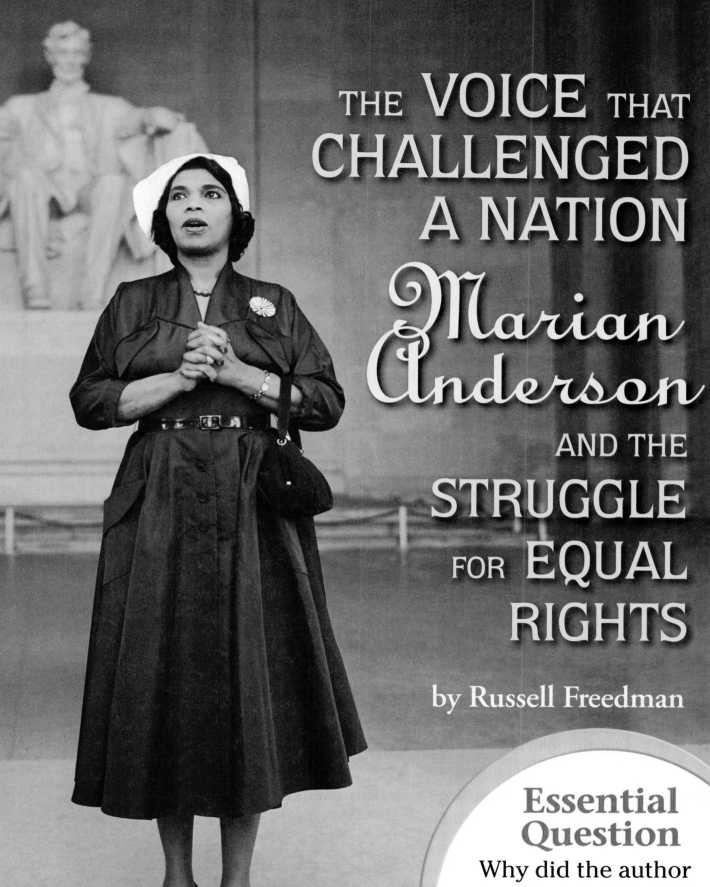

THE VOICE THAT CHALLENGED A NATION

Marian Anderson

AND THE STRUGGLE FOR EQUAL RIGHTS

by Russell Freedman

Essential Question

Why did the author write about a historic concert?

Marian Anderson, a renowned opera singer of the 1930s, has been barred by the Daughters of the American Revolution from performing at Constitution Hall because of her race. In protest, Eleanor Roosevelt, the First Lady, resigns from the DAR and arranges for Anderson to give a concert on the steps of the Lincoln Memorial.

"*I sang, I don't know how.*"

Marian Anderson was hurrying to the theater in San Francisco when she passed a newsstand and a headline caught her eye: MRS. ROOSEVELT TAKES STAND: RESIGNS FROM DAR. "I was on my way to the concert hall for my performance and couldn't stop to buy a paper," she recalled. "I did not get one until after the concert, and I honestly could not conceive that things had gone so far."

The controversy over Constitution Hall had started while Anderson was on a nationwide tour, and as she said later, she wasn't fully aware of what was happening until she spotted that San Francisco headline. At first she was very upset. "Music to me means so much, such beautiful things," she recalled, "it seemed impossible that you could find people who would curb you, stop you, from doing a thing which is beautiful."

Back at her San Francisco hotel she found a telegram from Sol Hurok, informing her of plans for a huge outdoor concert. Later, at Hurok's suggestion, she made a brief statement to reporters in the hotel lobby: "I am not surprised at Mrs. Roosevelt's action because she seemed to me to be one who really comprehended the true meaning of democracy. I am shocked beyond words to be barred from the capital of my own country after having appeared in almost every other capital in the world."

As Anderson continued with her scheduled tour, the furor over Constitution Hall "seemed to increase and follow me wherever I went." Reporters and photographers were waiting for her at every stop with a barrage of questions: "Do you feel insulted by this refusal?" "What is your attitude toward all this?" "What do you intend to do?"

> **STOP AND THINK**
>
> **Author's Craft** When Anderson says in the first paragraph on page 611 that she was not suited for "hand-to-hand combat," she is using a **metaphor**—describing one thing in terms of another. How might answering tough questions be like a physical fight?

But she was reluctant to speak out. "I did not want to talk," she recalled, "and I particularly did not want to say anything about the DAR. As I have made clear, I did not feel that I was designed for hand-to-hand combat, and I did not wish to make statements that I would later regret."

Anderson was not a person who enjoyed controversy or welcomed confrontations. Rather she was inclined to be generous in her judgments of others. "I was sorry for the people who had precipitated the affair," she later said. "I felt that their behavior stemmed from a lack of understanding . . . Could I have erased the bitterness, I would have done so gladly." She knew that many DAR members disagreed with the organization's official policy, and she did not want to condemn the entire group.

As she traveled across the country, plans for the Lincoln Memorial concert were moving forward. The National Park Service, a bureau of the Department of the Interior, prepared to handle the huge crowd that was expected. Arrangements were made for press coverage, for sound amplification, and for a coast-to-coast radio hookup that would broadcast the concert to the nation. For the first time in history a grand piano was carried up the Lincoln Memorial steps. Meanwhile, eighty-five national and local organizations, and more than three hundred prominent individuals, signed on as sponsors of the "Freedom Concert," as it was now called. A printed program, featuring lines from the Gettysburg Address, would be distributed by Boy Scouts, white and black, who circulated through the crowd.

Easter Sunday, April 9, 1939: Marian Anderson and her mother, Anna, lay a wreath at the Lincoln Memorial on the day of Anderson's historic concert.

Anderson had agreed to the concert, but not without hesitation and doubts. "I said yes, but the yes did not come easily or quickly. I don't like a lot of show, and one could not tell in advance what direction the affair would take. . . . The idea was sound, but it could not be comfortable to me as an individual. . . . [Yet] I could see that my significance as an individual was small in this affair. I had become, whether I liked it or not, a symbol, representing my people. I had to appear."

On Easter Sunday morning, April 9, accompanied by her mother and sisters, Marian rode the train from Philadelphia to Washington's Union Station. Since no hotel would take them, they had been invited to stay at the Washington home of Gifford Pinchot, the former governor of Pennsylvania. Early that afternoon, Marian and her accompanist, Kosti Vehanen, were driven to the Lincoln Memorial for a brief preconcert visit. The crowd had not yet started to arrive. They tried out the piano and examined the public address system, a battery of six microphones that would broadcast the event to those present at the Memorial and also to the national radio audience.

Later that day, shortly before the concert was scheduled to begin, Anderson and Vehanen returned to the Memorial in a handsome limousine with a motorcycle escort. Police were waiting to lead them from the car through a passageway that other officers kept open in the dense crowd. Marian had never felt as nervous as she did now: "My heart leaped wildly, and I could not talk. I even wondered whether I would be able to sing."

Entering the monument, they were taken to a small room where Interior Secretary Ickes was waiting. He went over the program with them. Then it was time to go out before the crowd.

Kosti Vehanen went first, moving to the piano to fasten down the music against the brisk afternoon breeze: "When I saw the immense crowd of seventy-five thousand people, then looked at the Steinway piano, I had a feeling that it would be of little use to begin to play, for I was sure that no one could possibly hear it. I also felt how really small a person seems when facing such a gathering, which stretched so far that I could scarcely see the end."

Then Marian was led to her seat on the green-carpeted platform of the Memorial by New York congresswoman Caroline O'Day and Assistant Secretary of the Interior Oscar Chapman. "No member of that audience will ever forget the sight of Miss Anderson emerging from a small anteroom beside [the] statue of Lincoln," Walter White remembered. "She was apparently calm, but those of us who knew her were aware of the great [agitation] beneath her serene exterior."

On the platform behind her, filling the two hundred places that had been reserved for distinguished guests, sat members of Congress, Supreme Court justices, and high-ranking government officials, along with Marian's mother, Anna, and her sisters, Ethel May and Alyse. Across from the elevated platform where Anderson was to stand as she sang was another platform for the film crews that would record the event. And nearby were countless photographers with their cameras at the ready.

The first name among the prominent sponsors listed in the program was "Mrs. Franklin D. Roosevelt," but Eleanor had decided that it was better not to attend. As the most famous, and controversial, woman in America, she did not want to draw attention to herself and upstage Marian Anderson.

Interior Secretary Ickes stepped up to the bank of microphones. "Genius draws no color line," he said. "She has endowed Marian Anderson with such voice as lifts any individual above his fellows, as is a matter of exultant pride to any race. . . . We are grateful to Miss Anderson for coming here to sing for us today."

Interior Secretary Harold L. Ickes greets Marian Anderson before introducing her to an outdoor audience of some 75,000 people.

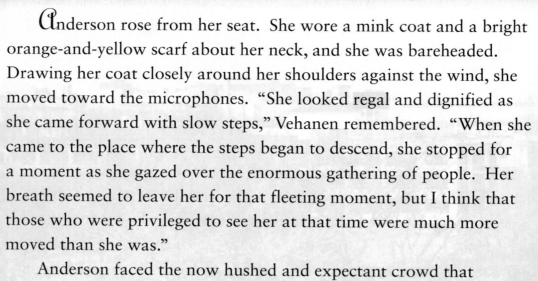

Anderson rose from her seat. She wore a mink coat and a bright orange-and-yellow scarf about her neck, and she was bareheaded. Drawing her coat closely around her shoulders against the wind, she moved toward the microphones. "She looked regal and dignified as she came forward with slow steps," Vehanen remembered. "When she came to the place where the steps began to descend, she stopped for a moment as she gazed over the enormous gathering of people. Her breath seemed to leave her for that fleeting moment, but I think that those who were privileged to see her at that time were much more moved than she was."

Anderson faced the now hushed and expectant crowd that stretched across the Mall from the base of the Lincoln Memorial all the way to the Washington Monument. Directly behind her, the great Lincoln Memorial was filled with shadow in the late-afternoon light. And the statue of Lincoln looked almost ready to speak.

"There seemed to be people as far as the eye could see," Anderson recalled. "I had a feeling that a great wave of good will poured out from these people, almost engulfing me. And when I stood up to sing . . . I felt for a moment as though I were choking. For a desperate second I thought that the words, well as I knew them, would not come. I sang, I don't know how."

"My feelings were so deep that I have never forgotten it, and I don't think until I leave this earth I will ever forget it," recalled opera and theater performer Todd Duncan. "Number one, I never have been so proud to be an American. Number two, I never have been so proud to be an American Negro. And number three, I never felt such pride [as] in seeing this Negro woman stand up there with this great regal dignity and sing.

615

"In back of me were the Tidal Basin and Washington Monument. Under my feet was the grass. To the side of me the walls were beautiful trees. The ceiling was the sky. And in front of me were those wonderful majestic stairs going up to the Lincoln Memorial. And there stood Miss Anderson. . . . The highlight of that day were the first words that she sang."

Closing her eyes, Marian Anderson began to sing, and her thrilling contralto voice carried across the Mall, touching every person who had come to hear her. Her opening number was "America," and the words "sweet land of liberty" poured from her almost as a prayer:

> *My country 'tis of thee,*
> *Sweet land of liberty,*
> *To thee we sing;*
> *Land where my fathers died,*
> *Land of the Pilgrims' pride,*
> *From every mountain-side*
> *Let Freedom ring!*

She did not use the word "I" as she sang. In her rendition "Of thee I sing" was replaced by "*To* thee *we* sing."

Then she sang "O mio Fernando," the aria that had won her the Lewisohn Stadium contest fourteen years earlier, followed by Schubert's "Ave Maria." After a brief intermission she sang three spirituals: "Gospel Train," "Trampin'," and "My Soul Is Anchored in the Lord," and finally, as an encore, she ended with another spiritual, "Nobody Knows the Trouble I See," a gentle lamentation that brought tears to the eyes of many in that hushed audience. "I have never heard such a voice," Ickes wrote in his diary.

As the last notes of the spiritual faded away, while the crowd was still under the spell of her voice, Anderson raised her hand and spoke a few words: "I am so overwhelmed," she said, "I just can't talk. I can't tell you what you have done for me today. I thank you from the bottom of my heart again and again."

✔ **STOP AND THINK**

Author's Purpose What do you think is the author's viewpoint of Anderson's abilities? How does his description of Anderson's performance on pages 614–616 support this view?

Then the spell was broken as great numbers of people, stirred by their own emotions, roared their acclaim and rushed toward Anderson to offer congratulations and good wishes, threatening to mob her. Walter White pushed his way to a microphone and pleaded with the crowd not to create a panic.

"As I did so, but with indifferent success, a single figure caught my eye in the mass of people below which seemed one of the most important and touching symbols of the occasion. It was a slender black girl dressed in somewhat too garishly hued Easter finery. Hers was not the face of one who had been the beneficiary of much education or opportunity. Her hands were particularly noticeable as she thrust them forward and upward, trying desperately, though she was some distance from Miss Anderson, to touch the singer. They were hands that despite their youth had known only the dreary work of manual labor. Tears streamed down the girl's dark face. Her hat was askew, but in her eyes flamed hope bordering on ecstasy. Life which had been none too easy for her now held out greater hope because one who was also colored and who, like herself, had known poverty, privation, and prejudice, had, by her genius, gone a long way toward conquering bigotry. If Marian Anderson could do it, the girl's eyes seemed to say, then I can, too."

As Walter White urged the surging crowd to stay back, the police were rushing Anderson back inside the Memorial. Even there well-wishers almost overwhelmed her, until finally the police were able to clear a passageway through the crowd and escort the singer to a waiting car.

For the rest of Marian Anderson's life, wherever she traveled and sang, people would come backstage after a performance and say, "You know, I was at that Easter concert."

STOP AND THINK

Question What question or questions do you have after reading this page?

Your Turn

In Times Past

Short Response The members of the United States Congress supported Marian Anderson by attending her performance. At the same time, the government allowed prejudice to limit people's opportunities in many parts of the country, including Washington, D.C. Write a paragraph that explains what this tells you about American society in the 1930s. SOCIAL STUDIES

Symbol of America

Make a Poster The song "America" celebrates liberty. Work in a small group to brainstorm a list of symbols that stand for the United States, such as the eagle and the Liberty Bell. Make a poster showing the symbols, and add captions to explain them. SMALL GROUP

The Power of One

Turn and Talk Discuss how the actions of Eleanor Roosevelt, Gifford Pinchot, and Interior Secretary Ickes, in "The Voice That Challenged a Nation," helped change history. Why do you think the author chose to write about these individuals in addition to describing Marian Anderson's historic performance? AUTHOR'S PURPOSE

Poetry

✔ TARGET VOCABULARY

conceive	prejudice
controversy	significance
distinguished	ecstasy
inclined	regal
agitation	serene

GENRE
Poetry uses the sound and rhythm of words in a variety of forms to suggest images and express feelings.

TEXT FOCUS
A **symbol** in poetry is a person, place, or thing that stands for an idea. For example, a stone might be a symbol of permanence.

LINES TO COURAGE

What represents courage to you? Maybe it is a symbol such as a monument to the bravery of others. Maybe it is a person who has achieved regal status for helping the poor. Maybe it is an emotion, like the serene feeling of helping someone, or the ecstasy after overcoming fear. These three poets each conceive of courage in a different way: facing problems, facing war, and facing controversy. As you read, compare their ideas of courage with your own. Then use your ideas to write your own poem of courage.

Life is mostly froth and bubble,
Two things stand like stone;
Kindness in another's trouble,
Courage in your own.

A. L. Gordon

WHISPERS TO THE WALL

Vietnam Veterans Memorial, Washington, D.C. Dedicated 1982

You are him from Maine,
him, from Montana,
and every him from sea
to sea and back.
Stewart, *Kelly*, *York*;
you are all of those,
who shrimped on boats,
flew planes,
studied, wrote,
collected,
kissed.

The brave ones spill
across your face;
an indelible trace
of young sons
who played baseball,
cards, guitars.
Thompson, *Sanchez*, *Vance*;
you know their favorite dish,
their first romance.

On silent nights, do they tell you
of boyhoods and Beatles,
bruised knees and hearts,
birthdays missed . . .
those who shrimped on boats,
flew planes,
studied, wrote,
collected,
kissed.

Rebecca Kai Dotlich

The Vietnam Veterans Memorial
has great significance as a tribute to
American soldiers who died during
the Vietnam War.

Who Could Tell?

¡Híjole!
Who could tell?

Who could tell
that Cesario Estrada Chávez,
the shy American
wearing a checkered shirt,
walking with a cane to ease his back
from the burden of the fields,
could organize so many people
to march for *La Causa,* The Cause?

Who could tell
that he with a soft *pan dulce* voice,
hair the color of mesquite,
and downcast, Aztec eyes,
would have the courage to speak up
for the *campesinos*
to get better pay,
better housing,
better health?

¡Híjole!
Who could tell?

Carmen T. Bernier-Grand

Write a Poem of Courage

César Chávez (1927–1993) faced prejudice as a child. His agitation for change led to better conditions for migrant workers. Write a poem about someone you know who has also shown courage. The person might be a distinguished hero, a friend, or a relative who is inclined to take on big challenges for a worthy cause.

Making Connections

 Text to Self

Speak Out More than seventy years have passed since Marian Anderson's famous concert. How do you think the concert should be remembered? Write a speech you might give to commemorate the 1939 event.

 Text to Text

Connect to Poetry Compare and contrast the ways the three poems in "Lines to Courage" treat the topic of courage. Then draw a picture illustrating the poem you connect with most strongly.

 Text to World

News Report Think about how the actions of Marian Anderson and César Chávez continue to have an impact on people today. Then describe an event from recent times that could not have happened before the civil rights movement. Share your report with a small group.

Grammar

What Are Comparative and Superlative Adjectives and Adverbs? A **comparative adjective** compares two persons, places, or things. To make comparative forms, add *er* to a short adjective and use the word *more* before a long adjective. A **superlative adjective** compares more than two persons, places, or things. To make superlative forms, add *est* to a short adjective and use the word *most* before a long adjective. You usually put the word *more* in front of an adverb to make a **comparative adverb** and *most* in front of an adverb to make a **superlative adverb**. The adjectives *good* and *bad* and the adverb *well* have special comparative and superlative forms.

Academic Language

comparative adjective
superlative adjective
comparative adverb
superlative adverb

Adjectives and Adverbs	Comparatives	Superlatives
simple (short adjective)	simpler	simplest
powerful (long adjective)	more powerful	most powerful
good (adjective)	better	best
bad (adjective)	worse	worst
joyfully (adverb)	more joyfully	most joyfully
well (adverb)	better	best

Turn and Talk **With a partner, read aloud each sentence below. Identify each comparative adjective, superlative adjective, comparative adverb, and superlative adverb.**

1 Was the Easter concert Anderson's greatest performance?

2 She spoke more emotionally after that show than after any other.

3 Who was dressed the most garishly of all?

4 The shorter of the two audience members clapped more vigorously than his companion.

Conventions When you compare two persons, things, or actions in your writing, be sure to use a comparative form. When you compare three or more, use a superlative form.

Incorrect Forms	Correct Forms
Ron is the best of the two trumpeters. He plays most energetically than the other.	Ron is the better of the two trumpeters. He plays more energetically than the other.

Connect Grammar to Writing

As you edit your persuasive essay, look for comparisons using adjectives or adverbs. Replace incorrect forms with correct ones.

Write to Persuade

✓ **Ideas** When you plan a **persuasive essay**, be aware of objections your audience might have. Think of convincing responses that will persuade readers to agree with you.

Orlando wanted to convince readers that cell phones have improved people's lives. As part of his planning, he created a chart exploring possible objections and responses to them. Later, he included this information in a persuasion chart to organize his essay.

Writing Process Checklist

▶ **Prewrite**

☑ Did I choose a position or goal I feel strongly about?

☑ Did I include strong reasons that will appeal to my audience?

☑ Did I give facts and examples to support each reason?

☑ Did I plan how to address possible objections?

☑ Did I arrange my reasons in a persuasive order?

Draft

Revise

Edit

Publish and Share

Exploring a Topic

Possible Objection	Response
• People annoy others when they talk on the phone. • Talking on cell phones distracts drivers, causing accidents.	*Ask* • ~~Tell~~ someone to move to another area to talk on the phone. • Cell phone use can be regulated.

Persuasion Chart

Position:

Cell phones have improved people's lives.

Reason: Families need to communicate.

Details: Might need permission to go somewhere after school

Reason: Good for emergencies

Details: Few pay phones are available. Can call for help right away

Objection: People who talk on their cell phones annoy others.

Response: Ask users to move to another area.

Objection: Talking on cell phones distracts drivers, causing accidents.

Response: Phone use can be regulated.

When I planned my persuasive essay, I included answers to possible objections.

Reading as a Writer

Which of Orlando's responses is more convincing? What possible objections and responses can you add to your own chart?

artificial

interaction

sensors

data

ultimate

domestic

uncanny

stimulus

literally

inaccessible

Vocabulary Reader

Context Cards

Vocabulary in Context

1 artificial

A robot does not have a real brain. Its intelligence is artificial, created by humans.

2 interaction

A controller allows the interaction between a player and video game. The game and player act on each other.

3 sensors

Sensors in devices detect information. If a camera's sensor doesn't detect enough light, it activates a flash.

4 data

A computer can sort through long lists of data, or information, often by converting it into ones and zeros.

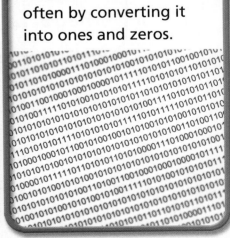

- **Study each Context Card.**

- **Tell a story about two or more pictures, using Vocabulary words of your choice.**

5 ultimate

The "last word" in technology is always replaced by a model that is the *new* ultimate version.

6 domestic

A robot might be programmed to wash dishes or do other domestic chores around the house.

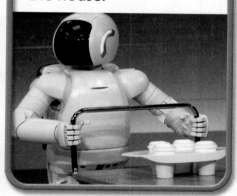

7 uncanny

In science fiction books and movies, robots often have uncanny, or weird, powers.

8 stimulus

In this robot's motion detector, movement is the stimulus that causes its lights to turn on.

9 literally

If a robot took the command "Make the bed" literally, or word for word, it might begin by sawing wood.

10 inaccessible

A robot can dive to an ocean depth that is inaccessible to people. Scuba divers could not go there.

Background

Living with Robots There is something fascinating and a little uncanny about robots. In science fiction stories, comic books, and movies, we have come to see robots as the ultimate form of interaction between people and machines—actual mechanical people. We imagine them responding to our orders with flat, artificial voices or with flashing, beeping sensors, doing domestic chores, and maybe taking a few things too literally, like "setting the table"—on its side!

In the following selection, you'll discover how robots really are helping people today, going to inaccessible or dangerous places, learning volumes of data, and performing complex actions at the stimulus of a computer's command.

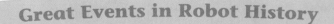

Great Events in Robot History

1783

Jacques de Vaucanson creates a mechanical duck that can flap its wings and eat grain.

1920

Czech playwright Karel Čapek invents the word *robot* for his play *R.U.R.* (Rossum's Universal Robots), shown here in a 1938 TV production.

1954

George Devol builds Unimate, the first industrial robot.

Comprehension

✔ **TARGET SKILL** **Sequence of Events**

As you read "Robotics," keep track of the sequence, or order, of events in the development of robots and in the work performed by individual robots. Using a flow chart like the one below to list the sequence of events will help you remember what you read.

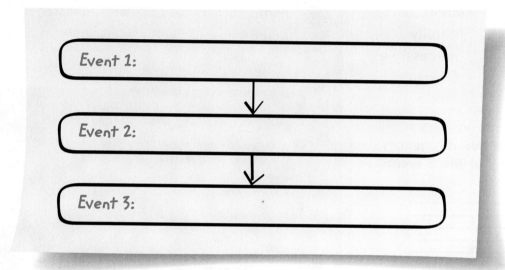

Event 1:

Event 2:

Event 3:

✔ **TARGET STRATEGY** **Visualize**

Forming mental images of the robots and the work they do can help you focus on, and keep track of, the sequence of events. Visualizing important details as you read is a good way of remembering the information.

Main Selection

MEET THE AUTHOR

HELENA DOMAINE

As a young girl, Helena Domaine saw Fritz Lang's classic robot movie of 1927, *Metropolis*, and became fascinated by the interaction between robots and humans. Today she writes science fiction and scientific nonfiction, and she is particularly interested in researching popular myths such as the Loch Ness monster, Bigfoot, and UFOs.

Robotics

by Helena Domaine

Essential Question

What events show how technology has changed?

Working Robots

There are a lot of places we'd like to go but can't. Dangerous places. Distant places. Inaccessible places. We can explore these places by sending in robots. These mechanical adventurers have computer brains that don't feel fear or panic. Killer levels of radioactivity? No problem. The black, airless vacuum of space? The crushing pressure of tons of ocean water? Tiny paths through ancient rock? Bring it on, say these brave new robots.

Andros 5, for example, handles live bombs for the Baltimore (Maryland) Police Department. Rosie was built by a team at Carnegie Mellon University in Pennsylvania. It can safely roll into highly contaminated nuclear facilities and wash them down or take them apart. Houdini might be considered Rosie's baby brother. This robot can enter hazardous waste storage tanks to clean them.

You Want Me to Go Where?

In 1994, the National Aeronautics and Space Administration (NASA) teamed up with scientists at Carnegie Mellon University and the Alaska Volcano Observatory. They sent a robot to explore an active volcano. Scientists explore volcanoes to learn how they work and how to read the warning signs of a volcanic eruption. An eight-legged robot named Dante II climbed down into Alaska's Mount Spurr, 90 miles (145 km) west of Anchorage. Dante's job was to explore the crater floor and take gas and soil samples. It was something that no human could have done.

Dante's designers knew the descent would be very tricky. The north wall of the volcano has a 1,000-foot (305-meter) drop. The south wall is steep and covered with rocks. Designers gave Dante servomotors, mechanisms that help Dante's main computer. The servomotors allow Dante to raise and lower each leg as the robot climbs over rocky surfaces. Dante's footpads and legs also have sensors. The sensors keep it from crashing into rocks or falling into holes.

Dante II makes its way beside a river in Alaska.

But even with all this technology, nobody trusted Dante to make its own decisions. Dante was connected to its human team by satellite and the Internet. Its main computer analyzed every step before it allowed the robot to go forward. Eventually Dante reached the floor of the crater, safe and sound.

As Dante gathered samples, the robot's cameras sent a three-dimensional view to the computer screens in front of the scientists at the volcano's rim. And thanks to something called Virtual Environment Vehicle Interface software, the scientists felt as if they were right there in the volcano with Dante.

But a near-perfect robotic adventure ended in a way familiar to anyone who's ever climbed a steep hill. Dante slipped in some loose dirt on the way out of the volcano and could not climb out. The science team had to call in a helicopter to rescue the robot.

STOP AND THINK

Visualize What details on this page help you clearly picture the robot's descent into the crater?

Unfortunately, no one can fly to Mars to save robots that get into trouble. NASA landed twin Rover robots, Spirit and Opportunity, on Mars in 2004. The robots were sent to explore the planet, collect soil and rock samples, and take pictures. Spirit and Opportunity are all alone on the red planet. They are millions of miles from Earth. And Mars is a far more hostile place than the inside of a volcano. Mars is very cold, averaging −67°F (−55°C). Its strong winds whip red dust across the rocky surface of the planet.

The Rovers' connection to NASA is tricky, too. Communications between the robots and NASA scientists are sent through millions of miles of space. The information travels via computer connections to orbiting spacecraft and antennas on Earth. As the Rovers roll across Mars, any helpful messages from their human teammates on Earth are delayed by several minutes. So the Rovers are designed to make many of their own choices. They are given jobs, but it is up to them to figure out how to get them done. The Rovers also have a "survival instinct" programmed into them. It helps them adapt to unexpected situations.

The Exploration Rovers collect rock and soil samples and take photographs on Mars.

The Incredible Shrinking Bot

Scientists at the California Institute of Technology are working on the designs for a tiny snake-bot to travel through the human gastrointestinal system (the stomach and intestines). As a doctor looks down a patient's throat for swelling or other signs of illness, the snake-bot would look at a patient's insides. A camera and sensors would help the snake-bot gather medical information for doctors. The snake-bot's information would help doctors diagnose disease. It may even help in therapy.

Miniature robots from New Mexico's Sandia Laboratory also explore tight spots.

But without question, the tiniest and most daring medical robots are being designed in Sweden. The Swedish micro-bots are smaller than the hyphen between *micro* and *bots* in this sentence. The micro-bots are made of silicon. The silicon is coated in gold and then covered in polymer (a plastic compound) that can shrink or swell. This allows the pieces of the robot to bend so it can pick things up and move them around.

The Swedish micro-bots are designed to operate in all kinds of fluids. The research team imagines a time in the near future when the micro-bots can be injected into the human bloodstream. Doctors hope the micro-bots will be able to clean up the plaque that causes heart attacks and break through the blood clots that cause strokes. The micro-bots could also remove bacteria. One day they may even fix disease-causing cells.

In the old sci-fi movie *Fantastic Voyage*, five scientists and their submarine, the *Proteus*, were shrunk to microscopic size. They were injected into the bloodstream of a fellow scientist. Their mission was to reach a blood clot in their friend's brain and save his life. What Hollywood imagined as movie fantasy in 1966 is becoming science fact.

Sandia researcher Doug Adkins designed the miniature robots to work in swarms, like insects. They communicate with each other and with a central station.

Artsy Robots

The Sony Corporation's QRIO robot took center stage—literally—in March 2004, when it conducted the Tokyo (Japan) Philharmonic Orchestra. QRIO can perform many tasks. But Sony, a Japanese electronics company, wanted to show off the robot's ability to control its motions. QRIO held a conductor's baton and led the human musicians through Beethoven's Symphony No. 5. Japanese automaker Toyota has also proudly produced a musical robot. The Toyota robot can play "When You Wish Upon a Star" on a trumpet. Toyota says it hopes to soon have an entire robot band ready to belt out tunes.

QRIO was designed to test controlled robotic movement.

Who's Got the Ball?

Robots aren't all work and no play. On May 4, 2003, robots from around the world played soccer in the International RoboCup Federation's American Open. The event was held at Carnegie Mellon University. Hiroaki Kitano established RoboCup in 1997. He hoped that it would lead to the development of robotic soccer players good enough to play against human athletes.

That first 1997 tournament was a little chaotic. The robots had a tough time finding the ball. They struggled to recognize their teammates and figure out which goal they were supposed to aim for. As engineers improved the robots' vision systems, play improved. By the 2001 games, the 8-inch (20-cm)-tall, wheeled robots in the Small League were doing better. They played two ten-minute halves on a field the size of a Ping-Pong table. Their soccer ball was an orange golf ball.

The Sony Corporation sends its Aibo team to the Open. Most RoboCup players are two-legged, but the Aibos are little robotic dogs. The Aibos kick the ball by getting down on their elbows. This position allows them to use both front paws. Play is slow and a bit goofy. The Aibos are, after all, still amateurs.

Aibos, robotic dogs, compete in a RoboCup soccer game.

Thinking Robots

Bertram, your robot butler, rolls into the living room and says in a flat voice, "Dinner is served." You're slouched down in a corner of the couch. "I'm not hungry, thanks," you answer. Your parents or friends might ask if you feel all right, or if there's anything they can get you. But Bertram has no reaction. He simply rolls back into the kitchen without a word and puts away the uneaten dinner. Bertram has understood your reply, but he can't respond to your tone of voice or your body language. And most people, Allison Bruce discovered, really don't like that about robots.

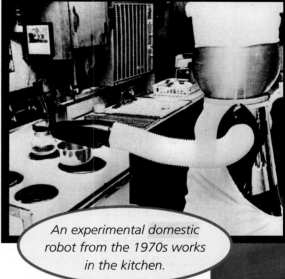

An experimental domestic robot from the 1970s works in the kitchen.

Bruce is a researcher at the Robotics Institute at Carnegie Mellon University. Bruce is part of the institute's Social Robot program. The program studies ways to improve interaction between humans and robots. In Bruce's experiment, a laptop computer was attached to a robot. The robot stood in the hall of a college classroom building and asked passing students a question. Sometimes the laptop screen would be blank, but sometimes it showed a face with a range of expressions.

Bruce was not really interested in the students' answers to the questions. What she was interested in was the students' willingness to stop and talk to the robot. She found that more students responded to the robot when it had a face.

Like Bruce, others who work with robots have realized that humans prefer robots they can relate to. They have developed robots that can show human emotions, such as anger, happiness, embarrassment, and sadness.

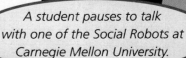

A student pauses to talk with one of the Social Robots at Carnegie Mellon University.

I Feel, Therefore I Am

Kismet the robot was designed and built by Cynthia Breazeal, a researcher at the Massachusetts Institute of Technology's (MIT's) Artificial Intelligence Laboratory. The lab is home to many kinds of interesting robots. But Kismet is not like the others. This robot can display emotion. Kismet's lips can pout or smile. His eyebrows can arch, and his ears can wiggle. A combination of clever computer programming and sophisticated engineering has given Kismet the ability to actually respond to a stimulus in an emotionally recognizable way.

If you say words of praise to Kismet, he will smile. Bright colors also earn a smile. So does his own reflection in a mirror. But raise your voice and scold Kismet, and his lips will sink into a frown. And when Kismet becomes overstimulated by too much noise or movement, he will withdraw, lowering his eyes and taking a kind of robotic time-out.

Kismet is lovable not just because of his blue golf-ball-sized eyes. Kismet interacts with people and shows he has "understood" them through his facial expressions. His success in relating to people may be reflected in the fact that everyone refers to Kismet as "he" instead of "it."

STOP AND THINK

Author's Craft When the author uses terms such as *polymer skin,* on page 641, she is using **jargon:** the specialized language of a field of study. How does the author help you understand this term?

Kismet was developed to interact with people.

Heads Will Roll!

His name is David Hanson. In 2003 he showed up at a science conference in Denver, Colorado, carrying a head. The head was backless and bald and bolted to a piece of wood. But it was still pretty. It had high cheekbones, blue eyes, and smooth rubber polymer skin. Hanson set the head down on a table. He plugged it into his laptop computer and tapped a few keys. Everyone stopped to watch what would happen.

Moments later, the head began to move, turning right and left. It smiled, sneered, and frowned. Hanson, a robot scientist at the University of Texas at Dallas, called the head K-bot. K-bot can mimic the major muscles in a human face. It has 24 servomotors under its specially developed skin. Digital cameras in its eyes watch the people who are curiously studying it, and software helps it to imitate what it sees.

David Hanson designed K-bot to express human emotions.

Hanson has built several robotic heads, but he isn't the only one. In Tokyo, Hiroshi Kobayashi's face robots, as he calls them, are also eerily lifelike. So is the head sitting in Fumio Hara's robotics lab at the Science University of Tokyo. Hara's robotic head can scan the face of the person standing in front of it. Then it can compare the face to those in its memory bank. Once the robot identifies which of six emotions the person is expressing, tiny machines under the robot's skin remold its face to mimic what it sees.

For Hara, heads are just the beginning. His goal is to design a robot that is interactive, friendly, and most of all, familiar. But do we really want a robot that looks just like us? Maybe not.

Fumio Hara poses with a skeleton of one of his face robots. The face robot's network of wires and pulleys are covered with a flexible skin.

In the late 1970s, Japanese robot engineer Masahiro Mori did some fascinating research on how human beings interact with robots. Mori discovered that people like friendly-looking mechanical robots. But Mori found that when robots look too much like humans, people stop liking them. Mori called this sudden shift the Uncanny Valley, the place where people begin to feel uncomfortable with humanlike robots.

✔ STOP AND THINK

Sequence of Events Read the third paragraph, and describe the sequence of events that takes place as robots become more humanlike.

Experience Is the Best Teacher

Engineers have begun building robots that can adapt to their environment. They operate on what are called patterns of behavior.

Most of these robots are quite small and behave a lot like insects. Insects don't really think. They rely on their senses and instincts to find food and survive. Like insects, the little insect-bots have been equipped for sensing their physical environment. But they have not been preprogrammed with any data about their environment. So when they are first turned on, they're brainless.

But the insect-bots' computers are programmed with separate "layers of behavior." The behavior layers help an insect-bot learn about its environment. The more it learns, the more it can do. Once the insect-bot has mastered one layer of behavior, the next higher layer of behavior kicks in. With each layer, the insect-bot gets better at dealing with the world around it.

At MIT, James McLurkin has built robot ants using these layers of behavior. But McLurkin's ant-bots are even more amazing because they are able to signal each other when they find ant-bot "food." In other words, the ant-bots learn how to work together to achieve a shared goal. The ultimate ant-bot, however, is yet to come—one that can communicate with real ants.

A robotic ladybug, developed by Sanyo Electric Company, sits on a leaf.

I believe," says Hans Moravec, a research professor at Carnegie Mellon, "that robots with human intelligence will be common during the next 50 years." Certainly, the Center for Intelligent Systems (CIS) at Vanderbilt University in Tennessee shows how close we are getting. The CIS has developed a robot called ISAC (for Intelligent Soft Arm Control). ISAC can express emotion and has both short-term and long-term memory. And because this robot's brain has been designed to "think" much like ours, ISAC may soon actually be able to dream.

It seems almost certain that in the future we will share our planet with robots. What we build in the lab will have the potential to become as smart as we are. It may even improve upon its own technology. Will we love these robots or fear them? Time will tell.

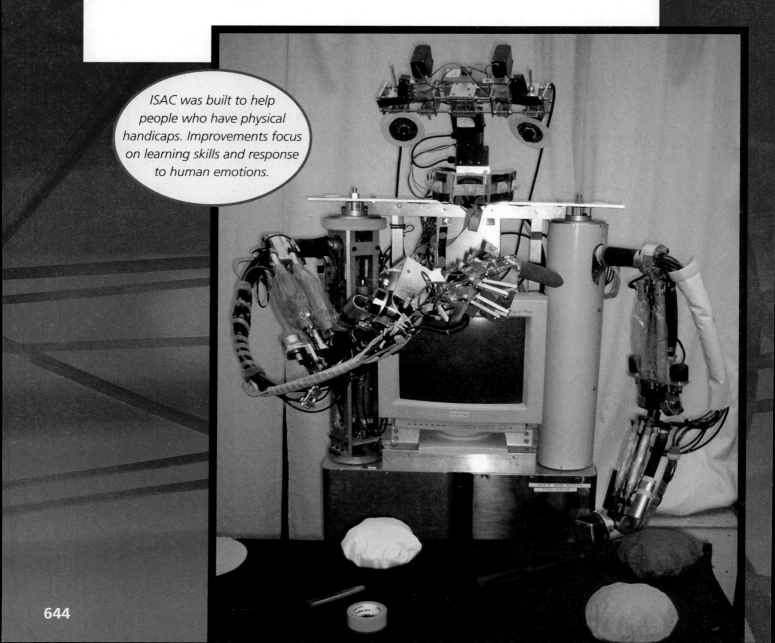

ISAC was built to help people who have physical handicaps. Improvements focus on learning skills and response to human emotions.

Your Turn

Good or Bad?

Write About Changes Do you think the current widespread use of robots to do work for people is a change for the better? Why or why not? Use details from the selection and your own knowledge to write a paragraph that explains your opinion. PERSONAL RESPONSE

Sweet Dreams

Create a Storyboard One of the robots mentioned in "Robotics" may soon be able to dream. What might that robot dream about? How might its dream be different from a human's dream? With a partner, create a storyboard that shows the robot's first dream. PARTNERS

Last Stop: Uncanny Valley

Turn and Talk With a partner, discuss how robots have developed over time. Based on facts from "Robotics" and the goals of robot scientists, what do you think robots are likely to be capable of in the future? At what point do you think robots will make you uncomfortable or even fearful? SEQUENCE OF EVENTS

DR. SNEED'S BEST FRIEND

by Nick James

Cast of Characters

Dr. Garcia
Dr. Watkins
Dr. Sneed
Sam

(It is Monday morning at a robotics laboratory in Portland, Oregon. Two scientists enter to find their co-worker, Dr. Sneed, hard at work.)

Dr. Garcia: *(looking around)* Wow, Sneed, it looks as if you've been working all weekend.

Dr. Watkins: Yes, I thought the data for our new project wasn't due until next week.

Dr. Sneed: *(nervously)* Well, actually, ah, I've been working on a top-secret project that requires my undivided attention. I didn't even have time to eat breakfast.

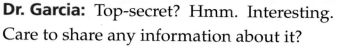

Dr. Garcia: Top-secret? Hmm. Interesting. Care to share any information about it?

Dr. Sneed: Impossible. All I can say is that it's about artificial intelligence.

Dr. Watkins: Well, that's what we all do. Come on, Sneed, you can trust us.

Dr. Sneed: (*pacing*) Fine, if you must know, the project concerns the use of sensors in a domestic setting. But I really can't go into detail.

Dr. Garcia: I have an uncanny feeling there is a lot more to it than that—but be mysterious if you want to. I've got work to do.

(*Later that morning, there is a knock at the door. A small robot enters, carrying an apple and a glass of milk.*)

Dr. Watkins: (*to the robot*) Hello, little dude. Can I help you?

Sam: (*in a flat, mechanical voice*) No, I do not require any help.

Dr. Sneed: (*rushing over to the robot*) Sam, what are you doing here?

Sam: I am delivering your apple and glass of milk, Dr. Sneed. A healthy snack!

Dr. Sneed: (*in an embarrassed whisper*) Sam, you were programmed to come here at noon. It's only nine o'clock.

Sam: I am sorry, Dr. Sneed. A stimulus in my motherboard overrode my internal clock.

Dr. Garcia: What's he talking about?

Sam: You did not eat breakfast, Dr. Sneed. I sensed that your stomach was growling.

Dr. Garcia: Well, Dr. Sneed, I see you've achieved a new interaction between human and machine.

Dr. Watkins: Yes, I always thought this kind of friendship from a robot was inaccessible. I suppose this is your top-secret project?

(*Dr. Sneed nods, embarrassed. He takes a big bite of the apple.*)

Sam: Goodbye, Dr. Sneed. (*He turns around and rolls toward the door.*)

Dr. Sneed: Hold on a second, Sam.

Sam: A second is not an object that I can hold, Dr. Sneed.

Dr. Sneed: I didn't mean it literally, Sam. Please go to my office and get two more apples for Dr. Garcia and Dr. Watkins.

Sam: A healthy snack. I will be right back.

(*Sam exits, stiffly. Dr. Watkins and Dr. Garcia stare at Dr. Sneed.*)

Dr. Garcia: You spent all weekend programming a robot to bring you food? That has to be the ultimate example of self-centered time-wasting!

Dr. Sneed: (*shrugging*) That's a matter of opinion. Besides, tomorrow he's making me macaroni and cheese. (*He smiles.*) It's my favorite.

Making Connections

Text to Self

My Robot Choose one of the robots mentioned in "Robotics." Write a short play scene in which the robot helps you do a typical activity in your life, whether for work or for fun.

Text to Text

Evaluate Robot Tasks The robots in "Robotics" and "Dr. Sneed's Best Friend" perform a variety of tasks. Which tasks do you think are most worthy of the time, effort, and resources required to develop a robot? Which are least worthy? Think about all of the robot tasks you have read about, and then list them from most to least important.

Text to World

Connect to Science Choose a type of robot that interests you, such as a robot that explores volcanoes or roams the planet Mars. Use print or online sources to find out more about that robot. Share your findings with the class.

Grammar

What Are the Mechanics of Writing? *Mechanics* refers to the correct use of **capitalization** and **punctuation**. You have learned to capitalize proper nouns and proper adjectives. You've also learned how to punctuate declarative, interrogative, imperative, and exclamatory sentences.

declarative sentence	proper noun period A robot named Dante II will descend into a volcano.
interrogative sentence	proper adjective question mark Which Alaskan volcano will it explore?
imperative sentence	period Let me see the viewing screen.
exclamatory sentence	exclamation point What strength that robot has!

An **interjection** is a word or words that show feeling. If it stands alone, follow it with an exclamation point. If it begins a sentence, set it off with a comma.

exclamation point

Wow! The robot is walking on red hot rock!

comma

Hey, its sensors have detected toxic fumes!

Try This! **Write the sentences below on another sheet of paper. Use correct capitalization and end punctuation. Place the correct punctuation after the interjection.**

1 Look at this photo of the martian landscape

2 Did a robot take that photo while on mars

3 Ooh What a breathtaking photo it is

4 I want to attend the california institute of technology

Conventions Your readers will have an easier time reading and understanding what you write if you use correct capitalization and punctuation.

Incorrect Capitalization and Punctuation	Correct Capitalization and Punctuation
will a robot be aboard the next american space vehicle. Hey here is an article about an upcoming flight to mars, According to the article, the passengers will be robots Give it a quick read, and then return it to me?	Will a robot be aboard the next American space vehicle? Hey, here is an article about an upcoming flight to Mars. According to the article, the passengers will be robots. Give it a quick read, and then return it to me.

Connect Grammar to Writing

As you edit your persuasive essay, correct any errors in capitalization or punctuation that you find.

Write to Persuade

✔ **Word Choice** The author of *Robotics* used persuasive language like *safely* and *without question* to persuade readers to agree with her. When you revise a **persuasive essay**, add strong words and phrases that will persuade readers to share your position.

As Orlando revised his essay on cell phones, he changed some of the words to make his argument more persuasive.

Writing Process Checklist

Prewrite

Draft

▶ **Revise**

☑ Did I state my position clearly?

☑ Did I order my reasons according to importance?

☑ Is my tone positive and polite?

☑ Is my language persuasive?

☑ Did I use a variety of sentence types?

☑ Did I end by summarizing reasons and calling on my audience to agree?

Edit

Publish and Share

Revised Draft

On a typical day, look around you.

How many

~~A lot of~~ people are talking on cell

phones? Today, cell phones are *widely* used

by both adults and kids. They are

one invention that has changed

for the better.

people's lives.

Final Copy

Cell Phones Are Beneficial
by Orlando Reyes

On a typical day, look around you. How many people are talking on cell phones? Today, cell phones are widely used by both adults and kids. They are one invention that has changed people's lives for the better.

For one thing, cell phones are the perfect way for families to share important information quickly. For example, if parents can't pick their kids up on time, or if kids want permission to go somewhere, they can call on a cell phone. Having a cell phone means that families can stay connected.

Another reason for people to have cell phones is in case of emergency.

In my final paper, I used persuasive language. I also made sure to proofread thoroughly.

Reading as a Writer

Which words and phrases are the most persuasive? Where can you add persuasive language to your own essay?

Read the next two selections. Think about the conclusions you can draw from the details given.

Lance Armstrong Keeps Going Strong

Lance Armstrong is known around the world as one of the United States' greatest athletes. He was born September 18, 1971, in Plano, Texas. Early on, he excelled at sports. At thirteen, he won the Iron Kids Triathlon. A triathlon is an event that combines three sports: running, swimming, and biking. At only sixteen, Lance Armstrong became a professional triathlete.

World Championships and the Olympic Games

During his final year of high school, Armstrong was invited to train in Colorado with the Junior U.S. National Cycling Team, for the 1990 Junior World Championship. In 1991, he won the U.S. National Amateur Cycling Championship, and in 1992, he went to his first of many Olympic Games.

After the 1992 Olympics, Armstrong became a professional cyclist. He finished last in his first race but continued to train. In 1993, he gained respect and earned prize money by winning several important races, including a stage in the Tour de France. The Tour de France is the most important event in cycling. Made up of several stages, this long-distance race lasts about three weeks and covers about 2,235 miles (3,600 km).

A Serious Illness and a New Foundation

In 1996, doctors discovered that Armstrong was in the advanced stages of cancer. To fight the disease, he had several operations and treatments with chemicals. In 1997, his doctors pronounced him "cancer free."

Lance Armstrong became a spokesperson for the fight against cancer. He started the Lance Armstrong Foundation, an organization that promotes cancer research and awareness. The Foundation sponsors the Ride for the Roses, an annual cycling event that is a favorite of cyclists.

Courage and Victory

Lance Armstrong felt a strong need to continue racing. With restored health and unstoppable courage, he set a goal of winning the Tour de France. In 1999, his dream came true. It was one of his greatest years as a cyclist.

Armstrong went on to win the Tour de France six more years in a row! In 2005, he became the only cyclist to have won the Tour de France seven times. After this amazing feat, he retired from cycling. His retirement was only temporary, though. In 2008, he announced that he would compete in the 2009 Tour de France. Because of his domination of the race, some people have jokingly called it the Tour de Lance.

The Tour de France

The Tour de France is the most famous and difficult bicycle race in the world. It was first held in 1903. It has taken place every year since, except during world wars. The race is held for three weeks in July. The course, number of stages, and distance traveled change every year. A typical race has twenty-one day-long stages, includes two days of rest, and covers about 2,235 miles (3,600 km).

The Tour de France racecourse circles the whole country. It occasionally goes briefly into other countries, such as Belgium, Italy, Germany, and Spain. Every year, up to 15 million fans line the roads to watch the race. Millions more view it on television. The race is so important to the French people that for them, Lance Armstrong, who has won the race often, is one of the most well-known Americans of modern times.

During the grueling race, athletes ride their bicycles for several hours every day. On the road, there is no stopping. Injuries are treated quickly so that no time is lost. Lunch is passed to the riders as they speed by, and they drink water as they pedal.

The course takes riders through all kinds of terrain. For days the cyclists speed across the flat countryside under the hot summer sun. They spend many more days biking over winding mountain roads. The hardest Tour de France stage, known as the "circle of death," is a treacherous ride in the Pyrenees Mountains. Mountain roads can climb 10,000 feet (3,050 m) in a single day. On the way down, the riders might be moving as fast as 70 miles (115 km) per hour. At such times, the race can be downright dangerous.

Because the Tour de France is so physically challenging, riders need a lot of energy. They use about 10,000 calories per day in the mountain stages and up to 7,000 calories per day in the flat stages. This means that each day, riders must take in up to five times the number of calories that they would normally get from food. It is a constant battle for cyclists to eat enough food to get the energy they need.

At last, riders begin the final stage of the race. The Tour de France ends in Paris. There, riders cycle along the most famous street in the city, the Champs-Élysées. The winner of the Tour de France is awarded the prestigious *maillot jaune* (may YOH zhohn), or yellow jersey, of victory.

Unit 5 Wrap-Up

The Big Idea

Changes Great and Small Think about how each of the selections in Unit 5 relates to the Big Idea, "Changing things for the better is worth the challenge." Choose the selection you can relate to most closely, and write an e-mail to a friend, explaining why the challenge and change described in that selection are important to you.

Listening and Speaking

A New World With a small group, talk about recent technological advances. Think of the inventions that have replaced typewriters, phonographs, many telephones, and other devices that were once the newest things. How have the inventions changed people's lives? Have there been negative changes as well as positive?

- MP3 players
- cell phones
- instant messaging
- hand-held game players

Glossary

This glossary contains meanings and pronunciations for some of the words in this book. The Full Pronunciation Key shows how to pronounce each consonant and vowel in a special spelling. At the bottom of the glossary pages is a shortened form of the full key.

Full Pronunciation Key

Consonant Sounds

b	**b**i**b**, ca**bb**age	m	a**m**, **m**an, du**mb**	y	**y**es, **y**olk, on**i**on
ch	**ch**ur**ch**, sti**tch**	n	**n**o, sudd**en**	z	ro**s**e, si**z**e, **x**ylophone, **z**ebra
d	**d**ee**d**, mail**ed**, pu**dd**le	ng	thi**ng**, i**nk**	zh	gara**g**e, plea**s**ure, vi**s**ion
f	**f**ast, **f**i**f**e, o**ff**, **ph**rase, rou**gh**	p	**p**o**p**, ha**pp**y		
		r	**r**oa**r**, **rh**yme		
g	**g**a**g**, **g**et, fin**g**er	s	mi**ss**, **s**au**c**e, **sc**ene, **s**ee		
h	**h**at, **wh**o	sh	di**sh**, **sh**ip, **s**ugar, ti**ss**ue		
hw	**wh**ich, **wh**ere				
j	**j**u**dg**e, **g**em	t	**t**igh**t**, stopp**ed**		
k	**c**at, **k**i**ck**, s**ch**ool	th	ba**th**, **th**in		
kw	**ch**oir, **qu**ick	th	ba**th**e, **th**is		
l	**l**id, need**l**e, ta**ll**	v	ca**v**e, val**v**e, **v**ine		
		w	**w**ith, **w**olf		

Vowel Sounds

ă	p**a**t, l**augh**	oi	b**oy**, n**oi**se, **oi**l	ŭ	c**u**t, fl**oo**d, r**ough**, s**o**me
ā	**a**pe, **ai**d, p**ay**	ou	c**ow**, **ou**t	û	c**ir**cle, f**ur**, h**ear**d, t**er**m, t**ur**n, **ur**ge, w**or**d
â	**ai**r, c**a**re, w**ea**r	o͞o	f**u**ll, b**oo**k, w**o**lf		
ä	f**a**ther, k**oa**la, y**a**rd	o͞o	b**oo**t, r**u**de, fr**ui**t, fl**ew**		
ĕ	p**e**t, pl**ea**sure, **a**ny			yo͝o	c**u**re
ē	b**e**, b**ee**, **ea**sy, p**ia**no			yo͞o	**a**b**u**se, **u**se
ĭ	**i**f, p**i**t, b**u**sy			ə	**a**go, sil**e**nt, penc**i**l, lem**o**n, circ**u**s
ī	r**i**de, b**y**, p**ie**, h**igh**				
î	d**ea**r, d**ee**r, f**ie**rce, m**e**re				
ŏ	h**o**rrible, p**o**t				
ō	g**o**, r**ow**, t**oe**, th**ough**				
ô	**a**ll, c**augh**t, f**o**r, p**aw**				

Stress Marks

Primary Stress ´: bi·ol·o·gy [bī **ŏl**´ ə jē]
Secondary Stress ´: bi·o·log·i·cal [bī´ ə **lŏj**´ ĭ kəl]

Pronunciation key and definitions © 2003 by Houghton Mifflin Company. Adapted and reprinted by permission from *The American Heritage Children's Dictionary.*

A

a·ban·don (ə **băn′** dən) *v.* To leave and not intend to return: *Derek will **abandon** his old car at the junkyard and buy a new one.*

a·brupt (ə **brŭpt′**) *adj.* Unexpected; sudden: *The television show came to an **abrupt** end when the thunderstorm caused the TV to lose its signal.*

a·bun·dance (ə **bŭn′** dəns) *n.* A great amount or quantity; a plentiful supply: *The heavy spring rains gave us an **abundance** of water for the summer.*

ac·cus·tomed (ə **kŭs′** təmd) *adj.* Used to; in the habit of: *Farmers are **accustomed** to working long days.*

af·firm (ə **fûrm′**) *v.* To give approval or validity to; confirm: *The appeals court **affirmed** the lower court's ruling.*

a·gil·i·ty (ə **jĭl′** ĭ tē) *n.* The quality and condition of being able to move quickly and easily; nimbleness: *The mountain climber showed remarkable **agility** in scaling the cliff.*

agility

ag·i·ta·tion (ăj′ ĭ **tā′** shən) *n.* **1.** Great emotional disturbance or excitement: *My dog barks in **agitation** when the mail arrives.* **2.** Energetic action to arouse public interest in a cause: *Abolitionists, in **agitation** against slavery, sparked a national debate prior to the Civil War.*

ag·o·ny (**ăg′** ə nē) *n.* Intense and prolonged pain or suffering: *Because of her injuries, she was in **agony**.*

aim (ām) *n.* Purpose; goal: *My **aim** is to be a writer when I grow up.*

al·ter (**ôl′** tər) *v.* To change or make different: *We **altered** our plans for the weekend after checking the weather.*

an·ces·tral (ăn **sĕs′** trəl) *adj.* Of, relating to, or inherited from an ancestor or ancestors: *Every living thing has an **ancestral** trait.*

a·non·y·mous (ə **nŏn′** ə məs) *adj.* Nameless or unnamed: *The prize was awarded by a panel of **anonymous** judges.*

apt·ly (**ăpt′** lē) *adv.* In a way that is exactly suitable; appropriately: *The boa constrictor, **aptly** named Squeeze, rested comfortably, awaiting his next meal.*

ar·chae·ol·o·gist (är′ kē **ŏl′** ə jĭst) *n.* A person who is an expert in archaeology: *Archaeologists use different tools to study cultures from the past.*

a·rise (ə **rīz′**) *v.* To come into being; appear: *We took advantage of opportunities as they **arose**.*

ă **rat** / ā **pay** / â **care** / ä **father** / ĕ **pet** / ē **be** / ĭ **pit** / ī **pie** / î **fierce** / ŏ **pot** / ō **go** / ô **paw, for** / oi **oil** / ŏŏ **book**

ar·ray (ə **rā′**) *n.* An impressively large number or group: *The cast for the play shows an impressive **array** of talents.*

ar·ti·fi·cial (är′ tə **fish′** əl) *adj.* **1.** Made by humans rather than occurring in nature. **2.** Not genuine or natural: *The flowers on the tables are made to look real, but they are **artificial**.*

art·is·try (är′ tĭ strē) *n.* **1.** Artistic quality or workmanship. **2.** Artistic ability: *Visitors to the museum observed the **artistry** of different paintings.*

as·cent (ə **sĕnt′**) *n.* The act of moving, going, or growing upward: *The climbers planned their **ascent** of the peak for a clear day so they could enjoy the views from the top.*

as·pect (ăs′ pĕkt) *n.* The way in which something can be viewed by the mind; an element or facet: *In prescribing a treatment, the doctor considered every **aspect** of the patient's history.*

B

bar·ren (băr′ ən) *adj.* **1.** Lacking plants or crops: *The drought left our farm with **barren** fields.* **2.** Empty; bare: *The volunteers worked to help make the neighborhood streets **barren** of litter and other trash.*

be·rate (bĭ **rāt′**) *v.* To scold severely; upbraid: *No one should **berate** a friend for something that isn't the friend's fault.*

bit·ter (bĭt′ ər) *adj.* **1.** Showing or proceeding from strong dislike or animosity: *The soldiers fought **bitterly** to win the war.* **2.** Resulting from grief, anguish, or disappointment: *Fans wept **bitterly** when the team lost the final match.*

bland (blănd) *adj.* Lacking distinctive character; dull; flat: *The politician's **bland** speech did not present any interesting ideas.*

blurt (blûrt) *v.* To say something suddenly without thinking: *The teacher accidentally **blurted** out the answer to the test question.*

brain·wash (brān′ wŏsh′) *v.* To persuade (a person) by intense means, such as repeated suggestions, to adopt a belief or behave in a certain way: *The TV commercials **brainwashed** me into buying the junk food.*

C

ca·reen (kə **rēn′**) *v.* To lurch or swerve while in motion: *As it moved down the icy road, the car was **careening** out of control.*

brainwash
Brainwash is a literal translation of a Chinese word meaning "to wash the brain." It first came into English as a military term during the Korean War.

barren

---

o͞o b**oo**t / ou **ou**t / ŭ c**u**t / û f**u**r / hw **wh**ich / th **th**in / th **th**is / zh vi**s**ion / ə **a**go, sil**e**nt, penc**i**l, lem**o**n, circ**u**s

ce·re·mo·ny (**sĕr′** ə mō nē) *adj.* ceremonial: A formal act or series of acts performed in honor of an event or special occasion: *The graduating students walked down the aisle in a **ceremonial** procession.*

clam·or (**klăm′** ər) *n.* A loud, continuous, and usually confused noise: *A **clamor** arose from the crowd as the rock star emerged onstage.*

complex

clus·tered (**klŭs′** tərd) *adj.* Gathered in groups: ***Clustered** around the fire, they held out their hands to get warm.*

coax (kōks) *v.* To persuade or try to persuade by gently urging: *The trainer **coaxed** the lion into the cage.*

col·lide (kə **līd′**) *v.* To strike or bump together with violent direct impact: *The car was badly damaged when it **collided** with the tree.*

com·mem·o·rate (kə **mĕm′** ə rāt′) *v.* To honor the memory of (someone or something), especially with a ceremony: *The crowd gathers in the park and **commemorates** the firefighters' sacrifice.*

com·plex (kəm **plĕks′**) *adj.* Consisting of many connected or interrelated parts or factors; intricate: *The **complex** wiring of a computer is hard to understand unless one is an expert.*

com·pre·hen·sion (kŏm′ prĭ **hĕn′** shən) *n.* **1.** The act or fact of understanding. **2.** The ability to understand something: *The tutor helped him improve his **comprehension** skills in English class through writing and reading lessons.*

com·pro·mise (**kŏm′** prə mīz′) *n.* A settlement of differences between opposing sides in which each side gives up some claims and agrees to some demands of the other: *By agreeing to share the cost, our neighbors reached a **compromise** over rebuilding the fence.*

con·ceive (kən **sēv′**) *v.* **1.** To form or develop in the mind. **2.** To imagine or think of: *The friends worked together to **conceive** a plan for turning the abandoned lot into a playground.*

con·cept (**kŏn′** sĕpt′) *n.* A general idea or understanding, especially one based on known facts or observation: *The **concept** that all matter is made up of atoms is well accepted.*

con·clu·sion (kən **klōō′** zhən) *n.* **1.** A judgment or decision reached by reasoning: *Scientists check their observations thoroughly to arrive at an accurate **conclusion**.* **2.** The end or finish: *At the **conclusion** of the play, the audience rose and cheered.*

ă rat / ā pay / â care / ä father / ĕ pet / ē be / ĭ pit / ī pie / î fierce / ŏ pot / ō go / ô paw, for / oi oil / o͝o book

con·di·tion (kən dĭsh′ ən) *n.*
1. A state of being or existence.
2. The existing circumstances: *Paul bundled up in his coat and hat before going out into the harsh conditions of the winter weather.*

con·front (kən frŭnt′) *v.* To come face to face with, especially in opposition: *He did not have an easy time confronting his fear of flying, but once he sat down in the airplane he started to relax.*

con·se·quence (kŏn′ sĭ kwĕns′) *n.* Something that follows from an action or condition; an effect; a result: *Having a large vocabulary was one of the consequences of so much reading.*

con·tempt (kən tĕmpt′) *n.* A feeling that a person or thing is inferior or worthless: *The two lawyers looked at each other with contempt in the courtroom because each thought the other's argument was worthless.*

con·test (kən tĕst′) *v.* To dispute; challenge: *Because the parking ticket had been given unfairly, he contested it in court.*

con·tro·ver·sy (kŏn′ trə vûr′ sē) *n.* A dispute, especially a public one between sides holding opposite views: *The debate between the candidates for class president started a controversy over who was better suited for the position.*

cred·it (krĕd′ ĭt) *n.* Recognition or approval for an act, ability, or quality: *The two authors share credit for the book's success.*

cul·mi·na·tion (kŭl′ mə nā′ shən) *n.* The highest point or degree, often just before the end; climax: *The culmination of the celebration was a huge display of fireworks.*

cul·prit (kŭl′ prĭt) *n.* A person or thing guilty of a fault or crime: *The culprit who took the basketball net should put it back.*

cul·tur·al (kŭl′ chər əl) *adj.* Of or relating to the arts, beliefs, customs, institutions, and all other products of human work and thought at a particular time and place: *Paris is the cultural center of France.*

cus·tom·ar·y (kŭs′ tə mĕr′ ē) *adj.* Established by custom; usual; habitual: *The customary place for a judge to sit is at the head of a courtroom.*

D

da·ta (dā′ tə) *pl. n.*
Information, usually in numerical form, suitable for processing by computer: *His job is to compile lists of information and input the data into a computer to be sorted.*

culprit
The word *culprit* is from Norman French, the language of English law courts from 1066 to 1362. In court, the prosecutor would say of the defendant, "Guilty *(culpable)*; ready *(prit)* to proceed." The court clerk abbreviated the phrase as *cul. prit,* and the term came to indicate the defendant.

ōō **boo**t / ou **ou**t / ŭ **cu**t / û **fu**r / hw **wh**ich / th **th**in / *th* **th**is / zh vi**s**ion / ə **a**go, sil**e**nt, penc**i**l, lem**o**n, circ**u**s

de·com·po·si·tion (dē kŏm pə zĭsh′ ən) *n.* The act or process of rotting or decaying: *Microbes caused the **decomposition** of dead plants on the forest floor.*

de·crep·it (dĭ krĕp′ ĭt) *adj.* Weakened, worn-out, or broken down because of old age or long use: *Tony's motorcycle grew **decrepit** over the years, so he could no longer use it.*

de·duce (dĭ dōōs′) *v.* To reach (a conclusion) by reasoning, especially from a general principle: *The engineers **deduced** from the laws of physics that the new airplane would fly.*

de·fy (dĭ fī′) *v.* To oppose or resist openly or boldly: *There is no good reason to **defy** school rules on the field trip.*

de·mean·or (dĭ mē′ nər) *n.* The way in which a person behaves; deportment: *As head librarian, she has a **demeanor** of quiet authority.*

de·pict (dĭ pĭkt′) *v.* To represent in or as if in a painting or words: *The artist **depicted** his subject in an accurate way, rather than create an abstract portrait.*

de·prive (dĭ prīv′) *v.* To prevent from having or enjoying; deny: *Heavy snow **deprived** the deer of food.*

des·per·a·tion (dĕs′ pə rā′ shən) *n.* The condition of having lost all hope: *In **desperation**, he heaved a shot from mid-court in one last effort to win the game.*

des·ti·ny (dĕs′ tə nē) *n.* The fortune, fate, or lot of a person or thing that is considered to be unavoidable: *Because Karen loved animals, she believed that growing up to be a veterinarian was her **destiny**.*

de·tached (dĭ tăcht′) *adj.* Marked by absence of emotional involvement: *She tried to ignore her emotions and keep a **detached** view of the problem.*

dig·ni·fied (dĭg′ nə fīd′) *adj.* Worthy of esteem or respect: *The volunteers helped clean the park in a **dignified** and polite manner.*

dis·close (dĭs klōz′) *v.* To make known (something previously kept secret): *The child promised not to **disclose** where the gifts were hidden.*

dis·may (dĭs mā′) *n.* A sudden loss of courage or confidence in the face of danger or trouble: *Being lost in the woods filled the hikers with **dismay**.*

dis·tinct (dĭ stĭngkt′) *adj.* Different from all others; separate: *Everybody in the talent show had a **distinct** talent.*

ă rat / ā **pay** / â **care** / ä **father** / ĕ **pet** / ē **be** / ĭ **pit** / ī **pie** / î **fierce** / ŏ **pot** / ō **go** /
ô **paw, for** / oi **oil** / ōŏ **book**

dis·tin·guished (dĭ **stĭng′** gwĭsht) *adj.* Recognized as excellent: *The college professor received an honorary degree for his **distinguished** teaching, talent, and dedication to students.*

di·vine (dĭ **vīn′**) *adj.* Of, from, or like God or a god; being in the worship or service of God: *Ancient civilizations often relied on **divine** advice to help them make decisions.*

dole·ful (**dōl′** fəl) *adj.* Filled with or expressing grief; mournful: *The cat's **doleful** cry in the rain was pitiful.*

do·mes·tic (də **mĕs′** tĭk) *adj.* Of or relating to the family or household: *Gathering in the living room to watch a movie together is one example of a **domestic** activity for families.*

dor·mant (**dôr′** mənt) *adj.* **1.** In an inactive state in which growth and development stop for a time. **2.** Not active but capable of renewed activity: *When the wind stilled, the windmill sat **dormant**.*

du·ra·ble (**door′** ə bəl) *adj.* Capable of withstanding wear and tear; sturdy: *Denim is a **durable** fabric used for work clothes.*

E

ec·sta·sy (**ĕk′** stə sē) *n.* Intense joy or delight: *After years of practice, the runner was in **ecstasy** over winning an Olympic medal.*

ed·i·to·ri·al (ĕd′ ĭ **tôr′** ē əl) *adj.* Of or relating to making (written material) ready for publication by correcting, revising, or marking directions for a printer: *The **editorial** department made numerous corrections to early drafts of the textbook.*

ee·rie (**îr′** ē) *adj.* Inspiring fear without a clear reason; strange and frightening: *The **eerie** old house made us feel uneasy.*

e·lab·o·rate (ĭ **lăb′** ə rĭt) *adj.* Having many details or parts: *The Great Wall of China was an **elaborate** building project.*

el·e·gant (**ĕl′** ĭ gənt) *adj.* Marked by or showing refinement, grace, and beauty in appearance or behavior: *The dancers moved in an **elegant** waltz across the stage.*

e·lu·sive (ĭ **loo′** sĭv) or (ĭ **loo′** zĭv) *adj.* **1.** Tending to escape: *The **elusive** wren kept flying away from our bird feeder.* **2.** Difficult to define or describe: *The idea seemed **elusive** when she tried to write it down on paper. It was hard for her to grasp.*

domestic

dormant

The word *dormant* means to "lie asleep, or as if asleep." It comes from the Latin word *dormīre*, meaning "sleep." Two related words are *dormitory*, "a room or building designed as sleeping quarters for a number of people," and *dormer*, from a French word meaning "sleeping room." Since sleeping rooms were usually on the top floor of a house, *dormer* gradually came to refer to a gable or window projecting from a sloping roof.

ōō b**oo**t / ou **ou**t / ŭ c**u**t / û f**u**r / hw **wh**ich / th **th**in / *th* **th**is / zh vi**s**ion / ə **a**go, sil**e**nt, penc**i**l, lem**o**n, circ**u**s

em·bod·y (ĕm **bŏd′** ē) *v.* **1.** To give a bodily form to. **2.** To make part of a system or whole: *The team leaders* **embodied** *the spirit of teamwork.*

em·brace (ĕm **brās′**) *v.* To take up willingly or eagerly: *We knew that the mayor would* **embrace** *our idea to clean up the community center playground.*

e·merge (ĭ **mûrj′**) *v.* To come into existence, arise; to become known for or as: *Both women and men would* **emerge** *as strong voices for change during the civil rights era.*

em·phat·i·cal·ly (ĕm **făt′** ĭk lē) *adv.* In a way that is forceful and definite in expression or action: *He* **emphatically** *denied the false allegations.*

equation

em·ploy (ĕm **ploi′**) *v.* To put to use or service: *In order to finish the project, the girl* **employed** *a strategy of working on it for one hour each night.*

em·u·late (ĕm′ yə lāt′) *v.* To strive to equal or excel, especially through imitation: *My mentor was an experienced pianist whose style I tried to* **emulate**.

en·gulf (ĕn **gŭlf′**) *v.* To swallow up or overwhelm by or as if by overflowing and enclosing: *The residents feared the floodwaters would* **engulf** *the land near the river.*

e·qua·tion (ĭ **kwā′** zhən) *n.* A mathematical statement asserting that two expressions are equal: *The math teacher wrote several* **equations** *on the blackboard for the students to learn.*

e·quiv·a·lent (ĭ **kwĭv′** ə lənt) *adj.* Equal, as in value, meaning, or force: *The wish of a king is* **equivalent** *to a command.*

e·rect (ĭ **rĕkt′**) *v.* To build; construct: *Six volunteers* **erected** *the heavy tent before we set up the rest of our camp.*

e·ven·tu·al (ĭ **vĕn′** chŏo əl) *adj.* Occurring at an unspecified future time; at last: *He did not worry about his missing keys because he knew that he would find them* **eventually**.

ex·as·per·ate (ĭg **zăs′** pə rāt′) *v.* To make angry or impatient; irritate greatly: *The dog's constant barking* **exasperated** *the neighbors.*

ex·ca·vate (ĕk′ skə vāt′) *v.* **1.** To make a hole in; hollow out. **2.** To remove by digging or scooping out: *Luisa decided to* **excavate** *the soil in her backyard before beginning her garden.*

ex·hil·a·rate (ĭg **zĭl′** ə rāt′) *v.* To cause to feel happy: *The young man felt a burst of* **exhilaration** *after helping to rebuild an abandoned house in his community.*

ă **r**a**t** / ā **p**a**y** / â **c**a**re** / ä **f**a**ther** / ĕ **p**e**t** / ē **b**e / ĭ **p**i**t** / ī **p**ie / î **f**ie**rce** / ŏ **p**o**t** / ō **g**o / ô **p**a**w, f**o**r** / oi **o**i**l** / ŏŏ b**oo**k

ex·panse (ĭk **spăns'**) *n.* A wide and open extent, as of surface, land, or sky: *Gazing out at the vast* **expanse** *of desert, the explorer wondered if he would be able to cross it.*

F

fal·ter (**fôl'** tər) *v.* **1.** To lose confidence or purpose; hesitate: *As the work became more difficult, she knew her determination would* **falter.** **2.** To move haltingly: *I might* **falter** *on this slippery path.*

fa·nat·ic (fə **năt'** ĭk) *n.* A person who is excessively or unreasonably devoted to a cause or belief: *The football* **fanatic** *covered his walls with posters of his favorite players.*

flair (flâr) *n.* Distinctive elegance or style: *The dancer had a certain* **flair** *that set her apart from everyone else.*

forge (fôrj) *n.* To give form or shape to, especially by means of careful effort: *Common goals can be used to* **forge** *a new friendship.*

frag·ment (**frăg'** mənt) *n.* A piece or part broken off from a whole: *I dropped the plate, and it shattered into* **fragments.**

frail (frāl) *adj.* Physically weak; not robust: *The* **frail** *child was at constant risk of getting injured.*

fray·ed (frād) *adj.* Worn away or tattered along the edges: *Because the cuffs of his jeans dragged on the ground as he walked, they quickly became worn and* **frayed.**

frig·id (**frĭj'** ĭd) *adj.* Extremely cold: *The house was* **frigid** *because they never turned on the heat.*

froth·ing (**frôth'** ĭng) *adj.* Foaming: *Oaxaca, Mexico is famous for its hot chocolate, which is served* **frothing** *in a traditional jar.*

frus·trate (**frŭs'** trāt) *v.* **1.** To prevent from accomplishing something. **2.** To bring to nothing: *The long wait at the airport brought* **frustration** *to many of the travelers, who were anxious to get to their destination.*

fun·da·men·tal (fŭn' də **měn'** təl) *adj.* Of, relating to, or forming a foundation; elemental; basic; primary: *A* **fundamental** *knowledge of mathematics should be part of every student's education.*

fu·ry (**fyoor'** ē) *n.* **1.** Violent anger; rage: *The batter threw his hat down in* **fury** *after striking out.* **2.** Violent and uncontrolled action: *The blizzard's* **fury** *caused roadways to be shut down to prevent car accidents.*

frayed

flair
In the Middle Ages, the French used the word *flair* to mean "odor or scent." The modern English meaning of "showiness" or "a special aptitude" may come from a hound's special ability to track a scent.

---

oō **boo**t / ou **out** / ŭ **cut** / û **fur** / hw **wh**ich / th **th**in / *th* **th**is / zh vi**s**ion / ə **a**go, sil**e**nt, penc**i**l, lem**o**n, circ**u**s

G

gen·u·ine·ly (jĕn′ yōō ĭn lē) *adv.*
Not falsely; truly or purely:
Oliver is not exaggerating; he
genuinely *believes every word of
the book.*

gloat (glōt) *v.* To feel or express
great, often spiteful pleasure:
Because she would **gloat** *after
each victory, the runner was disliked by her opponents.*

grim·ly (grĭm′ lē) *adv.*
Unrelentingly; rigidly: *Despite
his injury, the runner was* **grimly**
*determined to finish the mara-
thon.*

H

harsh (härsh) *adj.* **1.**
Unpleasant; rough. **2.**
Extremely severe: *The rain-
storm's* **harsh** *downpours and
severe winds caused flooding in
the city.*

her·i·tage (hĕr′ ĭ tĭj) *n.*
Something passed down from
preceding generations; a tradition: *Our country has a great*
heritage *of folk music.*

hov·er (hŭv′ ər) *v.* To stay floating, suspended, or fluttering in
the air: *The hummingbirds were*
hovering *over the flowers in our
backyard.*

I

im·mac·u·late·ly (ĭ măk′ yə lĭt lē)
adv. In a way that is perfectly
clean: *The operating room was
cleaned* **immaculately** *between
procedures.*

im·pend (ĭm pĕnd′) *v.* To be
about to occur: *Her retirement
is* **impending**, *so she may not be
with the company next year.*

im·plore (ĭm plôr′) *v.* **1.** To
appeal to (a person) earnestly
or anxiously. **2.** To plead or
beg: *The kids* **implored** *their
mother to buy them several new
toys at the mall.*

im·print (ĭm′ prĭnt) *n.* A marked
influence or effect; an impres-
sion: *The Mayan* **imprints** *on the
wall showed signs of early civilization.*

in·ac·ces·si·ble (ĭn ăk sĕs′ ə bəl)
adj. Not accessible; unable to
approach: *The toys on the shelf
were* **inaccessible** *to the little girl
because they were too high for
her to reach.*

in·clined (ĭn klīnd′) *adj.* Having
a preference or tendency; willing: *The car salesman was*
inclined *to negotiate prices with
shoppers. He wanted to help
them get the best deal possible.*

hover

incline
The word *incline*
contains the Latin
root *clīnāre*, meaning
"to lean." If you are
inclined to do some-
thing, you're leaning
in that direction.
Other words with the
same Latin root are
decline, meaning "to
bend or slope down-
ward" and also "to
politely refuse"; and
recline, meaning "to
lie back or down." If
you're not tired, you
may be inclined to
decline to recline!

ă rat / ā pay / â care / ä father / ĕ pet / ē be / ĭ pit / ī pie / î fierce / ŏ pot / ō go /
ô paw, for / oi oil / ōō book

in·i·tial·ly (ĭ nĭsh′ əl lē) *adv.* At the beginning; firstly: *The two women **initially** disliked each other but eventually became good friends.*

in·no·va·tion (ĭn′ ə vā′ shən) *n.* Something newly introduced: *Automatic transmission was a major **innovation** in automobiles.*

in·stinct (ĭn′ stĭngkt′) *n.* A natural talent or ability: *Parents usually have a natural **instinct** to protect their offspring.*

in·tense (ĭn tĕns′) *adj.* Existing in an extreme degree; very strong: *The wall was painted an **intense** blue; it overwhelmed every other color in the room.*

in·tent·ly (ĭn tĕnt′ lē) *adv.* In a way that shows concentration or firm purpose: *The girl searched through her house **intently**, determined to find her missing book.*

in·ter·act (ĭn′ tər ăkt′) *v.* To act on or affect each other: *Tennis is an example of an **interaction** between two or more people.*

J

jeop·ard·y (jĕp′ ər dē) *n.* Risk of loss or injury; danger: *He would be in **jeopardy** of getting hurt if he didn't wear his helmet while riding his bike.*

jos·tle (jŏs′ əl) *v.* To push and come into rough contact with while moving; bump: *The couple was **jostled** as they attempted to move across the crowded dance floor.*

ju·bi·lant (jōō′ bə lənt) *adj.* Full of joyful exultation; rejoicing: *A **jubilant** crowd celebrated their team's victory.*

jut (jŭt) *v.* To extend sharply outward or upward; project: *The branches of the huge tree **jutted** out over the street.*

L

lab·y·rinth (lăb′ ə rĭnth′) *n.* **1.** A maze. **2.** Something complicated or confusing in design or construction: *The inside of the cave was built to look like a **labyrinth** of secret pathways.*

like·li·hood (līk′ lē hŏŏd′) *n.* The chance of a thing happening; probability: *The **likelihood** of snow is very remote in July.*

lin·ger (lĭng′ gər) *v.* To be slow in leaving: *The children **lingered** in the toyshop until closing.*

lit·er·al·ly (lĭt′ ər ə lē) *adv.* Really; actually: ***Literally** millions of lives were saved by the vaccine.*

jostle
This word comes from the word *joust,* a sport that was popular in medieval times. In these contests, each mounted knight attempted to knock his opponent off of his horse using a weapon such as a lance.

ōō b**oo**t / ou **ou**t / ŭ c**u**t / û f**u**r / hw **wh**ich / th **th**in / *th* **th**is / zh vi**si**on / ə **a**go, sil**e**nt, pen**c**il, lem**o**n, cir**c**us

lit·er·ar·y (**lĭt′** ər ĕr′ ē) *adj.* Of or relating to writers or the writing profession: *The **literary** magazine published short stories, poems, and book reviews.*

loom·ing (**lo͞om′** ĭng) *adj.* In view, often with a threatening appearance: *The lookout stared ahead at the storm clouds that were **looming** in the distance.*

lore (lôr) *n.* The accumulated facts, traditions, or beliefs about something: *Achilles is a famous, god-like warrior in Greek **lore**.*

lu·nar (**lo͞o′** nər) *adj.* Of or relating to the moon: *The **lunar** mission was designed to send people to the moon.*

lurch (lûrch) *v.* To move suddenly and unsteadily; stagger: *The bumper cars **lurched** forward at the amusement park, steered by excited drivers of all ages.*

lush (lŭsh) *adj.* Having or covered in thick plant growth: *The homeowner worked hard to maintain a **lush** green lawn.*

lus·trous (**lŭs′** trəs) *adj.* Having luster; shining; gleaming: *Nancy wore a **lustrous** gown to her aunt's wedding.*

luxurious (lŭg **zho͝or′** ē əs) or (lŭk **sho͝or′** ē əs) *adj.* **1.** Fond of luxury. **2.** Costly; extravagant: *The **luxurious** apartment building she lived in offered an outdoor swimming pool, a garage, and a tennis court.*

M

ma·jes·tic (mə **jĕs′** tĭk) *adj.* Having or showing majesty: *The king and queen lived in a **majestic** palace surrounded by waterfalls and trees.*

ma·nip·u·late (mə **nĭp′** yə lāt′) *v.* To arrange, operate, or control by the hands or by mechanical means: *The pilot **manipulated** the airplane's controls.*

man·u·script (**măn′** yə skrĭpt′) *n.* The form of a book, paper, or article as it is submitted for publication in print: *The author sent the **manuscript** to the publisher after completing it.*

mas·sive (**măs′** ĭv) *adj.* **1.** Bulky, heavy, and solid. **2.** Unusually large or impressive: *The sea animals at the aquarium are housed in **massive** tanks that give them enough room to move around.*

maze (māz) *n.* A complicated and often confusing network of pathways: *The mouse found his way through the **maze** to get to the piece of cheese at the finish.*

mea·ger (**mē′** gər) *adj.* Lacking in quantity or richness; very little: *There was only a **meager** amount of popcorn left at the theater, so some people were not able to buy any for the movie.*

lush

maze

ă rat / ā pay / â care / ä father / ě pet / ē be / ĭ pit / ī pie / î fierce / ŏ pot / ō go /
ô paw, for / oi oil / o͝o book

men·ace (měn′ ĭs) *n.* A threat or a danger: *Just off the coast is a reef that is a menace to passing ships.*

men·tor (měn′ tôr) *n.* A wise and trusted advisor: *Katherine serves as a mentor to a number of the younger students in her school.*

mi·rac·u·lous (mĭ răk′ yə ləs) *adj.* Having the nature of a person, thing, or event that causes great admiration, awe, or wonder: *In one miraculous year, Albert Einstein revolutionized the way we think about physics.*

miss·ion (mĭsh′ ən) *n.* A group of persons sent to carry out an assignment: *My parents joined and international rescue mission.*

mo·tive (mō′ tĭv) *n.* An emotion or need that causes a person to act in a certain way: *Our motive in writing the book was to make people aware of the issue.*

mount (mount) *v.* **1.** To go upward; rise: *The shoppers rode the mounting stairs of the escalator.* **2.** To increase; grow higher: *Expenses are mounting, so we need to spend less.*

mul·ti·tude (mŭl′ tĭ tōōd′) *n.* A large number: *We faced a multitude of challenges but were able to overcome them all.*

mute (myōōt) *v.* To muffle or soften the sound of: *The additional insulation muted the sound of the people living next door.*

myth·i·cal (mĭth′ ĭ kəl) *adj.* **1.** Of or existing only in myths. **2.** Imaginary: *The new science fiction movie takes place in a mythical town.*

oc·cu·py (ŏk′ yə pī′) *v.* To seize possession of and maintain control over by force: *The soldiers patrolled the streets day and night, observing and occupying the land they had seized.*

op·tion (ŏp′ shən) *n.* The act of choosing; choice: *The flight attendant offered each passenger the option of chicken or beef.*

op·u·lent (ŏp′ yə lənt) *adj.* **1.** Having or showing great wealth; rich. **2.** Abundant; plentiful: *The queen's opulent dresses always included jewelry, fancy hats, and expensive shoes.*

or·a·cle (ôr′ ə kəl) *n.* A shrine in ancient Greece for the worship and consultation of a god who revealed knowledge or revealed the future: *In ancient civilization, people depended on oracles to tell about the future.*

o·rig·i·nate (ə rĭj′ ə nāt′) *v.* To come into existence; begin: *The idea of mass production originated in the United States.*

ōō b**oo**t / ou **ou**t / ŭ c**u**t / û f**u**r / hw **wh**ich / th **th**in / th **th**is / zh vi**s**ion / ə **a**go, sil**e**nt, penc**i**l, lem**o**n, circ**u**s

out·ly·ing (**out′** lī′ ĭng) *adj.* Lying outside the limits or boundaries of a certain area: *Kent visits his grandfather every weekend, who lives in an* **outlying** *suburb several miles from the city.*

P

par·al·lel (**păr′** ə lĕl′) *adj.* Matching feature for feature; corresponding: *The two companies are similar and have* **parallel** *business plans.*

par·tic·i·pant (pär **tĭs′** ə pənt) *n.* A person who joins with others in doing something or taking part: *All of the* **participants** *in the card game received ten cards from the deck.*

per·il·ous (**pĕr′** ə ləs) *adj.* Full of danger; hazardous: *The spy was sent off on a* **perilous** *mission during which her life would be in grave danger.*

per·me·ate (**pûr′** mē āt′) *v.* To spread or flow throughout: *The smell of baking cookies* **permeated** *the house.*

phe·nom·e·nal (fĭ **nŏm′** ə nəl) *adj.* Extraordinary; outstanding: *Jon has a* **phenomenal** *memory and remembers almost everything he has read.*

poise (poiz) *v.* To balance or hold in equilibrium: *The statue was* **poised** *on the pedestal.*

pon·der (**pŏn′** dər) *v.* To think about carefully; consider: *I* **pondered** *the meaning of my dream.*

pre·cede (prĭ **sēd′**) *v.* To come, exist, or occur before in time, order, position, or rank: *The host's introduction will* **precede** *the awards ceremony.*

pre·cise·ly (prĭ **sīs′** lē) *adv.* Exactly, as in performance, execution, or amount; accurately or correctly: *The surgeon worked* **precisely** *to repair the broken bone.*

pre·dom·i·nant (prĭ **dŏm′** ə nənt) *adj.* Greater than all others in strength, authority, or importance; dominant: *The team is* **predominantly** *made up of players from Guilford as there are only two players from other towns.*

prej·u·dice (**prĕj′** ə dĭs) *n.* An unpleasant judgment or opinion formed unfairly or before one knows the facts: *She had a strong* **prejudice** *against dogs. She did not like any breed.*

pres·sure (**prĕsh′** ər) *v.* To force, as by influencing or persuading: *The lineman broke through,* **pressuring** *the quarterback and forcing him to throw the ball away.*

pressure

The word root *press-* in English words and the English word *press* itself come from the past participle *pressus* of the Latin verb *premere,* "to squeeze, press." Thus, we have the noun *pressure* from the Latin noun meaning "a squeezing, as of the juice from grapes or of the oil from olives." We also have the verbs *compress,* "to squeeze together"; *depress,* "to squeeze down"; *express,* "to extract by pressure, expel, force"; and *impress,* "to press on or against, drive in, imprint."

ă **r**at / ā **p**ay / â **c**are / ä **f**ather / ĕ **p**et / ē **b**e / ĭ **p**it / ī **p**ie / î **fie**rce / ŏ **p**ot / ō **g**o / ô **p**aw, **for** / oi **oil** / o͝o **b**ook

pre·sum·a·bly (prĭ **zoo′** mə blē) *adv.* In a way that can be taken for granted; by reasonable assumption: *Presumably, he missed the train since we did not see him anywhere on the platform.*

prime (prīm) *v.* To make ready; prepare: *She described the questions he might be asked in order to **prime** the celebrity for the interview.*

prin·ci·ple (**prĭn′** sə pəl) *n.* A statement or set of statements describing natural phenomena or mechanical processes: *Scientific **principles** help us understand how the world works.*

pro·sper·i·ty (prŏ **spĕr′** ĭ tē) *n.* The condition of being successful, especially in money matters: *When the weather is good and soil conditions are right, farmers can enjoy times of great **prosperity**.*

pub·lish·ing (**pŭb′** lĭsh ĭng) *adj.* Related to preparing and issuing (something, such as a book) for public distribution or sale: *The **publishing** company produced novels, textbooks, and notebooks.*

pur·suit (pər **soot′**) *n.* The act or an instance of pursuing or chasing: *The cat ran quickly in **pursuit** of the mouse that fled.*

R

ran·dom (**răn′** dəm) *adj.* Having no specific pattern, purpose, or objective: *Although the numbers appeared to be **random**, there was a hidden pattern to them.*

rash (răsh) *adj.* Too bold or hasty; reckless: *The driver made a **rash** decision to run the red traffic light.*

re·cede (rĭ **sēd′**) *v.* To move back or away from a limit, point, or mark: *The floodwaters finally **receded**.*

re·cep·tion (rĭ **sĕp′** shən) *n.* **1.** A social gathering, especially one honoring or introducing someone: *The wedding **reception** took place in the hotel's ballroom.* **2.** A welcome, greeting, or acceptance: *The newcomer was given a friendly **reception**.*

rec·ol·lect (rĕk′ ə **lĕkt′**) *v.* To remember, to recall to the mind: *The formality with which he speaks **recollects** an earlier era.*

rec·re·a·tion (rĕk′ rē **ā′** shən) *n.* Refreshment of one's mind or body after work through some activity: *Reading a book is a **recreational** activity.*

re·flect (rĭ **flĕkt′**) *v.* To give evidence of the qualities of (someone): *Keeping your room neat **reflects** positively on you.*

ōo b**oo**t / ou **ou**t / ŭ c**u**t / û f**u**r / hw **wh**ich / th **th**in / *th* **th**is / zh vi**s**ion / ə **a**go, sil**e**nt, penc**i**l, lem**o**n, circ**u**s

re·gal (**rē'** gəl) *adj.* Of or relating to a king, royal: *The gifted speaker uplifted the crowd with his unselfish and **regal** manner of speech.*

regal

rel·ish (**rĕl'** ĭsh) *v.* To take pleasure in; enjoy: *As Andrea happily arose from bed, she was **relishing** the idea of going to the beach at dawn.*

re·luc·tant (rĭ **lŭk'** tənt) *adj.* Unwilling; averse: *Because they were having such a good time, the couple was **reluctant** to leave the party.*

rep·li·ca (**rĕp'** lĭ kə) *n.* **1.** A copy or reproduction of a work of art, especially one made by an original artist. **2.** A copy or reproduction, especially one smaller than the original: *Sean's toy airplanes are **replicas** of real airplanes.*

re·serve (rĭ **zûrv'**) *adj.* Kept back or saved for future use or a special purpose: *The family kept a **reserve** supply of food in case of emergencies.*

re·solve (rĭ **zŏlv'**) *v.* To find a solution to; solve: *The negotiator worked to **resolve** the conflict between the two countries.*

re·tain (rĭ **tān'**) *v.* To keep possession of; continue to have: *The new premier **retains** his post as minister of finance.*

re·vi·sion (rĭ **vĭzh'** ən) *n.* Changes or modifications made after reconsidering: *After the **revisions** had been made, the story was much more enjoyable to read.*

re·volt·ing (rĭ **vōlt'** ĭng) *adj.* Disgusting; repellent: *We were shocked by the **revolting** display of bad manners.* — *v.* **1.** Attempting to overthrow the authority of the state; rebelling. *In 1776, the American colonists were **revolting** against the British.* **2.** Opposing or refusing to accept something: *By refusing to incorporate her suggestions, we were **revolting** against her notion of what the front page should look like.*

rig·id (**rĭj'** ĭd) *adj.* Not changing shape or bending; stiff; inflexible: *The **rigid** iron frame provided the building with a solid structure.*

ru·di·men·ta·ry (roo' də **mĕn'** tə rē) *adj.* Of or relating to the basic principles or facts; elementary: *Before taking the class, he had only a **rudimentary** knowledge of economics.*

ruth· less (**rooth'** lĭs) *adj.* Showing no pity; cruel: *The robbers were **ruthless**.*

ă rat / ā pay / â care / ä father / ĕ pet / ē be / ĭ pit / ī pie / î fierce / ŏ pot / ō go /
ô paw, for / oi oil / oo book

S

sac·ri·fice (**săk′** rə fīs′) *v.* To give up one thing for another considered to be of greater value: *The brave soldier **sacrificed** his own life to save his comrades.*

sa·ga (**sä′** gə) *n.* **1.** A long adventure story written during the Middle Ages that deals with historical or legendary heroes, families, deeds, and events. **2.** A modern story that resembles a saga: *Troy's comic book series is a fictional **saga** about war in the seventeenth century.*

sal·vage (**săl′** vĭj) *v.* To save endangered property from loss: *The brothers hoped to **salvage** their parents' old home because they did not want it to be torn down.* — *n.* Goods or property saved from destruction.

sa·vor (**sā′** vər) *v.* To taste or smell, especially with pleasure: *The hungry family planned to **savor** each morsel of the feast.*

scho·las·tic (skə **lăs′** tĭk) *adj.* Of or relating to schools or education; academic: *The student was very proud of his **scholastic** achievement and studied hard in order to maintain it.*

scorn·ful (**skôrn′** fəl) *adj.* Full of or expressing scorn or contempt: *In a serious competition, people often speak **scornfully** about their opponents to challenge them or express their dislike.*

scrounge (skrounj) *v.* To obtain by rummaging or searching: *She was running late for school so she **scrounged** together an outfit as quickly as she could.*

sen·sor (**sĕn′** sər) or (**sĕn′** sôr) *n.* A device that responds to a particular type of change in its condition or environment: *The **sensors** in the porch lamp cause the lamp to light up every time someone steps onto the porch.*

se·rene (sə **rēn′**) *adj.* Peaceful and untroubled; calm: *The visitors to the library spoke in **serene** voices so that they would not disturb the readers.*

show·down (**shō′** doun′) *n.* An event, especially a confrontation, that forces an issue to a conclusion: *Superman readied himself for the **showdown** with his archenemy, Lex Luthor.*

shriv·eled (**shrĭv′** əld) *adj.* Shrunken or wrinkled: *Because they did not receive water, the plants in the desert became **shriveled** and died.*

sig·nif·i·cance (sĭg **nĭf′** ĭ kəns) *n.* The state or quality of being significant; importance: *The quilt holds great **significance** to the family. It has been passed down from generation to generation.*

scholastic

ōō b**oo**t / ou **ou**t / ŭ c**u**t / û f**u**r / hw **wh**ich / th **th**in / *th* **th**is / zh vi**s**ion / ə **a**go, sil**e**nt, penc**i**l, lem**o**n, circ**u**s

skep·ti·cal (**skĕp′** tĭ kəl) *adj.* Of, relating to, or characterized by a doubting or questioning attitude: *As she listened to her friend's tall tale, a **skeptical** expression formed on her face.*

som·ber (**sŏm′** bər) *adj.* Dark; gloomy: *The heavy thunderstorm made the neighborhood look gray and **somber**.*

so·phis·ti·cat·ed (sə **fĭs′** tĭ kā′ tĭd) *adj.* Elaborate, complex, or complicated: *The highly **sophisticated** technology was understood by only a few people in the world.*

sparse·ly (**spärs′** lē) *adv.* In a way that is not dense or crowded: *The **sparsely** vegetated tundra of the Arctic has few plants.*

spec·i·men (**spĕs′** ə mən) *n.* A sample, as of blood, tissue, or urine, used for analysis: *The doctor collected **specimens** of blood from each of the subjects in the research study.*

spite·ful (**spīt′** fəl) *adj.* Filled with, caused by, or showing spite; cruel: *The best friends were sorry that they had shared **spiteful** words with each other during an argument.*

sta·bi·lize (**stā′** bə līz′) *v.* To enable an object, such as a ship, to stay upright or return to an upright position after being tilted: *The keel on a sailboat helps to **stabilize** it.*

sta·ble (**stā′** bəl) *adj.* **1.** Not likely to change, change position, or change condition, firm: *Our house has a **stable** foundation.* **2.** Not likely to be affected or overthrown. *After years of civil war, the country was finally able to establish a **stable** government.* **3.** Firm or steady, as in purpose or character. *His friends knew they could always rely on him because he was so **stable**.* **4.** Mentally or emotionally sound; sane or rational. *Because of the professor's erratic behavior, some of his students wondered if he was **stable**.* **5.** Not known to decay; existing for an indefinitely long time, as an atomic particle. *Plutonium is not a **stable** element and the energy from its decay can be used in nuclear reactors.*

stead·fast (**stĕd′** făst′) *adj.* **1.** Not moving; fixed; steady. **2.** Firmly loyal or constant; faithful: *The runner stayed **steadfast** in his effort to win the race.*

stim·u·lus (**stĭm′** yə ləs) *n.* Something causing or regarded as causing a response: *Many hope the road repairs will be a **stimulus** to the state's economy.*

stri·dent (**strīd′** ənt) *adj.* Loud; harsh: *In the locker room, the coach talked to his players in a firm, **strident** tone to show that he was upset with the way they had played.*

sparsely

stable
Stable comes from an old French word related to the Latin word meaning "to stand." Something that is stable stands firm.

ă **r**a**t** / ā **pay** / â **c**a**re** / ä **fa**ther / ĕ **pet** / ē **be** / ĭ **pit** / ī **pie** / î **fie**rce / ŏ **pot** / ō **go** / ô **p**a**w**, f**or** / oi **oil** / ōō b**oo**k

sub·ject (səb **jĕkt'**) *v.* To cause to undergo: *The workers were **subjected** to the harsh rules of the workplace.*

sub·side (səb **sīd'**) *v.* To become less agitated or active: *The shouting between the two teams **subsided** when they came to an agreement over when to use the soccer field.*

sup·ple (**sŭp'** əl) *adj.* Easily bent or folded: *The wallet was made of **supple** leather so it opened and closed easily.*

sup·por·tive (sə **pôrt'** ĭv) *adj.* Giving support, sympathy, or encouragement: *My friends were **supportive** when I told them about my goals for this year.*

swiv·el (**swĭv'** əl) *v.* To turn or rotate on or as if on a pivot: *The child **swiveled** on his stool while sitting at the counter.*

T

taut (tôt) *adj.* Pulled or drawn tight: *The sails were **taut** with wind as the ship entered the harbor.*

teem (tēm) *v.* To be full of things; swarm or abound: *The pond water was **teeming** with microbes.*

tem·per·a·ment (**tĕm'** prə mənt) or (**tĕm'** pər ə mənt) *n.* The manner of thinking, behaving, or reacting in a way that is characteristic of a specific person: *The two best friends share different **temperaments** simply because they are different people.*

ten·den·cy (**tĕn'** dən sē) *n.* A characteristic likelihood: *Linen has a **tendency** to wrinkle.*

ten·sion (**tĕn'** shən) *n.* Unfriendliness or hostility between persons or groups: *The **tension** in the room kept building until finally an argument erupted.*

tor·rent (**tôr'** ənt) *n.* A swift flowing stream: *Every spring, the **torrent** flows down the mountain as the snow melts.*

trans·mis·sion (trăns **mĭsh'** ən) *n.* Something, such as a message, that is sent from one person, place, or thing to another: *The code-breaker deciphered each of the **transmissions** as it was intercepted.*

tre·mor (**trĕm'** ər) *n.* A shaking or vibrating movement, as of the earth: *The volcano's explosion could be felt through the **tremors** in the ground.*

tu·mult (**tōō'** mŭlt') *n.* A disorderly commotion or disturbance: *The fire in the theater created a **tumult** as everyone scrambled to get outside as quickly as possible.*

swivel

ōō b**oo**t / ou **ou**t / ŭ c**u**t / û f**u**r / hw **wh**ich / th **th**in / th **th**is / zh vi**si**on / ə **a**go, sil**e**nt, penc**i**l, lem**o**n, circ**u**s

U

ul·ti·mate (**ŭl′** tə mĭt) *adj.* The greatest extreme; the maximum: *The new camera model has more features than others, which makes it an **ultimate** leader in picture technology.*

un·af·fect·ed (ŭn′ ə **fĕk′** tĭd) *adj.* Not changed, modified, or affected: *The dinner party went as planned. It was **unaffected** by the people who showed up late.*

un·can·ny (ŭn **kăn′** ē) *adj.* Arousing wonder and fear, as if supernatural: *The computer-generated characters in the fantasy film had **uncanny** personalities that matched their supernatural abilities.*

un·der·state·ment (**ŭn′** dər stāt′ mənt) *n.* Lack of emphasis in expression, especially for rhetorical effect: *He often uses **understatement**, as in saying "not bad" to mean "very good."*

un·du·late (**ŭn′** jə lāt′) *v.* To move in waves or with a smooth wavy motion: *The fields of wheat were **undulating** in the breeze.*

un·earth (ŭn **ûrth′**) *v.* **1.** To bring up out of the earth; dig up. **2.** To bring to public notice; uncover: *Research scientists **unearthed** Mayan artifacts.*

un·pre·dict·a·bil·i·ty (ŭn′ prĭ dĭk′ tə **bĭl′** ĭ tē) *n.* The quality of being difficult to foretell or foresee: *Forming a plan to defend this team is difficult due to its **unpredictability**.*

un·ra·vel (ŭn **răv′** əl) *v.* **1.** To be separated, as thread: *The kite string **unravels** as the kite flies away.* **2.** To separate, as a problem or mystery: *Every day the author **unravels** a new clue in his detective novel.*

ur·gent (**ûr′** jənt) *adj.* Calling for immediate action or attention; pressing: *The **urgent** situation demanded immediate action.*

V

veer (vîr) *v.* To turn aside from a course, direction, or purpose; swerve: *The plane **veered** east to avoid the oncoming storm.*

ven·ture (**vĕn′** chər) *v.* To brave the dangers of: *The sailor was brave enough to **venture** the high seas in a light boat.*

ver·ti·cal (**vûr′** tĭ kəl) *adj.* Being or situated at right angles to the horizon; upright: *Most apartment buildings in New York City are tall and **vertical**, built this way to accommodate the many people who live there.*

---

understatement

The prefix *under-* has essentially the same meaning as the preposition *under*. For example, in words such as *underbelly, undercurrent, underlie,* and *undershirt, under-* denotes a position beneath or below. *Under-* also frequently conveys incompleteness or falling below a certain standard. Some examples are *undercharge, underdeveloped, underestimate,* and *underfeed.* Note that in this sense words beginning with *under-* often have counterparts beginning with *over-: overcharge, overestimate, overstate.*

ă r**a**t / ā p**ay** / â c**a**re / ä f**a**ther / ě p**e**t / ē b**e** / ĭ p**i**t / ī p**ie** / î f**ie**rce / ŏ p**o**t / ō g**o** /
ô p**aw**, f**o**r / oi **oi**l / o͞o b**oo**k

vig·or·ous·ly (vĭg′ ər əs lē) *adv.*
Forcefully and energetically: *To prepare for the upcoming season, the soccer players exercised vig-orously.*

void (void) *n.* An empty space; a vacuum: *The shuttle raced through the void of outer space.*

W

war·y (wâr′ ē) *adj.* On guard; watchful: *The lifeguard stood near the pool, looking warily at the swimmers to make sure they stayed safe in the water.*

wel·fare (wĕl′ fâr′) *n.* Health, happiness, and good fortune; well-being: *The government should promote the general welfare.*

wry (rī) *adj.* **1.** Twisted in an expression of displeasure or regret: *Tom shook his head with a wry half-smile when his dog dropped the torn newspa-per in his lap.* **2.** Funny in an understated or ironic way; dry: *Because she had a wry sense of humor, it took her friends a few moments to realize she was joking.*

ōō b**oo**t / ou **ou**t / ŭ **c**ut / û f**u**r / hw **wh**ich / th **th**in / *th* **th**is / zh vi**si**on / ə **a**go, sil**e**nt, penc**i**l, lem**o**n, circ**u**s

Acknowledgments

"The ACES Phone" by Jeanne DuPrau. Text copyright © 2005 by Jeanne DuPrau. Reprinted by permission of the author.

Airborn by Kenneth Oppel. Text copyright © 2004 by Kenneth Oppel. All rights reserved. Reprinted by permission of HarperCollins Publishers and the author.

All Alone in the Universe by Lynne Rae Perkins. Text and illustrations copyright © 1999 by Lynne Rae Perkins. Reprinted by permission of HarperCollins Publishers.

Adapted from *Any Small Goodness: A Novel of the Barrio* by Tony Johnston. Text copyright © 2001 by Roger D. Johnston and Susan T. Johnston as Trustees of the Johnston Family Trust. All rights reserved. Reprinted by permission of Blue Sky Press/Scholastic, Inc.

Bodies from the Ash: Life and Death in Ancient Pompeii by James M. Deem. Text copyright © 2005 by James M. Deem. All rights reserved. Reprinted by permission of Houghton Mifflin Harcourt Publishing Company.

The Boy Who Saved Baseball by John Ritter. Copyright © 2003 by John H. Ritter. Reprinted by permission of Philomel Books, a division of Penguin Young Readers Group, a member of Penguin Group (USA) Inc., 345 Hudson Street, New York, NY 10014, and Curtis Brown, Ltd. All rights reserved.

Children of the Midnight Sun: Young Native Voices of Alaska by Tricia Brown, photography by Roy Corral. Text copyright © 1998 by Tricia Brown. Photographs copyright © 1998 by Roy Corral. Reprinted by permission of Alaska Northwest Books, an imprint of Graphic Arts Center Publishing Company.

"Cloud Forest" from *Looking for Jaguar and Other Rain Forest Poems* by Susan Katz. Copyright © 2005 by Susan Katz. Reprinted by permission of HarperCollins Publishers.

The Emperor's Silent Army: Terracotta Warriors of Ancient China by Jane O'Connor. Copyright © 2002 by Jane O'Connor. Reprinted by permission of Viking Penguin, A Division of Penguin Young Readers Group, a Member of Penguin Group (USA) Inc., 345 Hudson Street, New York, NY 10014. All rights reserved.

First to Fly: How Wilbur and Orville Wright Invented the Airplane by Peter Busby, paintings by David Craig. Text, design, and compilation copyright © 2002 by Madison Press Books. Paintings copyright © 2002 by David Craig. Reprinted by permission of Madison Press Books.

The Fruit Bowl Project by Sarah Durkee. Text copyright © 2006 by Sarah Durkee. Reprinted by permission of Dell Publishing, a division of Random House, Inc., and Ed Victor, Ltd.

The Hero and the Minotaur by Robert Byrd. Copyright © 2005 by Robert Byrd. Reprinted by permission of Dutton Children's Books, a Division of Penguin Young Readers Group, a Member of Penguin Group (USA) Inc., 345 Hudson Street, New York, NY 10014. All rights reserved.

"Instructions for the Earth's Dishwasher" from *Earthshake: Poems from the Ground Up* by Lisa W. Peters. Copyright © 2003 by Lisa Westberg Peters. Reprinted by permission of HarperCollins Publishers.

Kensuke's Kingdom by Michael Morpurgo. Copyright © 1999 by Michael Morpurgo. Reprinted by permission of Scholastic, Inc. and Adams Literary.

Knots in My Yo-yo String by Jerry Spinelli. Copyright © 1998 by Jerry Spinelli. Cover photograph copyright © 1998 by Penny Gentieu. Map copyright © 1998 by Jenny Pavlovitz. Reprinted by permission of Alfred A. Knopf, a division of Random House Children's Books, a division of Random House, Inc.

"Lesson in Fire" by Linda Noel from *The Dirt is Red Here: Art and Poetry from Native California*, edited by Margaret Dubin. Text copyright © 2002 by Linda Noel. Reprinted by permission of Linda Noel.

"Long Trip" from *The Collected Poems of Langston Hughes* by Langston Hughes, edited by Arnold Rampersad with David Roessel, Associate Editor. Copyright © 1994 by the Estate of Langston Hughes. Reprinted by permission of Alfred A. Knopf, a division of Random House, Inc., and Harold Ober Associates, Inc.

"A Mighty Fine Fella" from *Nathaniel Talking* by Eloise Greenfield. Text copyright © 1988 by Eloise Greenfield. Reprinted by permission of the author.

"The Myers Family" from *Pass It Down: Five Picture-Book Families Make Their Mark*. Copyright © 2007 by Leonard S. Marcus. All rights reserved. Reprinted by permission of Walker & Company and Sterling Lord Literistic, Inc.

Number the Stars by Lois Lowry. Copyright © 1989 by Lois Lowry. Reprinted by permission of Houghton Mifflin Harcourt Publishing Company.

Onward: A Photobiography of African-American Explorer Matthew Henson by Dolores Johnson. Copyright © 2006 National Geographic Society. All rights reserved. Reprinted by permission of the National Geographic Society.

"The Princess Who Became a King" from *African Princess: The Amazing Lives of Africa's Royal Women* by Joyce Hansen. Text copyright © 2004 by Joyce Hansen. Painting copyright © 2004 by Laurie McGaw. Reprinted by permission of Hyperion Books for Children.

"Quitter" from *A Suitcase of Seaweed and Other Poems* by Janet S. Wong. Copyright © 1996 by Janet S. Wong. Reprinted by permission of Margaret K. McElderry Books, an imprint of Simon & Schuster Children's Publishing Division, and the author.

The Real Vikings: Craftsmen, Traders, and Fearsome Raiders by Melvin Berger and Gilda Berger. Copyright © 2003 by Melvin Berger. Reprinted by permission of The National Geographic Society.

"Reweaving the World Ohlone" by Stephen Meadows from *The Dirt is Red Here: Art and Poetry from Native California*, edited by Margaret Dubin. Text copyright © 2002 by Stephen Meadows. Reprinted by permission of the author.

Robotics by Helena Domaine. Copyright © 2006 by Helena Domaine. All rights reserved. Reprinted by permission of Lerner Publications Company, a division of Lerner Publishing Group, Inc.

"Science Friction" by David Lubar from *Tripping Over the Lunch Lady and Other Stories* edited by Nancy Mercado. Copyright © 2004 by David Lubar. Reprinted by permission of Dial Books for Young Readers, a Division of Penguin Young Readers Group, a Member of Penguin Group (USA) Inc., 345 Hudson Street, New York, NY 10014. All rights reserved.

The School Story by Andrew Clements and Brian Selznick. Text copyright © 2001 by Andrew Clements. Reprinted by permission of Simon & Schuster Books for Young Readers, an imprint of Simon & Schuster Children's Publishing Division.

"Song" by the Makah, translated by Frances Densmore in "Nookta and Quileute Music" from *Bureau of American Ethnology, Bulletin 124*. Reprinted by permission of Smithsonian Institution Libraries.

"A Song of Greatness," traditional Chippewa, translated by Mary Austin, from *The Children Sing in the Far West* by Mary Austin. Copyright © 1928 by Mary Austin. Copyright renewed 1956 by Kenneth M. Chapman & Mary C. Wheelwright. Reprinted by permission of Houghton Mifflin Harcourt Publishing Company.

Star in the Storm by Joan Hiatt Harlow. Copyright © 2000 by Joan Hiatt Harlow. All rights reserved. Reprinted by permission of Margaret K. McElderrry Books, an imprint of Simon and Schuster Children's Publishing Division.

"Super Samson Simpson" from *Something BIG Has Been Here* by Jack Prelutsky. Text copyright © 1990 by Jack Prelutsky. Reprinted by permission of HarperCollins Publishers.

Team Moon: How 400,000 People Landed Apollo 11 *on the Moon* by Catherine Thimmesh. Copyright © 2006 by Catherine Thimmesh. All rights reserved. Reprinted by permission of Houghton Mifflin Harcourt Publishing Company.

The Voice that Challenged a Nation: Marian Anderson and the Struggle for Equal Rights by Russell Freedman. Copyright © 2004 by Russell Freedman. All rights reserved. Reprinted by permission of Houghton Mifflin Harcourt Publishing Company.

"We Have Our Moments" from *Sports Pages* by Arnold Adoff. Text copyright © 1986 by Arnold Adoff. Reprinted by permission of HarperCollins Publishers.

"Whispers to the Wall" by Rebecca Kai Dotlich. Text copyright © 2004 by Rebecca Kai Dotlich. Reprinted by permission of Curtis Brown, Ltd.

"Who Could Tell?" from *César: ¡Sí, Se Puede!* by Carmen T. Bernier-Grand. Copyright © 2004 by Carmen T. Bernier-Grand. Reprinted by permission of Marshall Cavendish Corporation.

Credits

Illustration
Cover ©Paul Morin. **TOC 8** Chris Gall. **TOC 12** ©Margaret Lee. **20** Andy Levine. **22–33** ©C.F. Payne. **39** Eric Sturdevant. **41** Jan Bryan-Hunt. **58–61** Chris Lensch. **63** Eric Sturdevant. **65** Jan Bryan-Hunt. **68** Bassino & Guy. **70–89** David Goldin. **89** (br) Ken Bowser. **91** Eric Sturdevant. **93** Sally Vitsky. **96–111** ©Suling Wang. **113** Bill Melvin. **115** Ken Bowser. **117** Eric Sturdevant. **122** Daniel Del Valle. **134–137** (bkgd) Andi Butler. **135–136** (props) Pam Thomson. **137** Ken Bowser. **139** Eric Studevant. **141** Ken Bowser. **150–163** ©Robin Eley. **165–166** Jeff Mangiat. **167** ©Robin Eley. **169** Eric Sturdevant. **171** Ken Bowser. **183** (bkgd) Joe LeMonnier. **188–191** (bkgd) George Angelini. **191** (br) Ken Bowser. **193** Eric Sturdevant. **195** Jan Bryan-Hunt. **198** Ortelius Design, Inc. **200–217** Macky Pamintuan. **219** Eric Sturdevant. **221** Sally Vitsky. **224** Argosy. **226–237** ©William Low. **239** Robert Schuster. **241** (tr) William Low. (br) Ken Bowser. **243** Ken Bowser. **248** (inset) Ortelius Design, Inc. **267** Ken Bowser. **276** Ortelius Design, Inc. **278–289** ©Chris Gall. **292** Patrick Gnan. **293** (t) Chris Gall. **295** Ken Bowser. **297** Sally Vitsky. **302–317** ©Greg Newbold. **320** Robert Schuster. **321** (br) Ken Bowser. (tr) Rob Schuster. **323** (tl) Ken Bowser. **325** Jan Bryan-Hunt. **339** David Fuller. **342–345** Christiane Beauregard. **345** Jim Kelly. **347, 349** Ken Bowser. **354–265** David Diaz. **369** (tr) David Diaz. (br) Ken Bowser. **371** Ken Bowser. **390–393** Heli Hieta. **393** (br), **395** Ken Bowser. **397** Jan Bryan-Hunt. **400** Ken Bowser. **404** (l) Ortelius Design, Inc. **408–415** (border) Patrick Gnan. **410, 413** Mike Jaroszko. **416–419** Jo Lynn Alcorn. **419** (tr) Mike Jaroszko. **421** Ken Bowser. **423** Chris Lensch. **426** Ortelius Design, Inc. **447** Ken Bowser. **449** Sally Vitsky. **452** Nenad Jakesevic. **468–471** Richard Raney. **471** (tr) David Klug. **473** Ken Bowser. **494–495** Ortelius Design, Inc. **494–497** (web browser) Robert Schuster. **499** Ken Bowser. **501** Jan Bryan-Hunt. **504** Karen Minot. **507** (border) Patrick Gnan. **519** Bill Melvin. **520** Ortelius Design, Inc. **521** Ken Bowser. **523** Eric Sturdevant. **525** Jan Bryan-Hunt. **528** Ken Bowser. **534–545** ©Margaret Lee. **549** (tr) Margaret Lee. (b) Ken Bowser. **551** Ken Bowser. **553** Jan Bryan-Hunt. **557** Sally Vitsky. **575, 577, 579** Ken Bowser. **582** Ortelius Design, Inc. **584–595, 599** ©James Bentley. **601** Ken Bowser. **603** Sally Vitsky. **608–618** Kent Barton. **623–624** Ken Bowser. **646–649** David Klug. **649** (tr), **651** Ken Bowser. **653** Sally Vitsky. **656** Ken Bowser.

Photography
Key: (t) top. (c) center. (l) left. (r) right
TOC 4 (b) ©DeBROCK/Robertstock/IPNStock. **TOC 10** (b) ©C.M. Dixon, Heritage Image Partnership Ltd. **U01–17** ©HMCo/Ken Karp Photography. **18** (tl) ©PhotoAlto/SuperStock. (tr) ©Jupiter Images/Brand X/Alamy. (bl) ©Andanson James/CORBIS SYGMA. (br) ©Masterfile. **19** (tl) ©Ron Chapple Stock/Alamy. (tc) ©Imagestate/Alamy. (tr) ©senior images/Alamy. (bl) ©FogStock/Alamy. (bc) ©Time & Life Pictures/Getty Images. (br) ©Photodisc/Getty Images. **20–21** (bkgd) ©Estelle Klawitter/zefa/Corbis. **22** (t) ©HMCo./Jon Crispin/Mercury Pictures. (b) ©Courtesy of C.F. Payne. **34–37** (bkgd) ©Eric van den Brulle/Getty Images. **34** (t) ©Erich Lessing/Art Resource. (b) ©Bildarchiv Preussischer Kulturbesitz/Art Resource, NY. **35** (tl) ©Werner Forman/CORBIS. (tr) ©Erich Lessing/Art Resource. (bl) ©Biblioteca Apostolica Vaticana/Alfredo Dagli Orti/The Art Archive. (br) ©Randy Smith. **36** (tl) ©Bettmann/CORBIS. (tr) ©Dorling Kindersley. (bl) ©Khaled Kassem/Alamy. **37** (tr) ©Photodisc (br) ©IStockphoto. **41** ©HMCo/Ken Karp Photography. **42** (tl) ©Blend Images/SuperStock. (tr) ©Hill Street Studios/Stock This Way/Corbis. (bl) ©Tim Mantoani/Masterfile. (br) ©Jim West/Alamy. **43** (tl) ©Corbis/AGE Fotostock. (tc) ©Luca Zamperdri/Jupiter Images. (tr) ©Bill Fritsch/Brand X/Corbis. (bl) ©Andersen Ross/Getty Images (bc) ©Digital Vision Ltd/SuperStock. (br) ©Blend Images/Superstock. **44–45** (bkgd) ©Bettmann/Corbis. **47** (t) ©Donald Gargano/Shutterstock. **48** (tl) ©J. Helgason/Shutterstock. (b) ©Bettmann/CORBIS. **49** ©VEER Thomas Francisco/Getty Images. **50** (l) ©George Silk/Getty Images. **50–51** (b) ©DeBROCK/Robertstock/IPNStock. 51 (tr) ©H. Armstrong/IPNStock. (br) ©H. Armstrong Robert/IPNStock. **52** ©Courtesy of Jerry Spinelli. **54–55** ©HMCo/Ken Karp Photography. **55** (inset) ©HMCo/Ken Karp Photography. **61** ©Bettmann/CORBIS. **63** ©Bettmann/CORBIS. **65** ©HMCo/Ken Karp Photography. **66** (tl) ©SuperStock, Inc/SuperStock. (tr) ©UK Alan King/Alamy. (bl) ©Hulton Archive/Getty Images. (br) ©David

Photography. **470** ©HMCo/Ken Karp Photography. **471** (tr) ©HMCo. **475** ©HMCo/Ken Karp Photography. **476** (br) AFP/Getty Images. (bl) Farming in Egypt by English School (20th century) Private Collection/ Look and Learn/ The Bridgeman Art Library. (bl) Grant Faint/Photographer's Choice/Getty Images. (tl) Kenneth Garrett/National Geographic/Getty Images. (tr) Mrs Nina de Garis Davies (1881-1965)/British Museum, London, UK/The Bridgeman Art Library **477** (br) DEA/S. Vannini/Getty Images. (tl) Lebrecht Music and Arts Photo Library/Alamy. (bc) Mike Copeland/Gallo Images Roots RF Collection/Getty Images. **478–479** (bkgd) ©Neil A. Meyerhoff Inc./Panoramic Images. **482** Sandro Vannini/Corbis. **483** (t) Erich Lessing/Art Resource, NY. (b) Mike Copeland/Gallo Images Roots RF collection/Getty Images. **484** Dennis Cox/Alamy. **485** (br) Erich Lessing/Art Resource, NY. (b) Mrs. Nina de Garis (1881-1965) Ashmolean Museum, University of Oxford, UK/ The Bridgeman Art Library. (t) Sandro Vannini/Corbis. **486** (r) Scala/Art Resource, NY **487** bygonetimes/Alamy. **488** Gordon Sinclair/Alamy. **489** Stephen Studd/Photographer's Choice/Getty Images. **490** Erich Lessing/Art Resource, NY. **491** Erich Lessing/Art Resource, NY. **492** Michele Burgess/ Corbis. **493** (b) Aroldo de Luca/Corbis. (c) Getty Images/ Photodisc. **494** (bc) ©Stocktrek Images/Alamy. **494–495** Getty. **496–497** Getty. **496** (bc) ©/Egyptian Museum Cairo/Gianni Dagli Orti/The Art Archive. **497** (tr) Getty. (br) ©Sally and Richard Greenhill/Alamy. **501** ©HMCo/ Ken Karp Photography. **502** (tr) ©Carl Wilhelm Gotzloff/ Getty Images. (bl) Mimmo Jodice/Corbis. (br) ©Grant Faint/Getty Images. (tl) ©Bryan Reinhart/Masterfile. **503** (tc) ©Atlantide Phototravel/Corbis. (tl) ©Werner Forman/ Art Resource, NY (tr) ©HH/Taxi/Getty Images. (bl) ©David Ball/CORBIS. (bc) ©De Agostini/Getty Images. (br) ©Photodisc/Getty Images. **504–505** ©After Antonio Niccolini/The Bridgeman Art Library/Getty Images. **506** ©Courtesy of James Deem. **506–507** (bkgd) ©Massimo Listri/CORBIS. **507** ©Bettmann/CORBIS. **508–509** ©Hulton Archive/Getty Images. **510** (tl) ©Alinari Archives/ The Image Works. (tr) ©Vanni Archive/CORBIS. **512** ©Andrew Bargery/Alamy. **512** ©Erich Lessing /Art Resource. **513** ©Roger-Viollet/The Image Works. **514** ©Alinari/Art Resource, NY. **515** ©Scott Olson/Getty Images. **516** ©Alinari Archives/The Image Works. **517** ©Werner Forman Archive. **517** (c) Corel Stock Photo Library - royalty free. **518–519** ©SuperStock, Inc./ SuperStock. **520–521** (bkgd) ©Robert Holmes/CORBIS. **521** ©General Photographic Agency/Stringer/Getty Images. **525** ©Alamy. **525** ©HMCo/Ken Karp Photography. **528** ©Michael Newman/PhotoEdit. **U05–529** (spread) ©Michael Javorka/Stone/Getty. **529** ©PBNJ Productions/ Getty Images. (inset) ©PBNJ Productions/Getty Images **530** (tl) ©Image Source/Corbis. (tr) ©ROBERTO SCHMIDT/ StaffAFP/Getty Images. (bl) ©Matthew Borkoski/Jupiter Images. (br) ©Antonio Scorza/Staff/Getty Images. **531** (tc) ©Morgan David de Lossy/Corbis. (tl) ©Hammond/ photocuisine/Corbis. (tr) ©Jim Cummins/CORBIS. (bl) ©Paul A. Souders/CORBIS. (br) ©The Gallery Collection/ Corbis. (bc) ©Jonathan Nourok/PhotoEdit. **532–533** ©Tim Pannell/Corbis. **534** (b) ©Courtesy of Margaret Lee. (t) ©HarperCollins Children's Books. **545** (b) ©Jupiterimages/ creatas/Alamy. (c) Stefano Bianchetti/Corbis. **546–547** (bkgd) ©A. Barrington Brown/Photo Researchers, Inc. **547** (inset) ©Omikron/Photo Researchers, Inc. **548–549** (bkgd) ©MedicalRF.com/Corbis. **548** (inset) ©Science Source/ Photo Researchers, Inc. **553** ©HMCo/Ken Karp Photography. **554** (tl) ©Tom Collicott/Masterfile. (tr)

©Peter M. Fisher/Corbis. (br) ©Bettmann/CORBIS. (bl) ©Bettmann/CORBIS. **555** (tl) ©John Chapple/ Contributor/Getty Images. (tc) ©Bill Stormont/Corbis. (tr) ©Superstock/AGE Fotostock. (bl) ©The Granger Collection, New York. (bc) ©Malcolm Fife/zefa/Corbis. (br) ©Douglas Peebles/CORBIS. **556–557** (bkgd) ©Chuck Place/Alamy. **556** (inset) ©The Granger Collection. **558** ©SAUL LOEB/Newscom. **560–561** ©Wright State University. **562–563** ©Wright State University. **564–565** ©(ARC (Ames Research Center) AC99-003-4/Nasa. **568– 569** ©Bettmann/CORBIS. **570–571** ©Bettmann/CORBIS. **571** (b) Artville. (c) BrandXPictures. **572** ©Tomorrow's Aeronautical Museum. **573–574** ©Tomorrow's Aeronautical Museum. **575** (tr) ©Underwood & Underwood/CORBIS. **579** ©HMCo/Ken Karp Photography. **580** (tl) ©Three Lions/Stringer/Hulton Archives/Getty Images. (tr) ©Swim Ink 2, LLC/CORBIS. (bl) ©Bettmann/CORBIS. (br) ©Fred Ramage/Stringer/ Hulton Archive/Getty Images. **581** (tl) Hulton Archive/Getty Images. **582–583** ©Knud Dyby Collection dyb.999 at The Danish American Archive and Library, Dana College, Blair, NE 68008. **584** (t) ©Courtesy of Lois Lowry. (b) ©Courtesy of James Bentley. **595** (b) Blend Images/Alamy. (c) Comstock. (t) Peter Dazeley/ Photographer's Choice/Getty Images. **596–597** (bkgd) ©United States Holocaust Memorial Museum. **597** (inset) ©USHMM, courtesy of Frihedsmuseet. **598–599** ©Courtesy of Lois Lowry. **599** (inset) ©Flip Schulke/ CORBIS. **603** ©HMCo/Ken Karp Photography. **604** (tr) ©Jack Moebes/CORBIS. (bl) ©Keystone/Stringer/Getty Images. (bl) National Atlas.gov/Library of Congress. (tl) ©Three Lions/Stringer/Getty Images. **605** (tc) ©Bettmann/ CORBIS. (tr) ©Bettmann/CORBIS. (bl) ©Bettmann/ CORBIS. (bc) ©CORBIS. (tl) ©Steve Schapiro/Corbis. (br) ©2007 Associated Press. **606–607** (bkgd) ©Bettmann/ CORBIS. **606** (inset) ©Bettmann/CORBIS. (medal) ©Courtesy of the NAACP. **608–609** ©Bettmann/CORBIS. **608** ©Evans Chan. **611** ©Marian Anderson Collection, Annenberg Rare Book & Manuscript Library, University of Pennsylvania. **613** ©Marian Anderson Collection, Annenberg Rare Book & Manuscript Library, University of Pennsylvania. **614–615** ©CORBIS. **617** ©Marian Anderson Collection, Annenberg Rare Book & Manuscript Library, University of Pennsylvania. **618–619** ©Ted Russell/ Getty Images. **619** (c) Corel Stock Photo Library. (b) Getty Images/Photodisc. (t) PhotoDisc. **620–621** (bkgd) ©Medioimages/Photodisc/Getty Images. **622–623** (bkgd) ©Bettmann/CORBIS. **623** ©United States Postal Service. **627** ©HMCo/Ken Karp Photography. **628** (tl) ©Getty Images. (tr) ©OJO Images/SuperStock. (bl) ©Ace Stock Limited/Alamy. (br) ©Jiri Moucka/Shutterstock. (tc) ©Toshiyuki Aizawa/Reuters/Corbis. **629** (tr) ©Lynn Goldsmith/CORBIS. (br) ©Alexis Rosenfeld/Photo Researchers, Inc. (tl) ©CMCD/PhotoDisc. (bl) ©Roger Ressmeyer/Corbis. (bc) ©image100/Corbis. **630–631** (bkgd) ©HMCo. **630** (l) ©Corbis. (b) ©Olympus, Robot Hall of Fame. (r)©BBC/Corbis. **632–645** (bkgd) ©Lawrence Manning/Corbis. **633** (c) ©Hanson Robotics. (tr) ©AFP/ Getty Images. (br) ©Hank Morgan/Photo Researchers, Inc. **635** (inset) ©Hank Morgan/Photo Researchers, Inc. **636** (br) ©Reuters/Corbis. (bl) ©AFP/Getty Images. **637** (tr) ©Getty Images News. (cr) ©Getty Images News. **638–639** (t) ©Ramin Talaie/Corbis. (b) ©Tucker Balch, GVU Center, Georgia Institute of Technology. **639** (tr) ©Hulton Archive/ Getty Images. (br) ©Alison Bruce, The Robotics Institute, Carnegie Mellon University. **640** ©Rick Friedman/Corbis. **641** ©David Hanson. **642** ©Peter Menzel. **643** (b)